THE POEMS OF
SIR JOHN DAVIES

THE POEMS OF
Sir John Davies

EDITED BY ROBERT KRUEGER

With Introduction and Commentary
by the Editor and Ruby Nemser

OXFORD
AT THE CLARENDON PRESS
1975

Oxford University Press, Ely House, London W. 1

GLASGOW NEW YORK TORONTO MELBOURNE WELLINGTON
CAPE TOWN IBADAN NAIROBI DAR ES SALAAM LUSAKA ADDIS ABABA
DELHI BOMBAY CALCUTTA MADRAS KARACHI LAHORE DACCA
KUALA LUMPUR SINGAPORE HONG KONG TOKYO

ISBN 0 19 812716 2

© *Oxford University Press 1975*

*Printed in Great Britain
at the University Press, Oxford
by Vivian Ridler
Printer to the University*

EDITOR'S PREFACE

THE poems of Sir John Davies have formed the most important collection of Elizabethan poetry by a single author to have remained unedited in this century. The purpose of the present work is to offer a critical edition of these poems and to include the main information necessary for beginning the study of them. As in any edition, the first task has been to determine the canon. That Davies's minor poems have received little attention in this century may in part reflect uncertainty among scholars about the validity of attributions made in 1876 by the only editor of the complete poems, Alexander B. Grosart. If so, it has been largely misplaced. Most of Grosart's attributions are correct. The present edition removes only a few poems that he included and adds to the canon which he established. The next task, establishing the texts, could for Davies's major poems be done with more assurance of reflecting the author's intent than is customary for Elizabethan poetry because of the unusually clear relationships between printed and manuscript copies. The texts of the minor poems, which usually derive from manuscript, depend on fewer witnesses and ones of less authority, but are seldom corrupt. Because questions of canon (where they arise) and of text differ among the poems, these are treated under marked headings at the beginning of the commentary to each poem. A reader uninterested in such questions may proceed in the commentary to discussion of sources, dates of composition, occasions, and to more general criticism and glosses.

The biography appearing in the introduction is longer than is now customary in editions, for two reasons. A reader of a twentieth-century critical edition should not need to refer to editions published a century ago for biographical information, yet the fullest biographies of Davies are found in Grosart's editions of the complete poems and complete works. Further, Davies is not a writer of sufficient standing to warrant biographical treatment in a separate book, nor are the facts known about his life during the years in which he wrote verse sufficient to justify a book-length biography. The present study uses and refers to all available information about Davies's life for the years until he became Solicitor-General for Ireland in 1603, at which time the records of his life multiply by the same ratio as the quantity and quality of his verse diminishes. To write here of Davies's political career after 1603 would little help a student of his poetry. Suggestions about Davies's place in the Elizabethan poetical tradition and an evaluation of his achievement appear in the critical introduction. The resulting edition attempts to serve as the basic text for students of the Elizabethan period interested in one of the silver poets of this golden age.

I am pleased to express here briefly the appreciation which I tried to convey more fully and directly to some of the persons and institutions that assisted in this study. I began work on an edition of Davies's complete poems as a postgraduate student at Oxford; I did not know that simultaneously Ruby Nemser was working on *Nosce Teipsum* at Harvard. Later, on her learning that I was preparing an edition with commentary for the press, she generously offered me a copy of her thesis to use its very full notes on *Nosce Teipsum* as I would. Not fully to use her discoveries would have been a disservice to readers; not to allow her full credit would have been a disservice to her. I then asked her to join me in working on the entire critical commentary and general introduction. The result, whatever its faults, is much better than I might have written on my own. Her discovery of the importance of Cicero's *De natura deorum* to Davies's *Orchestra* is but one example of her contribution. She also added much to my personal satisfaction in this work, for Davies's poetry is a scholarly island where few academicians elect to stop. To have a friend with whom to delight in Davies's excellencies, laugh at his blunders, or puzzle over his actions allows one to see the island more clearly, and as both green and tawny.

Both of us, and readers of this book indirectly, are indebted to the libraries of many institutions which allowed printing and citation of their manuscripts: All Souls College, Oxford; the Bodleian Library, Oxford; the British Museum; the Cambridge University Library; Chetham's Hospital, Manchester; Downing College, Cambridge; the Edinburgh University Library; the Folger Shakespeare Library; the Harvard University Library; the Henry E. Huntington Library; the Carl Pforzheimer Library; the Philip and A. S. W. Rosenbach Foundation. Their staffs have all been unfailingly helpful. The Right Honourable the Earl of Leicester, His Grace the Duke of Northumberland, and Dr. James Osborn have all allowed consultation of their manuscripts and quotation from them. I wish to thank them here.

We have received help from many scholars. Dr. Carolyn Bishop offered several suggestions on Davies's epigrams, as did Dr. P. B. Rogers on his *Gullinge Sonnets*. Mr. John Buxton and Dr. John Carey as doctoral examiners both read the edition of the complete poems with great care and made helpful corrections. The Revd. T. J. Childs kindly lent a copy of his thesis on Davies's *Nosce Teipsum* so that it might be easily consulted, as it frequently was. Miss Margaret Crum of the Bodleian Library cheerfully made her unsurpassed knowledge of Elizabethan manuscripts available on many occasions. One Saturday morning years ago, Professor I. Ll. Foster shared with an unknown postgraduate student his sherry and his knowledge of a manuscript in the Bodleian, while patiently translating its Welsh poems, and did it so gracefully that one might have supposed any scholar would have done the same. Mr. David Foxon was no less generous with his knowledge of bibliographical and textual matters. Mr. Frederic Sternfeld gave his assistance to an inquiry about some puzzling musical references; and Dr. James L. Sanderson has, over a long correspondence about Davies, been helpful on many occasions. Although they do not talk of it at school, receiving such generosity is one of the pleasures of scholarship.

It is perhaps hardest to find accurate expression of thanks to those to whom we owe most. Many evenings as the two of us wrote the commentary on Davies's poems, our conversations turned to those under whom we had, separately, undertaken the study of Davies's poetry, Professor Douglas Bush and Dame Helen Gardner. We shared anecdotes about the astonishing learning that flashed forth from them as naturally as if they had always known such things, as if they had needed no labour to be learned. There were stories, as well, of their generosity, and courage in supporting their students. We felt that they showed lives well lived. We would wish to thank them for that too.

Durham, North Carolina
11 June 1971

                                                    R. K.

CONTENTS

ABBREVIATIONS AND REFERENCES

(Abbreviations and symbols relating to textual matters
and to quotation from manuscript appear on page xxiii)

Batman	Stephen Batman, *Batman uppon Bartholome His Booke De Proprietatibus Rerum*, 1582.
B.M.	British Museum.
C.S.P.	*Calendar of State Papers.*
Calvin, *Inst.*	John Calvin, *The Institution of Christian Religion*, trans. T[homas] N[orton], 1561.
Chamberlain, *Letters*	*The Letters of John Chamberlain*, ed. Norman Egbert McClure, 2 vols., Philadelphia, 1939.
D.N.B.	*The Dictionary of National Biography.*
De nat. deor.	Cicero, *De natura deorum.*
Elizabethan Stage	E. K. Chambers, *The Elizabethan Stage*, 4 vols., Oxford, 1923.
F.A.	Pierre de La Primaudaye, *The Second Part of the French Academie*, trans. T[homas] B[owes], 1594.
F.Q.	Spenser, *The Faerie Queene*, ed. J. C. Smith, 2 vols., 1909.
Grosart, *Poems*	*The Complete Poems of Sir John Davies*, ed. Alexander B. Grosart, 2 vols., 1876.
Grosart, *Works*	*The Works in Verse and Prose of Sir John Davies*, ed. Alexander B. Grosart, 3 vols., 1869–76.
Harington	*The Letters and Epigrams of Sir John Harington*, ed. N. E. McClure, Philadelphia, 1930.
H.M.C.	*The Reports of the Historical Manuscripts Commission* and its appendices.
Hooker, *Laws*	Richard Hooker, *Of the Laws of Ecclesiastical Polity*, in *The Works of Mr. Richard Hooker*, ed. John Keble, 3 vols., Oxford, 1836.
Jonson, *Works*	*Ben Jonson*, ed. C. H. Herford and Percy Simpson, 11 vols., 1925–52.
Macrobius	*Commentary on the Dream of Scipio*, trans. William Harris Stahl, New York, 1952.
Martial	*Epigrams.*
Montaigne	*Montaigne's Essays*, trans. John Florio, 3 vols., Everyman's Library 440–442, 1910.
Mornay	Philippe de Mornay, *A Woorke concerning the Trewnesse of the Christian Religion*, trans. Sir Philip Sidney and Arthur Golding, 1587.

N. & Q.	*Notes & Queries.*
Nemesius	*Of the Nature of Man*, ed. William Telfer, Library of Christian Classics IV, 1955.
NHA	Poems Not Hitherto Ascribed to Davies (a section of the present edition).
Nichols	*The Progresses and Public Processions of Queen Elizabeth*, ed. John Nichols, 3 vols., 1823.
N.T.	*Nosce Teipsum.*
O.E.D.	*The Oxford English Dictionary.*
Ovid, *Met.*	*Metamorphoses.*
Pliny	*Natural History.*
PP	Poems Possibly by Davies (a section of the present edition).
R.E.S.	*Review of English Studies.*
Rollins	*A Poetical Rhapsody 1602–1621*, ed. Hyder Edward Rollins, 2 vols., 1931–2.
Shakespeare	Citations are from *The Complete Works*, ed. Alfred Harbage (Penguin Books, Baltimore, 1969); it uses the line references of Clark and Wright's Cambridge edition.
S.R.	*A Transcript of the Registers of the Company of Stationers of London between 1554–1640 A.D.*, ed. Edward Arber, 5 vols., 1875–94.
S.T.	*The Summa Theologica of St. Thomas Aquinas*, trans. Fathers of the English Dominican Province, 22 vols., 1911–25.
S.T.C.	*A Short-Title Catalogue of Books Printed in England, Scotland, and Ireland, and of English Books Printed Abroad, 1475–1640*, ed. A. W. Pollard and G. R. Redgrave, London, 1926.
Tilley	Morris Palmer Tilley, *A Dictionary of the Proverbs in England in the Sixteenth and Seventeenth Centuries*, 1950.
T.L.S.	*The Times Literary Supplement.*
Tusc.	Cicero, *Tusculan Disputations.*
Wood	Anthony Wood, *Athenæ Oxonienses*, ed. Philip Bliss, 4 vols., 1813–1820.

Note on citations and quotations

The following policies have been observed regarding citations and quotations.

1. Modern practice in the use of *i/j*, *ſ/s*, *u/v* has been followed when quoting from all manuscript and printed works.

2. Some abbreviations which appear in manuscripts and print have been silently expanded, as they would probably have been by an Elizabethan editor or printer. Many poems are set from manuscript: to have indicated in the texts of Davies's poems where all abbreviations were expanded would mar the appearance of the page and would hinder rather than assist the reader. If no indication of expanded abbreviations appears in the poetical texts, none need appear in quotations from other documents.

3. Place of publication is normally omitted in citing works published in England. If more than one edition appeared during the same year of publication, or if confusion is likely, the place of publication is then included.

4. Volume numbers usually appear in lower case. When a work is cited in which the reader is likely to be assisted by knowing volume, chapter or section, and page, the volume number appears in upper case roman, the chapter or section in lower case roman, and the page in arabic.

5. References to works by classical authors are to the Loeb editions unless otherwise specified.

6. In general, references are to 'standard editions' where these are likely to be readily available to readers. If they are not, references are to more readily available editions, the accuracy of which, however, has been compared with standard editions for the passages quoted.

GENERAL INTRODUCTION

CANON

In a letter of 23 December 1602 John Chamberlain wrote to Dudley Carleton,

> You like the Lord Kepers devises so yll, [Davies's *Lotterie*] that I cared not to get Master Secretaries that were not much better, saving a pretty dialogue of John Davies twixt a maide, a widow and a wife, which I do not thincke but Master Saunders hath seen, and no doubt will come out one of these dayes in print with the rest of his workes (*Letters*, i. 177–8).

The 'pretty dialogue' was printed six years later in Francis Davison's miscellany, *Poetical Rhapsody*, but it did not appear during Davies's lifetime 'in print with the rest of his workes'. The nearest Davies came to publishing his collected poems was to reprint in one volume in 1622 three poems that had previously appeared separately: *Nosce Teipsum*, *Orchestra*, and *Hymnes of Astræa*.

Indeed, about half of 'the rest of his workes' which remain today were not printed in his own lifetime. Some, like his bawdy epigrams, Davies the judge must have suppressed as consciously as Donne the preacher attempted to suppress some of his early work. Some poems were simply ignored and others forgotten. A. B. Grosart in his editions of 1869 and 1876 first attempted to gather the complete poems, and deserves credit for almost doubling the number of Davies's poems in print. He accepted a few as being by Davies that were in fact by other writers, but most of the canon Grosart established has proved sound. The authenticity of Davies's most important work is unquestioned, and that of the remainder I hope to have established beyond reasonable doubt. There remains, however, a number of peripheral poems, found in manuscript, about which present evidence does not allow a certain conclusion; these appear in the section 'Poems Possibly by Davies'.

The danger is less that an editor of Davies will include poems by others than that he will not discover all of Davies's work. Poets like Shakespeare and Donne attracted the work of others to their names; less important poets did not, and their names could easily have been dropped from the poems to which they were attached. Moreover, like other Elizabethans who aspired to or held important public positions,

Davies wrote poems for friends, for occasions, for advancement or amusement, but not usually for print. For example, he evidently sent Sir Christopher Yelverton, a fellow lawyer and judge, a group of scurrilous poems libelling Attorney-General Edward Coke. Yelverton would hardly have proved Davies's friend by passing on the poems to someone else while his name was still attached; and Yelverton himself in re-copying the poems would have had no particular need to record Davies's name, since he knew it. If similar circumstances arose elsewhere, very likely some of Davies's verse, especially satirical verse, has been lost or else exists today unattributed and unrecognized in manuscript. While the movement of manuscripts from private to public libraries has made possible a more complete edition today than would have been possible at any other time since Davies's own, the limits to the completeness of any edition of his poems should be realized.

The poems are too numerous, and the problems related to their canonicity too varied, to be discussed here. Instead, the authenticity of any poem which might be questioned is treated in the commentary to that poem.

TEXT

Most of Davies's poems have come to us in manuscripts or early printed texts relatively free from corruption, and these textual witnesses may be classified in four principal groups.

1. Texts given to the printer and in some cases probably overseen during printing by Davies. In this group are his major poems, *Nosce Teipsum*, *Orchestra*, *Hymnes of Astræa*, and the *Epigrammes*.

2. Poems copied in the Laing manuscript, apparently under the supervision of Davies's daughter, from his own papers. These include the *Psalmes*, the *Love Elegies*, and miscellaneous verse.

3. Manuscript copies in the possession of Davies's acquaintances, some of them probably taken from his own copies. His *Epithalamion*, *Orchestra*, *Contention*, unpublished epigrams, and a few miscellaneous poems appear in these manuscripts. They serve as copy-texts in the present edition for some poems, and are useful in providing corrections for others. Such manuscripts may have provided the texts for some of Davies's poems printed in Davison's *Poetical Rhapsody*.

4. The anonymous miscellanies in manuscript which contain one or several poems of Davies scattered among the poetry and prose of

other writers, copied from either printed or manuscript sources of varying authority simply because the owner wanted a copy of the poem. An editor of Davies may at times correct the text from these, but he seldom need depend on them for his copy-text.

As is evident, the character of the textual witnesses varies. It is simplest, therefore, to give a textual introduction for each poem—or, as for the epigrams, for a group of poems—rather than to attempt to summarize in one place the ways in which the texts for the more than two hundred poems have been derived. Such introductions will be found in the Commentary. To avoid repetition, printed and manuscript witnesses used in constructing the texts of a number of poems are characterized in detail in a Bibliography, but not in the individual textual introductions.

THE PRESENT EDITION

The present edition is in old spelling—not necessarily the spelling of Davies—but one that he would have been able to read without surprise. It generally follows the accidentals of punctuation, italics, capitalization, and line arrangements or layout of the copy-text being used. In some poems the textual witnesses are such that an editor can reproduce more accurately the accidentals that the author would have preferred by emending from witnesses other than the copy-text that received the author's correction. Consequently, these poems have received more emendation of accidentals than is normal in most old-spelling critical editions.

I have silently made certain alterations throughout, without indicating them in apparatus, commentary, or appendices. In Davies's text and titles, and in quoting other authors, I have expanded abbreviations and have adopted modern practice in the use of i/j, f/s, u/v, and ligatures. I have normalized the typography and punctuation of titles, marginal glosses, and speech headings, and I have corrected turned and wrong-fount letters. Display capitals are not usually reproduced; faulty spacing is corrected, and all texts are printed in roman type. Names of persons, places, and the Deity are capitalized. Certain minor scribal peculiarities of manuscrupts used as copy-texts, such as forming every initial l or c as a capital, have been normalized.

When my copy-text is a printed work, unless otherwise indicated,

I have reproduced its punctuation and noted any alterations. Most of these poems were prepared for the press by Davies. Where my copy-text is a manuscript, unless it is in Davies's holograph, the punctuation is my own, since the manuscripts vary extremely from one to another in their punctuation.

I have tried to omit entirely from the text and apparatus what Davies could not have written. Most of the press-variants found in various copies of printed editions used as copy-texts for the poems can be shown by independent manuscript witnesses to be compositors' errors that clearly do not represent Davies's words. (A list of these variants may be found in my doctoral thesis, 'A Critical Edition of the Complete Poems of Sir John Davies', deposited in the Bodleian Library, Oxford.) Only those press-variants deserving consideration in establishing the text appear in the apparatus.

In some instances I have altered accidentals such as capitalization, spelling, or type face, either for clarity, or because such alterations bring the text closer in my judgement to authorial intention. In all but four works, emendations of accidentals are made entirely on editorial judgement, and are indicated in the critical apparatus without citing the accidentals of witnesses other than the copy-text. In emending accidentals in *Nosce Teipsum*, *Orchestra*, *Hymnes of Astræa*, and the *Epigrammes*, the emendations are sometimes supported by other textual witnesses which seem more likely at those points to represent Davies's intentions than did the copy-text. The apparatus, however, does not include the accidentals of all witnesses used in constructing the texts of these four poems; an explanation of the policy followed with respect to each poem will be found in the textual introduction to that poem.

I alter spelling and punctuation where a reader is likely to be misled by the copy-text, and alter capitalization and italicization in the interests of consistency or of apparent authorial intention. I indicate elision between two words, not within a single word.

The critical apparatus has several functions. It first lists all witnesses used in establishing the text. Next, it shows all substantive departures from copy-text (which, unless otherwise indicated, provides the title and layout of the poem). Finally, it indicates what were, or may have been, Davies's first thoughts before putting the poem into final form. In presenting variants, the apparatus cites the readings of all textual witnesses for the variant listed. The readings themselves are in the spelling of the witness cited, except when several witnesses agree in a variant; then the spelling is that of the first witness listed.

The following abbreviations and symbols relating to textual matters and quotation from manuscript appear in the apparatus and elsewhere in the edition.

]	The reading to the left of the bracket is that of the copytext and all witnesses not mentioned to the right of the bracket.
Print	All printed witnesses.
MSS.	All manuscript witnesses.
All	All witnesses.
Σ	The sum of the unspecified witnesses.
om.	Material omitted by one or more witnesses.
ed.	An editorial emendation.
ital.	Material appears in italic type or italic (distinguished) handwriting.
rom.	Material appears in roman type or Secretary handwriting.
l.c.	Material appears in 'lower case', not capitalized.
m.	The reference is to a marginal gloss.
c	Corrected reading or corrected forme.
u	Uncorrected reading or uncorrected forme.
∧	A caret indicates the absence of punctuation.
~	A wavy dash replaces a word where punctuation only has been altered.
[ ]	Bracketed letters or words have been supplied by the editor.
[~~word~~]	A word bracketed and struck through indicates that the word was written and then deleted in manuscript.
\ /	A pair of slanting rules indicates an insertion above the line in a manuscript, or, accompanied by the previous symbol, a word written over a deleted word.
*	An asterisk indicates that a particular reading is discussed in the Commentary.

LIFE

On 16 April 1569 John Davies was christened with his father's name in the parish church of St. John the Baptist in Tisbury, Wiltshire. Elizabethan law required baptism within a month of birth, and usually it followed as soon as possible. The christening was probably attended by the infant's maternal grandparents, John and Agnes Bennett of Pitt House, Wiltshire, who were the highest ranking family in the parish, and whose handsome manor house was only about a mile from the church. Their daughter Mary had married, perhaps slightly beneath her station, John Davies, a gentleman and wealthy tanner who lived a few miles away at Chicksgrove. This was her third son, following Matthew and Edward, both born in 1566.[1]

The Davies family had been in Chicksgrove for the past two generations. John, the child's paternal grandfather, had come with Sir William Herbert, first Earl of Pembroke, from South Wales into Wiltshire.[2] He became lord of the manor at Chicksgrove, where, on the side of a valley overlooking a stream, he built a large stone house that still stands. Under its roof he and his wife Matilda (or Maud) Bridemore reared their large family, and there she died, to be buried a year after her grandson's christening in the parish church. The date of her husband's death is unknown, but their estate passed to their eighth child and youngest son, John, who held it until his death in 1580.

In 1580, then, Mary Bennett Davies was left a widow with five children, the two youngest, Edith and Mary, aged about nine and six. Fortunately, she was wealthy and gave her sons a good education. In 1674 the grandson of the poet wrote of him, 'His father died when hee was very young & left him with his 2 brothers \to his

---

[1] The present biography omits some minor details and speculations found in the biographies in A. B. Grosart's editions of Davies's *Works* (1869, ii. xvii–cxxiv), and *Poems* (1876, i. xi–lvi); and in Theodore John Childs, 'An Edition of "Nosce Teipsum" by Sir John Davies with an Introductory Account of his Work' (B.Litt. thesis Oxford, 1939), pp. 1–107; Avis Leone Kidwell, 'Sir John Davies' *Orchestra*, edited, with a Life of Davies' (Diss. Cornell, 1930), pp. [19–76]; and David Hadas, 'The Mind and Art of Sir John Davies' (Diss. Columbia, 1963), pp. 9–26. These biographers found most of the material used here. The present account generally indicates neither the first use of such material nor silent corrections of earlier biographies. The reader requiring fuller information will wish to consult these biographies for himself and will find the present account much in their debt.

The parish register at Tisbury records the births of John Davies, his brothers, and his sisters. Grosart, unfamiliar with the manner of entries in the register of the Middle Temple, London, erred in thinking the poet's father a lawyer who had studied at New Inn (*Poems*, i. xv–xix), as Childs, pp. 4–6, points out. John Aubrey indicates in Bodleian MS. Autog. d. 21, fol. 147, that the poet's father was a tanner, information he communicated to Anthony Wood for his life of Davies in *Athenæ Oxonienses* (1815), ii. 400–5. Reference to the poet as a tanner's son occurs in Benjamin Rudyerd, *Prince d'Amour* (1660), p. 83.

[2] Bodleian MS. Carte 62, fol. 590[r].

Mother/ to bee Educated. Shee therefore brought them up all to learning.'[1] No records survive to indicate the education received by her two daughters and Edward; Matthew, however, became a scholar at Winchester College in 1577, as did John in 1580.[2]

Even then Winchester was one of the finest schools in England: a near contemporary of Davies complained, 'Westminster Winchester and Eaton schollers think none schollers but themselves'.[3] Entrance to the school depended on a boy's ability, on patronage, and on geography, with students from the immediate area receiving preference. Once there, a boy's day began at five o'clock, when he arose to sing psalms in Latin in his room; it ended after an evening service in Latin in the chapel. During the day he wrote and spoke in Latin. The schoolmaster Christopher Johnson told his Winchester students in the 1560s:

The speech of youth we wish to be Latin, of all even of those who are buried in the obscurity of the lowest classes, nor anyone to use his native language except when it shall be necessary. This custom must be especially preserved and practiced in the upper forms, must both be decreed by law, and preserved with severity and castigation. When the boys come to school and when they return home, when they play together, when they walk together, whenever they meet, let their speech be Latin or Greek. Let there be no place for lenience if anyone offends against this criminally.[4]

Although Johnson allows Greek, Winchester stressed Latin more strongly. In later years Davies wrote letters in Latin and often quoted Latin tags, but left no record of having known Greek.

His earliest reading at school was in the Latin classics. He would soon have been reading Plautus and Terence, whose comedies were

---

[1] Carte MS. 62, fol. 590ʳ. Grosart (*Poems*, i. xiii) considered fols. 590–1, notes about the life of Sir John Davies, to be 'rough jottings by the Historian' Thomas Carte, but they are headed 'May 2d 1674', and were thus written before Carte was born. Comparison with similar notes in the same hand in uncatalogued Hastings Papers (Genealogy) in the Henry E. Huntington Library reveals these folios to be notes made by Theophilus Hastings, seventh Earl of Huntingdon, son and heir to Lucy, Countess of Huntingdon, Davies's daughter and sole heir. As he was born after the poet's death, his information necessarily derives from family conversation and from Davies's papers, which he inherited. His correspondence from 1673 to 1675 shows that he invited Sir William Dugdale to study the family papers before writing about the Huntingdons and Sir John Davies in *The Baronage of England*.

[2] Thomas Frederick Kirby, *Winchester Scholars* (1888), pp. 147–9.

[3] Quoted in A. K. Cook, *About Winchester College* (1917), p. 285.

[4] Quoted in T. W. Baldwin, *William Shakspere's Small Latine & Lesse Greeke* (Urbana, 1944), i. 333. Baldwin's chapter 14 on Winchester discusses reading and regulations, as do Arthur F. Leach, *A History of Winchester College* (1899), and A. K. Cook.

favourite reading in the lower forms of Elizabethan schools. Many years later, in 1612, Davies draws a moral from their works in explaining the character of the Irish:

Lastly, this Oppression did of force and necessity make the Irish a craftie people: for such as are oppressed and live in slavery, are ever put to their shifts; *Ingenium mala saepe movent*; And therefore, in the old Comedies of *Plautus & Terence*, the Bondslave doth always act the cunning and Craftie part.[1]

At Winchester he probably also read Cicero's *De Oratore*, *De Amicitia*, *De Senectute*, and *Paradoxa*, Virgil's *Georgics* and *Bucolics*, Erasmus's *De Duplice Copia* and *Verborum ac Rerum*, Juvenal's *Satires*, Lucian's dialogues in Latin translation, Ovid's *Fasti*, *Tristia*, and *Metamorphoses*, and Martial's *Epigrams*.

Of these and all authors, Virgil and Cicero are most often quoted in Davies's later prose, but it was his reading and imitation of Martial's epigrams that most clearly influenced Davies's poetry. Winchester considered writing Latin epigrams an excellent exercise for students, and Martial an excellent model. In Martial Davies found colloquial vigour combined with urbane detachment, and close, realistic description used to delineate general vices—characteristics sympathetic to Davies's temperament, as we can see from their reappearance in his English epigrams a decade or more later. The strong influence of Martial on Wykehamists in this period is evident from the fact that the most important epigrammatists of the 1590s were scholars together at Winchester: among the fifty scholars enrolling at Winchester between 1577 and 1581 were John Owen, John Hoskyns, John Davies, and Thomas Bastard.[2]

Composing Latin verse was a daily activity at Winchester. T. W. Baldwin writes of a day in Christopher Johnson's class: 'The boys are exhorted to model upon the style of Cicero as the best. They are given eight distichs, each meaning "it dawned". They were then probably expected to invent for themselves a few more ways to get the sun up.'[3] The emphasis, in keeping with Renaissance aesthetic, was not upon originality of theme but upon inventiveness and cleverness in execution. Winchester boys were to avoid idle time by thinking of ways to get the sun up in verse; ten years after Winchester, Davies was to spend fifteen days in writing almost a thousand lines of verse to set the world dancing in his *Orchestra*.

---

[1] Grosart, *Works*, ii. 107.   [2] Kirby, pp. 142–50.   [3] Baldwin, p. 334.

Davies studied at Winchester for five years, then proceeded to the Queen's College, Oxford, where his entry is recorded on 15 October 1585.[1] Here he no longer needed to rise at five o'clock to sing psalms, and if his life was still closely regulated—playing football or attending plays by travelling companies was forbidden, for example—he now studied the trivium and parts of the quadrivium, and listened to and participated in disputations. If Anthony Wood is correct, at Oxford Davies 'laid a considerable foundation of academical literature, partly by his own natural parts (which were excellent) and partly by the help of a good tutor'.[2]

He stayed at Oxford only about a year and a half, too briefly to take a degree, and then proceeded to London to begin studying law.[3] For at least a year he studied at New Inn, an Inn of Chancery where he prepared himself for its affiliated Inn of Court, the Middle Temple, where his entry is recorded on 10 February 1587/8.[4] London offered not only freedom from the high walls and confining regulations of an Oxford college but the delights of bear-baiting and public playhouses; and an ambitious, observant, intelligent youth aspiring to the law would have been attracted to it as the centre of government. The royal court was here, and to and from the monarch ran the threads of compliment and favour that created power. Davies could share vicariously in the excitement of important decisions and events, could observe the important persons who manipulated events, could

> . . . hear poor rogues
> Talk of court news; and . . . talk with them too—
> Who loses and who wins; who's in, who's out.
> (*King Lear*, v. ii. 13–15)

He could also write satirical epigrams about them and others for the pleasure of his friends and wits at the Inns of Court. For an aspiring young man, the next best place to the royal court was an Inn of Court.

[1] *Register of the University of Oxford*, ed. Andrew Clarke (1887), II. ii. 147. Hadas in 'The Mind and Art of Sir John Davies' (Diss. Columbia 1963), p. 13, reports that the Winchester College archives confirm Davies's attendance at Queen's.

[2] Wood, ii. 400.

[3] The John Davies who took his degree from Magdalen College in 1590 must have been the student of county Monmouth who was admitted to Magdalen in 1585. See *Alumni Oxonienses*, ed. Joseph Foster (4 vols., 1891), i. 380 and *Register* (1888), II. iii. 160.

[4] Charles Henry Hopwood, ed., *Middle Temple Records* (1904), i. 296. Davies's fee on entry was twenty shillings, the fee set for those who had spent a year or more at New Inn.

Partly because of its four Inns of Court, London at this time was described as 'the third Universitie of England'.[1] During the term Middle Temple students attended the Law Courts; between terms they studied under Readers, advanced members who by their knowledge of the law had been raised above the rank of utter barrister. The basis of instruction was primarily disputation, conducted in the great hall of the Inn. In the evenings the judges, serjeants-at-law, and barristers entered wearing their robes, and were seated according to their ranks at the high table. Seated at tables running laterally from high table were the students, who wore dark gowns. A fire in the centre of the room offered heat and some light; between it and the high table was the abacus, or low table where the speaker stood. Following dinner, a speaker presented a discourse interpreting a point of law. The judges, barristers, and students were then expected to enter debate with the speaker until, if possible, a consensus was reached. In this setting Davies spent many of his evenings for nearly a decade. He was seemingly a gifted and serious student, for he was advanced to the rank of utter barrister on 4 July 1595, after the minimum allowable time, seven years.[2]

Many members of the Inns came not to study the law but to enjoy the company. Young noblemen, courtiers, and adventurers were offered membership and sometimes took up residence; thus the Inns performed some functions of a modern men's club—companionship, conversation, good dining, and good company among men of financial or political power or powerful minds. During Davies's years in residence, the membership of the Middle Temple included the writers Fulke Greville, Sir Henry Wotton, Sir Thomas Overbury, and the dramatists John Marston and John Ford; aldermen Robert Lee and John Watts, later Lord Mayors of London; the soldiers Sir Francis Vere and Sir Thomas Norris; and seamen Richard Hakluyt, Sir John Hawkins, and Sir Martin Frobisher.[3]

The four Inns provided the training and conversation and, during their long vacations, the opportunity for travel from which future leaders gained experience and learning. In the autumn of 1592 three close friends at the Temple—Davies, Richard Martin, and William Fleetwood—travelled together in Holland. England had for years

---

[1] Sir George Buc, *The Third Universitie of England* (1631), in John Stow, *Annales* (1631), p. [1063].

[2] *Middle Temple Records*, i. 354.

[3] John Hutchinson, *A Catalogue of Notable Middle Templars* (1902).

been offering steady sympathy and intermittent assistance to the Protestant Dutch in their war against Catholic Spain, England's chief rival. As a result, young men crossed the Channel, some to fight as Protestant crusaders, like Sidney; others to observe, like Davies and his friends. Davies observed the men of war, their works and words, and treated some of them in his epigrams. Epigram 24 mocks a man newly returned from combat whose speech is clogged with the jargon of battle:

> Gallus hath bin this Sommer in Friesland,
> And now returned he speakes such warlike wordes,
> As if I coulde their English understand,
> I feare me they would cut my Throat like swordes.
> He talkes of counterscarfes and casomates,
> Of parapets, curteynes, and Pallizadois,
> Of flankers, Ravelings, gabions he prates,
> And of false brayes, and sallies and scaladose.

The students of law also met men of their own profession. Two letters to Paul Merula from Davies following his return to England reveal that he and his friends visited this eminent legal scholar in Holland.[1] In this, his earliest extant correspondence, he thanks Merula for his hospitality and informs him that, as requested, he has delivered Merula's letter to William Camden. As interesting as the contents of the letters are the attitudes and characteristics of Davies's personality which they reveal. While he shows some self-consciousness in his apology for the style of Fortescue and other early English legal writers, and in his characteristically Elizabethan sense of the literary superiority of his own age to earlier times, he also proves to be as easy in offering metaphorical compliments in private letters written in Latin as he was later to become when offering them publicly in English verse. Thus, for example, he alludes to Merula's having set aside legal studies to assume the Chair of History at Leiden University:

Mihi vero in barbaro, ac tristi ac ab omnibus humanioribus litteris abhorrente Iuris nostri municipalis studio sudandum est: cum interea domino meo hilares ac urbanae Musae Nectar et ambrosiam cum affluentia omni ac abundantia apponant.

---

[1] For Davies's letters see Bodleian MS. D'Orville 52, fols. 49–50. For Merula's see B.M. MS. Cotton Julius C. v., fol. 49, printed by Thomas Smith in *V. Cl. Gulielmi Camdeni et Illustrium Virorum ad G. Camdenum Epistolæ* (1691), pp. 48–9.

His shorter letter warrants quotation in full as an example of Davies's style and interests:

Et humanitas vestra erga me, et desiderium meum gratificandi vobis et opportunus Willielmi Fleetwoodi reditus postulant, imo flagitant ut has ad vos nunc temporis exarem; quanquam pauci admodum effluxerunt dies ex quo alias dederim. At vero cum litteris hisce praeter vota et amorem meum, libellum transmisi, Laudes Iuris nostri Municipalis comparationemque cum Iure Civili nimis (vereor) invidiosam continentem. Librorum nostrorum omnium commodissimum qui transmitteretur censebam, utpote qui Latine scriptus sit (quanquam ut vides, caractere anglico excuses) cum caetera fere omnia ingentia volumina obsoleto ac corrupto sermone gallico tradantur. Iste vero commentariolus si horridus atque incultus sit ac habeat in se pleraque barbara, antiquata et Iuris nostri propria vocabula, id aetatis illius rusticitati ac inscitiae in quam humaniores litterae emortuae omnes fuerunt, tribuendum est. annum enim circiter Millesimum quadringentesimum, quinquagesimum vixit D. de Forti Scuto et commentarium istum scripsit, quem si dominus perlegere dignetur, atque ut benevolentiae meae gratificetur sententiam de eo suam per literas mihi renunciet, equidem curabo ut multo luculentior ac politior ea de re liber ad dominum deferatur. vale. e Medio Templo Londini XVI Kalend. Apriles 1592.

in omnibus amicitiae officijs humanitati
vestrae obsequentissimus
Io: Davys.

This was Davies's only journey outside the British Isles. London, the scene and subject of many of his epigrams, was his milieu, and both the company and education that it provided encouraged him to write verse. Renaissance education was largely rhetorical, and Davies, taught to write verse at Winchester, and schooled in disputation and rhetoric at Oxford, had entered at the Middle Temple a society in which professional advancement depended both on knowledge of the law and the ability to argue persuasively.

Legal disputation at the Middle Temple was paralleled by theological debate. In 1584, a few years before Davies's arrival, Richard Hooker was appointed Master of the Temple, its highest clerical post. As the previous Master had been too ill to preach, the sermons had been given mostly by Walter Travers, the Lecturer of Temple Church and a man of considerable oratorical power and powerfully Calvinist doctrine. The arrival of Hooker initiated a pattern of counterpointed sermons, with Hooker and Travers preaching to one another as well as to their audiences. In the words of Izaak Walton, As St. Paul withstood St. Peter to his face, so did they withstand each other in their Sermons: for, as one has pleasantly expressed it, 'The forenoon sermon spake Canterbury; and the afternoon Geneva.'[1]

These debates ended when Archbishop Whitgift forbade Travers to preach, and removed Hooker in 1591 at his own request: 'I am weary', Hooker wrote to him, 'of the noise and oppositions of this place; and indeed, God and Nature did not intend me for contentions but for study and quietness.'[2] Out of the disagreements, however, as Hooker acknowledged, came his *Laws of Ecclesiastical Polity*. And what Hooker found disagreeable many lawyers found exciting. Since church attendance was required, Davies must have heard many of the exchanges, and would have had ample opportunity to talk with both men. We cannot know whether he was influenced by their debates in 1591, but eight years later, when he published *Nosce Teipsum*, his statements on divine and natural law clearly indicated the ascendency of Hooker's views.

The Inns encouraged poets as well as disputants and preachers. John Donne later wrote poetry and preached sermons at nearby Lincoln's Inn; Sir Walter Raleigh took membership in the Middle Temple for the company it offered. In a period when most literate men seem at some time to have attempted verse, the Inns of Court were gathering places for men of letters—one of the reasons Ben Jonson called them 'the noblest nourceries of humanity, and liberty, in the kingdome'.[3] In this society of men who lived by skill with words, Davies developed simultaneously as a clever lawyer and a clever poet. And his poetry was ready to serve his professional advancement.

The Inns of Court were closely tied to government. Parliamentary committees sometimes met at the Inns, and from the Inns during the reigns of Elizabeth and James, men like Bacon, Ellesmere, and Burleigh rose to title and position and governance. In Elizabeth's reign six Speakers of the House of Commons came from the Middle Temple alone. Such men were models for Davies, and for one of them he did what may have been his earliest extant literary writing: 'A Conference between a Gentleman Usher and a Post', a clever prose entertainment, was reportedly presented before the Queen by the Lord Treasurer Burleigh on 10 May 1591.[4] When Burleigh's

---

[1] 'The Life of Mr. Richard Hooker', *Lives*, ed. Alfred W. Pollard (1925), p. 328.
[2] Ibid., p. 335.
[3] Dedication, *Every Man Out of his Humour* (1599), *Works*, iii. 421.
[4] John Nichols (ed.), *The Progresses and Public Processions of Queen Elizabeth* (1823),

granddaughter, Elizabeth Vere, married the Earl of Derby in January 1595, Davies provided an epithalamion, probably for recitation as an entertainment.

From 1593 to 1599 Davies wrote almost all the poems for which he is known. Many, like his decorative *Epithalamion*, his condolatory sonnet to Egerton on the death of his wife, and his *Hymnes of Astræa* and *Nosce Teipsum*, both dedicated to the Queen, were written to or for powerful persons. Even his *Orchestra*, although addressed to Richard Martin, was evidently later adapted to serve as an entertainment for the Queen. He satisfied the expectation that a poet in the 1590s would write sonnets by his *Sonnets to Philomel*, and he entertained himself, his friends, and a considerable public in London with his graphic and often coarse epigrams, largely composed by November 1594. These topical verses, so easily and carelessly rhymed, were most responsible for his contemporary literary reputation.

Davies's life during these years was centred at the Temple. While the Middle Temple Records take no notice of daily affairs, they indicate that, despite ordinances to the contrary, eight Middle Templars, including Fleetwood, Martin, and Davies, in 1591, 'broke the ordinance [forbidding Candlemas riots] by making outcries, forcibly breaking open chambers in the night and levying money as the Lord of Misrule's rent'.[1] When at Candlemas two years later the three were again responsible for riots, Davies was kept 'out of Commons' and Martin and Fleetwood both expelled temporarily.[2] Martin and Fleetwood were Davies's most frequent companions during his years at the Temple; and Martin, renowned among his contemporaries for remarkable grace and charm, exercised more evident sway over Davies than any other person. For him Davies in 1594 wrote *Orchestra*; in his dedication he calls Martin 'mine-owne-selves better halfe, my deerest frend', and in his conclusion, one 'To whom I owe my service and my love'. Martin was esteemed by other poets as well: Donne was his associate; Jonson calls him his friend in dedicating *The Poetaster* to him, and Hoskyns wrote the lines appearing on his tomb in the Temple Church. John Aubrey describes him as 'a very handsome man, a gracefull speaker, facetious, and well-beloved'.[3] His speech was so graceful that the Sheriffs of London

---

iii. 74–8. Nichols gives this date without citation; B.M. MS. Harl. 286, fol. 248, from which he takes his text, has no date.

[1] Records, i. 318.   [2] Ibid. 326–7.   [3] Brief Lives (1898), ii. 48.

chose him to welcome James I to the city in 1603. And he was so well liked by the Middle Templars that they elected him their 'Prince of Love' to rule during the revels leading to Candlemas Day, 1597/8. Like the Gray's Inn entertainment surrounding the Prince of Purpool described in *Gesta Grayorum*, these festivities included lavish costumes, assumed identities, banqueting, speeches, and plays, with the mock royal court here presided over by the Prince of Love. Martin's reign was described at length by his contemporary at the Temple, Benjamin Rudyerd, who praised Martin as

of a cheerful and gracious countenance . . . tall bodied, and well proportioned; of a sweet and fair conversation to every man that kept his distance. Fortune never taught him to temper his own Wit or Manhood . . . of a noble and high spirit . . . so wise, that he knew how to make use of all his Subjects, and that to their own contentment; so Eloquent in ordinary speech, by extraordinary practice, . . . that . . . study could not mend it. He was very fortunate and discreet in the love of Women; a great lover and complainer of company, having more judgement to mislike, then power to forbear.[1]

Rudyerd and others described Davies very differently in conversation and in epigrams where, under the name 'Matho', Davies's face, walk, and verse are all mocked:

Jo: Davys goes wadling with his arse out behinde as though he were about to make every one that he meetes, a wall to pisse against. . . . he never walkes but he carries a clokebag behind him / his arse sticks out soe farr.

· · ·

In Mathonem

Matho the dauncer with the maple [i.e. pock-marked] face
Intreated was to revell in a maske,
Wherefore, unto a shopp he hyed a pace
& for a visard speedyly did aske.
The shopp was hangd with glasses on each syde;
Quoth he, how do you that same visard sell?
(Taking his face which in a glasse he spyed
For a trew vizard, as he might do well)
For Matho masking needes no vizard weare,
Who for a face doth still a vizard beare.

[1] *Prince d'Amour* (1660), pp. 89–90. Further citations are made from this edition, which is a better transcript of the original manuscript, B.M. Harl. 1576, pp. 556–63, than the edition of 1841. Davies's identity and role in the festivities were pointed out by P. J. Finkelpearl in 'Sir John Davies and the "Prince d'Amour"', *N. & Q.* ccviii (1963), 300–2 and ccix (1964), 37.

In eundem

Mathon why sholdst thou thincke our Comon Lawe
None can into an ordered method drawe,
Since thy rude feete, whose gate confusion wrought,
Weare by greate paynes to ordered dauncinge brought?[1]

Though Rudyerd was a prejudiced witness, it appears that Davies
had a pock-marked face, awkward carriage, and clumsy gait. No
records concerning Davies anywhere suggest that he was handsome
or graceful.

The friendship between Davies and Martin appears then not to have
been between social equals, but between a magnetic, attractive, ad-
mired Prince of Love, and an awkward, homely, bright, and talented
but possibly peevish satirist, son of a tanner from a rural village.
Yet the poet of the cosmic dance was not content with his too distant
and elliptical orbit; and, unable to move closer, at the moment of
Martin's greatest magnetism as Prince of Love, Davies broke loose
without followers into terrible solitude and isolation.

The Candlemas festivities of 1597/8 brought the dissolution of
the friendship and the demise of Davies's fortunes. These festivities
were chronicled by Benjamin Rudyerd, whose account, however
biased or facetious, shows Davies increasingly seeking the attention
of his fellows, with his every effort becoming more desperate, and
being more mockingly rebuffed. In place of the name *Erophilus*, which
Davies gave himself in imitation of the Earl of Essex, Rudyerd's
account jibes at Davies's posture by calling him *Stradilax*. It attacks
his verse and decorum:

> *Stradilax* . . . ran down amongst them, like *Laocoon ardens*; and with a most
> urious and turbulent action, uttered these two Proverbs, the one borrowed
> from a Smith, the other from a Clown.[2]

In the same way that his own epigrams attacking others were doubt-
less posted in the city,

> there was a Libel set up against him in all the famous Places of the City, as
> Queen-Hithe, Newgate, the Stocks, Pillory, Pissing Conduit; and (but that

[1] Prose from John Manningham's diary, where Manningham seems uncertain
whether Rudyerd or Thomas Overbury was the speaker: B.M. MS. Harl. 5353,
fol. 127ᵛ. First epigram from MS. *Ro*, second from MS. *Che*. These two epigrams and
two others attacking Davies are printed, and their probable authorship by Rudyerd
discussed, by James L. Sanderson, 'Epigrames p[er] B[enjamin] R[udyerd] and Some
More "Stolen Feathers of Henry Parrot" ', *R.E.S.* xvii (1966), 241–55. Capitaliza-
tion and punctuation of epigrams supplied.

[2] pp. 78–9.

the Provost Marshall was his inward friend) it should not have missed Bridewell.[1]

He is accused of public drunkenness, of penning dull speeches, of having garish taste (he reportedly wore a gown of orange taffeta), of making an indecent address which offended the noble ladies present, and finally, of having 'practised factiously against the Prince, and earnestly stirred enmity betwixt him and the *Lincolnians*'. The friction between Davies and his associates intensified as the festivities progressed toward Candlemas Day, 2 February. Davies, increasingly isolated as he struggled for favour and inclusion, watched his every attempt to recover his position lead to new failure as his control over his fortunes slipped beyond him. He failed utterly, and on 9 February took his revenge. The Minutes of the Middle Temple tell the story:

9 Feb. 1597[/8]. While the Masters of the Bench and other fellows were quietly dining publicly in the Hall, John Davyes, one of the Masters of the Bar, in cap and gown, and girt with a dagger, his servant and another with him being armed with swords, came into the Hall. The servant and the other person stayed at the bottom of the Hall, while he walked up to the fireplace and then to the lower part of the second table for Masters of the Bar, where Richard Martyn was quietly dining. Taking from under his gown a stick, which is commonly called 'a Bastianado', he struck Martyn on the head with it till it broke, and then running to the bottom of the Hall he took his servant's sword out of his hand, shook it over his own head (*super caput suum proprium quatiebat*), and ran down to the water steps and jumped into a boat. He is expelled, never to return.[2]

Martin was not badly injured, but Davies was ruined. He had at a stroke lost his profession, his future, and the society of his friends. One wonders if during the imprisonment which followed he could view his situation with the lightheartedness attributed to him by a contemporary manuscript:

Davis beinge committed to prison for a quarrell betweene him and Martin, wrote as ensueth.

> Now Davis for a birde is in,
> But yet it is but for a Martin. (PP 2)

The day after his assault on Martin his rooms in the Middle Temple were given to someone else; and, following his release from prison, he left London.

---

[1] p. 80.   [2] *Records*, i. 379–80.

His grandson many years after would record Davies's actions in the following way:

Upon a quarell between him & Mr Martin before the Judges where Hee strooke Mr Martin hee was Confined & made a prisoner; after which in discontent hee retired into the Country & writt that Excellent poeme of his *Nosce teipsum* which was so well aprooved on by [~~him~~] the Lord Mountjoy after Lord Deputy of Irland & Earle of Devonshire that by his advise hee publisht it & dedicated itt to Queen Elizabeth to whom Hee presented it being introduced by the aforsaide Lord his pattron & this first Essay of his pen was so well rellisht that the Queen encouraged him in his Studdys promising him preferment & had him sworn her servant in Ordinary.[1]

John Aubrey probably had this period in mind when he wrote,

He was of the Middle Temple and after he had been there fo⟨r a⟩ time he considered with himselfe he wanted more University learning, ⟨and⟩ spent some more time there again (then only wearing his cloake.)[2]

Martin wrote an anagram making Davies adviser to the most famous betrayer:

Dauis / . Aduis / . Iudas . // Martin.[3]

And John Hoskyns, who had once shared rooms with Davies at the Temple, but now shared with Martin, asked,

Shall a soldier for a blowe with his hand given in warr to a captaine bee disgraced, & shall a lawyer for the bastinadoe given in a hall of court to his companion be advanced? We that profess lawes maintaine outrage? & they that breake all lawes, yet in this observe civillity?[4]

Obviously Hoskyns felt Davies should not be advanced, yet Davies began immediately attempting to repair his fortunes. Though he had been disbarred, he maintained his wit and pen, and the records of the next five years are of two kinds: letters to powerful persons asking their assistance in reinstating him to the Temple, and verses, entertainments, and speeches to and for those persons.

From many contemporary references it is clear that Davies's literary reputation rested mainly on his epigrams.[5] Yet these, along

---

[1] Carte MS. 62, fol. 590ʳ.

[2] Bodleian MS. Autog. d. 21, fol. 147. Aubrey also reports in this letter to Elias Ashmole that his great uncle knew and remembered Davies at Oxford. Apart from the time of his expulsion, Davies is not known to have left the Temple for an extended period until 1603, when he began residence in Ireland.

[3] B.M. Harl. MS. 5353, fol. 12ᵛ (slashes reproduce MS. punctuation).

[4] *The Life, Letters, and Writings of John Hoskyns*, ed. Louise Brown Osborn (New Haven, 1937), p. 135.

[5] Some of the many references to his epigrams include John Harington, *The Metamorphosis of Ajax* [1596], ed. Elizabeth Story Donno (New York, 1962), p. 103;

with several works by other writers which were similarly topical, coarse, or satiric, were publicly burned by ecclesiastical order on 4 June 1599, when it was decreed that no epigrams or satires be printed in future.[1] By the time the smoke rose before Stationers' Hall, however, 'the English Martiall' had already turned to other verse.

The family tradition that Davies wrote his verse-treatise on immortality, *Nosce Teipsum*, following his banishment from the Middle Temple seems true; among the few autobiographical lines in all his verse are those in the first elegy of *Nosce Teipsum* describing Affliction taking him by the ear to give him golden instruction (*N. T.* 149–56). If he could write *Orchestra* during fifteen days in 1594, he could surely write *Nosce Teipsum*, a poem twice its length, in the year following his dismissal. On 14 April 1599 it was entered in the Stationers' Register. It gave Davies a means of demonstrating public reformation and new-found seriousness in a poem lucid, ordered, and soundly and eminently didactic. It so well satisfied the Renaissance aesthetic of making moral instruction pleasing that it was reprinted six times during the next quarter century. Although we do not know if the Queen, skilled in maintaining hopes without granting promises, actually advanced Davies or had him sworn her servant because of his poem (as his grandson believed), Davies wrote twenty-six acrostics on her name, the *Hymnes of Astræa*, later in 1599. She may well have been as pleased with this flattery as with the philosophy of *Nosce Teipsum*.

Davies wrote to others as well. In 1599 he sent verses to Sir Thomas Egerton, Lord Keeper of the Great Seal, on the death of his wife. Beautiful manuscript copies of *Nosce Teipsum* with fulsome dedicatory verses were sent, probably shortly before printing, to Edward Coke, Attorney-General, and to Henry Percy, ninth Earl of Northumberland. Northumberland had been a fellow member of the Middle Temple, and evidently helped Davies during the difficult year following dismissal, for Davies asks,

> Then to what Spirit shall I these noates commend?
> But unto that which doth them best expresse?
> Who will to them more kind Protection lend?
> Then Hee, which did protect Mee in distresse?
> (*To . . . Northumberland,* lines 25–8)

and Harington's epigrams 112 and 388, *Letters and Epigrams*, ed. Norman Egbert McClure (Philadelphia, 1930); Thomas Bastard, *Chrestoleros* (1598), book ii, epigram 15; Edward Guilpin, *Skialetheia* (1598), epigram 20; Francis Meres, *Palladis Tamia* (1598), fol. 284[r]; Ben Jonson, epigram 18 in *Works*, viii. 32.

[1] *S.R.* iii. 677–8.

Letters and verses went to others in positions of influence. At the request of Sir Michael Hicks, who had befriended a number of literary men, Davies wrote verses to be inscribed on trenchers for Thomas Sackville, Lord Buckhurst, to whom Hicks was secretary. Since Buckhurst was the Lord Treasurer, Davies was, in his words, 'glad of any occasion of being made knowne to that noble gentleman' and indicated he would willingly alter his verses, if requested to.[1]

Elizabeth the Queen, Egerton the Lord Keeper, Buckhurst the Lord Treasurer—a powerful contingent, to which should be added a fourth, the Queen's Secretary of State, Sir Robert Cecil, to whom Davies wrote:

About 6 of clock this evening, my Lord of Cumberland signified your Honour's pleasure to me, that I should instantly conceive a speech for introduction of the Barriers. I have done it with a running pen, and a more running head, being distracted with a 100 parts of this business, all the little particularities being left to the care and provision of two of us. I hope we shall perform it with all circumstances, but for the substance of the matter, I mean the dancing and striking of the Barriers, I make no doubt but we shall show ourselves honest men and not shame ourselves.

This speech doth nothing satisfy me, and therefore much less will it seem passable in your Honour's judgment, but this is the effect of that which was intended to bring in the Barriers. I humbly beseech your Honour to let your eye pass a little over it, and to let me know what your judgment mislikes, and I shall quickly correct it. The gentleman that is to speak it must not know that it comes from me, for then he will never learn it. I am not ambitious to be reputed the author of a speech, but am zealous to have things done according to your Honour's pleasure.[2]

The speech is lost, but the date was probably 1601.[3] As before, Davies's purpose was clear: he was anxious, not to become known as an author, but to please. For a time Davies could see no results from his efforts to be reconciled to Martin and restored to the Temple. He relied only on hope, as he wrote to Cecil in a letter which Sir Walter Greg has called 'the most ingenious begging letter of a begging age':

having your Memory charged with so many great besonesses, there is no reason why you should remember such a Trifle as I am. howbeit the experience which I have had of your honourable favour doth begett in me a strong faith & assurance that you have not forgotten me. / & therfore I should much

---

[1] B.M. Lansdowne MS. 88, art. 2, fol. 4ʳ.
[2] *H.M.C. Hatfield* [9], xi. 544.
[3] *Elizabethan Stage*, iii. 269.

forgett my Self, If I should not remember to præsent my humble Thanks & devotion unto you who, I doubt not, like a good Angell, have er this donne me \a/ great benefit though it be yet invisible & unknowne unto me [or, me*n*].[1]

In a letter endorsed 16 June 1601 Davies wrote asking one last attempt from Cecil:

Right honorable Sir, I hold it a necessary Duty to praesent my humble thanks to your Lordship for the special favour you were pleasd to show me, the last day, at York house. / which, though it hath not yet effected that good which your Lordship wisht it should, yet it reflected much grace uppon me another way. / for many that were praesent did valew me the better, when they saw so great & worthy a personage have such respect & care of me. / my Lord chief Justice praetended he could not end the busines, bycause my adversary was absent. that lett is removd, for he is now returned to towne & will not depart till the end of the terme. /

Therfore, though I make so precious an accompt of your Lordships words, as I am sorry & ashamed that they should be spent in vayne, \ &/ in so trifling a besones yet I humbly beseech your Lordship to cast one Sun-beame more of your favour uppon me in this behalf; which if \it/ clear not my disgrace, I will draw a clow'd over me, & \so/ rest untill I may overcome it either by time or by Desert./ In the meane time vowing that all the affections of my hart, & powers of my braine, shalbee ever dedicated to your honors Service. /

Your Lordships to serve you in all
humble Dutyes
Jo: Davys.[2]

The letter brought results, for on 8 July 1601 John Chamberlain wrote: 'The Lord Cheife Justice and Master Secretarie have taken great paines to compound the quarrel twixt Martin and Davies which they have effected to the satisfaction of both parts.'[3] While Chief Justice Popham and Secretary Cecil reconciled Martin and Davies to one another, it was the insistence of Lord Keeper Egerton that effected Davies's return to the Temple, to which Egerton wrote on 30 June 1601:

My harty commendacions. Havinge hertofore both spoken pryvately unto some of you, & written to you all in generall, for the restoringe of Mr Jo: Davis to the bencfitt of your societye: I doe somewhat marvell, that I have hitherto neither found any effect of my request, nor receyved from you any

---

[1] W. W. Greg (ed.), *English Literary Autographs 1550–1650* (1928), part ii, item 47.
[2] B.M. MS. Lansdowne 88, art. 17, fol. 34.
[3] Chamberlain, *Letters*, i. 126.

aunswer of my lettres. The tyme that he hath ben alredy sequestred from your house, semeth (in mine opinion) a sufficient punnishment, and the Repentance which he hath shewd, a reasonable satisfaction for his offence. Whereof I have thought fitt once againe to putt you in minde, and ernestly to moove you to take consideracion thereof. And so, expectinge now some present satisfaccion from you in his behalf, I bidd you hartily farewell.[1]

The combined weight of this authority was too much. The Temple, which had concluded its entry for 9 February 1597/8 with 'He is expelled, never to return', on 30 October 1601 accepted his apology, which was made before the Chief Justice, the Chief Baron of the Exchequer, several serjeants-at-law, and the assembled members, among them Richard Martin, who accepted the apology as well.[2] After three and a half years of seclusion and attendance to the poetical needs of influential people, Davies had, as he said, 'allreaddye suffered muche damage and disgrace', and was now restored, in his words, to the 'Societye amongest whom I have had my chiefest education, and from whence I expect my best preferment'.[3]

He found preferment outside the Temple. When Elizabeth's last Parliament opened on 27 October 1601 Davies sat for the Borough of Corfe Castle, Dorset,[4] a seat undoubtedly achieved with the support of some powerful person. The most important question that session concerned parliamentary efforts to remove 'the monopolies'— monopolies usually in the trade, sale, or manufacture of items ranging from salt and vinegar to leather and lace ruffs which were granted by the monarch as rewards to favourites or former servants, and which were detested by the Commons and the people. The procedural question was crucial: should the House seek their removal by passing a Bill or by petitioning the Queen? Davies argued for the bolder course. By tradition and precedent, he said, the monarchy had limited its powers by allowing Parliament to assemble; thus it was no encroachment on royal prerogative to proceed by Bill.

Mr. Davies said: God hath given Power to Absolute Princes, which he Attributeth to Himself; *Dixi quod Dii estis*: And, as Attributes unto them, he hath given them Majesty, Justice, and Mercy. Majesty, in respect of the Honour that the Subject sheweth unto his Prince. Justice, in respect he can do no Wrong: Therefore, the Law is, I. Hen. 7. That the King cannot commit

---

[1] Huntington MS. 2522.
[2] *Records*, i. 416 and Lord Stowell, 'Observations . . . [on a] Petition of Sir John Davies', *Archaeologia* (1827), xxi. 107–12.
[3] Stowell, 111, 112.
[4] House of Commons, *Members of Parliament* (1878), part i, p. 438.

a Disseisin. Mercy, in respect he giveth Leave to his Subjects, to Right themselves by Law. And therefore, in the 44 Ass. an Indictment was brought against Bakers and Brewers; for that, by colour of License, they had broken the Assize: Wherefore, according to that Precedent, I think it most fit, to Proceed by Bill, and not by Petition.[1]

A later speech, among the boldest given in that session, concluded:

And therefore, let us do Generously and Bravely, like Parliament-Men; and our selves send for Them, and their Patents, and Cancel them before their Faces; Arreign them, as in times past, at the Bar, and send them to the Tower; there to remain, until they have made a good Fine to the Queen, and made some part of Restitution to some of the Poorest that have been oppressed by them.[2]

The Queen, shrewdly assessing the mood of the Commons, avoided a direct confrontation which might have endangered her prerogative by cancelling the most offensive monopolies and suggesting that others be tested in the courts. When her decision was reported in Commons, the barrister Davies was among those who wanted it recorded in writing. His argument for entering her reply in the *Commons Journals* demonstrates his brilliance and wit in extemporaneous speaking:

That which was deliver'd . . . from Her Sacred self, I think to be Gospel; that is, Glad Tydings. And as the Gospel is Written and Registred, so I would have that also: For Glad Tydings come to the Hearts of the Subjects.[3]

While he was outside the society of the Temple, Davies's scholarly concerns and pleasure in friendly disputation were especially fulfilled by his membership of the Society of Antiquaries, a group which included such eminent scholars, historians, and judges as William Camden, Sir Robert Cotton, John Stow, Francis Thynne, and Davies's close friend Sir John Dodderidge. Many of its members were of the Middle Temple; all, as 'antiquaries', were interested in the history of early England and the development of English customs and institutions. At gatherings the members each read a paper or offered a discourse on a single, agreed topic of discussion. At the close, Sir Robert Cotton took up and kept the speakers' manuscripts.[4] Those extant by Davies treat a variety of topics: the

---

[1] Heywood Townshend, *Historical Collections* (1680), pp. 241–2.
[2] Ibid., p. 244.   [3] Ibid., p. 258.
[4] Thomas Hearne discusses the society and prints some of its papers in *A Collection of Curious Discourses* (2 vols., 1771). The papers themselves are now B.M. MS. Cotton Faustina E. v; Davies's speech on epitaphs, in his holograph, appears on

Antiquity, Use, and Ceremonies of Lawful Combats in England
(given 22 May 1601); the Antiquity and Office of the Earl Marshal
of England (12 February 1602/3); and the Antiquity, Authority, and
Succession of the High Steward of England (1 or 4 June 1603). Of
special interest is his speech of 3 November 1600 on Epitaphs, as
it reveals his literary taste and standards of judgement. It is the
speech of an English humanist showing respect for tradition, especially
English literary tradition ('I say & I say it confidently no Age [have]
\no countrey/ in the world can show better Epitaphs then those
which were made above 400 yeare since uppon princes of this king-
dome'), yet a sense of literary superiority regarding the epitaphs of
his own 'late refined age' to medieval epitaphs, one of which he
characterizes as 'some what monkish in kind yet it wants not an
eloquency & a kind of grace'. Throughout his speech Davies shows
a desire to trace the current literary tradition to its classical pre-
cedents, with which he is familiar, and a willingness to judge current
practice not by conformity with rules but according to results. His
opening remarks define the form and matter of epitaphs, and, paren-
thetically, of epigrams:

An Epitaph is a monument of the dead; it is a kind of poeme though not a
perfect poeme, but as an Italian calls it a mote or Atome of poeticus, poeticus
Atomus. there is no precise art or imitation required in \itt/; and \therefore/
Aristotle in his booke of poetry speakes not of it. Yett in this Apish Age
wherein there ar so many imitatores stultus pecus, there ar divers \that/ prae-
scribe rules of making epitaphes, and \that allow of none except they/ conteyn
as many parts as a demonstrative oration. as the praise of the party buried,
\what a great losse or/ misse the world hath of him; \thereuppon/ a mourn-
full lamentation, then a comfort to the world and lastly an exhortation
to imitate his vertues. And all this besides must be exprest shortly, and
clearly. Others will have his name his Age his state, his deserts his gifts
of body and mind and his death \sett forth;/ and so wold have it a breef
story or description of his life, and death;
    This forsooth shold be the matter of an Epitaph. for the forme they will
have it of one peece, and \as it were/ one maine conceit \with the parts con-
tinued chayned and depending. \besides it/ must be no verse but a kind of
metricall prose seeming so by the strange transposition of the wordes; which
must likewise tast nothing of the moderne but \all/ al'antiche;
    I speake not this as if I lov'd not antiquities \which were Aie venerable /,

fols. 168–71, and in Hearne, i. 238–45, where, however, its authorship is unidentified.
Quotations that follow are from the manuscript, as Hearne's text has omissions.

I reverence them as I wold Reverence Adam if he were alive, but I speake this \for/ honor of \our/ English Epitaphes I meane the ancient Epitaphes of England, which I will mayntayne to be good Epitaphes, and yet ar they not cutt out according to this measure, but as they ar divers so have they divers formes and \yet none without a Generall grace/. The only Rule that is ob-serv'd in them is that which is Required in an Epigrame, Witt and brevitie and that which Plato in his Common-wealth required in an Epitaph. that an epitaph shold not be above 4 lines.

Davies's interest in English literary history and antiquities in this period reflects only part of his lifelong interest in British history. In an undated letter to Sir Robert Cotton he referred to their forth-coming journey together to Cambridge 'to see the ancient Seat of Robert le Bruis'; in 1605 he wrote sending Cotton maps of principal Irish cities;[1] and when in 1612 he published *A Discoverie of the True Causes why Ireland was never entirely subdued nor brought under Obedience of the Crowne of Englande Untill his Majesties Happie Raigne*, he wrote with familiarity (though not respect) regarding Irish history and customs.

After his return to the Temple in 1601, he did not stop writing verse for those who had helped restore him. When Egerton and Cecil entertained the Queen at their houses in 1602, Davies wrote *A Lotterie* and *A Contention* as entertainments; he continued to celebrate the beauty of the Virgin Queen, then near seventy. *The Humble Petition* calls her 'Beawtyes rose and vertues booke', and *A Maids Hymne* identifies her as

> Sacred virginity, unconquered Queene . . .
> O fresh Immortall baye, untroubled well,
> Or violett which untouch't doest sweetest smell.

But even so, like the others, he knew well that the Virgin Queen would soon be gone without an English heir; and while the hymns and entertainments honouring virginity were played, many eyes were looking north. When the Queen died on 24 March 1603 Davies left immediately for Scotland. As John Chamberlain complained on 30 March, 'There is much posting that way and many run thether of theyre owne errand, as yf yt were nothing els but first come first served, or that preferment were a goale to be got by footmanship: among whom . . . [is] John Davies the poet.'[2] Some who could not themselves go sent letters: on 28 March Francis Bacon wrote one

---

[1] B.M. MS. Cotton Julius C. iii, fols. 133–4.
[2] Chamberlain, *Letters*, i. 189.

of his several extant letters to Davies, here asking him to commend his name to the King.[1] Davies himself was well received, as Anthony Wood later reported:

Upon the death of Q. Elizabeth, he, with the lord Hunsdon, went into Scotland to congratulate K. James as her lawful successor; and being introduced into his presence, the king enquired the names of those gentlemen who were in the company of the said lord, and he naming John Davies among, who stood behind, them, the king straitway asked, whether he was *Nosce Teipsum*? and being answered that he was the same, he graciously embraced him, and thenceforth had so great a favour for him, that soon after he made him his solicitor and then his attorney-general in Ireland.[2]

On 12 April Chamberlain reported 'John Davies is sworne his [the King's] man', news disapproved by John Manningham, who had known Davies at the Middle Temple, and recorded in his diary: 'Jo: Davis reports that he is sworne the Kings man./. that the K: shewed him great favors / inepte / (he slaunders while he prayses)./'[3] Davies, doubtless elated at his change of fortune, celebrated the entry of the King and Queen into England with two poems, *The Kinges Welcome* and *To the Queene*. On Fortune's cap he was the very button.

From then on he continued to enjoy her favours, and largely abandoned his muse. On 18 October 1603 he was knighted in Dublin.[4] On 25 November he was appointed Solicitor-General for Ireland, where he served under the Lord Deputy Sir Charles Blount, Lord Mountjoy, who, according to Davies's grandson, had suggested that Davies dedicate *Nosce Teipsum* to Queen Elizabeth.[5] With his arrival in Ireland the records of his life and Davies's own prose writings and correspondence multiply, but for the student of his poetry these hold little interest, for he scarcely wrote further verse. Professor G. A. Wilkes observed in 1962 that the pages of Grosart's edition of Davies's prose works that appeared in 1876 were still uncut in most copies he had seen;[6] similarly, none of Davies's verse written after 1603 has ever been thought worth notice in critical discussions. A brief summary of Davies's later years will therefore suffice here.

---

[1] *The Letters and the Life of Francis Bacon*, ed. James Spedding (1868), iii. 65.

[2] Wood, ii. 401.

[3] Chamberlain, *Letters*, i. 192; B.M. MS. Harl. 5353, fol. 127ᵛ.

[4] *C.S.P. 1603–24 (Carew Papers)* [78], p. 383.

[5] Rowley Lascelles, *Liber Munerum Publicorum Hiberniae* (1852), I. ii. 75; Carte MS. 62, ibid.

[6] 'The Poetry of Sir John Davies', *Huntington Library Quarterly*, xxv (1962), 298.

From Solicitor-General he was advanced to become Attorney-General on 19 April 1606.[1] In both positions Davies's duties were many and his industry prodigious. He travelled throughout Ireland administering Jacobean justice to a conquered but obstreperous people. When he acted as a justice of the assize, like others in his position he travelled with fifty or sixty mounted troops and over a hundred foot-soldiers for protection. Of the peasants he encountered in the countryside, Davies once reported that they greeted him as amazedly as the ghosts in hell looked upon Aeneas on seeing him alive in that place. The power of legal officers was such that if a jury returned a verdict which the officers of the Crown did not approve the jury could be punished. On 17 November 1609, for example, as Attorney-General he was involved in a trial with Lord Chief Justice Winche in which four of the jurors returned a verdict of innocent against several Irishmen being tried for treason. In consequence the jurors were each fined £100, pilloried in Dublin, and punished with the loss of one ear 'for acquitting the said traitors contrary to the clear evidence that they had been in open rebellion'.[2]

Davies was one of the architects of James's policy in Ireland. He shared responsibility for planning 'the plantation of Ulster', which brought Scots and English to northern Ireland and has brought intermittent disruption ever since. He showed little respect or appreciation for Irish culture and tradition, but when his writings on Ireland are compared with those of Spenser he appears the more humane writer. Like most of his English contemporaries and all the political administrators in Ireland, he sought to extirpate Catholicism. He disagreed with the adopted policy of great severity toward Irish Catholic leaders only because he thought attention should be centred instead on converting the masses, who would be more malleable than their leaders. Though severe, his policies were no more so than those of his superiors. Dispensing British justice in Ireland meant, in large part, preserving James's rule.

James himself undoubtedly approved of Davies. The King spoke highly of Davies's achievements in Ireland and received familiar letters from him.[3] He made Davies King's Serjeant in 1612, consulted him on Irish affairs during Davies's frequent journeys to London, and personally specified that Davies should be Speaker of the House when the Irish Parliament opened in 1613. Yet even a king's word

---

[1] *Liber Munerum*, I. ii. 73.   [2] *H.M.C. Egmont* [63], I. i. 35.
[3] Carte MS. 62, fol. 590ᵛ; *H.M.C. Hastings* [78], iv. 5.

may be opposed: when the Irish Catholics insisted on placing their own man in the Speaker's chair, the corpulent Davies was simply picked up by his supporters and placed atop him.[1]

On 21 June 1619 Davies wrote to Buckingham asking to be removed from his position as Attorney-General and on 30 October 1619 he was replaced.[2] Of his service in Ireland one twentieth-century historian has written,

He was the animating spirit of the Irish Government at an epoch of singular importance in Irish history. For not merely was Davis the trusted and most efficient instrument of the Irish policy of King James . . . but he was in a large degree the guiding spirit of the Irish administration by which that policy was directed . . . He at once entered on a career as an Irish law officer of almost unexampled duration and of quite unrivalled importance.[3]

He also served King James by writing two works widely circulated in manuscript, though not printed during his lifetime: one a defence of Prince Charles's title to the duchy of Cornwall, the other a treatise defending the royal prerogative and James's right to levy impositions. The Davies who in 1601 had urged the Commons, 'let us do Generously and Bravely, like Parliament-Men; and our selves send for them, and their Patents, and Cancel them before their Faces', had in the years since amassed immense wealth and lands through royal favour, and had gained respect for the system that had allowed him to succeed.

His wealth and position enabled him to marry Eleanor, daughter of George Touchet, Lord Audley, Earl of Castlehaven, early in 1609.[4] She proved to be a visionary who was consulted by the Queen, and who prophesied many important events with such embarrassing accuracy that she was considered dangerous or mad, and, in years after Davies's death, was imprisoned for a time. She evidently failed to foresee that she would be ill suited to Davies, who was rationalist in religion, worshipful toward authority, respectful of precedent, and, by the time she met him, unsympathetic to anything revolutionary. Though Davies wrote hundreds of letters that have survived, no correspondence with Eleanor remains. She, however, recounted in her prophetical writings that she had foreseen her husband's death, and had gone into mourning for him three years in advance:

[His] doom I gave him in letters of his own name (JOHN DAVES, JOVES HAND)

---

[1] *C.S.P. 1603–24 (Carew Papers)*, pp. 270–5, 278–85.
[2] Bodleian MS. Fortescue 245; *Liber Munerum*, ibid.
[3] C. Litton Falkiner, 'Sir John Davis', *Essays Relating to Ireland* (1909), pp. 33, 36.
[4] Chamberlain, *Letters*, i. 288.

within three years to expect the mortal blow; so put on my mourning gar-
ment from that time: when about three days before his sudden death, before
all his servants and friends at the table, gave him pass to take his long sleep,
by him thus put off, 'I pray weep not while I am alive, and I will give you
leave to laugh when I am dead.'[1]

They had three children: two sons John and Richard, one of whom
was mute and both of whom died young, and a daughter Lucy, who
was Davies's heir.[2] Born 20 January 1612/13, she was married before
her eleventh birthday to Ferdinando Hastings, later Earl of Hunting-
don, at the house of the Countess Dowager of Derby in Harefield,
where twenty years earlier the Countess and Sir Thomas Egerton
had given an entertainment for Queen Elizabeth that was written
by Davies. Because the marriage was without a licence the two
were remarried in Davies's house in Englefield, Berkshire. Davies
spent many of his last years there or at his house in the Strand, and
he often wrote to the Earl of Huntingdon about affairs in Parliament
while he represented Hindon, Wiltshire, and later Newcastle under
Lyme in the Commons.

The tanner's son became a lawyer and a knight; the knight married
a lady; their daughter became a countess. Here, in its way, was a
success story. Moreover, Davies would have become Lord Chief
Justice. He had bought his robes,[3] but on 8 March 1626, the
night before he was to sit on the high bench, he died, as his wife
had predicted. His funeral sermon was preached by John Donne, his
body laid in St. Martin-in-the-Fields.[4]

THE POEMS

A recent critic counsels against praising the poetry of Sir John Davies
for the wrong reasons,[5] excellent advice that reminds us that his
verse has often been appreciated for qualities it did not possess, so
that there is an unfortunate discrepancy between critical comment
and the poetry. Grosart praised 'the deep and original thinking'
of *Nosce Teipsum*, which even T. S. Eliot called the product of an

[1] Quoted by George Ballard, *Memoirs of Several Ladies of Great Britain* (1752),
p. 274.
[2] Carte MS. 62, fol. 590ᵛ.
[3] Bodleian MS. Wood F. 39, fol. 375ʳ.
[4] Carte MS. 62, fol. 590ᵛ.
[5] G. A. Wilkes, 'The Poetry of Sir John Davies', *Huntington Library Quarterly*, xxv
(1962), 283-98.

independent mind; and it has been suggested that the repeated publication of that poem during the seventeenth and eighteenth centuries was due to the belief that it effectively rebutted materialism.[1] In our time, E. M. W. Tillyard has written of *Orchestra* as if it were a serious exposition of the concept of order,[2] and many writers discuss it as an indirect and therefore delightful treatment of the same material that *Nosce Teipsum* expounds directly, and by implication, undelightfully. This is too serious a view of *Orchestra*, and as naïve as Grosart's defence of the originality of *Nosce Teipsum*. But if Tillyard mistook *Orchestra* because of his own involvement in propounding the Elizabethan world-picture, he saw Davies correctly as a minor poet who reflects his age as great poets never do.

Davies seems never to have taken any attitude to poetry higher than that of a schoolboy composing Latin verses on assigned themes; anyone who has performed such exercises knows that neither the originality nor the profundity of one's ideas has much bearing on one's skill in composition. While the latter is no contemptible achievement, it is not necessarily the mark of a great classicist or poet. Professor Wilkes quite rightly isolates 'invention' as the motive behind *Orchestra*: he mentions 'the cleverness of the analogies, the ingenuity of their elaboration, the brilliance with which the whole undertaking is sustained'.[3] This merely rhetorical approach to poetry is one outstanding feature of Davies's work; another is the amazing skill of the performance. The result, however, is a body of poetry that, inspired by technical considerations, arouses in the reader primarily admiration of the technique: poetry excellent in its kind, but irretrievably minor. There is, nevertheless, a great difference between a minor poet and a bad poet, and Davies's ability to give pleasure by his poetry claims for it our continued attention.

An extremely versatile technician, Davies wrote, experimented in, even helped to introduce many popular types of poetry. He is a major practitioner of the 'elegy' both amorous and philosophical. Early in antiquity the term 'elegy' came to mean almost any kind of reflective poetry; its main vehicle was the elegiac distich (a hexameter followed by a pentameter), used in love poems, other expressions of emotion or reflection, didactic poetry, and epigram. Thus *Nosce Teipsum* belongs to an established genre of didactic poetry, the tra-

---

[1] Richard H. Perkinson, 'The Polemical Use of Davies' *Nosce Teipsum*', *Studies in Philology*, xxxvi (1939), 597–608.
[2] *The Elizabethan World Picture* (1943), pp. 96–8   [3] p. 289.

dition of works like Hesiod's *Works and Days*, Virgil's *Georgics*, and Lucretius' *De Rerum Natura*. Sidney regards it as a lower form of poetry:

The second kinde, is of them that deale with matters Philosophicall, either morall as *Tirteus, Phocilides, Cato*; or naturall, as *Lucretius*, and *Virgils Georgikes*; or Astronomicall as *Manilius* and *Pontanus*; or Historicall as *Lucan* . . . But bicause this second sort is wrapped within the folde of the proposed subject, and takes not the free course of his own invention, whether they properly bee Poets or no, let *Gramarians* dispute; and goe to the third indeed right Poets.[1]

Much of the didactic poetry of Davies's time preserves a formal fiction, as in Daniel's *Musophilus*, a debate between Musophilus and Philocosmus. The treatise in verse is less usual; the undated treatises of Fulke Greville are the best known ones besides Davies's poem on the soul.

For the classical elegiac metre, Davies substitutes the quatrain with alternate rhyme in both *Nosce Teipsum* and the four 'Elegies of Love'. His sonnets are usually based on the quatrain (most are loosely Shakespearian), perhaps indicating that Davies regarded the sonnet as a form of epigram and saw its relation also to classical love-elegies. But Davies wrote in other forms as well. Like many of his contemporaries, he tried his hand at versifying the Psalms, and the workmanship of his couplets entitles them to a high place. The *Ten Sonnets to Philomel* are respectable if not inspired, and the restraint with which he stops after ten is rare and praiseworthy. The *Gullinge Sonnets* lead the revolt against Petrarchism by mocking its feckless lovers and their predictable and extravagant techniques for describing their idealized griefs. The satire is so subtle that but for the warning in the dedication to Sir Anthony Cooke, we might easily take them for serious poems, however silly. He also uses the sonnet form in his epithalamion, one of the earliest in English, and for other kinds of satire: the eleven satires on Sir Edward Coke's marriage constitute a mock sonnet sequence. Of the popular Elizabethan modes, only pastoral is not represented; Davies seems entirely and happily an urban poet.

Besides the two long poems *Orchestra* and *Nosce Teipsum*, Davies's main success lies in the field of epigram, where he displays clearly his character as a poet of the City and also his great versatility.

---

[1] *The Defence of Poesie* in *The Complete Works of Sir Philip Sidney*, ed. Albert Feuillerat (1923), iii. 9.

Unlike the epigrams of many of his contemporaries, his are not all satiric. The lots composed for the entertainment at Harefield and the verses inscribed on trenchers for Lord Buckhurst correspond to the original Greek epigram, used for inscriptions. Some purposes of the classical epigram, both Greek and Latin, are satisfied in Davies's use of the sonnet, a verse-form found frequently in the published *Epigrammes*, which reflect the influence of Martial the satirist. But Martial wrote other kinds of epigrams: eulogies, compliments, descriptions, acknowledgements, verses to set forth an idea or to accompany a gift; and Davies similarly wrote a sonnet to Egerton, probably to accompany the gift of a book, the sonnet 'Of Faith' and the 'Sonnet sent with a Booke', and two complimentary sonnets for the publication of a book by his friend George Chapman. Since for Davies the sonnet assumes the functions of the classical love-elegy, he may be said to be merely extending the range of the sonnet to other elegiac forms.

In the epigram in particular, Davies is an innovator. Guilpin acknowledges this in calling him 'our English Martiall' (*Skialetheia*, Ep. 20), and the *Epigrammes* show that Davies saw himself in that light: he mocks the 'new-fangled' Ciprius for praising 'olde George Gascoines rimes' (Ep. 22); he refers to the eclipsing of Heywood's reputation 'since my light muse arose' (Ep. 29); in the first epigram he explains 'what an Epigramme doth meane'; and the second he devotes to explaining the 'new terme', *gull*.

Davies is not an innovator in prosody. He does not introduce new metres; nor, though capable of 'creating' the sixteen-line stanza of the *Hymnes of Astræa*, does he produce wonders comparable to the Spenserian stanza or the strophes of Spenser's *Epithalamion*; nor does he, like Sidney, experiment with Greek metre or quantitative verse. He does, however, use an immense variety of stanzaic forms: the rhyme royal of *Orchestra*; the different types of sonnets; the sixain of *A Hymne in Praise of Musicke* with its quatrain and closing couplet, and that of *The Humble Petition* in tercets rhyming *aab*; the couplets of his *Psalmes*. Saintsbury greatly admired the *Hymnes of Astræa*, praising the 'two fives and a six of almost Caroline quaintness and elegance'.[1] And Saintsbury and Eliot have both commented on the excellence of the quatrain in *Nosce Teipsum*, Eliot indeed considering Davies to be unsurpassed even by Gray.[2]

---

[1] *A History of English Prosody* (1908), ii. 106.
[2] 'Sir John Davies', *On Poetry and Poets* (1957), p. 135.

That Davies and Gray are by common consent the best practi-
tioners of the quatrain stems from their having used it for statement
rather than for narrative, as Davenant and Dryden did. *Pace* Eliot,
there can be no doubt that Gray's *Elegy* is a better poem than *Nosce
Teipsum*: the content is emotive rather than expository. But it does not
surpass *Nosce Teipsum* in versification; it reveals too clearly the ten-
dency, inherent in its tone of melancholy, to pass over into listless-
ness. The reader becomes too conscious that the pentameter is
maintained largely by disyllabic adjectives. The point is, of course,
academic; the common reader will never love *Nosce Teipsum*, and
although Gray could never have produced and sustained the latter,
Davies could not have written Gray's *Elegy*. The comparison simul-
taneously points to Davies's technical superiority and reminds us
that other values are more important in poetry.

The relative lack of emotional charge is not merely the difference
between *Nosce Teipsum* and Gray's *Elegy*, but the characteristic note of
all Davies's poetry. T. S. Eliot attributes to Davies the gift 'for turn-
ing thought into feeling',[1] but he is wrong. Comparison of the
following passages renders incomprehensible Eliot's assertion that
Davies has here surpassed Pope:[2]

> Much like a subtill Spider which doth sit,
> In middle of her Web which spreadeth wide;
> If ought do touch the utmost threed of it,
> She feeles it instantly on every side.
>
> <div align="right">(<i>N.T.</i> 1061–4)</div>
>
> The spider's touch, how exquisitely fine!
> Feels at each thread, and lives along the line.
>
> <div align="right">(<i>An Essay on Man</i>, i. 217–18)</div>

The sensuousness of Pope's lines, with their concision, delicate as-
sonance, and the effect of vibration that comes from the closing
alliteration, inevitably excels Davies's rather bald and prosaic
statement. Lest this seem too hard on Davies, it should be noticed
that even in material as hackneyed as that of the *Hymnes*, Davies
occasionally gives the impression of passionate sincerity. Moreover,
if a thought is intrinsically emotive, Davies is far too competent to
ruin it:

> What can we know? or what can we discerne?
> When Error chokes the windowes of the mind.
>
> <div align="right">(<i>N.T.</i> 57–8)</div>

[1] p. 136.   [2] p. 134.

On the whole, however, there is little feeling in Davies's poetry. He commits himself only to writing well, not to expressing his own feelings or those of others. No other poet seems so little disturbed by upheaval around him; except for the reference to his recent affliction in *Nosce Teipsum*, he introduces no passion into his poems. The poems for which he is best known are those that can be carried by the combination of intellect and versification: the rational and expository *Nosce Teipsum*, the wholly impersonal *Orchestra*, and the comic epigrams. The last never display anger, or even a desire to reform. The observer and the reader remain at the exact distance needed for humour: close enough to see the comic details, but too far for emotional identification with the subjects. Davies's worst poems are those that involve emotional effect, the love poems.

Davies is predominantly and successfully an occasional poet, in the widest sense of 'occasional': most of his poems arise from some external stimulus or are written to accomplish some external purpose. This statement obviously applies to the contents of the section 'Occasional Poems and Poems from Entertainments': they are written for special occasions. The entertainments may have been written to order, not for money but for the favour of influential people; in a letter thanking Lord Buckhurst's secretary for having recommended him for the *Verses upon Trenchers*, Davies says he is obliged 'bycause I am glad of any occasion of being made knowne to that noble gentleman whom I honour & admire exceedingly'.[1]

The *Hymnes of Astræa* are very likely occasional in the strict sense. Entered in the Stationers' Register on the anniversary of the Queen's accession, they were probably presented to Elizabeth for that occasion and then given to John Standish for publication. *Orchestra*, too, was a response to an external impetus, Martin's request, and probably was planned as an entertainment.

Even *Nosce Teipsum* is probably occasional in the broad sense. The tale of conversion promulgated by Wood has a fine ring; it may be the story that Davies told his daughter, since it is repeated by her son.[2] But the kind of spiritual crisis that story suggests does not usually burst out into 2,000-line versifications of works of popular theology. Davies was probably sobered by the consequences of his attack on Martin; *Nosce Teipsum* is not, however, the working-out of a conversion to sobriety and religion, but the attempt to demonstrate it.

[1] See Commentary, pp. 415–16.
[2] See Commentary on *Nosce Teipsum*, p. 324.

As Professor Wilkes says, 'in 1599 [it] offered a way to respectability that Davies would be unwilling to refuse'.[1]

The most spontaneous of Davies's works, and those least directed toward effecting some external change, are the satiric epigrams; a paradoxical conclusion, since satire is of all modes the one most tied to its specific subject or occasion. Even the satire seems incidental to them; Davies is not angry or indignant, nor does he appear, as Hall or Guilpin does, bent on reforming or eliminating the 'generall vice' he purports to attack. The epigrams stand alone in originating in no more serious impetus than the desire to display cleverness. Had Davies stopped writing poetry when he was called to the Bar, the right-minded would have found little to approve, and we would not think of him as part of the team of Davies and Daniel; *Orchestra*, after all, appears in one light as the companion to the epigrams, in another when accompanied by *Nosce Teipsum*.

The earlier Davies has none of the later one's sobriety; he darts about quickly, full of delight at his own wit. In many ways he is like Spenser, even in the epigrams, where characters and their quirks rush through an imagined London rather as the citizens do in Spenser's *Epithalamion*. *Orchestra* in particular reminds us of Spenser. It uses a rather long, ornate stanza for narrative, one that Spenser uses for *The Ruines of Time* and *The Fowre Hymnes* (although *Orchestra* antedates the publication of Spenser's *Hymnes*, it contains verbal similarities). It resembles *The Faerie Queene* in its pictorial qualities, its Ovidian myth-making such as the birth of dancing, and the appearance of personifications; and it brings Spenser to mind also because its theme is one of the essential elements of *The Faerie Queene*: a delight in motion so encompassing that the rejection of it at the end of the *Cantos of Mutabilitie* comes as a great shock. Both poems celebrate ordered motion.

The similarity reaches its zenith with the introduction of Concord and Comeliness. The latter, 'chyld of order sweet' (*Orch.* 113), is so basic to the ideals of *The Faerie Queene* that Spenser uses 'comely' throughout to express general approval, from the squire Reverence in the House of Holiness, 'in comely sad attire' (*F.Q.* I. x. 7) to the Graces who bestow on men 'all gracious gifts'

> Which decke the body or adorne the mynde,
> To make them lovely or well favoured show,

> As comely carriage, entertainement kynde,
> Sweete semblaunt, friendly offices that bynde.
> (F.Q. VI. x. 23)

And Concord is the major social virtue of The Faerie Queene, for virtue is marked by charity and harmony:

> O goodly golden chaine, wherewith yfere
> The vertues linked are in lovely wize.
> (F.Q. I. ix. 1)

But then Saintsbury points out that we cannot and need not divide Davies into two poets, when he calls Nosce Teipsum more Spenserian than Orchestra.[1] Both writers strive for smooth, melodious lines, and Davies achieves his aim throughout Nosce Teipsum. Although this similarity may be obscured by the difference in diction, it is undeniable. The archaic diction and the extensive use of alliteration and assonance give Spenser's verse richness. The plainness of Davies's diction emphasizes the smooth flow of his verse.

The smoothness and clarity of Davies's writing come from the way in which he treats ideas as well as from the verse and diction. He not merely clarifies, he simplifies ideas to fit into the compass of the verse. The reduced thought, freed of complexity, ambiguity, and uncertainty, lends itself to expression in simple words and melodious lines. Bacon complains of Ciceronian prose that it hinders philosophical inquiry 'because it is too early satisfactory to the mind of man, and quencheth the desire of further search, before we come to a just period'.[2] The charge applies to Davies's poetry, especially Nosce Teipsum, where the ideas are so simple and so easily presented as to leave the impression of completeness and incontrovertibility.

The unimpassioned control of ideas, the smoothness of verse, and the use of largely denotative language create a divergence between Davies and his major contemporaries, who show more awareness of conflict and complexity, and whose words suggest things that lie outside their compass and arouse the imagination. Lyly's euphuism explores while it defines, explores the very process of defining. At the moment when it fixes shifting reality by alliteration and parallelism, it suggests by antithesis the area outside the verbal limits. The style of Sidney's Arcadia seems designed not merely to delight by ornament,

---

[1] p. 106.
[2] The Advancement of Learning, ed. G. W. Kitchin (Everyman's Library), p. 25.

but to suggest the problems that hedge the perception of reality and the mere description of appearance. *Astrophil and Stella* is polarized between the sonnet's momentary definition of the lover's experience and the recognition that the experience itself persists in all its defiance of reason.

Even Spenser, whose long stanza permits great explicitness, uses evocative words that arouse the reader's imagination to supply what the word cannot. And certainly Donne's poetry, subordinating the verse to the rhythm of speech, prevents any set of limits from establishing itself over the thought; the language disrupts old limits, the analogies suggest new directions, and the reader is led from one vantage-point to another, as the poet denies him the comfort of a single or simple view. Davies's poetry, however, is explicit rather than suggestive, the thought not compressed but simplified, the metaphors entirely illustrative. It is a form in which to state and clarify accepted ideas, not one to suggest new viewpoints or directions to new knowledge.

Nosce Teipsum in particular has always reminded readers of later neo-classical poetry. We should bear in mind the possibility that the continued popularity of the poem into the eighteenth century rested not merely on the acceptability of the contents but on the style. Although Nahum Tate's preface to the edition of 1697 refers to a continuing interest in the reign of Elizabeth, the Elizabethan style probably seemed rather outlandish to his contemporaries and successors; but the vocabulary and versification of *Nosce Teipsum* would have seemed familiar and contemporary. Just over a century later Chalmers confirms this by his comment that in versification Davies 'has anticipated the harmony which the modern ear requires more successfully than any of his contemporaries'.[1] And in his essay on Davies, devoted largely to *Nosce Teipsum*, T. S. Eliot repeatedly remarks how atypical the vocabulary is in the period; he speaks of 'a taste in language remarkably pure for his age', and 'a language of remarkable clarity and austerity'.[2]

The marks of *Nosce Teipsum*, as of much neo-classical poetry, are ease and clarity. The verse-form itself contributes to both these qualities; Davenant chose it for *Gondibert* at least partly for the readers' convenience: 'I beleev'd it would be more pleasant to the Reader, in a Work of length, to give this respite or pause, between every *Stanza*

[1] Ed., *Works of the English Poets* (1810), v. 78.
[2] *On Poetry and Poets*, pp. 136 and 133, respectively.

... than to run him out of breath with continu'd *Couplets*.'[1] For Davies, the quatrain has the advantage not just of respite, but of room for expansion:

> Then doth th'aspiring *Soule* the body leave,
> Which we call *death*; but were it known to all
> What *life* our *Soules* do by this *death* receave,
> Men would it *Birth*, or *Gaole deliverie* call.
>
> (*N.T.* 1881–4)

In this typical example the event is followed by an interpretation that includes two possible metaphors. The idea is stated simply and expanded until it is perfectly clear. Davies obviously could have written *Nosce Teipsum* in couplets by giving up a great deal of the expansion. As he has written it, the ideas do not rush past the reader, requiring that he stop and explain them to himself; they walk forward sedately and turn slowly before him. The leisureliness of the author's method permits the reader to proceed very quickly.

Perhaps the outstanding feature of *Nosce Teipsum* is that the figures of speech, even the plays on words, operate not for their own sakes but to clarify the thought. Rarely does a figure even invite one to linger and contemplate it. Usually the analogies reduce the abstractions of theory to concrete and familiar objects:

> When *Reasons* lampe which like the *Sunne* in skie,
> Throughout *Mans* litle world her beames did spread,
> Is now become a Sparkle, which doth lie
> Under the Ashes, halfe extinct and dead.
>
> (*N.T.* 61–4)

Even when Davies indulges in word-play that turns the reader aside to admire the poet's wit, the excursion is brief, and closely connected to the thought:

> She within *Listes* my raunging mind hath brought,
> That now beyond my self I list not go;
> My selfe am *Center* of my circling thought,
> Onely *my selfe* I studie, learne, and *know*.
>
> (*N.T.* 165–8)

The pun on 'list' is ornamental, not illustrative, but it is intrinsically part of the stanza and the argument; hitherto the poet has decried the human tendency to look outward, but he now shows that in affliction,

---

[1] Preface to *Gondibert: An Heroick Poem* (1651), p. 25.

the mind retires within herself. Under her tutelage, 'list' is confined within lists, and 'raunging' disciplined into circling.

The discipline that confines the poet's wit to the clearly relevant is another neo-classical feature in *Nosce Teipsum*. 'Wit in the Poet', says Dryden,

is no other then the faculty of imagination in the writer, . . . which searches over all the memory for the species or Idea's of those things which it designs to represent . . . 'Tis not the jerk or sting of an Epigram, nor the seeming contradiction of a poor Antithesis, . . . nor the gingle of a more poor *Paranomasia*: . . . but it is some lively and apt description, dress'd in such colours of speech, that it sets before your eyes the absent object, as perfectly and more delightfully then nature.[1]

Davies's use of figures conforms more closely to Dryden's definition of wit than to Elizabethan practice.

The pervasive figurativeness of *Nosce Teipsum* directs attention to a principal difference between poetry and prose. Sidney's insistence that metre is extrinsic to prose is borne out by his practice; in particular, the parts of *Arcadia* told from the narrator's point of view abound in expressions like 'so to speak' and 'as it were', which in classical Roman prose constitute the writer's notice that the language is figurative. For the Romans and for many Elizabethans educated in Latin, poetry is figurative, prose is not. Davies's contemporaries probably recognized at once the generic implications of his writing. For them, at least, *Nosce Teipsum* was more than just philosophy in verse.

So it should be for us. T. S. Eliot points out that it is not very good philosophy;[2] indeed, if it were, it would probably not be poetry at all. The poem is orderly, but not closely reasoned, and has got away with great gaps in the train of thought because the verse carries the reader from line to line, stanza to stanza, not from idea to idea. The rather scrappy philosophy depends entirely on the verse, to which the specific theories are accidental, not essential.

Professor Wilkes calls *Nosce Teipsum* 'a brilliant exploitation of the resources of verse for argument and persuasion'.[3] While the poem appears to be so divided that the first elegy is rhetorical or persuasive, and the second argumentative, in fact persuasion and argument, rhetoric and logic, are combined at all points. Argument and logic

---

[1] 'An Account of [*Annus Mirabilis*]', in *The Poems of John Dryden*, ed. James Kinsley (1958), i. 46.
[2] p. 136.   [3] p. 298.

are found in the first elegy, and the second depends heavily on the
power of good verse to persuade the reader that the argument is
sound and convincing. Throughout the poem the method and pace
of exposition are so smooth that the reader would finish without
having time to be bored even if the verse were excruciatingly dull—
which it is not. In the following passage, predominantly mono-
syllabic, end-stopped lines, reinforced by parallel structure, give
surprising force to pure clichés:

> So do the *Winds* and *Thunders* cleanse the Aire,
> So working Seas, settle and purge the wine;
> So lopt and pruned Trees do florish faire;
> So doth the fire the drossie Gold refine.
>
> (*N.T.* 157–60)

The smoothness of the verse comes from its comparative regularity,
the matching of speech-stress to verse-stress within the permissible
variations of iambic pentameter, and the sparing use of caesura. These
features are apparent even in the worst stanza of the poem, which
cannot be ruined by analysis or redeemed by versification:

> Lastly Nine things to *Sight* required are;
> The *power* to see, the *light*, the *visible thing*,
> Being not too *small*, too *thinne*, too *nigh*, too *farre*,
> *Cleere space*, and *time* the forme distinct to bring.
>
> (*N.T.* 993–6)

The enumeration here makes the second and third lines extremely
heavy, especially since the speech stress on 'too' makes four feet of
the third line virtually spondaic. But Davies lightens the verse as much
as possible by using the trisyllabic 'required' and the extra-metrical
disyllable 'visible'. The absence of a caesura in the first line and
the very early one in the fourth permit the lines to run smoothly.
And all this material is covered with minimal distortion of syntax;
Wordsworth himself could not quarrel with the word order.

Davies also provides a great deal of metrical variation, by occa-
sionally inverting feet in different lines; by sometimes using spon-
dees; by varying the position of the caesura. The stress moves freely
because heavily stressed words and polysyllables appear in dif-
ferent places from line to line, subtly changing the rhythm. Davies's
versification gives rise to real beauties of melody:

> So when the roote and fountaine of mankind,
> Did draw corruption, and Gods curse by sinne;

This was a charge, that all his heires did bind,
And all his of-spring grew corrupt therein.
                                    (*N. T.* 773–6)

The outstanding virtue of *Nosce Teipsum* is not passion or originality of
ideas or prosody but readability; anyone conversant with Elizabethan
vocabulary will find no obstacles to quick reading and easy com-
prehension. Add clarity, wit, and a 'genius for versification',[1] the
marks of all Davies's poetry, and the result is not first-rate poetry,
but excellence at a lower rank.

The same clarity and wit appear in the epigrams (the contents of
the published *Epigrammes* and the sections 'Epigrams from Manu-
script' and 'Poems Not Hitherto Ascribed to Davies'), although they
differ radically from *Nosce Teipsum* in their brevity, the spontaneity of
their composition, their humour, and the directness of their observa-
tion. The last contrasts sharply with Davies's other poetry, where
the images are habitually derived from tradition, or more often, from
books. The imitations of Martial are no exception, as Davies replaces
the customs and personages of Rome with local and contemporary
details. Despite these differences, however, the epigrams display
the same essential characteristics of Davies's workmanship: the in-
tellectuality manifest in the detachment of the satiric observer, the
fundamental regularity of the verse, the consonance of form with
content and purpose.

In an address on epigrams and epitaphs to the Society of Antiquaries
in 1600, Davies states that the only rules governing the epigram are
that it must be brief and witty;[2] this leaves the writer free to choose
form and content. Probably, therefore, Davies's choice of genre and
of specific content represents his natural inclination to write poetry
as a display-case for wit, humour, and mastery of form, directed
towards arousing laughter and admiration in the audience. The
epigrams embody also one of the poet's ideals, revealed in the sub-
ject-matter and in the implied character of the observer; between
the subject and the observer is set a great gap in sophistication.

The ideal is Castiglione's *sprezzatura*, depicted by counter-example.
Like many elements in Davies's poetry, it suggests the Restoration,
specifically the comedies, where the same lapses are held up to ridi-
cule. The absence of plot in the epigrams eliminates the dramatic
emphasis on love and sexual conquest; another difference is in social

[1] Eliot, p. 136.
[2] B.M. MS. Cotton Faustina E. v., fol. 168ʳ.

context, marked by the absence from the epigrams of any women except prostitutes. But these differences are accidental; the essential characteristics are the same: the comic use of *sprezzatura*, the satire upon foibles and vulgarity rather than vice, and the light-hearted, humorous attitude towards sex—about half of Davies's jokes concern lechery, syphilis, cuckoldry, and the aspects of physiology that are barred from polite conversation for reasons of tact or decency.[1]

The faceless but audible 'hero' of the epigrams, the pattern of perfection, is a man whose reason so thoroughly controls his will, his affections, his body, and the world around him that he presents to the world an unflawed surface, invulnerable and impassible. Apparently born with physical, mental, social, and economic endowments, he is sophisticated when we meet him; his language is polished—indeed epigrammatic. He is never at a loss for words or short of money, he cannot be cheated, cuckolded, or infected with venereal disease; nor can he be seen through, embarrassed, or overawed. If he has passions or weaknesses, they elude discovery. Without perceptible effort, he dresses well, speaks well, thinks well, looks good, smells good, and feels good.

Against this standard all the gulls are measured, and are inevitably mocked for falling short. The epigrams ridicule any ripple that disturbs the surface, any glimpse of a frightened face behind the mask. The general object of humour is discrepancy: between the view a person has of himself and the clearer view of the observer; between the impression he wants to make and the one he achieves (like the unhappy Gella, who would like to be thought beautiful); between the surface he presents and the contradictory reality that the observer sees. Thus the epigrams laugh at pretension, hypocrisy, stupidity, but also at naïveté and such physical disadvantages as ugliness, skin-disease, bad breath, and poor teeth. The standard is neither moral nor tolerant, but at this remove from the individuals attacked, we are undisturbed by the cruelty, and can appreciate the comedy.

The *persona* of the epigrams likes telling jokes. Through the epigrams Davies sought a reputation for wit, either in his perception and description of a situation funny in itself (comedy derived from displaying someone in an awkward position), or in his ability to discover

---

[1] The absence of all references to adultery in the published *Epigrammes* suggests that the personages of the epigrams were readily recognizable, so that adultery, which has social as well as personal implications, was too weighty to be joked about publicly.

the humour in an apparently serious or neutral situation (where the comedy arises from incongruity or the unexpectedness of the humorous vision), or in the cleverness with which he invents jokes. Thus the epigrams fall into three categories. In the first, the poem simply describes the event; e.g. 'In Leucam'. In the second, the poem describes a situation and caps it with a pointed statement of the humour: e.g. 'In Rufum', where the couplet only summarizes the body of the poem. The humour of the first group arises wholly from the situation; that of the second is partly situational and partly verbal. The third kind is entirely verbal. Davies creates humour by using a surprising analogy or a pun, as in the lines on Septimus the aged lecher (Ep. 35):

> Septimus lives, and is like Garlicke seene,
> For though his head be white, his blade is greene.
> This olde mad coult deserves a Martires praise,
> For he was burned in Queene Maries dayes.

The comparison of Septimus's continued prowess to martyrdom recalls Donne's conjunction of religious and sexual imagery, with one important exception: the connection depends not on a metaphysical vision but upon the second meaning of 'burned'. Recognizing the pun, the reader also realizes that only one of the two senses applies, for 'Septimus lives'. Donne's puns require that both meanings be kept in mind (e.g. 'covering' in 'Elegy XIX', line 48, meaning both clothing and intercourse), as is true also of the paradoxes of Donne's poetry. Thus, even in works that have wit as their end, Davies uses it as a device for adornment, whereas Donne uses it for the analysis and often destruction of accepted concepts.

The prosody of the epigrams is like that of *Nosce Teipsum*. One similarity is the frequency of the quatrain with alternate rhyme: most of the epigrams consist of between one and five quatrains with or without a closing couplet; and the form next in frequency is the Shakespearian sonnet (with some variation in the number of rhymes), which is built of such quatrains.

The verse of the epigrams does not flow as smoothly as in *Nosce Teipsum*, but we may fairly attribute the greater roughness to intention, not failure. The leisurely smoothness of *Nosce Teipsum* would not suit the epigram at all; it would counteract the requisite brevity, and interfere with the fast pace that humour requires: a joke succeeds because it takes the hearer by surprise, because its pace gives him no time to think about what lies beneath the surface, and because it relieves a state of tension. Euphony and fluent verse also dull the reader's alertness to wit, and counteract the colloquial tone traditional in the genre.

Epigram, therefore, demands speed in movement and a certain roughness and informality in tone, achieved largely by language: by abrupt, conversational beginnings, and by colloquialism, slang, and obscenity:

> When Marcus comes from Mins, he stil doth sweare
> By, come on seaven, that all is lost and gone,
> But thats not true, for he hath lost his hayre
> Onely for that he came too much on one.
>
> (Ep. 21)

The directness with which Davies calls a spade a spade produces roughness of tone even without harsh sound: 'The false knave Flaccus' (Ep. 18), or 'Stinking with dogges, and muted all with haukes' (Ep. 43), or the following description of Lady Hatton:

> A widdowe fayre, and fresh, and fat, and full
> Well fed, well taught, well used from her wadle.
>
> (NHA 7)

The most important devices, however, belong either to sound or metrics. The epigrams are not cacophonous, but they contain many harsh sounds. Large numbers of unvoiced spirants, stops, and sibilants strike the ear; every line contains at least one of these, and many lines seem to hiss and spit like angry cats: the speaker feints at doffing his cap to Cineas, 'Which he perceiving seems for spite to burst' (Ep. 33). Here the front vowels reinforce the effect of the consonants.

The harshness of sound often combines with prosodic devices to prevent smoothness; when the monosyllables (and Davies's poetry is largely monosyllabic) begin and end in unvoiced sounds including many sibilants, they eliminate any possibility of mellifluousness: e.g. 'Catch at my cap'. Even rougher in effect are the spondees or virtual spondees, like 'buffe jerkin', or 'harsh noise', composed of clipped monosyllables.

Finally, Davies disrupts smoothness by using the caesura far more often than in any of his other works. Whereas in *Nosce Teipsum* he uses it sparingly, in the epigrams he breaks line after line:

> Gella, if thou dost love thy selfe, take heede,
> Lest thou my rimes, unto thy lover reade,

> For straight thou grinst, and then thy lover seeth,
> Thy canker-eaten gums, and rotten teeth.

(Ep. 11)

In spite of differences in technique between the epigrams and *Nosce Teipsum*, we see the same eye for form and the same fine ear; indeed, sometimes the same techniques are used with different effects and aims.

In *Orchestra*, which falls between these two works chronologically, appears the smoothly flowing yet varied verse of *Nosce Teipsum* combined with the wit and vivacity that give life to epigrams. As a result, the rhythm of *Orchestra* reflects the theme with absolute fidelity, even to the paradox implicit in the image of the cosmic dance, which Marston points out:

> *Yee gracious Orbs, keepe the old measuring,*
> *All's spoyld if once yee fall to capering.*[1]

That is, the universe does not move with the speed and energy of dancers; its motion is not sudden or rash. Nor is the poetry of *Orchestra*; it runs quickly, partly to support the idea of dancing, partly perhaps in the hope that the readers will be borne along too rapidly to reflect upon and recognize the audacity of the metaphor.

They did, of course, and dismissed it as an intellectual caper. Of their opinions, little remains except the contemptuous remarks of enemies like Marston, Rudyerd, and Jonson. *Orchestra* was eclipsed in the 1590s by Davies's reputation for epigram (recorded not only in the epigrams of Harington and Guilpin, but in Meres's *Palladis Tamia*).[2] After that period, Davies was *Nosce Teipsum*; and in succeeding times the sage and serious, like Alexander Chalmers in 1810, followed the Elizabethans in dismissing *Orchestra* as a trifle, however pleasing.[3]

The scholars of the twentieth century have at last accorded *Orchestra* its share of critical esteem. Not, unfortunately, because we like trifles, but because it is supposed to couch in a pleasant fiction the eternal verities of the Elizabethan faith.[4] This view simply inverts

---

[1] *The Scourge of Villainie* (1598), satire xi. 35–6, in *The Poems of John Marston*, ed. Arnold Davenport (1961), p. 168.

[2] See footnote 5, p. xxxvi.

[3] Loc. cit.

[4] See E. M. W. Tillyard, *The Elizabethan World Picture* (1943), and ed., *Orchestra* (1945), *passim*; C. S. Lewis, *English Literature in the Sixteenth Century* (1954), p. 526; David Hadas, 'The Mind and Art of Sir John Davies' (Diss. Columbia, 1963), *passim*.

the sentimental reasoning that called *Nosce Teipsum* beautiful because it was edifying into the assertion that *Orchestra*, being beautiful, must be edifying.

In fact, *Orchestra* is Davies's best joke. His contemporaries considered it frivolous at best. Thomas Nashe refers to it in a discussion of frivolous writers: the poet 'capers it up to the spheares in commendation of daunsing'.[1] Marston's attack on Curio says:

> Prayse but *Orchestra*, and the skipping art,
> You shall commaund him, faith you have his hart
> Even capring in your fist. A hall, a hall,
> Roome for the Spheres, the Orbes celestiall
> Will daunce *Kemps Jigge*. They'le revel with neate jumps
> A worthy Poet hath put on their Pumps?[2]

As Wilkes points out, the language of the dedication to Martin ('this suddaine, rash, halfe-capreol of my wit') shows Davies's concurrence in these opinions.[3] Hoskyns cites *Orchestra* as an example of rhetorical amplification; it is erroneous to take the amplifying details as the theme itself.[4]

The better one knows *Orchestra*, the more conscious one becomes of its essential levity. The reader familiar with the *Odyssey* immediately recognizes the first description of Antinous as parodic. To one who recognizes the sources, the echoes of Lucian and Cicero function as pointers in the margin. For Lucian's dialogues are often illustrative exercises; *The Dance* is mock-encomium, the genre that, by praising the insignificant or contemptible, prepares the rhetorician to argue on all sides of any question. And any Elizabethan who had ploughed through *De natura deorum* must have laughed heartily to see Davies adduce the material that in Cicero's work demonstrates the existence of God as evidence of the respectability of ballroom-dancing.

More signals of the humorous intent are scattered throughout this poem which the author dashed off in two weeks. Terpsichore is invoked explicitly as the 'light Muse'. And there are hidden allusions, and puns of varying quality, in stanzas 3, 4, 7, 13, 19, 34, 43, and 49. Recognizing the joke, Davies's serious-minded contemporaries treated it as they felt it deserved: they ignored it, meanwhile buying

---

[1] *Lenten Stuffe* (1599), in *Works*, ed. Ronald B. McKerrow, iii. 177.
[2] *The Scourge of Villainie*, satire xi. 27–32, ibid., pp. 167–8.
[3] p. 287.
[4] See Commentary on *Orchestra*, p. 360.

up five editions of *Nosce Teipsum*. The change in taste that has re-
versed the positions of the two poems is probably an improvement,
provided that we do not try to justify our preference for *Orchestra*
by attributing to it what it does not possess. The mental tyranny
that exalts a literary creation merely for the usefulness of its content,
whether scholarly, political, social, or theological, is destructive to
literature and criticism.

Orchestra is good reading, partly because its images are delightful,
but in the main because the theme imposes no special burden upon
the poet's versification; the suitability of the theme to his natural
style makes the poem the only example in the canon of perfect
consonance between inclination and necessity. Therefore *Orchestra*
contains not just lines and stanzas of admirable melody, but moments
that penetrate beyond the ear by their beauty:

> What eye doth see the heav'n but doth admire
> When it the movings of the heav'ns doth see?
> My selfe, if I to heav'n may once aspire,
> If that be dauncing, will a Dauncer be.
>   (*Orch.* 26)

This is clearly the craftsman of *Nosce Teipsum*, writing exceptionally
regular verse with subtle rhythmic variations. Even more typical
of the verse of *Orchestra* is the following stanza:

> Of all their wayes I love *Mæanders* path,
> Which to the tunes of dying Swans doth daunce,
> Such winding sleights, such turnes and tricks he hath,
> Such Creekes, such wrenches, and such daliaunce,
> That whether it be hap or heedlesse chaunce,
>   In this indented course and wriggling play
>   He seemes to daunce a perfect cunning *Hay*.
>   (*Orch.* 53)

This stanza displays the features peculiar to *Orchestra*: the swiftness
achieved by more frequent and longer polysyllables, the occasional
variation of enjambment and inversion. Davies's inclination to meta-
phor is here, and his clarity of language; the aptness of metaphor
notable in *Nosce Teipsum* appears here combined with the unexpected
turn which forms so important a part of comedy in the epigrams.
Tillyard, who saw the essential qualities of *Orchestra* even though he
took it too seriously, pointed out in this stanza the attainment of

freshness in the expression of 'the stalest schoolboy stock', and the admixture of 'sheer outrageousness':

What could be fresher than *indented course* or *wriggling play*? and yet they come out of the bottom of the bag. And what more nonsensical than the notion of the waters of the Meander keeping time with their unbroken flow to the defunctive music of large numbers of the *Cycnus Asiaticus*? But Davies is so gay, so certain of not being gainsaid that the reader is forced to agree that the Meander (although neither party has seen it) is the best of all rivers . . . Davies deals mainly with the accumulated doctrines of many ages yet in rhythms that embody youthful vitality.[1]

For an amplifying poem, Davies chooses a stanza that gives him ample room for ornament. For once, the ornament (though apt) impedes the narrative, a departure from Davies's usual practice that reminds us that the poem was composed and printed at the height of the fashion for Ovidian poetry.[2] Like other Ovidian poems, *Orchestra* is marked by sensuousness, pictorial decoration, and a love story based on mythology. But the choice of rhyme royal suggests that Davies is once more mocking poetic fashion, for as Hallett Smith says, 'the general rule, enunciated for example by King James of Scotland and by Gascoigne, [laid down] that this stanza was to be used for tragic matters, complaints, and testaments'.[3] In adopting the stanza of *The Mirror for Magistrates* and *The Rape of Lucrece*, and introducing as heroine Penelope, a traditional pattern of chastity,[4] Davies seems again to have raised the flag of parody.

Tillyard, to whose work the critical esteem of *Orchestra* is due, calls it not a great but 'a lucky poem'; perhaps the Latin *felix* best describes the happy concurrence of statement and expression, as well as the mood we may extract from it. The poem emanates optimism based on the security of a limited and regular world, an absolute confidence that nothing can 'rend that Adamantine chaine'. The comfortable certainty *de rerum natura* that enables Davies to play light-heartedly with the idea of cosmic order has often stirred men to nostalgia for an age of faith. A. H. Bullen has pointed out the probable echoes of *Nosce Teipsum* in Arnold's poetry,[5] but no one has hitherto observed the reference to *Orchestra* (st. 49) in 'Dover Beach':

---

[1] *Five Poems* (1948), pp. 32–3.
[2] Hallett Smith, *Elizabethan Poetry* (1952), p. 93.
[3] Ibid., p. 113.
[4] On Penelope as a model of chaste womanhood, see Smith, p. 120 n.
[5] *Some Longer Elizabethan Poems* (1903), pp. x–xi.

The Sea of Faith
Was once, too, at the full, and round earth's shore
Lay like the folds of a bright girdle furl'd.

(ll. 21–3)

Arnold speaks sadly of the loss of Davies's assurance that the sea
and all the universe 'Musick and measure both doth understand', an
error, indeed, but less painful then the uncertainty Arnold saw around
him.

   Arnold uses *Orchestra* as a reflection of a faith; by implication, he
too sees Davies as a representative of his age. That is a fundamental
truth: Davies's poems will never again be read for edification, nor
spontaneously for pleasure. His readers will always be students of the
Elizabethan period. Nevertheless, that audience, equipped with the
learning that breaks the barriers between ages, will reap a perhaps
unexpected measure of enjoyment. They will begin with the dis-
covery that *Nosce Teipsum* is easy and painless to get through, and
continue perhaps, to admire the wit of an epigram, or to enjoy the
lyrical grace of the *Hymnes of Astræa*, or to take pleasure in the many
delights of *Orchestra*; and their enjoyment in his verse will thereby
be little different from that found by the Elizabethans themselves.

THE POEMS

NOSCE TEIPSUM

This Oracle expounded in two Elegies.
1. Of Humane knowledge.
2. Of the Soule of Man, and the immortalitie thereof.

Title in printed texts and manuscripts.

To the right noble, valorous, and learned Prince,
Henry Earle of Northumberland.

The strongest and the noblest argument
To prove the Soule immortall, rests in this;
That in no mortall thing it finds content,
But seekes an object that aeternall is.

If any Soule hath this immortall Signe,   5
(As every Soule doth show it, more or lesse)
It is your *Spirit*, *Heröick*, and *divine;*
Which this trew noate most lively doth expresse;

For being a Prince, and having Princely blood
The noblest of all Europe in your vaines;   10
Having youth, wealth, Pleasure, and every Good
Which all the world doth seek with endlesse paynes,

Yet can you never fixt your thoughts on these;
These cannot with your heav'nly mind agree;
These momentary objects cannot please   15
Your winged Spirit, which more aloft doth flee./

It only longs to learne, and know the Truth;
The Truth of every thing, which never dies;
The Nectar which praeserves the Soule in youth,
The Manna which doth minds immortalize . ./   20

These noble studdies, more ennoble you,
And bring more honor to your race and name
Then Hot-Spurs fier, which did the Scots subdew,
Then Brabants Lion, or Great Charles his fame;

Then to what Spirit shall I these noates commend?   25
But unto that which doth them best expresse?
Who will to them more kind Protection lend?
Then Hee, which did protect Mee in distresse?

To the right noble etc.   *Text and punctuation from MS. AC, in author's holograph.*
   27 [can] will

To my honorable Patron and frend
Ed. Cooke Esqr her Majesties Atturney Generall.

Great *Procurator* of your Princes state,
Who useth, as her owne, your hands, and eies;
Who by your tongue all causes doth debate,
That twixt her subjects and her self do rise;

Watchman of her Praerogative and Crowne,   5
An Atlas, and a piller of her Throne;
Grace to the Law, and honor to the Gowne,
Whose fortunes still with vertues wings have flowne;

Heere I praesent to your clear Judgments eie;
Which the lawes knotts and riddles both discerne;   10
And to your rich and copious Memorie
Which never lost the thing it once did learne;

Heer some imperfect noates I do praesent
Of those high powers, which that Great power above
Hath unto you in such perfection lent,   15
As they in meaner spirits do envy move./

But you whose worth, and honorable place
Above the power of envie doth you raise;
Lift up my worthles muse with your good Grace
Which would avoid contempt, yet seekes no praise.   20

[*Dedication.*]

To my most gracious dread Soveraigne.

To that *cleare Majestie*, which in the North
Doth like another Sunne in glorie rise;
Which standeth fixt, yet spreds her heavenly worth,
Loadstone to Hearts, and Loadstarre to all Eyes:

To my honorable etc.   *Text and punctuation from MS.HH, in author's holograph.*
[*Dedication.*] To my most etc.   *Printed texts: 1599, 1622. MSS.: AC, HH, H573*   **Text**
from 1599; punctuation from AC.

Like Heav'n in all; like th' Earth in this alone,   5
  That though great States by her support do stand,
  Yet she her selfe supported is of none,
  But by the Finger of th' Almighties hand:

To the divinest and the richest minde
  Both by Arts purchase, and by Natures Dower,   10
  That ever was from Heaven to Earth confin'd,
  To shew the utmost of a Creatures power:

To that great Spirit which doth great Kingdomes move:
  The sacred Spring whence *Right* and *Honor* streames,
  Distilling *Vertue*, shedding *Peace* and *Love*   15
  In every place, as *Cynthia* sheds her beames:

I offer up some sparkles of that fire,
  Whereby we *reason, live, and move and bee*;
  These sparkes by nature evermore aspire,
  Which makes them to so *high* a *Highnesse* flee.   20

Faire *Soule*, since to the fairest bodie knit
  You give such lively life, such quickning power,
  Such sweete celestiall influence to it,
  As keepes it still in youths immortall flower:

(As where the *Sunne* is present all the yeare,   25
  And never doth retire his golden ray,
  Needes must the Spring be everlasting there,
  And every season like the Mon'th of May.)

O many, many yeares may you remaine
  A happie Angell to this happie Land: 30
  Long, long may you on earth our Empresse raigne,
  Ere you in Heaven a glorious Angell stand:

Stay long (sweet Spirit) ere thou to Heaven depart,
  Which mak'st each place a Heaven wherein thou art.

                Her Majesties least and   35
                unworthiest Subject,

            John Davies.

15 *Peace AC, H573, 1622: l.c. Σ*   20 a *MSS.:* an *Print*   25 *Sunne AC,*
H573: rom. Σ

Nosce Teipsum.

Of Humane Knowledge.

Why did my parents send me to the schooles
    That I with knowledg might enrich my mind?
    Since the *desire to know* first made men fooles,
    And did corrupt the roote of all mankind.

For when Gods hand had written in the harts,   5
    Of the first Parents, all the rules of good:
    So that their skill enfusd, did passe all Arts,
    That ever were before, or since the Flood;

And when their reasons eye was sharpe, and cleere,
    And (as an Eagle can behold the Sunne)   10
    Could have approch't the'*eternall light* as neere,
    As th'intellectuall Angels could have done;

Even then to them, the *Spirit of lies* suggests,
    That they were blind, because they saw not Ill;
    And breathes into their incorrupted breasts   15
    A curious *wish*, which did corrupt their *will*.

For that same Ill they straight desir'd to know;
    Which Ill, being nought but a defect of good,
    In all Gods works the Divell could not show,
    While Man their Lord in his perfection stood.   20

So that them selves were first to do the Ill,
    Ere they thereof the knowledge could attaine;
    Like him that knew not poisons power to kill,
    Untill by tasting it him selfe was slaine.

Even so, by tasting of that Fruite forbid,   25
    Where they sought *knowledge*, they did *error* find:
    Ill they desir'd to know, and Ill they did,
    And to give *Passion* eyes, made *Reason* blind.

Nosce Teipsum.   *Text as for immediately preceding Dedication,* 'To my most etc.'
  25 that] the *MSS.*

For then their minds did first in passion see,
    Those wretched shapes of *Miserie*, and *Woe*,   30
    Of *Nakednesse*, of *Shame*, of *Povertie*,
    Which then their owne experience made them know.

But then grew *Reason* darke, that *she* no more
    Could the faire Formes of *Truth*, and *Good* discerne:
    Battes they became, that *Eagles* were before,   35
    And this they got by their *desire to learne*.

But we their wretched Ofspring, what do we?
    Do wee not still tast of the fruite forbid?
    Whiles with fond, fruitelesse curiositie,
    In bookes prophane, we seeke for knowledge hid?   40

What is this *knowledge*? but the Skie-stolne fire,
    For which the *Thiefe* still chaind in Ice doth sit?
    And which the poore rude *Satyre* did admire,
    And needs would kisse, but burnt his lips with it?

What is it? but the cloud emptie of Raine,   45
    Which when *Joves* Guest embrac't, he Monsters got?
    Or the false *Pailes*, which oft being fild with paine,
    Receiv'd the water, but retain'd it not?

Shortly what is it? but the fierie *Coach*
    Which the *Youth* sought, and sought his death withall?
    Or the *Boyes* wings, which when he did approch   51
    The *Sunnes* hote beames, did melt and let him fall?

And yet, alas, when all our Lampes are burnd,
    Our Bodies wasted, and our Spirits spent,
    When we have all the learned *Volumes* turnd,   55
    Which yeeld mens wits both helpe, and ornament;

---

34 *Truth*, and *Good AC*, *HH* ('good' altered to 'Good' in Davies's hand in *AC*): *Good
and Truth 1599, 1622, H573*   37 Ofspring, *1599*: ~ᴧ *AC*   38 wee not
MSS.: not wee *Print*   40 bookes prophane] prophane bookes *MSS.*   41 Skie
Σ: Shie *1599*   45 emptie of Raine *MSS.*: of emptie Raine *Print*   49 *Coach
AC*, *H573*: rom. *Σ*   55 *Volumes 1622*, *AC*, *H573*: l.c. *Σ*

What can we know? or what can we discerne?
　　When *Error* chokes the windowes of the mind;
　　The diverse formes of things how can we learne,
　　That have bene ever from our birth-day blind?　　　　60

When *Reasons* lampe which like the *Sunne* in skie,
　　Throughout *Mans* litle world her beams did spread,
　　Is now become a Sparkle, which doth lie
　　Under the Ashes, halfe extinct and dead:

How can we hope, that through the Eye and Eare,　　　65
　　This dying Sparkle, in this cloudie place,
　　Can recollect those beames of knowledge cleare,
　　Which were enfus'd, in the first minds by grace?

So might the heire, whose father hath in play,
　　Wasted a thousand pounds of auncient rent,　　　　70
　　By painfull earning of one grote a day,
　　Hope to restore the patrimonie spent!

The wits that div'd most deepe, and soar'd most hie,
　　Seeking Mans powers, have found his weaknes such:
　　"Skill comes so slow, and life so fast doth flie,　　　75
　　"We learne so litle, and forget so much.

For this, the wisest of all Morall men,
　　Said *he knew nought, but that he nought did know*;
　　And the great mocking Maister, mockt not then,
　　When he said, *Truth was buried deepe below*.　　　　80

For how may we to other things attaine?
　　When none of us his owne soule understands?
　　For which the Divell mockes our curious braine,
　　When *know thy selfe*, his oracle commands.

For why should we the busie Soule beleeve,　　　　85
　　When boldly she concludes of that, and this?
　　When of her selfe she can no judgement geve,
　　Nor how, nor whence, nor where, nor what, she is?

All things without, which round about we see,
    We seeke to know, and have therewith to do: 90
    But that whereby we *reason, live, and be,*
    Within our selves, we strangers are theretoo.

We seeke to know the moving of each *Spheare,*
    And the straunge cause of th'ebs and flouds of *Nile:*
    But of that clocke, which in our breasts we beare,   95
    The subtill motions, we forget the while.

We that acquaint our selves with every *Zoane,*
    And passe both *Tropikes,* and behold both *Poles;*
    When we come home, are to our selves unknowne,
    And unacquainted still with our owne *Soules.*   100

We studie *Speech;* but others we perswade;
    We *Leech-craft* learne, but others Cure with it;
    We'interpret *Lawes,* which other men have made,
    But reade not those, which in our harts are writ:

Is it because the minde is like the eye,   105
    (Through which it gathers knowledge by degrees)
    Whose rayes reflect not, but spread outwardly,
    Not seeing it selfe, when other things it sees?

No doubtlesse: for the minde can backward cast
    Upon her selfe her understanding light;   110
    But she is so corrupt, and so defac't,
    As her owne image doth her selfe affright.

As is the fable of that Ladie faire,
    Which for her lust was turnd into a Cow;
    When thirstie to a streame she did repaire,   115
    And saw her selfe transformd she wist not how;

At first she startles, then she stands amaz'd,
    At last with terror she from thence doth flie;
    And loathes the watrie glasse wherein she gaz'd,
    And shunnes it still, though she for thirst do die.   120

92 theretoo *AC* (*JD*): thereto *Σ*   93 *Spheare MSS.*: spheare *Print*   94 *Nile*
1622, AC, H573: rom. Σ   100 still] moste *MSS.*   103 We' *ed.*: We *All*
110 her selfe *Σ*: het selfe *1599c*

Even so *Mans soule*, which did Gods Image beare,
   And was at first, faire, good and spotlesse pure;
   Since with her *sinnes* her beauties blotted were,
   Doth of all sights, her owne sight least endure.

For even at first reflection she espies,   125
   Such strange *Chymeraes*, and such Monsters there,
   Such Toyes, such *Antikes*, and such Vanities,
   As she retires, and shrinks, for shame, and feare.

And as the man loves least at home to bee,
   That hath a sluttish house haunted with *Sprites*;   130
   So she impatient her owne faults to see,
   Turnes from her selfe, and in strange things delites.

For this, few *know themselves*: for merchants broke
   View their estate with discontent and paine;
   And *Seas* are troubled, when they do revoke   135
   Their flowing waves, into themselves againe.

And while the face of outward things we find,
   Pleasing, and faire, agreable, and sweete;
   These things transport, and carrie out the mind,
   That with her selfe, her selfe can never meete.   140

Yet if *Affliction* once her warres begin,
   And threat the feeble *Sense* with sword and fire;
   The *Mind* contracts her selfe, and shrinketh in,
   And to her selfe she gladly doth retire.

As *Spiders* toucht seeke their webs inmost part;   145
   As *Bees* in stormes unto their hives returne;
   As *Blood* in danger gathers to the hart,
   As *Men* seeke Towns, when foes the Country burne.

If ought can teach us ought, *Afflictions* lookes
   (Making us looke into our selves so neare)   150
   Teach us to *know our selves*, beyond all bookes,
   Or all the learned *Schooles* that ever were:

147 *Blood AC, H573: rom. Σ*   148 *Men AC, H573: rom. Σ*

This *Mistresse* lately pluckt me by the Eare;
   And many'a golden lesson hath me taught;
   Hath made my *Senses* quicke, and Reason cleare,   155
   Reformd my Will, and rectifide my Thought.

So do the *Winds* and *Thunders* cleanse the Aire,
   So working Seas settle and purge the wine;
   So lopt and pruned Trees do florish faire;
   So doth the fire the drossie Gold refine.   160

Neither *Minerva*, nor the learned *Muse*,
   Nor Rules of *Art*, nor *Precepts* of the wise,
   Could in my braine those beames of skill enfuse,
   As but the glaunce of this *Dames* angrie eyes.

She within *Listes* my raunging mind hath brought,   165
   That now beyond my selfe I list not go;
   My selfe am *Center* of my circling thought,
   Onely *my selfe* I studie, learne, and *know*.

I know my Bodi's of so fraile a kinde,
   As force without, feavers within can kill;   170
   I know the heavenly nature of my mind,
   But tis corrupted both in *wit* and *will*:

I know my *Soule* hath power to know all things,
   Yet is she blind and ignorant in all;
   I know I'am one of *Natures* litle kings,   175
   Yet to the least and vilest things am thrall.

I know my life's a paine, and but a span,
   I know my *Sense* is mockt with every thing;
   And to conclude, *I know* my selfe a *Man*,
   Which is a *proud* and yet a *wretched* thing.   180

---

154 many' *ed.*: many *All*   157 and *MSS.*, *1602–1622*: *ital.* Σ   163 those]
these *AC*, *H573*   175 I' *ed.*: I *All*

Of the Soule of Man, and the Immortalitie thereof.

The lights of heaven, which are the worlds faire eyes,
    Looke downe into the world, the world to see;
    And as they turne, or wander in the skies,
    Survey all things, that on this *Center* bee.

And yet the *lights* which in my *towre* do shine,   185
    Mine *Eyes* which view all objects nigh and farre,
    Looke not into this litle world of mine,
    Nor see my face, wherein they fixed are.

Since *Nature* failes us in no needfull thing,
    Why want I meanes my inward selfe to see?   190
    Which sight the knowledge of my self might bring,
    Which to true wisedome is the first degree.

That *Powre* which gave my eyes, the world to view;
    To view my selfe enfus'd an *inward light*;
    Whereby my *Soule*, as by a Mirror true,   195
    Of her owne forme may take a perfect sight.

But as the sharpest *eye* discerneth nought,
    Except the *Sunne-beames* in the Aire do shine:
    So the best *Soule*, with her reflecting thought,
    Sees not her selfe, without some light divine.   200

O Light, which mak'st the Light, which makes the Day,
    Which setst the Eye without, and Mind within,
    Lighten my spirit with one cleare heavenly ray,
    Which now to view it selfe doth first begin.

For her true forme how can my Sparke discerne,   205
    Which dimme by *Nature*, *Art* did never cleere?
    When the great Wits, of whom all skill we learne,
    Are ignorant both *what* she is, and *where*.

---

186 view] see *MSS.: om. 1599u*   190 my *1622, HH:* mine *Σ*   198 *beames*
AC: rom. Σ   207 great *Σ:* gerat *1599*

One thinks the *Soule* is *Aire*, another *Fire*,
　　Another *Blood*, defus'd about the hart;　　　　　210
　　Another saith, the *Elements* conspire,
　　And to her *Essence* each doth give a part.

Musitians thinke our *Soules* are *Harmonies*,
　　Phisitions hold that they *Complexions* bee;
　　Epicures make them swarmes of *Atomies*,　　　215
　　Which do by chaunce into our Bodies flee.

Some thinke one generall *Soule* fils every braine,
　　As the bright *Sunne* sheds light in every Starre;
　　And others thinke, the name of *Soule* is vaine,
　　And that *we* onely *well mixt* bodies are.　　　220

In judgement of her *substance* thus they varie;
　　And thus they varie'in judgement of her *seate*;
　　For some her Chaire up to the *braine* do carrie,
　　Some thrust it downe into the *stomakes* heate:

Some place it in the Roote of life, the *Hart*,　　　225
　　Some in the *Liver*, fountaine of the Vaines;
　　Some say *she'is all in all, and all in part*,
　　Some say she'is not containd, but all containes.

Thus these great *Clerks*, their litle wisedome show,
　　While with their Doctrines they at *Hazard* play;　　　230
　　Tossing their light opinions to and fro,
　　To mocke the *Lewd*, as learnd in this as they.

For no craz'd braine could ever yet propound
　　Touching the *Soule* so vaine and fond a thought;
　　But some among these Maisters have bene found,　　　235
　　Which in their *Schooles* the selfe same thing have taught.

---

210 *Blood 1622*: l.c. Σ　　222 varie' *ed.*: varie *All*　　223 *braine* H573: *rom.* Σ
227 *she'* H573, HH: *she* Σ　　　228 she' HH: she Σ　　contaínes. *1599*: ∼, *AC*
229 *Clerks AC, HH: rom.* Σ

God onely wise, to punish pride of Wit,
    Among mens wits hath this confusion wrought;
    As the proud *Towre*, whose points the clouds did hit,
    By Tongues confusion was to ruine brought.   240

But *thou*, which didst *Mans soule* of nothing make,
    And when to nothing it was fallen agen,
    "To make it new, the Forme of Man didst take,
    "And *God* with *God*, becam'st a *Man* with Men:

Thou that hast fashioned twise this *Soule* of ours,   245
    So that she is by double title thine,
    Thou onely knowest her nature and her powers,
    Her subtile forme thou onely canst define.

To judge her selfe, she must her selfe transcend,
    As greater Circles comprehend the lesse;   250
    But she wants powre her owne powres to extend,
    As fettred Men can not their strength expresse.

But thou bright morning Starre, thou rising *Sunne*,
    Which in these latter times hast brought to light,
    Those mysteries, which since the world begun,   255
    Lay hid in darknesse, and eternall night;

Thou, *like the Sunne*, dost with indifferent *Ray*
    Into the *Pallace* and the *Cottage* shine,
    And shew'st the *Soule* both to the *Clarke* and *Lay*,
    By the cleere *Lampe* of thy' *Oracles* divine.   260

This Lampe, through all the Regions of my braine,
    Where my *Soule* sits, doth spread such beames of grace,
    As now me thinks, I do distinguish plaine,
    Each subtill line of her immortall face.

241 *Mans soule MSS., 1622*: *Mans-soule* Σ   243 *Quotation marks in 1622 only.*
254 latter *1622, AC, HH*: later Σ   255 which *AC, HH*: that Σ   257 *Ray*
AC: ray *Print*: *Ray H573, HH*   259 *Clarke H573: rom.* Σ   *Lay AC, H573*:
lay *1599c*: Lay Σ   *260 thy' *HH, H573*: thy Σ   *Oracles MSS.*: *Oracle Print*
262 grace, *1599*: ∼; *AC*

The soule a substance, and a *spirit* is,
    Which *God* him selfe doth in the Bodie make;
    Which makes the *Man*, for every Man from this,
    The *nature* of a *Man*, and *name* doth take.

*What the
Soule is.*

And though this Spirit be to the Bodie knit
    As an apt meane, her powers to exercise,   270
    Which are *life*, *motion*, *sense*, and *will* and *wit*,
    Yet she *survives*, although the Bodie *dies*.

She is a substance, and a reall thing,
  1 Which hath it selfe an actuall working might:
  2 Which neither from the *Senses* power doth spring,
  3 Nor from the Bodies humors tempred right.

*That the
Soule is a
thing subsis-
ting by itself
without the
Bodie.*

She is a *Vine*, which doth no propping need
    To make her spread her selfe, or spring upright;
    She is a *Starre*, whose beames do not proceed,
    From any *Sunne*, but from a *native* light.   280

For when she sorts things *present* with things *past*
    And thereby things *to come* doth oft foresee;
    When she doth *doubt* at first, and *choose* at last,
    These acts her owne, without the Bodie, be.

*1.
That the
Soule hath a
proper opera-
tion without
the Bodie.*

When of the deaw (which th'*eye* and *eare* do take   285
    From flowers abroad, and bring into the braine)
    She doth within both waxe, and hony make;
    This worke is hers, this is her proper paine.

When she from sundrie Acts one skill doth draw,
    Gathering from diverse fights one Art of warre;   290
    From many Cases like, one Rule of law,
    These her Collections, not the *Senses*, are.

When in th'effects she doth the Causes know,
    And (seing the streame) thinks where the spring doth rise;
    And (seeing the branch) conceives the roote below,   295
    These things she viewes, without the Bodies eyes.

281 *For when* ed.: rom. *All*   285 th' *MSS.*: the *Print*

When she without a *Pegasus* doth flie,
　　Swifter then lightnings fire from *East* to *West*;
　　About the *Center*, and above the *skie*;
　　She travels then, although the bodie rest:　　　　300

When all her works she formeth first within,
　　Proportions them, and sees their perfect end,
　　Ere in act doth anie part begin;
　　What instruments doth then the bodie lend?

When without hands she thus doth *Castels* build,　　305
　　Sees without eyes, and without feete doth runne;
　　When she digests the World, yet is not fild;
　　By her owne power these miracles are done.

When she defines, argues, devides, compounds,
　　Considers *vertue*, *vice* and *generall things*,　　310
　　And marrying diverse principles and grounds,
　　Out of their match a true Conclusion brings;

These Actions in her Closet, all alone,
　　(Retir'd within her selfe) she doth fulfill;
　　Use of her bodies Organs she hath none,　　　　315
　　When she doth use the powers of Wit, and Will.

Yet in the Bodies prison so she lyes,
　　As through the bodies windowes she must looke,
　　Her diverse powers of *Sense* to exercise,
　　By gathering Notes out of the *Worlds* great Booke:　　320

Nor can her selfe discourse, or judge of ought,
　　But what the sense Collects, and home doth bring;
　　And yet the power of her discoursing thought,
　　From these Collections, is a Diverse thing.

For though our eyes can nought but Colours see;　　325
　　Yet colours give them not their powre of sight;
　　So though these fruites of Sense her objects bee,
　　Yet she discernes them by her proper light.

303 doth] doe *MSS*.

The workman on his stuffe his skill doth show;
  And yet the stuffe gives not the man his skill;   330
  Kings their affaires do by their servants know,
  But order them by their owne royall will;

So though this cunning Mistresse and this Queene,
  Doth as her instruments the *Senses* use,
  To know all things that are *felt*, *heard* or *seene*,   335
  Yet she her selfe doth onely *judge*, and *choose*.

Even as our great wise *Empresse*, that now raignes,
  By *soveraigne* title over sundrie lands,
  Borrowes in meane affaires her *subjects* paines;
  Sees by their eyes, and *writeth* by their hands.   340

But things of waight and consequence indeed,
  Her selfe doth in her chamber them debate;
  Where all her Counsellers she doth exceed,
  As farre in judgement, as she doth in state.   344

Or as the man whom she doth now advance   *Sir Thomas*
  Upon her gracious *mercy seate* to sit,   *Egerton Lord*
  Doth common things of course, and circumstance,   *Keeper of the*
  To the Reports of common men commit;   *great Seale.*

But when the Cause it selfe must be decreed,
  Himselfe in person, in his proper Court,   350
  To grave and solemne hearing doth proceed;
  Of everie proofe, and every by-report:

Then like Gods Angell he pronounceth right,
  And milke and honie from his tongue do flow;
  Happie are they that still are in his sight,   355
  To reape the wisedome, which his lips do sow.

Right so the *Soule* which is a Ladie free,
  And doth the justice of her *State* maintaine,
  Because the *Senses* readie servants bee,
  Attending nigh, about her Court the braine.   360

345m. *Marginal gloss appears in 1602 only.*

By them the formes of outward things she learnes;
  For they returne into the fantasie,
  What ever each of them abroad discernes;
  And there enroll it, for the mind to see.

But when she sits to judge the good and Ill,   365
  And to discerne betwixt the false and true,
  She is not guided by the *Senses* skill,
  But doth each thing in her owne Mirror view.

Then she the *Senses* checks, which oft do erre,
  And even against their false reports decrees;   370
  And oft she doth condemne, what they preferre,
  For with a powre above the *Sense* she sees.

Therefore no *Sense* the precious joyes conceives,
  Which in her private Contemplations bee,
  For then the ravisht spirit the *Senses* leaves,   375
  Hath her owne powers, and proper actions free.

Her harmonies are sweete, and full of skill,
  When on the bodies instrument she playes;
  But the proportions of the *wit*, and *will*,
  Those sweete accords, are even the Angels layes.   380

These tunes of *Reason* are *Amphyons Lyre*,
  Wherewith he did the *Thebane* citie found;
  These are the notes wherewith the heavenly *Quire*,
  The praise of him which spreads the heavens, doth sound.

Then her *selfe being Nature* shines in this,   385
  That she performes her noblest works alone;
  "The *worke* the Touchstone of the *nature* is,
  "And by their operations things are knowne.

2.   *Are they not senslesse* then that thinke the soule
That the soule   Nought but a fine perfection of the *Sense*?   390
is more then a
perfection or   Or of the formes which *fancie* doth enrolle,
reflection of the   A *quicke resulting*, and a *consequence*?
sence.

370 reports] reporte *MSS.*   381 *Lyre AC, H573:* lyre Σ   384 spreads]
made *1622*   heavens *AC, HH:* heave *1599:* heaven *1622, H573*

What is it then that doth the *Sense* accuse,
   Both of *false judgements*, and *fond appetites*?
   Which makes us do what *Sense* doth most refuse?   395
   Which oft in torment of the *Sense* delights?

Sense thinks the *Planets spheres* not much a sunder;
   What tels us then their distance is so farre?
   Sense thinks the lightning borne before the thunder:
   What tels us then they both together are?   400

When Men seeme Crowes farre off upon a Towre,
   Sense saith th'are crows, what makes us think them men?
   When we in *Agues* thinke all sweete things sowre,
   What makes us know our tongs false judgement then?

What powre was that whereby *Medea* saw   405
   And well approv'd, and praisd the better course,
   When her rebellious *Sense* did so withdraw
   Her feeble powres, as she pursu'd the worse?

Did *Sense* perswade *Ulysses* not to heare
   The Mermaids songs, which so his men did please,   410
   As they were all perswaded through the eare,
   To quit the ship, and leape into the *seas*?

Could any powre of *Sense* the *Romane* move,
   To burne his owne right hand with courage stout?
   Could *Sense* make *Marius* sit unbound and prove,   415
   The cruell launcing of the knottie gout?

Doubtlesse in *Man* there is a *nature* found
   Beside the *Senses*, and above them farre;
   "Though most men being in sensuall pleasures drownd,
   "It seemes their *Soules* but in their *Senses* are.   420

399 thunder: *1599*: ~‸ *AC*   407 withdraw‸ *1599*: ~, *AC*   409 Did]
Could *MSS.* heare ‸ *1599*: ~, *AC*   420 their *Senses 1622, MSS.*: the *Senses 1599*

If we had nought but *Sense*, then onely they
    Should have sound mindes, which have their *senses* sound:
    But *wisedome* growes, when *senses* do decay,
    And *folly* most in quickest *sense* is found.

If we had nought but *sense*, each living wight   425
    Which we call *brute*, would be more sharpe then wee;
    As having *Senses apprehensive might*,
    In a more cleere, and excellent degree.

But they do want that *quicke discoursing power*,
    Which doth in us the erring *sense* correct: 430
    Therefore the *Bee* did sucke the painted flower,
    And *birds* of grapes the cunning shadow peckt.

Sense outside knowes, the *Soule* through all things sees;
    Sense Circumstance, she doth the *substance* view;
    Sense sees the barke, but she the life of trees,   435
    Sense heares the sounds, but she the Concords true.

But why do I the *Soule* and *Sense* devide?
    When *Sense* is but a powre, which she extends,
    Which being in diverse parts diversified,
    The diverse formes of objects apprehends.   440

This power spreads outward, but the roote doth grow
    In th'inward *Soule*, which onely doth perceive;
    For th'*eyes* and *eares* no more their objects know;
    Then glasses know what faces they receive.

For if we chaunce to fixe our thoughts elsewhere,   445
    Although our eyes be ope, we do not see.
    And if one power did not both see and heare,
    Our sights and sounds would alwayes double bee.

Then is the *Soule* a nature which containes,
    The powre of *Sense* within a greater powre,   450
    Which doth employ and use the *Senses* paines;
    But sits, and rules, within her private bowre.

431 *Bee*_∧ 1599: ~, *AC*

If *she doth then* the subtill *Sense* excell,
   How grosse are they that drowne her in the blood?
   Or in the bodies humours tempered well,
   As if in them such high perfection stood?

       3.
       That the soule
       is more then the
       temperature of
       the humours of
       the bodie.

As if most skill in that *Musitian* were,
   Which had the best, and best tun'd instrument,
   As if the Pensill neate, and Colours cleere,
   Had powre to make the Painter excellent.   460

Why doth not Beutie then refine the wit?
   And good Complexion rectifie the will?
   Why doth not Health bring wisedome still with it?
   Why doth not Sicknesse make men brutish still?

Who can in *Memorie*, or *wit*, or *will*,   465
   Or *aire*, or *fire*, or *earth*, or *water* find?
   What *Alchimist* can draw with all his skill,
   The *Quintessence* of these out of the mind?

If th'*Elements* which have nor *life*, nor *sense*,
   Can breed in us so great a powre as this: 470
   Why give they not them selves like excellence?
   Or other things wherein their mixture is?

If she were but the bodies qualitie,
   Then would she be with it *sicke, maimd* and *blind*;
   But we perceive where these privations bee,   475
   A *healthie, perfect,* and *sharpe-sighted* mind.

If she the bodies nature did partake,
   Her strength would with the bodies strength decay;
   But when the bodies strongest sinewes slake,
   Then is the *Soule* most active, quicke and gay.   480

If she were but the bodies accident,
   And her sole *being* did in it subsist,
   As *white in snow*, she might her selfe absent,
   And in the bodies Substance not be mist.

  453 *doth*] do *AC*, *H573*   467 *Alchimist AC*, *H573*: rom. *Σ*   483 *snow,*
1599: ~; *AC*

But *it* on *her*, not *she* on *it* depends,   485
　　For *she* the body doth sustaine and cherish,
　　Such secret powers of life to it she lends,
　　That when they faile, then doth the bodie perish.

Since then the *Soule workes by her selfe alone*,
　　Springs not from sense, nor *humours well agreeing*;   490
　　Her nature is peculiar, and her owne.
　　She is a *substance*, and a *perfect being*.

*That the soule
is a spirit.*　But *though* this substance be the roote of *Sense*,
　　Sense knowes her not, which doth but *bodies* know:
　　She is a spirit and heavenly Influence,   495
　　Which from the fountaine of Gods spirit doth flow.

She is a spirit, yet not like *aire*, or *wind*,
　　Nor like the *spirits* about the *heart* or *braine*,
　　Nor like those spirits which *Alchimists* do find,
　　When they in every thing seeke gold, *in vaine*.   500

For she all *natures* under heaven doth passe,
　　Being like those spirits which Gods bright face do see,
　　Or like *himself*, whose *image* once she was,
　　Though now, alas, she scarce his *shadow* bee.

Yet of the *formes* she holds the first degree,   505
　　That are to grosse materiall bodies knit;
　　Yet she her selfe is *bodilesse* and free,
　　And though confin'd, is almost infinit.

*That it can
not be a bodie.*　*Were she a bodie*, how could she remaine
　　Within this bodie, which is lesse then she?   510
　　Or how could she the worlds great shape containe,
　　And in our narrow breasts contained be?

All *bodies* are confin'd within some place;
　　But *she* all place within her selfe confines:
　　All *bodies* have their measure and their space,   515
　　But who can draw the *Soules* dimensive lines?

495 and heavenly *1622*, *AC*, *HH*: and a heavenly *1599*　　　499 *Alchimists*
AC, *H573*: rom. *Σ*　　　　　　　509 *Were she H573*: rom. *Σ a ed.*: rom. *All*
511 Or] And *MSS*.

No *bodie* can at once two formes admit,
　　Except the one the other do deface;
　　But in the *Soule* ten thousand formes do sit,
　　And none intrudes into her neighbours place. 520

All *bodies* are with other bodies fild;
　　But she receives both heaven and earth together,
　　Nor are their formes by rash incounter spild,
　　For there they stand, and neither toucheth ether.

Nor can her wide Embracements filled bee: 525
　　For they that most and greatest things embrace,
　　Enlarge thereby their minds Capacitie,
　　As streames enlarg'd, enlarge their Channels space.

"*All things receiv'd do such proportion take,*
　　"*As those things have wherein they are receiv'd*: 530
　　So little glasses, little faces make,
　　And narrow webs, on narrow frames be weav'd.

Then what vast bodie must we make the *mind*?
　　Wherein are men, beasts, trees, towns, seas and lands?
　　And yet each thing a proper place doth find, 535
　　And each thing in the true proportion stands.

Doubtlesse this could not be, but that she turnes
　　Bodies to spirits by *sublimation* strange;
　　As fire converts to fire, the thinge it burnes,
　　As we our meates into our nature change. 540

From their grosse *matter* she abstracts the *formes*,
　　And drawes a kind of *Quintessence* from things;
　　Which to her proper nature she transformes,
　　To beare them light on her celestiall wings.

This doth she when from things *particular*, 545
　　She doth abstract the *universall kinds*;
　　Which bodilesse, and immateriall are,
　　And can be lodg'd but onely in our minds.

528 their *MSS.*: the *Print*　　　529-30 *Quotation marks, inserted in Davies's hand,*
appear in AC only.　　539 thinge *AC* (*altered from* things *in Davies's hand*): things *Σ*

And thus from diverse *accidents* and *acts*
   Which do within her observation fall,   550
   She goddesses and powres divine abstracts,
   As *Nature*, *Fortune*, and the *Vertues* all.

Againe, how can she severall *bodies* know
   If in her selfe a *bodies* forme she beare?
   How can a Mirror sundrie faces show,   555
   If from all shapes and formes it be not cleare?

Nor could we by our eyes all colours learne,
   Except our eyes were of all colours voide:
   Nor sundrie tasts can any tongue discerne
   Which is with grosse and bitter humours cloide: 560

Nor may a man of *passions* judge aright,
   Except his mind be from all passions free;
   Nor can a *Judge* his office well acquite,
   If he possest of either partie bee.

If lastly this quicke powre a bodie were,   565
   Were it as swift as is the *wind*, or *fire*;
   (Whose *Atomies* do th'one downe side-wayes beare,
   And make th'other in *Pyramids* aspire)

Her nimble bodie yet in *time* must move;
   And not in instants through all places slide;   570
   But she is nigh, and farre, beneath, above,
   In point of time which thought can not devide.

Sh'is sent as soone to *China* as to *Spaine*,
   And thence returnes as soone as she is sent,
   She measures with one time, and with one paine,   575
   An ell of Silke, and heavens wide-spreading Tent.

As then the *Soule* a substance hath alone,
   Besides the bodie, in which she is confin'd;
   So hath she not a *bodie* of her owne,
   But is a *spirit*, and *immateriall mind*.   580

552 *Fortune* ... *Vertues* A C, H573: l.c. Σ   568 th' A C, HH: the Σ

Since *body and soule* have such diversities,
    Well might we muse, how first their match began;
    But that we learne, that *he* that spread the skies,
    And fixt the earth, first formd the *Soule* in man.

That the Soule is created immediatly by God. Zach. 12. 1.

This true *Prometheus* first made man of earth,   585
    And shed in him a beame of heavenly Fire;
    Now in their mothers wombes before their birth,
    Doth in all sonnes of men their *Soules* inspire.

And as *Minerva* is in fables said,
    From *Jove* without a mother to proceed: 590
    So our true *Jove*, without a mothers aide,
    Doth daily millions of *Minervaes* breed.

Then neither from eternitie before,
    Nor from the time when *Times* first point begun,
    Made he all *Soules*, which now he keepes in store,
    Some in the Moone, and others in the Sunne: 596

Erronious opinions of the creation of soules.

Nor in a *secret cloister* doth he keepe
    These virgin spirits, untill their mariage day;
    Nor locks them up in Chambers where they sleepe,
    Till they awake, within these beds of Clay.   600

Nor did he first a certaine number make,
    Infusing part in *beasts*, and part in *men*,
    And, as unwilling farther paines to take,
    Would make no more then those he formed then:

So that the widow *Soule*, her *body* dying,   605
    Unto the next borne *body* maried was;
    And so by often chaunging and supplying,
    Mens *soules* to *beasts*, and beasts to men did passe.

These thoughts are fond: for since the bodies borne
    Be more in number farre then those that die,   610
    Thousands must be abortive and forlorne,
    Ere others deaths to them their *soules* supply.

583 learne, 1599: ~; *AC*   593 *ital. ed.: rom. All*   593m. *Erronious*]
Haereticall AC, HH: marginal note om. H573   604 formed *MSS.*: framed *Print*
605 her] the *AC*, H573   608 *beasts AC: rom.* Σ

But as *Gods handmayde*, *Nature* doth create
  Bodies in time distinct, and order due,
  So God gives *soules* the like successive date,   615
  Which *him selfe* makes in bodies formed new:

Which *him selfe* makes of no materiall thing;
  For unto Angels he no power hath given,
  Either to forme the shape, or stuffe to bring,
  From *aire*, or *fire*, or *substance of the heaven*.   620

That the
Soule is not
traduced from
the parents.

Nor *he* in this doth *Natures* service use,
  For though from bodies she can bodies bring,
  Yet could she never soules from soules *traduce*,
  As fire from fire, or light from light doth spring.

Alas, that some that were great lights of old,   625
  And in their hands the *lampe* of God did beare,
  Some reverend Fathers, did this error hold,
  Having their eyes dim'd with religious feare.

The principall
objection.

For *when* (say they) by rule of faith we find
  That everie *soule* unto her *body* knit,   630
  Brings from the mothers wombe the *sinne of kind*,
  The roote of all the ill she doth commit:

How can we say that God the *Soule* doth make,
  But we must make him author of her sinne?
  Then from mans soule she doth beginning take,   635
  Since in mans soule Corruption did begin.

For if God make her, first he makes her ill;
  Which God forbid our thoghts should yeeld unto;
  Or makes the bodie her faire forme to spill,
  Which of it selfe it had no powre to do.   640

Not *Adams bodie*, but his *soule* did sinne,
  And so her selfe unto corruption brought:
  But our poore *Soule* corrupted is within,
  Ere she hath sinn'd either in act or thought.

621 *Nor he* ed.: *rom. All*   621m. *Marginal gloss omitted here in 1619–22. 1622*
adds gloss to lines 625–8: 'Objection that the soule is extraduce.'   629 *ital. ed.:*
rom. All   629m. *The principall objection MSS.: om. Print*

And yet we see in her such powres divine,   645
  As we could gladly thinke, *from God she came*;
Faine would we make him author of the wine,
  If for the dregs we could some other blame.

Thus these good men with holy *Zeale* were blind;   *The answer to*
  When on the other part the *Truth* did shine,   *the objection.*
Whereof we do cleere demonstrations find,   651
  By light of *nature*, and by light *divine*.

None are so grosse as to contend for this,
  That soules from bodies may traduced bee:
Betweene whose natures no proportion is,   655
  When roote and branch in nature still agree.

But many subtill wits have justifi'd,
  That *Soules* from *Soules* spiritually may spring;
Which if the nature of the *Soule* be try'd,
  Will even in nature prove as grosse a thing.   660

For all things made, are either made of nought,   *Reasons drawne*
  Or made of stuffe, that ready made doth stand: *from nature.*
Of nought no creature ever formed ought,
  For that is proper to th'*Almighties* hand.

If then the *Soule* another *Soule* do make,   665
  Because her power is kept within a bound,
She must some former stuffe or *matter* take,
  But in the *Soule* there is no *matter* found.

Then if her heavenly *Forme* do not agree,
  With any *matter* which the world containes;   670
Then she of nothing must created bee,
  And to *create*, to God alone pertaines.

Againe if *soules* do other *soules* beget,
  Tis by themselves, or by the bodies powre:
If by themselves, what doth their working let,   675
  But they might *soules* engender every houre?

649 *Zeale AC*, H573: zeale Σ   650 *Truth AC*, H573: truth Σ   661 *ital.*
ed.: *rom. All*   664 *Almighties AC*, H573: rom. Σ

If by the bodie, how can *wit* and *will*
   Joyne with the bodie onely in this act;
   Since when they do their other works fulfill,
   They from the body do themselves *abstract*?   680

Againe if *Soules* of *Soules* begotten were,
   Into each other they should change and move;
   And *change* and *motion* still *corruption* beare,
   How shall we then the *Soule* immortall prove?

If lastly *Soules* did generation use,   685
   Then should they spread incorruptible seed;
   What then becomes of that which they do loose,
   When th'acts of generation do not speed?

And though the Soule *could* cast spirituall seed,
   Yet *would* she not, because she *never dies*;   690
   For mortall things desire their *like* to breed,
   That so they may their kind immortalize.

Therefore the Angels sonnes of God are nam'd,
   And marrie not, nor are in mariage given;
   Their spirits and ours, are of one *substance* fram'd,   695
   And have one Father, even the *Lord of heaven*;

Who would at first, that in each other thing,
   The *earth* and *water* living *soules* should breed;
   But that *Mans soule*, whom he wold make their king,
   Should from him selfe immediatly proceed.   700

And when he tooke the *woman* from *mans* side,
   Doubtlesse himselfe inspir'd her *soule* alone;
   For tis not sayd, he did mans *soule* devide,
   But tooke *flesh of his flesh, bone of his bone.*

Lastly, God being made Man for Mans owne sake,   705
   And being like Man, in all, except in Sinne:
   His Bodie from the *Virgins* wombe did take,
   But all agree, *God form'd his soule within.*

696 heaven; *1599*: ~. *AC*

Then is the *Soule* from God: so *Pagans* say,
　　Which saw by natures light her heavenly kind; 710
　　Naming her *kin to God, and Gods bright ray,*
　　A Citizen of heaven to earth confin'd.

But now I feele they plucke me by the eare,
　　Whom my young *Muse* so boldly termed blind;
　　And crave more heavenly light, that cloud to cleare, 715
　　Which makes them thinke, God doth not make the mind.

God doubtlesse makes her, and doth make her good, *Reasons*
　　And graffes her in the bodie there to spring; *drawne from*
　　Which though it be corrupted, flesh and blood *divinitie.*
　　Can no way to the *Soule* corruption bring. 720

And yet this *Soule* (made good by God at first,
　　And not corrupted by the Bodies ill)
　　Even in the Wombe is sinfull and accurst,
　　Ere she can *judge* by *wit,* or *choose* by *will.*

Yet is not God the Author of her Sinne, 725
　　Though Author of her *being,* and *being there,*
　　And if we dare to judge our *Judge* herein,
　　He can condemne us, and himselfe can cleere.

First God from infinite eternitie
　　Decreed what *hath bene, is,* or *shall be* done, 730
　　And was resolv'd, that every Man should bee,
　　And in his turne his race of life should runne:

And so did purpose all the *Soules* to make
　　That ever *have bene* made, or *ever shall*;
　　And that their *being* they should onely take 735
　　In humane bodies, or not *be* at all.

---

717 *God* H573: rom. Σ　　719 corrupted, *1599*: ～∧ *AC*　　blood∧ *1599*: ～, *AC*
721–2 *Parentheses from 1599; om. AC.*　　723 sinfull Σ: sinfulll *1599*　　724 *ital.*
1622: rom. Σ

Was it then fit, that such a weake event,
  (*Weakenesse it selfe*, the sinne, and fall of Man)
  His Counsels execution should prevent,
  Decreed and fixt before the world began?   740

Or that one *penall law* by *Adam* broke,
  Should make God breake his owne *eternall law*,
  The setled order of the world revoke,
  And change all formes of things which he foresaw?

Could *Eves* weake hand, extended to the tree,   745
  In sunder rend that *Adamantine chaine*,
  Whose golden linkes, *effects*, and *causes* bee,
  And which to Gods owne chaire doth fixt remaine?

O could we see, how cause from cause doth spring,
  How mutually they linckt, and folded are,   750
  And heare, how oft one disagreeing string
  The harmonie doth rather make, then marre:

And view at once, how *death* by *sinne* is brought,
  And how from *death* a better *life* doth rise,
  How this Gods *justice*, and his *mercy* tought,   755
  We this decree would praise as right and wise.

But we that measure times by first and last,
  The sight of things successively do take;
  When God on all at once his view doth cast,
  And of all times doth but one *instant* make.   760

All in *him selfe* as in a *glasse* he sees,
  For *from him, by him, through him all things bee;*
  His sight is not discoursive by degrees,
  But seeing the whole each single part doth see.

He lookes on *Adam* as a *roote* or *well*,   765
  And on his heires as *branches* and as *streames*,
  He sees *all* men, as *one* man, though they dwell
  In sundrie Cities, and in sundrie Realmes.

And as the *roote* and *branch* are but one *tree*,
　　And *well* and *streame* do but one *river* make;　　770
　　So if the *roote* and *well* corrupted bee,
　　The *streame* and *branch* the same corruption take.

So when the roote and fountaine of mankind,
　　Did draw corruption, and Gods curse by sinne;
　　This was a charge, that all his heires did bind,　　775
　　And all his of-spring grew corrupt therein.

And as when th'hand doth strike, the Man offends,
　　For *part from whole, law severs not in this;*
　　So *Adams* sinne to the whole kind extends,
　　For all their Natures are but part of his.　　780

Therefore this *sinne of kind*, not personall
　　But reall, and hereditarie was,
　　The guilt whereof and punishment to all,
　　By course of Nature, and of Law doth passe.

For as that Easie law was given to all,　　785
　　To auncestor, and heire, to first, and last;
　　So was the first transgression generall,
　　And all did plucke the fruite, and all did tast.

Of this we find some footsteps in our Law,
　　Which doth her Roote from God and Nature take;　　790
　　Ten thousand Men she doth together draw,
　　And of them All one Corporation make.

Yet these and their Successors are but one,
　　And if they gaine, or loose their liberties;
　　They harme or profite not themselves alone,　　795
　　But such as in succeeding times shall rise.

And so the Auncestor, and all his heires,
　　Though they in number passe the starres of heaven,
　　Are still but one; his *forfeitures* are theirs,
　　And unto them are his *advancements* given.　　800

796 times *MSS.*: time *Print*　　799 one; *1599*: ~, *AC*

His Civill acts do bind and barre them all,
    And, as from *Adam* all corruption take,
    So if the Fathers crime be *capitall*,
    In all the *blood* law doth *corruption* make.

Is it then just with us to disinherit   805
    The unborne Nephewes, for the Fathers fault?
    And to advaunce againe for one mans merit,
    A thousand heires, that have deserved nought?

And is not Gods decree as just as ours?
    If he for *Adams* sinne his sonnes deprive,   810
    Of all those native vertues, and those powres,
    Which he to him, and to his race, did give?

For what is this contagious sinne of kind?
    But a privation of that grace within,
    And of that great, rich, dowrie of the mind,   815
    Which all had had, but for the first mans sinne?

If then a man on light conditions gaine
    A great estate, to him and his for ever;
    If wilfully he forfeit it againe,
    Who doth bemone his heire? or blame the giver?   820

So though God make the *Soule* good, rich, and faire,
    Yet when her forme is to the body knit,
    Which makes the Man, which Man is *Adams heire*,
    Justly forthwith he takes his grace from it.

And then the *Soule* being first from nothing brought,   825
    When Gods grace failes her, doth to nothing fall;
    And this *declining pronesse unto nought*,
    Is even that sinne, that we are borne withall.

Yet not alone the first good qualities,
    Which in the first *Soule* were, deprived are,   830
    But in their place the contrary do rise,
    And reall spots of sinne her beautie marre.

810 sinne] synnes *MSS.*   817 gaine‸ *1599:* ~, *AC*   829–32 *Stanza missing in MSS.*

Nor is it strange, that *Adams* ill desart,
 Should be transferd unto his guiltie Race;
 When *Christ* his grace, and justice doth impart, 835
 To men unjust, and such as have no grace.

Lastly the *Soule* were better so to bee,
 Borne slave to sinne, then not to be at all:
 Since (if she do beleeve) one sets her free,
 That makes her mount, the higher for her fall. 840

Yet this the curious wits will not content.
 They yet will know, since God foresaw this ill,
 Why his high providence did not prevent,
 The declination of the first mans will!

If by his word he had the current stayd, 845
 Of *Adams* will, which was by nature free;
 It had bene one, as if his word had sayd,
 I will henceforth, that *Man no man shall bee.*

For what is Man without a moving mind?
 Which hath a judging *wit*, and choosing *will*? 850
 Now if Gods power should her election bind,
 Her motions then would cease and stand all still.

And why did God in man this *Soule* infuse,
 But that he should his maker *know* and *love*?
 Now if *love* be compeld, and cannot chuse, 855
 How can it gratefull or thank-worthie prove?

Love must free hearted bee, and voluntarie,
 And not enchaunted, or by Fate constraind;
 Not like that love which did *Ulisses* carie
 To *Circes* Ile, with mightie charmes enchaind. 860

Besides were we unchangeable in *will*,
 And of a *wit* that nothing could misdeeme,
 Equall to God, whose wisedome shineth still
 And never erres, we might our selves esteeme.

*834 transferd unto his guiltie Race] imputed to his guiltlesse race *MSS.*
839 do] will *MSS.* 840 for *1622, MSS.*: from *1599* 864 erres, *1599*:
~; *AC*

So that if man would be unvariable,   865
   He must be God, or like a Rocke or Tree,
   For even the perfect Angels were not stable,
   But had a fall more desperate then wee.

Then let us praise that Power, which makes us bee
   Men as we are, and rest contented so;   870
   And knowing mans fall was Curiositie,
   Admire Gods counsels, which we cannot know.

And let us know, that God the maker is,
   Of all the *Soules* in all the men that bee;
   Yet their Corruption is no fault of his,   875
   But the first Mans, that broke Gods first decree.

Why the soule   *This substance*, and this *spirit*, of *Gods owne making*,
is united to the   Is in the bodie plac't, and planted here,
body.   "That both of God, and of the world partaking,
   "Of all that is, man might the image beare.   880

God first made Angels bodilesse, pure, minds;
   Then other things, which mindlesse bodies bee;
   Last he made Man, th'*Horizon* twixt both kinds,
   In whom we do the worlds abridgement see.

Besides, this world below did need *one wight*,   885
   Which might thereof distinguish every part,
   Make use thereof, and take therein delight,
   And order things with Industrie and Art.

Which also God might in his works admire,
   And here beneath yeeld him both prayer and praise,   890
   As there above the holy Angels Quire,
   Doth spread his glorie, with spirituall layes.

Lastly the bruite unreasonable wights,
   Did want a *visible king* on them to raigne;
   And God himselfe thus to the world unites,   895
   That so the world might endlesse blisse obtaine.

869 bee‸ *1599*: ~, *AC*   879–80 *Quotation marks in 1622 only.*   888 In-
dustrie *1622*: *l.c. Σ*   894 want . . . on] lacke . . . ore *HH*

But how shall we this *union* well expresse?
 Nought tyes the *Soule*, her subtiltie is such,
 She moves the bodie which she doth possesse,
 Yet no part toucheth, but by *vertues* touch.

*In what maner
the soule is
united to the
bodie.*

900

Then dwels she not therein as in a tent;
 Nor as a Pilot in his Ship doth sit;
 Nor as a Spider in her Web is pent;
 Nor as the Waxe retaines the print in it;

Nor as a Vessell water doth containe;
 Nor as one Liquor in another shed;
 Nor as the heate doth in the fire remaine;
 Nor as a voice throughout the aire is spred;

905

But as the faire, and cheerefull *morning light*,
 Doth here, and there, her silver beames impart,
 And in an instant doth her selfe unite
 To the transparent Aire, in all and part:

910

Still resting whole, when blowes the Aire devide;
 Abiding pure when th'Aire is most corrupted;
 Throughout the Aire her beames dispersing wide,
 And when the Aire is tost, not interrupted;

915

So doth the piercing *Soule* the bodie fill;
 Being all in all, and all in part diffus'd,
 Indivisible, incorruptible still,
 Not forc't, encountred, troubled or confus'd.

920

And as the *Sunne* above the light doth bring,
 Though we behold it in the Aire below;
 So from th'eternall light the *Soule* doth spring,
 Though in the Bodie she her powers do show.

*Howe the
Soule doth
exercise her
powers in the
body.*

But as this worlds *Sunne* doth effects beget
 Diverse, in diverse places every day;
 Here *Autumnes* temperature, there *Summers* heate,
 Here flowrie *Spring-tide* and there *Winter* gray;

925

---

919 incorruptible *1622*: uncorruptible *Σ*: uncorrupted *1619* 921 *MSS. place
marginal gloss here; printed texts place it at next stanza.*

Here *Even*, there *Morn*, here *Noon*, there *Day*, there *Night*;
    Melts wax, dries clay, makes floures some quick, some
                                                    dead;   930
    Makes the *More* black, and th'*Europæan* white,
    Th'*American* tawnie, and th'*East Indian* red;

So in our litle world this *Soule* of ours,
    Being onely one, and to one bodie tyed,
    Doth use on diverse objects, diverse powers,   935
    And so are her effects diversified.

The vegetative   Her *quickning* power in every living part
or quickening   Doth as a Nurse, or as a Mother serve;
power.   And doth employ her *Œconomicke Art*,
                    And busie care, her houshold to preserve.   940

Here she *attracts*, and there she doth *retaine*,
    There she *decocts*, and doth the food prepare,
    There she *distributes* it to every vaine,
    There she *expels* what she may fitly spare.

This power to *Martha* may compared bee,   945
    Which busie was the *houshold things* to do;
    Or to a *Dryas* living in a Tree,
    For even to Trees this power is proper too.

And though the *Soule* may not this power extend
    Out of the Body, but still use it there;   950
    She hath a power which she abroad doth send,
    Which viewes and searcheth all things every where.

The Power of   *This power is Sense*, which from abroad doth bring,
Sense.   The *colour*, *tast*, and *touch*, and *sent*, and *sound*;
                    The *quantitie*, and *shape* of every thing,   955
                    Within th'earths Center, or heavens Circle found.

This Power in parts made fit, fit objects takes,
    Yet not the things, but Formes of things receives,
    As when a Seale in Waxe impression makes,
    The print therein, but not it selfe, it leaves.   960

    929 here] there *HH*   *Night* ed.: night *1599*, *MSS.*: Night *1622*   939 *Œcono-
micke AC (JD)*: oeconomicke *1599*

And though things sensible be numberlesse,
   But onely five the *Senses* Organs bee;
   And in those five All things their Formes expresse,
   Which we can *touch*, *tast*, *smelle*, or *heare*, or *see*.

These are her windowes through the which she viewes   965
   The *light of knowledge* which is lifes load-starre;
   "And yet whiles she these spectacles doth use,
   "Oft worldy things seeme greater then they are.

First the two *Eyes*, which have the *Seeing* power,   *Sight.*
   Stand as one watchman, Spie, or Sentinell;   970
   Being plac'd aloft within the Heads high Tower,
   And though both see, yet both but one thing tell.

These Mirrors take into their litle space,
   The formes of *Moone*, and *Sunne*, and every *Starre*,
   Of every Bodie, and of every place,   975
   Which with the worlds wide Armes embraced are.

Yet their best object, and their noblest use,
   Hereafter in another world will bee;
   When God in them shall heavenly light infuse,
   That face to face they may their *Maker* see.   980

Here are they guides which do the Bodie leade,
   Which else would stumble in eternall night;
   Here in this world, they do much knowledge *reade*,
   And are the Casements which admit most light.

They are her farthest reaching Instrument;   985
   Yet they no beames unto their Objects send,
   But all the rayes are from their Objects sent,
   And in the *Eyes* with pointed Angles end.

If th'objects be farre off, the rayes do meete
   In a sharpe point, and so things seeme but small;   990
   If they be neare, their rayes do spread and fleete,
   And make broade points, that things seeme great withall.

964 *smelle* ed. (*Capell*): *feele All*   965 her *MSS.*: the *Print*   987 their]
the *MSS.*

Lastly Nine things to *Sight* required are;
    The *power* to see, the *light*, the *visible thing*,
    Being not too *small*, too *thinne*, too *nigh*, too *farre*,   995
    Cleere space, and *time* the forme distinct to bring.

Thus see wee how the *Soule* doth use the Eyes,
    As Instruments of her quicke power of sight;
    Hence do th'Arts *Opticke*, and faire *painting* rise,
    Painting which doth ingenious minds delight.   1000

Hearing. *Now* let us heare how she the *Eares* employes;
    Their office is the troubled Aire to take,
    Which in their Mazes formes a sound, or noise,
    Whereof her selfe doth true distinction make.

These wickets of the *Soule* are plac'd on hie,   1005
    Because all sounds do lightly mount aloft;
    And that they may not pierce too violently,
    They are delayed with turnes, and windings oft.

For should the voice directly strike the braine,
    It would astonish, and confuse it much;   1010
    Therefore these plaits and folds the sound restraine,
    That it the Organ may more gently touch.

As Streames which with their winding banks do play,
    Stopt by their Creeks, run softly through the plaine,
    So in the Eares labrinth the voyce doth stray,   1015
    And doth with easie motion touch the braine.

It is the slowest, yet the daintiest *Sense*,
    For even the *eares* of such as have no skill,
    Perceive a discord, and conceive Offence,
    And knowing not what'is good, yet find the ill.   1020

And though this *Sense* first gentle *Musicke* found,
    Her proper object is *the speech of men*;
    But that speech chiefly, which Gods herralds sound,
    When their Tongs utter, what his Spirit did pen.

    994 *thing ed.: rom. All*   996 *space* H573: *rom. Σ*   *1000 ingenious *MSS.*:
all gentle *Print*   1013 play, *1599*:~ₐ *AC*   1018 skill, *1599*: ~; *AC*
1021 found, *1599*: ~; *AC*

Our *Eyes* have lids, our *Eares* still ope we see,   1025
    Quickly to heare how every tale is proved;
    Our *Eyes* still move, our *Eares* unmoved bee,
    That though we'heare quicke, we be not quickly moved.

Thus by the Organs of the *Eye* and *Eare*,
    The *Soule* with knowledge doth her selfe endew;   1030
    "Thus she her prison may with pleasure beare,
    "Having such prospects All the world to view.

These Conduit pipes of knowledge feed the mind;
    But th'other three attend the Bodie still;
    For by their services the *Soule* doth find,   1035
    What things are to the Bodie good, or ill.

The Bodies life with meates and Aire is fed;   *Taste.*
    Therefore the *Soule* doth use the *tasting* power
    In Veines, which through the Tong and Palate spred
    Distinguish every rellish sweete, and sower.   1040

This is the Bodies *Nurse*; but since mans wit
    Found th'art of *Cookerie* to delight this *Sense*,
    More bodies are consum'd, and kild with it,
    Then with the sword, famine, or pestilence.

Next in the Nosthrils she doth use the *smell*,   *Smelling.*
    As God the *breath* of *life* in them did give,   1046
    So makes he now this power in them to dwell,
    To judge all Aires, whereby we *breath* and *live*.

This *Sense* is also mistresse of an Art,
    Which to soft people sweete perfumes doth sell;   1050
    Though this deare Aire doth little good impart,
    "Since they smell best, that do of nothing smell.

And yet good *sents* do purifie the braine,
    Awake the Fancie, and the Wits refine,
    Hence old *Devotion Incense* did ordaine,   1055
    To make mens spirits more apt for thoughts divine.

1028 we' *ed.*: we *All*   1031–2 *Quotation marks in 1622 only.*   1036 Bodie‸
1599: ∼, *AC*   ill. *1599:* ∼, *AC*   1042 this *MSS.*: his *Print*   1047 this
1622, MSS.: his *1599*   *1051 Aire *MSS.*: Art *Print*   1056 apt] fitt *MSS.*

Feeling.   *Lastly the Feeling power,* which is Lifes roote,
    Through ev'ry living part it selfe doth shed;
    By *sinewes,* which extend from head to foote,
    And like a Net ore all the bodie spred.   1060

Much like a subtill Spider which doth sit,
    In middle of her Web which spreadeth wide;
    If ought do touch the utmost threed of it,
    She feeles it instantly on every side.

By *touch* the first pure qualities we learne   1065
    Which quicken all things, *hote, cold, moyst,* and *drie*;
    By *touch hard, soft, rough, smooth* we do discerne,
    By *touch sweete pleasure,* and *sharpe paine* we trie:

These are the outward Instruments of *Sense,*
    These are the *Guards* which every thing must passe;   1070
    Ere it approch the minds intelligence,
    Or touch the Phantasie, *wits looking glasse.*

The Imagina- And yet these Porters which all things admit,
tion or common   Them selves perceive not, nor discerne the things;
Sense.   One *Common* power doth in the forehead sit,   1075
    Which all their proper formes together brings.

For all those *Nerves* which *spirits of Sense* do beare,
    And to those outward Organs spreading go,
    United are as in a Center there,
    And there this power those sundry forms doth know.

Those outward Organs present things receive   1081
    This inward *Sense* doth absent things retaine;
    Yet straight transmits all formes she doth perceive,
    Unto a higher region of the *braine*;

The Phantasie. Where *Phantasie,* neare handmaid to the mind,   1085
    Sits, and beholds, and doth discerne them all;
    Compounds in one, things diverse in their kind,
    Compares the blacke, and white, the great and small.

1058 ev'ry *AC* (*JD*): every *1599*   1060 ore all *MSS.*: all ore *Print*
1077 those] theis *HH, H573*   1083 formes] things *MSS.*   1084 *braine;*
ed.*:* ~. *1599, AC*   1085 *Phantasie, 1599:* ~ₐ *AC*

Besides those single formes she doth esteeme,
   And in her Ballance doth their values trie;   1090
   Where some things good, and some things ill do seeme,
   And neutrall some in her *phantasticke* eye.

This busie power is working day and night;
   For when the outward *Senses* rest do take,
   A thousand Dreames, phantasticall, and light,   1095
   With fluttering wings do keepe her still awake.

Yet alwayes all may not before her bee;   *The sensative*
   Successively she this, and that intends;   *memory.*
   Therefore such formes as she doth cease to see,
   To *Memories* large volume she commends.   1100

This *Lidger Booke* lyes in the braine behind,
   Like *Janus eye*, which in his *poll* was set;
   The *Lay-mans Tables*, *Storehouse of the mind*,
   Which doth remember much, and much forget.

Here *Senses Apprehension* end doth take;   1105
   As when a Stone is into water cast,
   One Circle doth another Circle make,
   Till the last circle, touch the banke at last.

But though the *apprehensive power* do pawse,   *The passions*
   The *Motive* vertue then begins to move: *of Sense.*
   Which in the heart below doth *passions* cause,   1111
   Joy, *griefe*, and *feare*, and *hope*, and *hate*, and *love*.

These *passions* have a free Commaunding might,
   And diverse Actions in our life do breed;
   For all Acts done without true reasons light,   1115
   Do from the passion of the *Sense* proceed.

But sith the *Braine* doth lodge these powers of *Sense*,
   How makes it in the heart those passions spring?
   The mutuall love and kind intelligence,
   Twixt heart and braine this *sympathy* doth bring.   1120

1090 her] a *HH*   1091 some . . . ill *ed.*: som . . . il *1599* (*full line*)
1097 before *AC, HH*: afore *Σ*   1102 *eye AC, HH*: rom. *Σ*   1113 *passions*
MSS.: rom. *Print*   1118 those] these *MSS.*   1119 love and *MSS.*: love,
the *Print*

From the kind heate which in the heart doth raigne,
    The *spirits* of life do their beginning take,
    These *spirits* of life ascending to the braine,
    When they come there, the *spirits* of *Sense* do make.

These *spirits* of *Sense* in Phantasies high Court,   1125
    Judge of the formes of *Objects* ill or well;
    And so they send a good or ill report,
    Downe to the heart, where all Affections dwell.

If the report be *good*, it causeth *love*,
    And longing *hope*, and well assured *joy*,   1130
    If it be *ill*, then doth it *hatred* move,
    And trembling *feare*, and vexing *griefes* annoy.

Yet were these naturall affections good,
    (For they which want them *blocks* or *divels* be)
    If *reason* in her first perfection stood,   1135
    That she might *Natures* passions rectifie.

The motion of life.

Besides an other *Motive* power doth rise,
    Out of the hart, from whose pure blood do spring
    The *vitall Spirits*, which borne in *Arteries*,
    Continuall motion to all parts do bring.   1140

The locall motion.

This makes the pulses beate, and lungs respire,
    This holds the synewes like a bridles Raines,
    And makes the bodie to advaunce, retire,
    To turne, or stop, as she them slacks, or straines.

Thus the *Soule* tunes the *bodies* Instrument,   1145
    These harmonies she makes with *life*, and *sense*;
    The organes fit are by the bodie lent,
    But th'actions flow from the *Soules* influence.

The intellec-tual powers of the soule.

But now I have a *will*, yet want a *wit*,
    To'expresse the workings of the *wit*, and *will*;   1150
    Which though their roote be to the bodie knit,
    Use not the body, when they use their skill.

1124 make. 1599: ∼, *AC*   1138 spring *ed.*: ∼, *1599, AC*   1139 *Spirits,*
... *Arteries, 1599:* ∼ₐ ... ∼ₐ *AC*   1144 turne, or] turne, and *MSS.*
1150 To' *MSS.*: To *Print*

These powers the nature of the *Soule* declare,
  For to mans *Soule* these onely proper bee;
  For on the earth no other wights there are,   1155
  Which have these heavenly powers, but only wee.

The *wit*, the pupill of the *Soules* cleare eye,   *The wit or*
  And in mans world the onely shining *Starre*,   *understanding.*
  Lookes in the mirrour of the phantasie,
  Where all the gatherings of the *Senses* are.   1160

From thence this power the shapes of things abstracts,
  And them within her *passive part* receives,
  Which are enlightned by that part which *acts*,
  And so the formes of single things perceives.

But after by discoursing to and fro,   1165
  Anticipating, and comparing things,
  She doth all universall natures know,
  And all *effectes* into their *causes* brings.

When she *rates* things, and moves from ground to ground,
  The name of *Reason* she obtaines by this;   *Reason.*
  But when by reasons she the truth hath found,   1171
  And *standeth fixt*, she *Understanding* is.   *Understanding.*

When her assent she *lightlie* doth encline
  To either part, she is *Opinion light*;   *Opinion.*
  But when she doth by principles define   1175
  A Certaine truth, she hath *true Judgements* sight.   *Judgement.*

And as from *Senses*, *Reasons* worke doth spring;
  So manie *Reasons*, *understanding* gaine,
  And manie *understandings*, *knowledge* bring,
  And by much *knowledge*, *wisdome* we obtaine.   1180

So many staires we must ascend upright,
  Ere we attaine to *wisdomes* high degree:
  So doth this earth eclipse our reasons light,
  Which else in instants would like Angels see.

1156 powers, *1599:* ~‚ *AC*   wee. *1599:* ~, *AC*   1157 *wit, 1599:* ~‚ *AC*
1158 the *HH, 1622:* th' *Σ*   1171 reasons] reason *1622, AC*   1172 *Under-*
standing *AC, 1622: l.c. Σ*   1173 encline‚ *1599:* ~, *AC*   1174 *Opinion AC:*
l.c. *Σ*   1177 *Senses, ed.:* ~‚ *AC, 1599*

Yet hath the *Soule* a dowrie naturall,   1185
    And *sparcks of light* some common things to see;
    Not being a *blanck*, where nought is writ at all,
    But what the writer will may written bee.

For nature in mans hart her lawes doth pen,
    Prescribing *truth* to *wit*, and *good* to *will*,   1190
    Which do *accuse*, or else *excuse* all men,
    For every thought, or practise, good, or ill.

And yet these sparks grow almost infinite,
    Making the world, and all therein their food;
    As fire so spreads, as no place holdeth it,   1195
    Being nourisht still, with new supplies of wood.

And though these sparks were almost quencht with sinne,
    Yet they whom that *Just one* hath Justifide,
    Have them encreased with heavenly light within,
    And like the *widowes oyle* still multiplide.   1200

The power of
will.

And as this *wit* should goodnesse trulie know,
    We have a *will* which that true good should chuse;
    Though *will* do oft, when *wit* false formes doth show,
    Take *ill* for *good*, and *good* for *ill* refuse.

The Relations
betwixt wit
and will.

Will puts in practise what the *wit* deviseth;   1205
    Will ever acts, and *wit* contemplates still;
    And as from *wit* the power of *wisdome* riseth,
    All other vertues daughters are of *will*.

Will is the *Prince*, and *wit* the Counsellour,
    Which doth for common good in Councell sit;   1210
    And when *wit* is resolv'd, *will* lends her power
    To execute, what is advisd by *wit*.

Wit is the minds chief Judge, which doth Comptroule
    Of *fancies* Court the judgements false and vaine;
    Will holds the royall Scepter in the *Soule*,   1215
    And on the passions of the hart doth raigne.

1186 things] thing *MSS.*   1202 *will 1622, MSS.:* wit *1599*

Will is as Free an any Emperour;
   Nought can restraigne her *gentle* libertie;
   No Tyrant, nor no Torment hath the powre,
   To make us *will*, when we *unwilling* bee.   1220

To these high powers a Store-house doth pertaine,   *The intellect-*
   Where they all Arts, and generall Reasons lay;   *uall memorie.*
   Which in the *Soule* even after death remaine,
   And no *Lethæan* Flud can wash away.

This is the *Soule*, and these her vertues bee;   1225
   Which though they have their sundry proper ends,
   And one exceeds another in degree,
   Yet each on other mutually depends.

Our wit is geven, *Almightie* God to *know*,   *The relations*
   Our *will* is given, to *love* him being *knowne*; *of the powers*
   But God could not be *knowne* to us below,   *of the Soule*
   But by his *works*, which through the *sense* are shown. *one to another.*

And as the *wit* doth reape the fruits of *sense*,
   So doth the *quickning* powre the *senses feed*;
   Thus while they do their sundrie gifts dispence,   1235
   The best the service of the least doth need.

Even so the King his Magistrats do serve;
   Yet commons feede both Magistrate and King;
   The commons peace the Magistrats preserve,
By borrowed power, which from the Prince doth spring.   1240

The *quickning power* would *be*, and so would rest;
   The *sense* would not *be* only, but *be well*;
   But *wits* ambition longeth to be *best*,
   For it desires in endlesse blisse to dwell.

And these three powers, three sorts of men do make;   1245
   For some like plants, their veines do only fill;
   And some like beasts, their senses pleasure take;
   And some like Angels do Contemplate still.

1225 these *1622, MSS.*: those *1599*   1229 geven, *1599*: ~∧ *AC*
1229m. *Marginal gloss om. Print*   1238 King; *1599*: ~, *AC*

Therefore the fables turnd some men to flowers;
    And others did with brutish formes invest;   1250
    And did of others make Celestiall powers,
    Like Angels, which still travell, yet still rest.

Yet these three powrs, are not three *Soules* but one;
    As one, and two, are both contain'd' in *three*;
    Three being one number by it selfe alone,   1255
    A shadow of the blessed Trinitie.

An Acclama-   O *what* is man (great maker of mankind)
tion.   That thou to him so great respect dost beare?
                  That thou adornst him with so bright a mind?
                  Mak'st him a king, and even an Angels peere?   1260

O what a livelie life! what heavenly power!
    What spreading vertue! what a sparkling Fire!
    How great, how plentifull, how rich a dowre,
    Do'st thou within this dying Flesh inspire!

Thou leav'st thy print in other workes of thine,   1265
    But thy whole image thou in man hast writ;
    There cannot be a creature more divine,
    Except like thee it should be infinit.

But it exceeds mans thought to think how high
    God hath raizd *man*, since *God a man* became;   1270
    The Angels do admire this *mysterie*,
    And are astonisht when they view the same.

That the   Nor *hath he* given these blessings for a day,
soule is   Nor made them on the bodies life depend;
immortall, and   The *Soule* (though made in time) *Survives for aye*,   1275
cannot die.   And, though it hath beginning, sees no end.

Her onely *end* is *never ending blisse*,
    Which is *th'eternall Face of God to see;*
    Who *last of ends,* and *first of causes is,*
    And to do this she must *eternall* bee.   1280

1273 *Nor hath MSS.: rom. Print   he AC, HH: rom. Σ*   1277 *blisse AC, H573:*
rom. Σ

How senslesse then, and dead a *Soule* hath hee,
    Which *thinks* his *Soule* doth with his bodie dye?
    Or *thinks* not so, but so would have it bee,
    That he might sinne with more securitie.

For though these light and vicious persons *say*,   1285
    Our *Soule* is but a smoke or aiery blast,
    Which during life doth in our nosthrils play,
    And when we die, doth turne to wind at last.

Although they *say*, come *let us eate and drinke*,
    Our life is but a sparke, which quicklie dyes,   1290
    Though thus they *say*; they know not what *to thinke*,
    But in their minds ten thousand doubts arise.

Therefore no heretikes desire to spread
    Their light opinions, like these *Epicures*;
    For so their staggering thoughts are comforted,   1295
    And other mens assent their doubt assures.

Yet though these men against their conscience strive;
    There are some sparkles in their flintie breasts;
    Which cannot be extinct, but still revive,   1299
    That though they would, they cannot quite be *beasts*.

But who so makes a mirror of his mind,
    And doth with patience view himselfe therein;
    His *Soules* eternitie shall cleerly find,
    Though th'other beauties be defac't with sinne.   1304

First in mans minde we finde an appetite   1. *Reason.*
    To *learne*, and *know the truth* of everie thing;   *Drawne from*
    Which is connaturall, and borne with it,   *the desire of*
    And from the *Essence* of the *Soule* doth spring.   *knowledge.*

With this *desire* she hath a native *might*
    To finde out everie truth, if she had time,   1310
    Th'innumerable effectes to sort aright,
    And by degrees, from cause to cause to clime.

1305 *minde 1622, AC, H573: rom. Σ*   1312 *cause*² ∧ *1599:* ∼, *AC*

But since our life so fast away doth slide,
   As doth a hungry Eagle through the wind;
   Or as a Ship transported with the tide,   1315
   Which in their passage leave no print behind;

Of which swift, litle, time, so much we spend,
   While some few things we through the sense do straine;
   That our short race of life is at an end,
   Ere we the principles of skill attaine;   1320

Or God (which to vaine ends hath nothing done)
   In vaine this *appetite* and *power* hath given,
   Or else our knowledge, which is here begon,
   Hereafter must be perfected in heaven.

God never gave a *power* to one whole kind,   1325
   But most part of that kinde did use the same,
   Most eyes have perfect sight, though some be blind,
   Most leggs can nymbly run, though some be lame.

But in this life, no *Soule* the truth can know
   So perfectly, as it hath power to do;   1330
   If then perfection be not found below,
   An higher place, must make her mount thertoo.

2. Reason.   *Againe*, how can she but immortall bee?
Drawn from   When with the motions of both *will* and *wit*,
the motion of   She still aspireth to eternitie,   1335
the Soule.   And never rests till she attaine to it?

Water in Conduit pipes can rise no higher
   Then the well head, from whence it first doth spring;
   Then since to'eternall God she doth aspire,
   She cannot be, but an eternall thing.   1340

"All moving things to other things do move,
   "Of the same kind, which shewes their nature such:
   So *earth* fals downe, and *fire* doth mount above,
   Till both their proper Elements do touch.

1332 thertoo *AC (JD)*, HH *(JD)*: therto *1599*   1334 of both] both of *MSS.*
1339 to' *AC*: to *Σ*

And as the moisture which the thirstie earth   *The Soule*
   Suckes from the sea, to fill her emptie veines,   *compared to a*
   From out her wombe at last doth take a birth,   *River.*
   And runnes a *Nymph* along the grassie plaines;

Long doth she stay, as loath to leave the land
   From whose soft side she first did issue make;   1350
   She tastes all places, turnes to every hand,
   Her flowrie bankes unwilling to forsake;

Yet *nature* so her streames doth leade and carry,
   As that her course doth make no finall stay,
   Till she her selfe unto the *Ocean* marry,   1355
   Within whose watry bosome first she lay;

Even so the *Soule* which in this earthy mould
   The Spirit of God doth secretlie infuse;
   Because at first she doth the earth behould,
   And onely this materiall world she viewes;   1360

At first her *mother earth* she holdeth dere,
   And doth embrace the world, and worldly things;
   She flyes close by the ground, and hovers here,
   And mounts not up with her celestiall wings:

Yet under heaven she cannot light on ought,   1365
   That with her heavenly *nature* doth agree;
   She cannot rest, she cannot fixe her thought,
   She cannot in this world contented bee.

For who did ever yet in *honor*, *wealth*,
   Or *pleasure of the Sense* contentment find?   1370
   Who ever ceasd' to wish, when he had *health*?
   Or having *wisdome*, was not vext in mind?

Then as a *Bee* which among weeds doth fall,
   Which seeme sweet floures, with lustre fresh, and gay,
   She lights on that, and this, and tasteth all,   1375
   But pleasd' with none, doth rise and sore away;

1361 her *1622*: our *Σ*   1366 That] Which *MSS.*   1370 *pleasure*ₐ
1599: ~, *AC*   find? *1599*: ~; *AC*   1376 away; *1599*: ~, *AC*

So when the *soule* finds here no true content;
    And like *Noahs Dove*, can no sure footing take,
    She doth returne from whence she first was sent,
    And flyes to *him* that first her wings did make.   1380

Wit seeking *truth*, from cause to cause ascends,
    And never rests, till it the *first* attaine;
    Will seeking *good*, finds many middle ends,
    But never stayes, till it the *last* do gaine.

Now God the *Truth*, and *first of causes* is,   1385
    God is the *last good end*, which lasteth still;
    Being *Alpha* and *Omega* nam'd for this,
    Alpha to *wit*, *Omega* to the *will*.

Sith then her heavenly kind she doth bewray,
    In that to God she doth directly move;   1390
    And on no mortall thing can make her stay,
    She cannot be from hence, but from *above*.

And yet this *first true cause*, and *last good end*,
    She cannot heere so *well*, and *truly*, see,
    For this perfection she must yet attend,   1395
    Till to her *maker* she espoused bee.

As a *Kings* daughter, being in person sought
    Of diverse Princes which do Neighbour neare.
    On none of them can fixe a constant thought,
    Though she to all do lend a gentle eare;   1400

Yet can she love a Forraine *Emperour*,
    Whom of great worth, and powre she heares to be,
    If she be woo'd but by *Embassadour*,
    Or but his *letters*, or his *picture* see.

For well she knowes, that when she shalbe brought,   1405
    Into the *Kingdome* where her *spouse* doth raigne,
    Her eyes shall see, what she conceiv'd in thought,
    Him selfe, his state, his glorie, and his traine:

1378 *Dove AC*, H573: *rom.* Σ   1380 that] which *MSS.*   1387-8 *Omega*
AC (*JD*): *l.c. 1599*   1394 heere *1622*, HH, H573: heare Σ   1404 *picture*]
pictures *1622*

So while the *virgin Soule* on *Earth* doth stay,
    She woo'd and tempted is ten thousand wayes,   1410
    By these great powers which on the *earth* beare sway,
    The *wisedome of the world, wealth, pleasure, praise*;

With these sometime she doth her time beguile,
    These do by fits her phantasie possesse;
    But she distasts them all within a while;   1415
    And in the sweetest finds a Tediousnesse.

But if upon the worlds Almightie king,
    She once do fixe her humble loving thought;
    Which by his *picture* drawne in every thing,
    And *sacred messages*, her *love* hath sought;   1420

Of him she thinks she cannot thinke too much,
    This hony tasted still, is ever sweete;
    The pleasure of her ravisht thought is such
    As almost here she with her blisse doth meete;

But when in heaven she shall his *Essence* see,   1425
    This is her *soveraigne good*, and *perfect blisse;*
    Her longings, wishings, hopes all finisht bee,
    Her joyes are full, her Motions rest in this.

There is she Crownd with garlands of *content*,
    There doth she *Manna* eate, and *Nectar* drinke;   1430
    That presence doth such high delights present,
    As never tongue could speake, not hart could think.

For *this* the better *Soules* do oft despise
    The bodies death, and do it oft desire;
    For when on ground the burthened ballance lyes,
    The emptie part, is lifted up the higher.

3. Reason.
*From contempt
of death in the
better sort of
spirits.*

But if the bodies death the *Soule* should kill,
    Then death must needs *against her nature* bee;
    And were it so, all *Soules* would flie it still,
    "For Nature hates, and shunnes her contrarie.   1440

1430 *ital. MSS.: rom. Print*   1437 kill, *1599:* ~; *AC*   1439 so,
1599: ~; *AC*

For all things else, which Nature makes to bee,
   Their *being* to preserve are chiefly taught;
   For though some things desire a chaunge to see,
   "Yet never thing did long to turne to nought.

If then by death the *Soule* were quenched quite,   1445
   She could not thus against her nature runne;
   Since every senslesse thing, by Natures light,
   Doth preservation seeke, destruction shunne.

Nor could the worlds best spirits so much erre,
   (If death tooke all) that they should all agree,   1450
   Before this life, their *honor* to preferre;
   For what is praise to things that nothing bee?

Againe, if by the bodies prop she stand,
   If on the bodies life her life depend;
   As *Meleagers* on the fatall brand;   1455
   The bodies good she onely would intend.

We should not find her halfe so brave, and bold,
   To leade it to the warres, and to the Seas,
   To make it suffer watchings, hunger, cold,
   When it might feed with plenty, rest with ease.   1460

Doubtlesse all *Soules* have a surviving thought,
   Therefore of death we thinke with quiet mind:
   But if we thinke of *being turnd' to nought*,
   A trembling horror in our *Soules* we find.

4. Reason.
From the
feare of death
in the wicked
Soules.

And as the better spirit, when she doth beare   1465
   A scorne of death, doth shew she cannot dye;
   So when the wicked *Soule* deaths face doth feare,
   Even then she proves her owne Eternity.

For when deaths forme appeares, she feareth not
   An utter quenching, or extinguishment;   1470
   She would be glad to meete with such a lot,
   So that she might all future ill prevent.

1472 So that *MSS.*: That so *Print*

But she doth doubt, what after may befall,
  For natures law accuseth her within,
  And saith T'is true, that is affirm'd by all,   1475
  That after Death there is a paine for sinne.

Then she which hath bene hudwinckt from her birth,
  Doth first her selfe within deaths mirrour see;
  And when her bodie doth returne to earth,
  She first takes care, how she along shalbe.   1480

Who ever sees these irreligious men,
  With burthen of a sicknesse, weake, and faint;
  But heares them talking of religion then,
  And vowing of their *Soules* to every Saint?

When was there ever cursed *Atheist* brought   1485
  Unto the *Gibbet*, but he did adore
  That blessed power, which he had set at nought,
  Scorn'd, and blasphemed all his life before?

These light, vaine persons, still are drunke, and mad,
  With surfettings and pleasures of their youth;   1490
  But at their deaths they are fresh, sober, sad,
  Then they discerne, and then they speake the truth.

If then all *Soules*, both good, and bad do teach,
  With generall voyce, that *Soules* can never dye;
  T'is not mans flattering glose, but *natures speach*,   1495
  Which like *Gods* oracle, can never lye.

Hence springs that universall strong desire,   *5. Reason.*
  Which all men have of Immortalitie;   *From the*
  Not some Few spirits unto this thought aspire,   *generall desire*
  But all mens minds in this united bee.   *of Immortality.*
    1500

Then this desire of Nature is not vaine;
  "She covets not Impossibilities;
  "Fond thoughts may fall into some Idle braine,
  "But one *Assent* of all is ever wise.

1486 *Gibbet*, 1599: ~? AC

From hence that generall care, and studie springs,　　1505
　　That *launching* and *progression of the mind*,
　　Which all men have so much of Future things,
　　As they no joy do in the present find.

From this desire that maine desire proceeds,
　　Which all men have surviving Fame to gaine,　　1510
　　By *Tombes*, by *Bookes*, by memorable *Deedes*,
　　(For she that this desires doth still remaine.)

Hence lastly springs Care of posterities,
　　For things their kind would everlasting make;
　　Hence is it, that old men do plant young Trees,　　1515
　　The fruite whereof another age shall take.

If we these Rules unto our selves apply;
　　And view them by reflection of the mind;
　　All these true notes of Immortalitie,
　　In our *Hearts Tables* we shall written find.　　1520

6. Reason.
From the very
doubt and dis-
putation of
Immortalitie.

And though some impious wits do questions move,
　　And doubt if *Soules* immortall be or no,
　　That *doubt* their Immortalitie doth prove,
　　Because they seeme immortall things to know.

For he which reasons on both parts doth bring,　　1525
　　Doth some things mortall, some immortall call;
　　Now if himselfe were but a mortall thing,
　　He could not Judge immortall things at all.

For when we Judge, our minds we mirrours make;
　　And as those glasses which materiall bee,　　1530
　　Formes of materiall things do onely take,
　　For thoughts, or minds, in them we cannot see.

So when we God and Angels do conceive,
　　And thinke of *truth*, which is eternall too;
　　Then do our minds immortall formes receive,　　1535
　　Which if they mortall were, they could not do.

1506 *progression*] *progressing* HH　　1511 *Bookes,* 1599: ~ ∧ *AC*　　1529 Judge,
1599: ~ ∧ *AC*　　1534 too *ed.*: to *1599*

And as if beasts conceivd' what Reason were,
   And that conception could distinctly show;
   They should the name of *reasonable* beare,
   For without *Reason*, none could *reason* know.   1540

So when the *Soule* mounts with so high a wing,
   As of eternall things she *doubts* can move;
   She proofes of her eternitie doth bring,
   Even when she strives the contrary to prove.

For even the *thought* of Immortalitie,   1545
   Being an act done without bodies aide;
   Shewes that her selfe alone could move, and bee,
   Although the body in the grave were laide.

And if her selfe she can so lively move,
   And never need a forraine helpe to take;   1550
   Then must her motion everlasting prove,
   "Because her selfe she never can forsake.

But though corruption cannot touch the mind,   *That the*
   By any cause that from it selfe may spring;   *Soule cannot be*
   Some outward cause *fate* hath perhaps designd,   *destroyed.*
   Which to the *Soule* may utter quenching bring.   1556

Perhaps her *cause* may cease and she may die;   *Her cause*
   God is her *cause*, his *word* her maker was,   *ceaseth not.*
   Which shall stand fixt for all eternitie,
   When heaven and earth shall like a shadow passe.   1560

Perhaps some thing repugnant to her kind   *She hath no*
   By strong *Antipathy* the *Soule* may kill;   *contrary.*
   But what can be *contrarie* to the mind,
   Which holds all *contraries* in concord still?

She lodgeth heate, and cold, and moist and drye,   1565
   And life, and death, and peace, and warre, together;
   Ten thousand fighting things in her do lye,
   Yet neither troubleth, or disturbeth either.

Perhaps for want of foode the *Soule* may pine:
  But that were strange, since all things *bad* and *good*,   1570
  Since all Gods creatures *mortall* and *divine*,
  Since *God himselfe* is her eternall food.

  Bodies are fed with things of mortall kind,
    And so are subject to mortalitie;
    But *truth*, which is eternall, feeds the mind,   1575
    The *tree of life* which will not let her dye.

Yet violence perhaps the *Soule* destroyes,
    As lightning or the *Sun-beames* dimme the sight;
    Or as a thunder-clap, or Cannons noyse,
    The powre of hearing doth astonish quite.   1580

  But high perfection to the *Soule* it brings,
    T'encounter things most excellent and high;
    For when she viewes the best and greatest things,
    They do not hurt, but rather cleare her eye.

  Besides, as *Homers Gods* gainst Armies stand,   1585
    Her subtle forme can through all dangers slide;
    Bodies are captive, *minds* endure no band,
    "And will is free, and can no force abide.

But lastly, *Time* perhaps at last hath power,
    To spend her lively powers, and quench her light;   1590
    But old God *Saturne*, which doth all devour,
    Doth cherish her, and still augment her might.

  Heaven waxeth old, and all the *Spheares* above,
    Shall one day faint, and their swift motion stay;
    And *Time* it selfe, in *Time* shall cease to move,   1595
    Onely the Soule survives, and lives for aye.

  "Our bodies every footstep that they make,
    "March towards death, untill at last they dye,
    "Whether we worke, or play, or sleep, or wake,
    "Our life doth passe, and with *times* wings doth flie; 1600

1575 *truth*, 1599: ~ₐ *AC*   1586 dangers] daunger *AC, H573*   1589 *lastly*,
1599: ~ₐ *AC*

But to the *Soule* Time doth perfection give,
    And ads fresh lustre to her beautie still;
    And makes her in eternall youth to live,
    Like her which Nectar to the Gods doth fill.

The more she lives, the more she feeds on *truth*,   1605
    The more she feeds, her *strength* doth more increase;
    And what is *strength*, but an effect of *youth*,
    Which if *time* nurse, how can it ever cease?

But now these *Epicures* begin to smile,   *Objections*
    And say my doctrine is more false then true;   *against the*
    And that I fondly do my selfe beguile,   *Immortalitie of*
    While these receiv'd opinions I ensue.   *the Soule.*

For what? say they, doth not the *Soule* wax old?   *1. Objection.*
    How comes it then that aged men do doate?
    And that their braines grow sottish, dull, and cold, 1615
    Which were in youth the onely spirits of noate?

What? are not *Soules* within themselves corrupted?
    How can there Idiots then by Nature bee?
    How is it that some wits are interrupted?
    That now they dazled are, now clearely see?   1620

These Questions make a subtle Argument   *Answer.*
    To such as thinke both *Sense* and *reason* one,
    To whom, nor agent from the Instrument,
    Nor power of working, from the worke is knowne.

But they that know that wit can show no skill,   1625
    But when she things in *Senses* glasse doth view,
    Do know, if accident this glasse do spill,
    It *nothing sees*, or *sees the false for true.*

For if that region of the tender braine,
    Where th'inward sense of phantasie should sit,   1630
    And th'outward senses gatherings should retaine,
    By nature, or by chaunce, become unfit;

Either at first uncapable it is,
 And so few things or none at all receives;
 Or mard by accident, which haps amisse,   1635
 And so amisse it every thing perceives;

Then as a cunning Prince that useth *Spies*,
 If they returne no newes, doth nothing know;
 But if they make advertizement of Lyes,
 The Princes Counsels all awrie do go;   1640

Even so the *Soule* to such a body knit,
 Whose inward senses undisposed bee,
 And to receive the formes of things unfit,
 Where nothing is brought in, can nothing see;

This makes the Idiot which hath yet a mind,   1645
 Able to *know* the truth, and *chuse* the good,
 If she such figures in the braine did find,
 As might be found, if it in temper stood;

But if a *Phrensie* do possesse the braine,
 It so disturbes, and blots the formes of things,   1650
 As phantasie proves altogether vaine,
 And to the wit no true relation brings;

Then doth the wit admitting all for true,
 Build fond conclusions, on those idle grounds;
 Then doth it flie the good, and ill pursue,   1655
 Beleeving all, that this false *Spie* propounds.

But purge the humors, and the rage appease,
 Which this distemper in the fancie wrought;
 Then shall the *wit*, which never had disease,
 Discourse, and Judge, discreetly as it ought.   1660

So though the clouds eclips the *Suns* faire light,
 Yet from his face they do not take one beame;
 So have our eyes their perfect power of sight,
 Even when they looke into a troubled streame.

1640 Counsels *1622*: Counsells *HH*: Councells *AC*, *H573*: counsell *1599*
1659 shall *1622*: will *1599u*, *MSS.*: will *1599c*, *1619*

Then these defects in *Senses* organes bee,   1665
   Not in the *Soule*, nor in her working might,
   She cannot loose her perfect power to see,
   Though mists, and clouds do choke her window light.

These Imperfections then we must impute
   Not to the Agent, but the Instrument;   1670
   We must not blame *Apollo*, but his lute,
   If false accords from her false strings be sent.

The *Soule* in all hath one Intelligence,
   Though too much moisture in an Infants braine,
   And too much drinesse in an old mans sense,   1675
   Cannot the prints of outward things retaine;

Then doth the *Soule* want worke, and idle sit,
   And this we *childishnesse* and *dotage* call;
   Yet hath she then a quicke and active wit,
   If she had stuffe, and tooles to worke withall.   1680

For, give her organes fit, and objects faire,
   Give but the aged man the yong mans sense;
   Let but *Medea Æsons* youth repaire;
   And straight she shewes her wonted excellence.

As a good harper stricken farre in yeares   1685
   Into whose cunning hands the gowte is fall;
   All his old Crotchets in his braine he beares,
   But on his harpe playes ill, or not at all.

But if *Apollo* take his gowte away,
   That he his nymble fingers may applie;   1690
   Apolloes selfe will envie at his play,
   And all the world applaud his minstralsie.

Then *dotage* is no weakenesse of the mind,
   But of the *Sense*; for if the mind did wast,
   In all old men we should this wasting find,   1695
   When they some certaine terme of yeares had past;

1666 nor *HH*: or *Σ*

But most of them, even to their dying howre,
   Retaine a mind more lively, quick, and strong,
   And better use their understanding power,
   Then when their braines were warme, and limmes were
                             yong;   1700

For though the body wasted bee and weake;
   And though the leaden forme of earth it bears;
   Yet when we heare that halfe-dead body speake,
   We oft are ravisht to the heavenly *Spheares*.

2. Objection.   *Yet, say* these men, if all her organes dye,   1705
   Then hath the *Soule* no power her powers to use;
   So in a sort her powers extinct do lye,
   When unto *act* she cannot them reduce.

And if her powers be dead, then what is she?
   For since from every thing some *powers* do spring,   1710
   And from those powers some *acts* proceeding bee,
   Then kill both *power*, and *act*, and kill the *thing*.

Aunswer.   *Doubtlesse* the bodies death, when once it dies,
   The instruments of sense, and life doth kill;
   So that she cannot use those faculties,   1715
   Although their roote rest in her substance still.

But as the body living, *wit* and *will*
   Can *judge*, and *chuse*, without the bodies ayde;
   Though on such objects they are working still,
   As through the bodies organs are convayde;   1720

So when the body serves her turne no more,
   And all her *Senses* are extinct and gone;
   She can discourse of what she learn'd before,
   In heavenly contemplations all alone.

So if one man well on a lute doth play,   1725
   And have good horsemanship, and learnings skill;
   Though both his lute and horse we take away,
   Doth he not keepe his former learning still?

1701 bee *AC* (*JD*): be *1599*   1705 *ital. MSS.: rom. Print*   1717 *wit*_∧
1599: ~, *AC*   *will*_∧ *1599*: ~, *AC*   1724 contemplations] contemplation
HH

He keeps it doubtlesse; and can use it too;
    And doth both th'other *skils* in power retaine;   1730
    And can of both the proper actions do,
    If with his lute, or horse he meete againe.

So though the instuments by which we live
    And view the world, the bodies death do kill;
    Yet with the body they shall all revive,   1735
    And all their wonted offices fulfill.

But how till then shall she her selfe imploy?   3. *Objection.*
    Her spies are dead, which brought home newes before;
    What she hath got and keepes she may enjoy,
    But she hath meanes to understand no more.   1740

Then what do those poore *Soules* which nothing get?
    Or what do those which get and cannot keepe?
    Like Buckets bottomlesse which all out let;
    Those *Soules* for want of exercise, must sleepe.

See how mans *Soule* against it selfe doth strive;   *Aunswer.*
    Why should we not have other meanes to know?   1746
    As children, while within the wombe they live,
    Feede by the navill, here they feede not so.

These children, if they had some use of sense,
    And should by chance their mothers talking heare,   1750
    That in short time, they shall come forth from thence,
    Would feare their birth, more then our death we feare.

They would cry out; if we this place shall leave,
    Then shall we breake our tender navill strings:
    How shall we then our nourishment receive?   1755
    Since our sweet food no other conduit brings?

And if a man should to these babes reply;
    That into this faire world they shalbe brought,
    Where they shall see, the *Earth*, the *Sea*, the *Sky*,
    The glorious *Sun*, and all that God hath wrought;   1760

1729 too *ed.*: to *1599*   1751 shall] should *MSS.*   1753 shall] should
HH   1758 shalbe] shold bee *HH*   1759 *Earth AC*: earth *Σ*   *Sky AC*:
sky *Σ*   1760 wrought; *1599*: ~. *AC*

That there ten thousand dainties they shall meete,
   Which by their mouths they shal with pleasure take;
   Which shalbe cordiall too, aswell as sweete,
   And of their little lymbes, tall bodies make;

This would they thinke a fable, even as we   1765
   Do thinke the *Storie* of the *golden age*;
   Or as some sensuall spirits amongst us be,
   Which hold the *world to come, a faigned stage.*

Yet shall these infants after find all true,
   Though then thereof they nothing could conceive;   1770
   Assoone as they are borne, the world they view,
   And with their mouthes the nurses milke receive.

So when the *Soule* is borne (for death is nought
   But the *Soules* birth, and so we should it call);
   Ten thousand things she sees beyond her thought,   1775
   And in an unknowne maner knowes them all.

Then doth she see by Spectacles no more,
   She heares not by report of double spies,
   Her selfe in instants doth all things explore,
   For each thing present, and before her lyes;   1780

4. Objection.   *But still* this crew with questions me pursues,
   If *Soules* deceasd (say they) still living bee,
   Why do they not returne to bring us newes,
   Of that strange world, where they such wonders see?

Aunswer.   *Fond men*, if we beleeve that men do live,   1785
   Under the *Zenith* of both frozen *Poles*,
   Though none come thence advertizement to give,
   Why beare we not the like faith of our *Soules*?

The *Soule* hath here on earth no more to do,
   Then we have businesse in our mothers wombe;   1790
   What child doth covet to returne thereto?
   Although all children first from thence do come.

1764 little *AC* (*JD*): litle *1599*

But as *Noahs* pigeon which returnd no more
    Did shew she footing found for all the flud;
    So (when good *Soules* departed through deaths dore   *1795*
    Come not againe) it shewes their dwelling good.

And doubtlesse such a *Soule* as up doth mount
    And doth appeare before her Makers face,
    Holds this vile world in such a base account,
    As she lookes downe, and scornes this wretched place.

But such as are detruded downe to hell,   *1801*
    Either for shame, they still themselves retire,
    Or tyed in chaines, they in close prison dwell,
    And cannot come, although they much desire.

Well well, say these vaine spirits, though vaine it is,   *5. Objection.*
    To thinke our *Soules* to heaven or hell do go,   *1806*
    Politique men, have thought it not amisse,
    To spread this *lye*, to make men vertuous so.

Do you then thinke this *morall vertue* good?   *Aunswer.*
    I thinke you do, even for your private gaine;   *1810*
    For common wealths by *vertue* ever stood;
    And common good the private doth containe.

If then this *vertue* you do love so well,
    Have you no meanes her practize to maintaine?
    But you this *lye* must to the people tell,   *1815*
    That good *Soules* live in joy, and ill in paine?

Must *vertue* be preserved by a *lye*?
    Vertue and *Truth* do ever best agree:
    By this it seemes to be a veritie,
    Since the effects so good, and vertuous bee.   *1820*

For as the Divell father is of lyes,
    So vice and mischiefe do his lyes ensue,
    Then this good doctrine did not he devise,
    But made this *lye*, which saith it is not true.

1798 And‸ *1599:* ∼, *AC*   1806 go, *1599:* ∼‸ *AC*

For *how* can that be false which every tong,   1825
   Of every mortall man affirmes for true;
   Which truth hath in all ages bene so strong,
   As lodestone-like, all harts it ever drew.

For not the *Christian* nor the *Jew* alone,
   The *Persian*, nor the *Turke* acknowledge this;   1830
   This mysterie to the wild *Indian* knowne,
   And to the *Canniball*, and *Tartar* is.

This rich *Assirian* drugge growes everywhere,
   As common in the *North*, as in the *East*,
   This docrine doth not enter by the *eare*,   1835
   But of itselfe is native in the breast.

None that acknowledge God or providence,
   Their *Soules* eternitie did ever doubt;
   For all *religion* takes her roote from hence,
   Which no poore naked nation lives without.   1840

For since the world for man created was;
   (For onely man the use thereof doth know)
   If man do perish like a withered grasse,
   How doth Gods wisdome order things below?

And if that wisdome still wise ends propound,   1845
   Why made he man of other creatures king?
   When (if he perish here) there is not found,
   In all the world so poore and vile a thing?

If death do quench us quite, we have great wrong,
   Since for our service all things else were wrought;   1850
   That *Dawes*, and *Trees* and *Rocks* should last so long,
   When we must in an instant passe to nought.

But blest be that *great power* that hath us blest,
   With longer life then heaven or earth can have,
   Which hath enfusd into our mortall brest   1855
   Immortall powers, not subject to the grave.

1827 hath in all ages] in all ages hath *H573* (*Davies altered reading in AC from that
of H573 to that of text above.*) 1829 nor *AC, HH*: or *Σ*   1830 nor *ed.*: or *All
the*] *om. AC, H573*   1844 below? *1599*: ~. *AC*   1855 our *1622, MSS.*: one *Σ*

For though the *Soule* do seeme her grave to beare,
   And in this world is almost buried quick;
   We have no cause the bodies death to feare,
   "For when the shell is broke out comes a chick.   1860

For *as* the *Soules Essentiall* powers are three,   *Three kinds of*
   The *quickning* power, the *power of Sense*, and *Reason*, *life aun-*
   Three kinds of life to her designed bee,   *swerable to the*
   Which perfect these three powers, in their due season. *three powers of*
                                                      the soule.

The first life in the mothers wombe is spent,   1865
   Where she her *nursing power* doth onely use,
   Where when she finds defect of nourishment
   Sh'expels her body; and this world she viewes.

This we call *Birth*: but if the child could speake
   He *death* would call it, and of nature plaine   1870
   That she would thrust him out naked and weake,
   And in his passage pinch him with such paine.

Yet out he comes, and in this world is plac't;
   Where all his *Senses* in perfection bee,
   Where he finds flowers to smell, and fruits to tast,   1875
   And sounds to heare, and sundry formes to see:

When he hath past some time upon this Stage,
   His *reason* then a little seemes to wake,
   Which though she spring when sense doth fade with age,
   Yet can she here no perfect practise make.   1880

Then doth th'aspiring *Soule* the body leave,
   Which we call *death*; but were it knowne to all
   What *life* our *Soules* do by this *death* receave,
   Men would it *Birth*, or *Gaole deliverie* call.

  1857 do] doth *MSS.*   1858 is] seemes *AC, H573*   1859 death should
engender rather hope then feare *HH*   1860 a] the *HH*   1871 would]
should *HH*

In this third life Reason will be so bright   1885
   As that her sparke will like the *Sun-beames* shine,
   And shall of God enjoy the reall sight,
   Being still increast by influence divine.

An Acclama-
tion.

O ignorant poore man what doost thou beare
   Lock't up within the Casket of thy breast?   1890
   What Jewels, and what riches hast thou there?
   What heavenly treasure in so weake a cheast?

Looke in thy *Soule*, and thou shalt *beauties* find
   Like those which drownd *Narcissus* in the floud;
   Honor and *Pleasure* both are in thy mind,   1895
   And all that in the world is counted *good*.

Thinke of her worth and thinke that God did meane,
   This worthy mind, should worthy things embrace;
   Blot not her beauties with thy thoughts uncleane;
   Nor her dishonor with thy passions base.   1900

Kill not her *quickning power* with surfettings,
   Mar not her *sense* with Sensualities,
   Cast not her serious *wit* on idle things,
   Make not her free *will* slave to vanities.

And when thou thinkst of her *eternitie*,   1905
   Thinke not that *death*, against her nature is;
   Thinke it a *birth*: and when thou goest to die
   Sing like a Swan, as if thou wentst to blisse.

And if thou like a Child didst feare before,
   Being in the darke where thou didst nothing see;   1910
   Now I have brought thee *torch-light*, feare no more,
   Now when thou Diest, thou canst not hudwinkt bee.

1898 This] that *AC*, *H573*   1902–4 Sensualities/vanities] Sensualitie/
vanitie *1599u, 1619–22, H573.* (*In AC Davies altered rejected reading to that of text given
here.*)   1903 serious] curious *HH*   things, *1599:* ~‚ *AC*   1909 before,
1599: ~‚ *AC*   1911 thee *1619–1622, HH, H573:* the *1599, AC*

And thou my *Soule*, which turnst thy Curious eye
   To view the beames of thine owne forme divine,
   Know that thou canst know nothing perfectly,   1915
   While thou art Clouded with this flesh of mine.

Take heed of *over-weening*; and compare
   Thy Peacocks feet with thy gay Peacocks traine;
   Studie the best and highest things that are,
   But of thy selfe an humble thought retaine.   1920

Cast downe thyselfe, and onely strive to raise
   The glorie of thy Makers sacred name;
   Use all thy powers that blessed power to praise,
   Which gives thee power to *be*, and *use the same*.

FINIS.

HYMNES OF ASTRÆA
IN
ACROSTICKE VERSE

Title from Printed Texts.

Hymnes of Astræa.

HYMNE I.

Of Astræa.

E arly before the day doth spring,
L et us awake my Muse, and sing;
I t is no time to slumber,
S o many Joyes this time doth bring,
A s time will faile to number.   5

B ut whereto shall we bend our Layes?
E ven up to Heaven, againe to raise
T he Mayde, which thence descended
H ath brought againe the golden dayes,
A nd all the world amended.   10

R udenesse it selfe she doth refine,
E ven like an Alchymist divine,
G rosse times of Iron turning
I nto the purest forme of gold:
N ot to corrupt, till heaven waxe old,   15
A nd be refin'd with burning.

HYMNE II.

To Astræa.

E ternall Virgin, *Goddesse* true,
L et me presume to sing to you.
I *ove*, even great *Jove* hath leisure
S ometimes to heare the vulgar crew,
A nd heares them oft with pleasure.   5

Hymnes of Astræa.   *Printed texts: HA1599, 1619, 1622.   Text from HA1599.*

B lessed *Astræa*, I in part
E njoy the blessings you impart,
T he *Peace*, the milke and hony,
H umanity, and civill *Art*,
A richer *Dower* then money.

                                                          10

R ight glad am I that now I live,
E ven in these daies whereto you give
G reat happinesse and glorie;
I f after you I should be borne,
N o doubt I should my birth day scorne,   15
A dmiring your sweete storie.

HYMNE III.

To the Spring.

E arth now is greene, and heaven is blew,
L ively Spring which makes all new,
I olly Spring doth enter,
S weete young Sun-beames do subdue
A ngry, aged Winter.   5

B lasts are mild, and Seas are calme,
E very medow flowes with Balme,
T he earth weares all her riches,
H armonious birdes sing such a Psalme
A s eare and hart bewitches.   10

R eserve (sweete Spring) this Nymph of ours
E ternall garlands of thy flowers,
G reene garlands never wasting;
I n her shall last our *states* faire spring,
N ow and for ever flourishing,   15
A s long as heaven is lasting.

Hymne III.　　　　　2 new, *ed.*: ∼‸ *HA1599*　　　　　3 enter, *ed.*: ∼‸ *HA1599*
5 Winter *ed.*: *l.c. HA 1599*

HYMNE IV.

To the Moneth of May.

E ach day of thine, sweete moneth of May,
L ove makes a solemne holy-day:
I will performe like dutie,
S ince thou resemblest every way
A *stræa* Queene of beautie.　　　　5

B oth you fresh beauties do partake,
E ithers aspect doth Sommer make:
T houghts of young Love awaking
H earts you both do cause to ake,
A nd yet be pleasd with *aking*.　　　　10

R ight deare art thou, and so is shee,
E ven like attractive Sympathie,
G aines unto both like dearenesse;
I weene this made Antiquitie
N ame thee, Sweete *May* of *Majestie*,　　　　15
A s being both like in *clearenesse*.

HYMNE V.

To the Larke.

E arly, chearfull, mounting Larke,
L ights gentle Usher, mornings clarke,
I n merrie Notes delighting:
S tint awhile thy Song, and harke,
A nd learne my new Inditing.　　　　5

B eare up this Hymne, to heav'n it beare,
E ven up to heav'n, and sing it there,
T o heav'n each morning beare it;
H ave it set to some sweete Sphere,
A nd let the Angels heare it.　　　　10

Hymne V. 1 Early, *ed.*: ∼ₐ *HA1599*

R enownd *Astræa*, that great name,
E xceeding great in worth and fame,
G reat worth hath so renownd it,
I t is *Astræas* name I praise,
N ow then, sweete Larke, do thou it raise,   15
A nd in high Heaven resound it.

HYMNE VI.

To the Nightingale.

E very night from Even till Morne
L oves Quirister amidde the thorne
I s now so sweet a Singer,
S o sweete, as for her Song I scorne
A pollos voice, and finger.   5

B ut Nightingale since you delight
E ver to watch the Starrie night,
T ell all the Starres of heaven,
H eaven never had a Starre so bright,
A s now to earth is given.   10

R oyall *Astræa* makes our Day
E ternall with her beames, nor may
G rosse darkenesse overcome her;
I now perceive why some do write,
N o countrie hath so short a night,   15
A s England hath in sommer.

HYMNE VII.

To the Rose.

E ye of the garden, Queene of flowers,
L oves Cuppe wherein he Nectar poures,
I ngendred first of Nectar:
S weete nurse-child of the Springs young howres,
A nd Beauties faire Character.   5

Hymne VI. 8 Tell *1622*: To *Σ*

B est Jewell that the earth doth weare,
E ven when the brave yong Sun drawes neare,
T o her hoate Love pretending;
H imselfe likewise like forme doth beare,
A t rising and descending.   10

R ose of the Queene of love belov'd;
E nglands great Kings divinely mov'd,
G ave Roses in their Banner;
I t shewed that Bewties Rose indeede,
N ow in this age should them succeede,   15
A nd raigne in more sweet manner.

HYMNE VIII.

To all the Princes of Europe.

E *urope*, the Earthes sweete Paradise:
L et all thy Kings that would be wise,
I n *Politique Devotion*:
S aile hither to observe her eyes,
A nd marke her heavenly motion.   5

B rave Princes of this civill age,
E nter into this pilgrimage:
T his Saints tongue is an oracle,
H er eye hath made a Prince a Page,
A nd workes each day a Miracle.   10

R aise but your lookes to her, and see
E ven the true beames of Majestie,
G reat Princes, marke her duly;
I f all the world you do survey,
N o forehead spreades so bright a Ray,   15
A nd notes a Prince so truly.

Hymne VIII. 4 hither to *Σ*: hitherto *HA1599*

HYMNE IX.

To Flora.

E mpresse of flowers, tell where a way
L ies your sweet Court this merry *May*,
I n *Greenewich* garden Allies:
S ince there the heavenly powers do play,
A nd haunt no other Vallies.   5

B ewty, *Vertue*, *Majestie*,
E loquent Muses, three times three,
T he new fresh houres and Graces,
H ave pleasure in this place to be,
A bove all other Places.   10

R oses and Lillies did them draw,
E r they divine *Astræa* saw;
G ay flowers they sought for pleasure:
I n steede of gathering crownes of flowers,
N ow gather they *Astræas* Dowers,   15
A nd beare to heaven that treasure.

HYMNE X.

To the Moneth of September.

E ach Moneth hath praise in some degree;
L et May to others seeme to be
I n Sense the sweetest Season;
S eptember thou art best to me,
A nd best dost please my reason.   5

B ut neither for thy Corne nor Wine
E xtoll I those mild dayes of thine,
T hough corne and wine might praise thee;
H eaven gives thee honor more divine,
A nd higher fortunes raise thee.   10

Hymne IX. 6 *Vertue ed.: l.c. HA 1599*

R enownd art thou (sweet moneth) for this,
E mong thy dayes her birth day is,
G *race, plentie, peace* and *honor*
I n one faire houre with her were borne,
N ow since they still her Crowne adorne,   15
A nd still attend upon her.

HYMNE XI.

To the Sunne.

E ye of the world, fountaine of light,
L ife of day, and death of night,
I humbly seeke thy kindnesse:
S weet, dazle not my feeble sight,
A nd strike me not with blindnesse.   5

B ehold me mildly from that face,
E ven where thou now dost runne thy race,
T he Spheare where now thou turnest;
H aving like *Phaeton* chang'd thy place,
A nd yet hearts onely burnest.   10

R ed in her right cheeke thou dost rise;
E xalted after in her eyes,
G reat glorie there thou shewest:
I n thother cheeke when thou descendest,
N ew rednesse unto it thou lendest,   15
A nd so thy Round thou goest.

HYMNE XII.

To her Picture.

E xtreame was his Audacitie,
L ittle his Skill that finisht thee,
I am asham'd and Sorry,
S o dull her counterfait should be,
A nd she so full of glory.   5

Hymne XI. 9 *Phaeton* 1622: *rom. HA1599*   Hymne XII. 1 Audacitie, *ed.*: ∼;
HA1599

B ut here are colours red and white,
E ach lyne, and each proportion right;
T hese Lynes, this red, and whitenesse,
H ave wanting yet a life and light,
A Majestie, and brightnesse.   10

R ude counterfait, I then did erre,
E ven now, when I would needes inferre,
G reat boldnesse in thy maker:
I did mistake, he was not bold;
N or durst his eyes her eyes behold;   15
A nd this made him mistake her.

HYMNE XIII.

Of her Mind.

E arth now adiew, my ravisht thought
L ifted to heav'n, sets thee at nought;
I nfinit is my longing,
S ecrets of Angels to be taught,
A nd things to heav'n belonging.   5

B rought downe from heav'n of Angels kind,
E ven now do I admire her mind:
T his is my contemplation,
H er cleare sweet *Spirit* which is refind,
A bove Humane *Creation*.   10

R ich Sun-beame of th'æternall light,
E xcellent *Soule*, how shall I wright;
G ood Angels make me able;
I cannot see but by your eye,
N or, but by your tongue, Signifie,   15
A thing so Admirable.

HYMNE XIV.

Of the Sun-Beames of her Mind.

E xceeding glorious is this starre;
L et us behold her Beames a farre
I n a side lyne reflected;
S ight beares them not when neare they are
A nd in right lines directed.   5

B ehold her in her vertues beames,
E xtending Sun-like to all Realmes;
T he Sunne none viewes too nearely;
H er well of goodnesse in these streames,
A ppeares right well and clearely.   10

R adiant vertues, if your light
E nfeeble the best Judgements sight,
G reat splendor above measure
I s in the minde, from whence you flow:
N o wit may have accesse to know,   15
A nd view so bright a treasure.

HYMNE XV.

Of her Wit.

E ye of that mind most quicke and cleare,
L ike Heav'ns eye, which from his spheare,
I nto all things pryeth,
S ees through all things every where,
A nd all their natures tryeth.   5

B right Image of an Angels wit,
E xceeding sharpe, and swift like it,
T hings instantly discerning:
H aving a Nature infinit,
A nd yet increasd by learning.   10

R ebound upon thy selfe thy light,
E njoy thine owne sweete precious sight:
G ive us but some reflection;
I t is enough for us, if wee
N ow in her speech, now pollicie,   15
A dmire thine high perfection.

HYMNE XVI.

Of her Will.

E ver well affected *will*,
L oving *goodnesse*, Loathing *ill*,
I nestimable Treasure:
S ince such a power hath power to spill,
A nd save us at her pleasure.   5

B e thou our Law, sweet *will*, and say
E ven what thou wilt, we will obay
T his Law, if I could reade it:
H erein would I spend night and day,
A nd study still to plead it.   10

R oyall *free will*, and onely *free*,
E ach other *will* is Slave to thee:
G lad is each *will* to serve thee:
I n thee such Princely power is seene,
N o Spirit but takes thee for her Queene,   15
A nd thinkes she must observe thee.

HYMNE XVII.

Of her Memorie.

E xcellent Jewels would you see,
L ovely Ladies? come with me,
I will (for love I owe you)
S hew you as rich a Treasurie,
A s East or West can shew you.   5

B ehold, if you can judge of it,
E ven that great Store-house of her wit;
T hat bewtifull large Table:
H er *memorie* wherein is writ
A ll Knowledge admirable.   10

R eade this faire booke, and you shall learne
E xquisite Skill if you discerne,
G aine heav'n by this discerning;
I n such a memorie divine,
N ature did forme the *Muses* nine,   15
A nd *Pallas* Queene of Learning.

HYMNE XVIII.

Of her Phantasie.

E xquisite curiositie,
L ooke on thy selfe with judging eye,
I f ought be faultie leave it,
S o delicate a phantasie
A s this, will straight perceive it.   5

B ecause her temper is so fine,
E ndewed with harmonies divine:
T herefore if discord strike it,
H er true proportions do repine,
A nd sadly do mislike it.   10

R ight otherwise a pleasure sweete,
E ver she takes in actions meete;
G racing with smiles such meetnesse;
I n her faire forehead beames appeare:
N o Sommers day is halfe so cleare,   15
A dornd with halfe that sweetnesse.

HYMNE XIX.

Of the Organs of her Minde.

E clipsed she is, and her bright rayes
L ie under vailes, yet many wayes
I s her faire forme revealed;
S he diversly her selfe conveyes,
A nd cannot be concealed.   5

B y Instruments her powers appeare
E xceedingly well tun'd and cleare:
T his Lute is still in measure,
H olds still in tune, even like a spheare,
A nd yeelds the world sweet pleasure.   10

R esolve me, Muse, how this thing is,
E ver a bodie like to this
G ave heav'n to earthly creature?
I am but fond this doubt to make,
N o doubt the Angels bodies take,   15
A bove our common nature.

HYMNE XX.

Of the Passions of her Heart.

E xamine not *th'inscrutable Hart*,
L ight *Muse* of her, though she in part
I mpart it to the Subject;
S earch not, although from heav'n thou art,
A nd this an Heavenly object.   5

B ut since she hath a hart, we know
E ver some passions thence do flow,
T hough ever rul'd with Honor;
H er Judgement raignes, they waite below,
A nd fixe their eyes upon her.   10

R ectified so, they in their kind
E ncrease each Vertue of her mind,
G overn'd with mild tranquillitie;
I n all the Regions under Heav'n,
N o State doth beare it selfe so even,   15
A nd with so sweet facilitie.

HYMNE XXI.

Of th'innumerable Vertues of her Mind.

E re thou proceede in this sweet paines,
L earne *Muse* how many drops it raynes
I n cold and moist *December*;
S umme up *May* flowers and *Augusts* graines,
A nd grapes of mild *September*.   5

B eare the Seas sands in memorie,
E arths grasses, and the starres in Skie,
T he little moates which mounted
H ang, in the beames of *Phœbus* eye,
A nd never can be counted.   10

R ecount these numbers numberlesse,
E re thou her vertue canst expresse,
G reat wits this count will cumber;
I nstruct thy selfe in numbring Schooles;
N ow Courtiers use to begge for fooles,   15
A ll such as cannot number.

HYMNE XXII.

Of her Wisedome.

E gle-eyed Wisedome, lifes Loadstarre,
L ooking neare on things a farre;
I *oves* best beloved daughter,
S howes to her Spirit all things that are,
A s *Jove* himselfe hath taught her.   5

Hymne XXI. 13 cumber; *ed.*: ∼ *,HA1599*

B y this straight Rule she rectifies
E ach thought that in her hart doth rise:
T his is her cleare true mirror,
H er *looking glasse*, wherein she spies
A ll formes of Truth and Error.   10

R ight princely Vertue, fit to raigne,
E nthroniz'd in her Spirit remaine,
G uiding our fortunes ever;
I f we this Starre once cease to see,
N o doubt our State will Ship-wrackt be,   15
A nd torne and sunke for ever.

HYMNE XXIII.

Of her Justice.

E xil'd *Astræa* is come againe,
L o here she doth all things maintaine
I n *number, waight*, and *measure*:
S he rules us with delightfull paine,
A nd we obey with pleasure.   5

B y *Love* shee rules more then by *Law*,
E ven her great *mercy* breedeth awe:
T his is her Sword and Scepter,
H erewith she hearts did ever draw,
A nd this Guard ever kept her.   10

R eward doth sit in her right hand:
E ach Vertue thence takes her Garland
G ather'd in Honors garden:
I n her left hand (wherein should be
N ought but the Sword) sits Clemencie,   15
A nd conquers Vice with pardon.

Hymne XXII. 8 mirror, *ed.*: ∼ₐ *HA1599*   Hymne XXIII. 6 *ital. 1622: rom.*
HA1599

HYMNE XXIV.

Of her Magnanimitie.

E ven as her State, so is her Mind,
L ifted above the vulgar kind:
I t treades proud Fortune under,
S un-like it sits above the wind,
A bove the stormes, and Thunder.   5

B rave Spirit, large Heart, admiring *nought*,
E steeming each thing as it ought,
T hat swelleth not, nor shrinketh:
H onor is alwaies in her thought,
A nd of great things she thinketh.   10

R ocks, Pillars, and heav'ns Axel-tree,
E xemplifie her Constancie;
G reat changes never chaunge her:
I n her Sexe feares are wont to rise,
N *ature* permits, *Vertue* denies,   15
A nd scornes the face of *daunger*.

HYMNE XXV.

Of her Moderation.

E mpresse of kingdomes though she be,
L arger is her Soveraigntie,
I f she her selfe do governe;
S ubject unto her selfe is shee,
A nd of her selfe true Soveraigne;   5

B ewties Crowne though she do weare,
E xalted into Fortunes chaire,
T hron'd like the Queene of Pleasure:
H er Vertues still possesse her Eare,
A nd counsell her to Measure.   10

Hymne XXIV. 6 *nought*, ed.: ~ₐ HA 1599   15 ital. 1622: *rom.* HA 1599

R eason, if she incarnate were,
E ven Reasons selfe could never beare
G reatnesse with Moderation;
I n her one temper still is seene,
N o libertie claimes she as Queene,   15
A nd showes no alteration.

HYMNE XXVI.

To Envie.

E nvie go weepe, my Muse and I
L augh thee to scorne; thy feeble Eye
I s dazled with the glorie
S hining in this gay poesie,
A nd litle golden Storie.   5

B ehold how my proud quil doth shed
E ternall *Nectar* on her head:
T he pompe of Coronation
H ath not such power her fame to spread,
A s this my admiration.   10

R espect my Pen as free and franke,
E xpecting not Reward nor Thanke;
G reat wonder onely moves it;
I never made it mercenary;
N or should my Muse this burthen carie   15
A s hyr'd, but that she loves it.

FINIS.

ORCHESTRA

Title: Orchestra Or a Poeme of Dauncing. Judicially prooving the true observation of time and measure, in the Authenticall and laudable use of Dauncing. Ovid. Art. Aman. lib. 1. Si vox est, canta: si mollia brachia, salta: Et quacunque potes dote placere, place. *1596*: Orchestra. Or A Poeme expressing the Antiquitie and Excellencie of Dauncing. In a Dialogue betweene Penelope, and one of her Wooers. Not finished. *1622*: A Poem of Dauncinge. *LF*

89

[*Dedications.*]

To his very Friend, Ma. Rich: Martin.

To whom shall I this dauncing Poeme send,
This suddaine, rash, halfe-capreol of my wit?
To you, first mover and sole cause of it,
Mine-owne-selves better halfe, my deerest frend.
   O would you yet my Muse some Honny lend   5
   From your mellifluous tongue, whereon doth sit
   Suada in majestie, that I may fit
   These harsh beginnings with a sweeter end.
You know, the modest Sunne full fifteene times
Blushing did rise, and blushing did descend,   10
While I in making of these ill made rimes,
My golden howers unthriftily did spend.
   Yet if in friendship you these numbers prayse,
   I will mispend another fifteene dayes.

To the Prince.

SIR, whatsoever *YOU* are pleas'd to doo
It is your speciall Praise, that you are bent,
And sadly set your Princely mind thereto:
Which makes *YOU* in each thing so excellent.
   Hence is it, that *YOU* came so soone to bee   5
   A Man at Armes in every point aright;
   The fairest Flowre of noble Chivalrie;
   And of Saint *George* his Band the bravest Knight.
And hence it is, that all your youthfull Traine
In activenesse, and Grace, *YOU* doe excell,   10
When *YOU* doe Courtly Dauncings entertaine.
Then Dauncings Praise may bee presented well
   To *YOU*, whose action adds more praise thereto,
   Then all the *Muses* with their Penns can doo.

To his very Friend etc. *Printed text: 1596. MS.: LF. Text from 1596.*
   Title. om. very *and* Ma. *LF*   3 it, *ed.:* ∼ˌ *1596*   8 sweeter] better *LF*
13 these numbers] this number *LF*
To the Prince. *Text: 1622. Layout supplied.*

Orchestra
Or
a Poeme of Dauncing.

I

Where lives the man that never yet did heare
Of chast *Penelope*, *Ulisses* Queene?
Who kept her faith unspotted twenty yeere
Till he returnd that far away had beene,
And many men, and many townes had seene:
    Ten yeere at siedge of *Troy* he lingring lay,
    And ten yeere in the *Midland-sea* did stray.

2

Homer, to whom the Muses did carouse,
A great deepe cup with heavenly Nectar filld
The greatest, deepest cup in *Joves* great house,
(For *Jove* himselfe had so expresly willd)
He dranke off all, ne let one drop be spilld;
    Since when, his braine that had before been dry,
    Became the welspring of all Poetry.

3

Homer doth tell in his aboundant verse,
The long laborious travailes of the *Man*,
And of his Lady too he doth reherse,
How shee illudes with all the Art she can,
Th'ungratefull love which other Lords began;
    For of her Lord false Fame long since had sworne,
    That *Neptunes* Monsters had his carcasse torne.

Orchestra Or a Poeme of Dauncing. *Printed texts: 1596, 1622. MS.: LF. Text from 1596, except for stanzas 127[A]–132[A] and all marginal glosses, which are found in 1622 only.*

   1.3 Who] which *LF*   1.5 ital. *1622: rom. 1596*   1.6 yeere] yeares *LF*
1.7 ital. *LF: rom. Print*   2.5 off *1622: of 1596:* up *LF*   3.2 *Man 1622:*
man *1596*   3.5 ungratefull . . . which] unwellcome . . . that *LF*

4

All this he tells, but one thing he forgot,
One thing most worthy his eternall song,
But he was old, and blind, and saw it not,
Or else he thought he should *Ulisses* wrong,
To mingle it, his Tragick acts among.
    Yet was there not in all the world of things,
    A sweeter burden for his Muses wings.

5

The Courtly love *Antinous* did make,
Antinous that fresh and jolly Knight,
Which of the gallants that did undertake
To win the Widdow, had most wealth and might,
Wit to perswade, and beautie to delight.
    The Courtly love he made unto the Queene,
    Homer forgot as if it had not beene.

6

Sing then *Terpsichore*, my light Muse sing
His gentle Art and *cunning curtesie*:
You, Lady, can remember every thing,
For you are daughter of Queene Memorie,
But sing a plaine and easie Melodie:
    For the soft meane that warbleth but the ground,
    To my rude eare doth yield the sweetest sound.

7

One onely nights discourse I can report,
When the great Torch-bearer of heaven was gone
Downe in a maske unto the *Oceans* Court,
To revell it with *Tethis* all alone;
Antinous disguised and unknowne

4.3 old, and blind] blynd and old *LF*   5.7 beene. *ed.:* ~, *Print*
6.1 Singe then my Muse skilfull *Terpsicore* singe *LF*   6.2 *ital. 1622: rom. 1596*
6.3 You, Lady, *ed.:* ~ₐ ~ₐ *Print*   thing, *ed.:* ~ₐ *Print*   6.6 For the soft
meane] For longest tyme *LF*   6.7 eare] eares *LF*   7.1 One onely] Only
one *LF*   7.2 When] what tyme *LF*   7.3 *Oceans LF: rom. Print*

Like to the spring in gaudie Ornament
Unto the Castle of the Princesse went.

8

The soveraigne Castle of the rocky Ile
Wherein *Penelope* the Princesse lay,
Shone with a thousand Lamps, which did exile
The shadowes darke, and turn'd the night to day,
Not *Joves* blew Tent what time the Sunny ray
   Behind the bulwarke of the earth retires
   Is seene to sparkle with more twinckling fiers.

9

That night the Queene came forth from far within,
And in the presence of her Court was seene,
For the sweet singer *Phæmius* did begin
To praise the Worthies that at *Troy* had beene;
Somwhat of her *Ulisses* she did weene
   In his grave Hymne the heav'nly man would sing,
   Or of his warres, or of his wandering.

10

Pallas that houre with her sweet breath divine
Inspir'd immortall beautie in her eyes,
That with cœlestiall glory she did shine,
Brighter then *Venus* when she doth arise
Out of the waters to adorne the skies;
   The wooers all amazed doe admire,
   And check their owne presumptuous desire.

11

Onely *Antinous* when at first he view'd
Her starbright eyes that with new honour shind,
Was not dismayd, but there-with-all renew'd

8.3 which] that *LF*   8.4 The shadowes darke *1622*: The dim darke
shades *Σ*   9.2 her] the *LF*   9.4 *Troy 1622: rom. 1596*   10.6 The] Her
LF   11.3 Was not dismayd, but] nothinge amased *LF*

The noblesse and the splendour of his mind;
And as he did fit circumstances find,
Unto the Throne he boldly gan advance,
   And with faire maners, wooed the Queene to dance.

12

GOddesse of women, sith your heav'nlinesse
  Hath now vouchsaft it selfe to represent
To our dim eyes, which though they see the lesse
Yet are they blest in their astonishment,
Imitate heav'n, whose beauties excellent
   Are in continuall motion day and night,
   And move thereby more wonder and delight.

13

Let me the mover be, to turne about
Those glorious ornaments that Youth and Love
Have fixed in your every part throughout,
Which if you will in timely measure move,
Not all those precious Jemms in heav'n above
   Shall yield a sight more pleasing to behold,
   With all their turnes and tracings manifold.

14

WIth this, the modest Princesse blusht and smil'd,
  Like to a cleare and rosie eventide;
And softly did returne this answere mild,
Faire Sir; you needs must fairely be denide
Where your demaund cannot be satisfied.

11.4 noblesse and the splendour] nobleness and splendor *LF*   13.2 that]
which *LF*   13.3 your₍ *LF*: you, *Print*   13.5 those] the *LF*   13.7 with
their aspects and turninges manifold *LF*
14.1–7   With this the modest Princes blusht & smild,
                 like the sweete eveninge of a Sommers Daye,
                 and softly did returne this awnswer milde,
                 daunce (gentill Sir) I neither can nor maye,
                 I never Lov'd my weaknesse to [displaye] bewraye
                    By counterfeitinge madnesse when I might,
                    With sober carriage beare my selfe aright. *LF*

My feete, which onely nature taught to goe,
Did never yet the Art of footing know.

15

But why perswade you me to this new rage?
(For all disorder and misrule is new,)
For such misgovernment in former age
Our old divine Forefathers never knew,
Who if they liv'd, and did the follies view
    Which their fond Nephews make their chiefe affaires,
    Would hate themselves that had begot such heires.

16

SOle heire of Vertue, and of Beautie both,
  Whence commeth it (*Antinous* replies)
That your imperious vertue is so loth
To graunt your beautie her chiefe exercise?
Or from what spring doth your opinion rise
    That Dauncing is a frenzie and a rage,
    First knowne and us'd in this new-fangled age?

17

The Antiqui-
tie of Dancing.

Dauncing (bright Lady) then began to be,
When the first seedes whereof the world did spring,
The Fire, Ayre, Earth and Water did agree,
By Loves perswasion, Natures mighty King,
To leave their first disordred combating;
    And in a daunce such measure to observe,
    As all the world their motion should preserve.

18

Since when they still are carried in a round,
And changing come one in anothers place,
Yet doe they neyther mingle nor confound,

15.1 But wherfore should men love this newe found rage *LF*   15.5 the]
their *LF*   16.1 *Display capital ed.*: Sole *Print*   17.1 *Dauncing 1622: rom.*
1596   17.2 spring, *1622:* ~ₐ *1596*   17.3 Water *1622: l.c. 1596*   17.4
perswasion] perswasions *LF*

But every one doth keepe the bounded space
Wherein the daunce doth bid it turne or trace:
   This wondrous myracle did Love devise,
   For Dauncing is Loves proper exercise.

19

Like this, he fram'd the Gods eternall bower,
And of a shapelesse and confused masse
By his through-piercing and digesting power
The turning vault of heaven formed was:
Whose starrie wheeles he hath so made to passe,
   As that their movings doe a musick frame,
   And they themselves, still daunce unto the same.

20

Or if this (All) which round about we see
(As idle *Morpheus* some sicke braines hath taught)
Of undevided *Motes* compacted bee,
How was this goodly Architecture wrought?
Or by what meanes were they together brought?
   They erre that say they did concur by chaunce,
   Love made them meete in a well-ordered daunce.

21

As when *Amphion* with his charming Lire
Begot so sweet a *Syren* of the ayre,
That with her Rethorike made the stones conspire
The ruines of a Citty to repayre,
(A worke of wit and reasons wise affayre)
   So Loves smooth tongue, the *motes* such measure taught
   That they joyn'd hands, and so the world was wrought.

18.4 doth keepe the] observes his *LF*   18.6 devise, *1622:* ~, *1596*
19.1 he] Love *LF*   19.4 formed *Σ:* framed *1596*   19.6 frame, *1622:* ~,
1596   20.3 *Motes 1622:* motes *1596*   20.4 goodly] godly *LF*
20.6 They rave and lye that saye it was by chaunce *LF*   21.2 *Syren LF: rom.*
Print   21.3 That] as *LF*   21.6 *motes 1622: rom. 1596*

22

How justly then is Dauncing termed new
Which with the world in point of time begun?
Yea Time it selfe (whose birth *Jove* never knew
And which indeed is elder then the Sun)
Had not one moment of his age outrunne
 When out leapt Dauncing from the heape of things,
 And lightly rode upon his nimble wings.

23

Reason hath both their pictures in her Treasure,
Where *Time the measure of all moving is*;
And Dauncing is a moving all in measure:
Now if you doe resemble that to this
And think both one, I think you think amis:
 But if you judge them Twins, together got,
 And Time first borne, your judgment erreth not.

24

Thus doeth it equall age with *age* injoy,
And yet in lustie youth for ever flowers,
Like Love his Sire, whom Paynters make a Boy,
Yet is he eldest of the heavn'ly powers;
Or like his brother Time, whose winged howers
 Going and comming will not let him dye,
 But still preserve him in his infancie.

25

This said; the Queene with her sweet lips divine
Gently began to move the subtile ayre,
Which gladly yielding, did it selfe incline
To take a shape betweene those rubies fayre
And being formed, softly did repayre
 With twenty doublings in the emptie way,
 Unto *Antinous* eares, and thus did say.

22.3 Yea] When *LF*   **22.4** indeed is elder *1622*: is far more auncient *Σ*
23.2 *ital. 1622: rom. 1596*   **23.3** measure: *ed.*: ∼, *Print*   **23.4-5** if you
doe . . . think . . . I think you think] who so doth . . . thinkes . . . perhappes he
thinkes *LF*   **24.1** *age 1622: rom. 1596*

26

WHat eye doth see the heav'n but doth admire
When it the movings of the heav'ns doth see?
My selfe, if I to heav'n may once aspire,
If that be dauncing, will a Dauncer be:
But as for this your frantick jollitie,
    How it began, or whence you did it learne,
    I never could with reasons eye discerne.

27

Antinous aunswered: Jewell of the Earth
Worthie you are that heav'nly Daunce to leade:
But for you think our dauncing base of birth
And newly borne but of a brainsick head
I will forthwith his antique Gentry read,
    And for I love him, will his Herault be
    And blaze his armes, and draw his Petigree.

28

When Love had shapt this world, *this great faire wight*   *The original*
That all wights else in this wide womb containes,   *of dauncing.*
And had instructed it to daunce aright,
A thousand measures with a thousand straines,
Which it should practise with delightfull paines
    Untill that fatall instant should revolve,
    When all to nothing should againe resolve:

29

The comly order and proportion faire
On every side did please his wandring eye,
Till glauncing through the thin transparent aire
A rude disordered rout he did espie
Of men and women, that most spightfullie
    Did one another throng, and crowd so sore,
    That his kind eye in pitty wept therefore.

26.1 heav'n] heavens *LF*   26.2 movings . . . heav'ns] motions . . . heaven
LF   26.5 jollitie, *ed.*: ~∧ *Print*   26.6 How] When *LF*   27.5 forthwith]
for sooth *LF*   28.1 *ital. 1622: rom. 1596*   28.2 this *1622:* his *Σ*   con-
taines, *ed.*: ~∧ *Print*   28.6 that] the *LF*   29.7 in] for *LF*

30

And swifter then the Lightning downe he came,
Another shapelesse *Chaos* to digest,
He will begin another world to frame,
(For Love till all be well will never rest)
Then with such words as cannot be exprest
 He cutts the troups, that all a sunder fling,
 And ere they wist, he casts them in a ring.

31

Then did he rarifie the Element
And in the center of the ring appeare,
The beames that from his forehead spreading went,
Begot an horrour and religious feare
In all the soules that round about him weare,
 Which in their eares attentivenesse procures
 While he with such like sounds their minds allures.

32

The speach of
Love perswad-
ing men to
learn Dancing.

How doth Confusions Mother, headlong Chance
Put reasons noble squadron to the rout?
Or how should you that have the governance
Of Natures children, heaven and earth throughout
Prescribe them rules, and live your selves without?
 Why should your fellowship a trouble be,
 Since mans chiefe pleasure is societie?

33

If sence hath not yet taught you, learne of me
A comly moderation and discreet,
That your assemblies may well ordered be
When my uniting power shall make you meet;
With heav'nly tunes it shall be tempered sweet:
 And be the modell of the worlds great frame,
 And you Earths children, *Dauncing* shall it name.

30.2 *Chaos LF: rom. Print* 30.6 that] and *LF* 30.7 he casts] to cast *LF*
31.3 spreading *Σ*: shining *1596* 31.7 sounds] wordes *LF* 33.2 a modera-
tion comly and discreete *LF* 33.4 meet; *ed.*: ~, *Print* 33.7 *Dauncing*
1622: rom. 1596

34

Behold the *World* how it is *whirled round*,
And for it is so *whirl'd*, is named so;
In whose large volume many rules are found
Of this new Art, which it doth fairely show:
For your quick eyes in wandring too and fro
    From East to West, on no one thing can glaunce,
    But if you marke it well, it seemes to daunce.

35

First you see *fixt* in this huge mirrour blew   *By the orderly*
Of trembling lights a number numberlesse,   *motion of the*
Fixt they are nam'd, but with a name untrue,   *fixed Stars.*
For they all move, and in a Daunce expresse
That *great long yeare* that doth containe no lesse
    Then threescore hundreths of those yeares in all
    Which the Sunne makes with his course naturall.

36

What if to you these sparks disordered seeme,
As if by chaunce they had been scattered there?
The Gods a solemne measure doe it deeme
And see a just proportion every where,
And know the points whence first their movings were;
    To which first points when all returne againe,
    The Axeltree of Heav'n shall breake in twaine.

37

Under that spangled skye, five wandring flames,   *Of the Planets.*
Besides the King of Day, and Queene of Night,
Are wheel'd around, all in their sundry frames,

34.1 *World 1622*: world *1596*   34.1–2 *ital. 1622: rom. 1596*   34.3 volume
many rules] vollumes many notes *LF*   34.4 it doth fairely show] I to you
will shewe *LF*   34.6 on . . . can] can on *LF*   34.7 it seemes] doth
seeme *LF*   35.1, 3, 5 *long*] large *LF*   36.1 if . . . sparks] though . . . Lightes *LF*
seeme, *ed.*: ∼ₐ *Print*   36.5 whence first their movings] from whence they
movinge *LF*   36.6 first points] when turninge *LF*   37.2 and] the *LF*
37.3 sundry] severall *LF*

And all in sundry measures doe delight:
Yet altogether keepe no measure right.
  For by it selfe, each doth it selfe advaunce,
  And by it selfe, each doth a Galliard daunce.

38

Venus the Mother of that bastard Love
Which doth usurpe the worlds great Marshals name,
Just with the Sunne her dainty feete doth move
And unto him doth all her jestures frame:
Now after, now afore, the flattering Dame
  With divers cunning passages doth erre,
  Still him respecting that respects not her.

39

For that brave Sunne the Father of the Day,
Doth love this Earth the Mother of the Night,
And like a revellour in rich aray
Doth daunce his Galliard in his Lemmans sight,
Both back, and forth, and side-wayes passing light,
  His Princely grace doth so the Gods amaze,
  That all stand still and at his beautie gaze.

40

But see the Earth, when hee approcheth neere,
How she for joy doth spring and sweetly smile;
But see againe her sad and heavie cheere
When changing places he retires a while:
But those black clouds he shortly will exile,
  And make them all before his presence flye
  As mists consum'd before his cheerfull eye.

  37.6 by it selfe] all alone *LF*   37.7 by it selfe] all aloane *LF*   38.4 her]
the *1622*   38.5 afore] before *LF*   *38.6 passages] traver fer [*sic*] *LF*
39.2 the Night] this night *LF*   39.4 his Galliard] a Galliard *LF*   *39.6
Princely *1622*: gallant *Σ*   so] all *LF*   40.1 hee *1622 (Errata list)*, *LF*: she
1596, 1622 (Text)   40.5 black] darke *LF*   40.7 mists consum'd] mist
consumes *LF*

41

Who doth not see the measures of the Moone
Which thirteene times she daunceth every yeare?
And ends her pavine thirteene times as soone
As doth her brother, of whose golden haire
She borroweth part and proudly doth it weare.
  Then doth she coylie turne her face aside,
    That halfe her cheeke is scarce somtimes discride.

42

Next her, the pure, subtile, and cleansing fire,   *Of the Fire.*
Is swiftly carried in a circle even:
Though *Vulcan* be pronounst by many a lyer
The onely halting God that dwells in heaven.
But that foule name may be more fitly given
  To your false fier that far from heav'n is fall
    And doth consume, wast, spoile, disorder all.

43

And now behold your tender Nurse the *Ayre*   *Of the Ayre.*
And common neighbour that *ay runns around*,
How many pictures and impressions faire
Within her emptie regions are there found,
Which to your sences Dauncing doe propound?
  For what are *Breath*, *Speech*, *Ecchos*, *Musick*, *Winds*,
    But Dauncings of the ayre in sundry kinds?

44

For when you breath, the *ayre* in order moves,
Now in, now out, in time and measure trew;
And when you speake, so well she dauncing loves,

41.4 haire *1622*: heire *1596*   41.5 proudly] comly *LF*   41.6 Yet is shee
Coye and turnes her face a side *LF*   41.7 discride] espied *LF*   42.1 pure,
subtile, and] pure and subtile *LF*   42.5 may] might *LF*   42.6 To your
false fyer that did from heaven fall *LF*   43.1 *Ayre 1622*: ayre *1596*
43.2 *ital. 1622: rom. 1596*   43.4 her] their *LF*   43.6 *Italics and capitals
(except* 'Ecchos') *from 1622.*   43.7 Dauncings] dawncinge *LF*   44.1 you
breath,] your breath‸ *LF*   ayre *1622: rom. 1596*   44.3 she *Σ*: the *1596*

That doubling oft, and oft redoubling new,
With thousand formes she doth her selfe endew:
   For all the words that from your lips repaire,
   Are nought but tricks and turnings of the aire.

45

Hence is her pratling daughter *Eccho* borne
That daunces to all voyces she can heare:
There is no sound so harsh that she doth scorne,
Nor any time wherein she will forbeare
The aiery pavement with her feete to weare.
   And yet her hearing sence is nothing quick,
   For after time she endeth every trick.

46

And thou sweet *Musick*, Dauncings only life,
The eares sole happines, the ayres best speach,
Loadstone of fellowship, charming rod of strife,
The soft minds Paradice, the sick minds Leach,
With thine owne tongue thou trees and stones canst teach
   That when the Aire doth daunce her finest measure,
   Then art thou borne the Gods and mens sweet pleasure.

47

Lastly, where keepe the *Winds* their revelry,
Their violent turnings and wild whirling hayes?
But in the Ayres tralucent gallery?
Where she her selfe is turnd a hundreth wayes,
While with those Maskers wantonly she playes;
   Yet in this misrule, they such rule embrace
   As two at once encomber not the place.

44.4–5   that ought shee dubleth and redubleth newe,
           and doth her selfe with thousand formes indewe *LF*
44.6 that] which *LF*   44.7 of] in *LF*   45.1 *Eccho 1622: rom. 1596*
45.2 daunces] dawnceth *LF*   45.4 will] doth *LF*   45.6 quick, *1622:* ∼ₐ *1596*
46.1 *Musick 1622: rom. 1596*   46.2 the] and *LF*   46.7 mens sweet] mans
best *LF*   47.1 *Winds 1622:* winds *1596*   revelry, *1622:* ∼ₐ *1596*
47.5 those] these *LF*

48

If then fier, ayre, wandring and fixed lights
In every province of th'imperiall skye,
Yeeld perfect formes of daۆcing to your sights,
In vaine I teach the eare, that which the eye
With certaine view already doth descrie.
   But for your eyes perceive not all they see,
   In this I will your sences maister bee.

49

For loe the *Sea* that fleets about the Land,   *Of the Sea.*
And like a girdle clips her solide wast,
Musick and measure both doth understand:
For his great Christall eye is alwayes cast
Up to the Moone, and on her fixed fast.
   And as she daۆceth in her pallid spheere,
   So daۆceth he about the Center heere.

50

Sometimes his proud greene waves in order set,
One after other flow unto the shore,
Which when they have with many kisses wet,
They ebb away in order as before;
And to make knowne his Courtly Love the more,
   He oft doth lay aside his three-forkt Mace,
   And with his armes the timerous Earth embrace.

51

Onely the Earth doth stand for ever still,
Her rocks remove not, nor her mountaines meete,
(Although some witts enrich with Learnings skill
Say heav'n stands firme, and that the Earth doth fleete
And swiftly turneth underneath their feete)

48.1 fier, ayre] ayer fyer *LF*   48.6 your . . . all] the . . . what *LF*   see,
1622: ∼ˌ *1596*   49.1 For loe . . . fleets] Likewise . . . flotes *LF*   *Sea 1622*:
rom. *1596*   49.2 like . . . her] as . . . the *LF*

Yet though the Earth is ever stedfast seene,
On her broad breast hath Dauncing ever beene.

52

Of the Rivers.

For those blew vaines that through her body spred,
Those saphire streams which from great hills do spring,
(The Earths great duggs: for every wight is fed
With sweet fresh moisture from them issuing)
Observe a daunce in their wide wandering:
    And still their daunce begets a murmur sweete,
    And still the murmur with the daunce doth meete.

53

Of all their wayes I love *Mæanders* path,
Which to the tunes of dying Swans doth daunce,
Such winding sleights, such turnes and tricks he hath,
Such Creekes, such wrenches, and such daliaunce,
That whether it be hap or heedlesse chaunce,
    In this indented course and wriggling play
    He seemes to daunce a perfect cunning *Hay*.

54

But wherefore doe these streames for ever runne?
To keepe themselves for ever sweet and cleare:
For let their everlasting course be donne
They straight corrupt and foule with mud appeare.
O yee sweet Nimphs that beauties losse doe feare,
    Contemne the Drugs that Phisick doth devise,
    And learne of Love this dainty exercise.

51.6 is ever stedfast seene] hath stedfast ever bene *LF*   51.7 hath Dauncing
ever beene] was ever dawncinge seene *LF*   52.1 that] which *LF*   52.2 hills
ed.: hils *Print* (*full line*)   *52.5 wide *ed.*: wild *Print*: Longe *LF*   52.7 & still
their murmor doth with their dawnce meete *LF*   53.1 In steed of all behold
Mæanders path *LF*   53.2 Which] That *LF*   53.5 hap] arte *LF*
53.6 this *Σ*: his *1596*   wriggling *1622*: wringling *1596*: whirlinge *LF*
53.7 *Hay 1622: rom. 1596*   54.1 these] those *LF*   54.5 yee] you *LF*

55

See how those flowers that have sweet Beauty too   *Of other*
(The onely Jewels that the Earth doth weare   *things upon*
When the young Sunne in bravery her doth woo)   *the earth.*
As oft as they the whistling wind doe heare,
Doe wave their tender bodies here and there;
   And though their daunce no perfect measure is,
   Yet oftentimes their musick makes them kis.

56

What makes the Vine about the Elme to daunce
With turnings, windings, and imbracements round?
What makes the Load-stone to the North advaunce
His subtile point, as if from thence he found
His chiefe attractive Vertue to redound?
   Kind Nature first doth cause all things to love,
   Love makes them daunce and in just order move.

57

Harke how the Birds doe sing, and marke then how
Jumpe with the modulation of their layes,
They lightly leape, and skip from bow to bow;
Yet doe the Cranes deserve a greater prayse
Which keepe such measure in their ayrie wayes,
   As when they all in order ranked are,
   They make a perfect forme triangular.

58

In the chiefe angle flyes the watchfull guide,
And all the followers their heads doe lay
On their forgoers backs, on eyther side,
But for the Captaine hath no rest to stay
His head forwearied with the windy way,
   He back retires, and then the next behind,
   As his Lieuetenaunt leads them through the wind.

55.3 when the fresh Sunn in [arbor] \spring tyme/ doth her woe *LF*   55.7 kis.
1622: ~, *1596*   56.2 imbracements] embracinges *LF*   56.5 redound]
rebownde *LF*   56.7 makes] made *LF*   57.1 then] them *LF*   57.2 Jumpe
with the] they jumpe with *LF*   58.3 their] the *LF*   58.4 rest] backe *LF*

59

But why relate I every singular?
Since all the worlds great fortunes and affaires
Forward and backward rapt and whirled are,
According to the musick of the spheares:
And Chaunce her selfe, her nimble feete upbeares
    On a round slipperie wheele that rowleth ay,
    And turnes all states with her imperious sway.

60

Learne then to daunce you that are Princes borne
And lawfull Lords of earthly creatures all;
Imitate them, and thereof take no scorne,
(For thys new Art to them is naturall)
And imitate the starres cælestiall.
    For when pale Death your vitall twist shall sever,
    Your better parts must daunce with them for ever.

61

Thus Love perswades, and all the crowne of men
That stands around doth make a murmuring;
As when the wind loosd from his hollow den,
Among the trees a gentle base doth sing,
Or as a Brooke through peebles wandering:
    But in their lookes they uttered this plaine speach,
    That they wold learn to daunce, if Love wold teach.

62

*How Love
taught men to
daunce.
Rounds, or
Countrey
Daunces.*

Then first of all, hee doth demonstrate plaine
The motions seaven that are in nature found,
Upward, and *downward*, *forth*, and *back againe*,
To this side, and *to that*, and *turning round*:
Whereof, a thousand brawles he doth compound,

---

*59.5 Chaunce] Chaunge *1622*   upbeares] upreares *LF*   59.7 imperious *1622*
(*Errata list*), LF: impetuous *1596*: imperuous *1622* (*Text*)   60.1 Princes]
princly *LF*   60.3 thereof take] thinke thereof *LF*   60.4 *Parentheses from*
1622; om. *1596*.   60.6 your *Σ*: you *1596*   61.2 doth] doe *LF*
61.3 his] the *LF*   61.6 But in their] Yet in theize *LF*   61.7 daunce, if
Love *1622*: daunce ͺ if love *1596*   62.1 hee doth] they do *LF*   62.3–4 *ital.*
*1622: rom. *1596*

Which he doth teach unto the multitude,
And ever with a turne they must conclude.

63

As when a Nimph arysing from the Land
Leadeth a daunce with her long watery traine
Downe to the Sea, she wries to every hand
And every way doth crosse the fertile plaine:
But when at last she falls into the maine
    Then all her traverses concluded are,
    And with the Sea her course is circulare.

64

Thus when at first Love had them marshalled
As earst he did the shapelesse masse of things,
He taught them *rounds* and *winding Heyes* to tread,
And about trees to cast themselves in rings.
As the two Beares whom the first mover flings
    With a short turne about heavens Axeltree,
    In a round daunce for ever wheeling bee.

65

But after these, as men more civill grew   *Measures.*
He did more grave and solemne measures frame,
With such faire order and proportion trew
And correspondence every way the same,
That no fault finding eye did ever blame:
    For every eye was moved at the sight
    With sober wondring, and with sweet delight.

66

Not those young Students of the heavenly booke,
Atlas the great, *Promethius* the wise,
Which on the Starres did all their lyfe-time looke

63.3 she] & *LF*   63.5 But when] untill *LF*   63.7 circulare. *ed.*: ∼,
Print   64.3 *ital. 1622*: *rom. 1596*   64.6 With] in *LF*   65.2 measures]
measure *LF*   65.5 did] might *LF*   *66.1 young *ed* : youg *1622*: old
1596, LF

Could ever find such measures in the skies,
So full of change and rare varieties;
   Yet all the feete whereon these measures goe,
   Are onely Spondeis, solemne, grave, and sloe.

67

But for more divers and more pleasing show,
A swift and wandring daunce he did invent,
With passages uncertaine to and fro,
Galliards.   Yet with a certaine aunswere and consent
To the quick musick of the Instrument.
   Five was the number of the Musicks feete,
   Which still the daunce did with five paces meete.

68

A gallant daunce, that lively doth bewray
A spirit and a vertue Masculine,
Impatient that her house on earth should stay
(Since she her selfe is fierie and divine)
Oft doth she make her body upward flyne,
   With loftie turnes and capriols in the ayre,
   Which with the lustie tunes accordeth fayre.

69

Currantoes.   What shall I name those currant travases,
That on a triple *Dactyle* foote doe run
Close by the ground with slyding passages,
Wherein that Dauncer greatest prayse hath won
Which with best order can all orders shun:
   For every where he wantonly must range,
   And turne, and wind, with unexpected change.

66.4 measures] measure *LF*   67–8 *Stanzas misnumbered* 70 *and* 71 *in* 1596.
67.1 divers] various *LF*   67.2 he *LF*: she *Σ*   67.4 Yet] but *LF*
67.6–7 was . . . did] is . . . doth *LF*   68.4 (. . .) *ed.*: ₐ . . . : *Print*   69.1 travases,
1622: ~ₐ *1596*   69.2 That] which *LF Dactyle 1622: rom. 1596*   69.3 by] to *LF*
69.4 won] fownde *LF*   69.5 can all orders] doth all order *LF*

70

Yet is there one, the most delightfull kind,   *Lavoltaes.*
A lofty jumping, or a leaping round,
Where arme in arme, two Dauncers are entwind,
And whirle themselves with strickt embracements bound,
And still their feet an *Anapest* do sound:
   An *Anapest* is all theyr musicks song,
   Whose first two feet are short, and third is long.

71

As the victorious *twinns* of *Læda*'and *Jove*
That taught the *Spartans* dauncing on the sands
Of swift *Eurotas*, daunce in Heav'n above,
Knit and united with eternall hands;
Among the Starres their double Image stands,
   Where both are carried with an equall pace
   Together jumping in their turning race.

72

Thys is the Net wherein the Sunns bright eye
Venus and *Mars* entangled did behold,
For in thys Daunce, their armes they so imply
As each doth seeme the other to enfold:
What if lewd wits another tale have told
   Of jealous *Vulcan*, and of yron chaynes,
   Yet this true sence that forged lye containes.

73

These various formes of dauncing, Love did frame,
And beside these, a hundred millions moe,
And as he did invent, he taught the same

70.1 one, *ed.:* ~∧ *Print*   70.3 are] were *LF*   70.5–6 *Anapest 1622:*
rom. 1596   70. 5 do] doth *LF*   71.1 *twinns 1622: rom. 1596*   *Læda*'
ed.: Læda Print: Led' *LF*   71.2 That] which *LF*   *Spartans LF: rom Print.*
sands ∧ *ed.:* ~, *Print*   71.3 *Eurotas, 1622:* ~∧ *1596*   71.4 hands] bandes *LF*
72.1 is ... wherein ... bright] was ... in which ... great *LF*   72.3 imply]
[imploye] applye *LF*   72.4 each *ed.:* ~, *Print*   72.5 if] though *LF*

With goodly jesture, and with comly show,
Now keeping state, now humbly honoring low.
    And ever for the persons and the place
    He taught most fit, and best according grace.

Grace in
Dauncing.

74

For Love, within his fertile working braine
Did then conceive those gracious Virgins three,
Whose civill moderation doth maintaine
All decent order and conveniencie,
And faire respect, and seemlie modestie:
    And then he thought it fit they should be borne,
    That their sweet presence dauncing might adorne.

75

Hence is it that these *Graces* painted are
With hand in hand dauncing an endlesse round:
And with regarding eyes, that still beware
That there be no disgrace amongst them found;
With equall foote they beate the flowry ground,
    Laughing, or singing, as their passions will,
    Yet nothing that they doe becomes them ill.

76

Thus Love taught men, and men thus learnd of Love
Sweet Musicks sound with feete to counterfaite,
Which was long time before high thundering *Jove*
Was lifted up to heav'ns imperiall seate.
For though by birth he were the Prince of *Creete*,
    Nor *Creete*, nor Heav'n, should that yong Prince have seen
    If Dancers with their Timbrels had not been.

    73.4 goodly . . . comly] comly . . . goodly *LF*   *74.2 Did] Doe *1622 Errata*
list.   74.3 civill] comly *LF*   *74.3 doth *LF*: did *Σ*   74.5 seemlie]
decent *LF*   74.6 then] nowe *LF*   74.7 dauncing] [~~bewty~~] \dauncing/ *LF*
75.1 *Graces 1622: rom. 1596*   75.5 flowry] flowringe *LF*   75.6 or] and
LF   75.7 Yet] for *LF*   76.1 of] to *LF*   76.3 high] the *LF*   76.5
were] was *LF*   *76.6 that] the *1622*: y̆ *1596*: y^t *LF*

77

Since when all ceremonious misteries,
All sacred Orgies and religious rights,
All pomps, and tryumphs, and solemnities,
All Funerals, Nuptials, and like publike sights,
All Parliaments of peace, and warlike fights,
   All learned Arts, and every great affaire
   A lively shape of Daunting seemes to beare.

The use and formes of Daunting in sundry affaires of mans life.

78

For what did he who with his ten-tong'd Lute
Gave Beasts and blocks an understanding eare?
Or rather into bestiall minds and brute
Shed and infus'd the beames of reason cleare?
Doubtlesse for men that rude and savage were
   A civill forme of daunting he devis'd,
   Wherewith unto their Gods they sacrifiz'd.

79

So did *Musæus,* so *Amphion* did,
And *Linus* with his sweet enchanting song,
And he whose hand the earth of monsters rid
And had mens eares fast chayned to his tong:
And *Theseus* too, his wood-borne slaves among,
   Us'd daunting as the finest pollicie
   To plant religion and societie.

80

And therefore now the Thracian *Orpheus* Lire
And *Hercules* him selfe are stellified;
And in high heav'n amidst the starry Quire
Daunting their parts continually doe slide:
So on the Zodiake *Ganimede* doth ride,
   And so is *Hebe* with the *Muses* nine
   For pleasing *Jove* with daunting, made divine.

77.4 like] such *LF*   78.3 into] in these *LF*   78.4 beames] beame *LF*
78.5 for men] to them *LF*   79.5 too, *LF*: to$_\wedge$ *Σ* among, *ed.*: $\sim_\wedge$ *Print*
80.6 *Muses LF*: rom. *Print*

81

Wherefore was *Proteus* sayd himselfe to change
Into a streame, a Lyon, and a tree,
And many other formes fantastique strange
As in his fickle thought he wisht to be?
But that he daunc'd with such facilitie.
  As like a Lyon he could pace with pride,
  Ply like a Plant, and like a River slide.

82

And how was *Cæneus* made at first a man,
And then a woman, then a man againe
But in a Daunce? which when he first began
Hee the mans part in measure did sustaine:
But when he chang'd into a second straine
  He daunc'd the womans part another space,
  And then return'd into his former place.

83

Hence sprang the fable of *Tiresias*
That he the pleasure of both sexes tryde:
For in a daunce hee man and woman was
By often change of place from side to side.
But for the woman easily did slide
  And smoothly swim with cunning hidden Art,
  He tooke more pleasure in a womans part.

84

So to a fish *Venus* herselfe did change,
And swimming through the soft and yeelding wave,
With gentle motions did so smoothly range
As none might see where she the water drave:
But this plaine truth that falsed fable gave
  That she did daunce with slyding easines,
  Plyant and quick in wandring passages.

81.3 many] twenty *LF*   83.5 did] must *LF*   83.7 a] the *LF*
84.2 soft] swift *LF*   84.4 As] that *LF*   84.5 falsed] forged *LF*
84.7 in wandring] & windinge *LF*   passages. *ed.*: ∼, *Print*

85

And merry *Bacchus* practis'd dauncing too,
And to the Lydian numbers rounds did make:
The like he did in th'Easterne India doo,
And taught them all when *Phœbus* did awake,
And when at night he did his Coach forsake:
   To honor heav'n, and heav'ns great roling eie
   With turning daunces, and with melodie.

86

Thus they who first did found a common-weale,
And they who first Religion did ordaine,
By dauncing first the peoples harts did steale,
Of whom we now a thousand tales doe faine.
Yet doe we now their perfect rules retaine,
   And use them still in such devises new
   As in the world long since their withering grew.

87

For after Townes and Kingdomes founded were,
Betweene great States arose well-ordered *war*,
Wherein most perfect measure doth appeare
Whether their well-set ranks respected are
In Quadrant forme or Semicircular:
   Or else the March, when all the troups advaunce
   And to the Drum in gallant order daunce.

88

And after warrs, when white-wing'd victory
Is with a glorious tryumph beautified,
And every one doth *Io Io* cry,
Whiles all in gold the Conquerour doth ride,
The solemne pompe that fils the Citty wide
   Observes such ranke and measure every where,
   As if they altogether dauncing were.

85.1 too *ed.*: to *Print*: so *LF*   85.4–5 did . . . did] doth . . . doth *LF*   86.5
now] still *LF*   86.6 still] nowe *LF*   87.1 were, *ed.*: ∼ₐ *Print*
87.2 war *1622: rom. 1596*   87.4 their] the *LF*   87.7 And to *Σ*: Unto
1596   Drumₐ *ed.*: ∼, *Print*

89

The like just order Mourners doe observe,
(But with unlike affection and attire)
When some great man that nobly did deserve
And whom his friends impatiently desire
Is brought with honour to his latest fire:
    The dead corps too in that sad daunce is mov'd,
    As if both dead and living, dauncing lov'd.

90

A diverse cause, but like solemnitie
Unto the Temple leades the bashfull bride,
Which blusheth like the Indian Ivorie
Which is with dip of Tyrian purple died:
A golden troope doth passe on every side
    Of flourishing young men and Virgins gay,
    Which keepe faire measure all the flowry way.

91

And not alone the generall multitude,
But those choise *Nestors* which in counsell grave
Of Citties, and of Kingdomes doe conclude,
Most comly order in their Sessions have:
Wherefore the wise *Thessalians* ever gave
    The name of Leader of their Countries daunce
    To him that had their Countries governaunce.

92

And those great Maisters of the liberall Arts
In all their severall Schooles doe Dauncing teach:
For humble Grammer first doth set the parts
Of congruent and well-according speach:
Which Rhetorick whose state the clouds doth reach,
    And heav'nly Poetry doe forward lead,
    And divers Measures, diversly doe tread.

89.3 that] which *LF*   89.6 too in that] so in their *LF*   90.4 Which]
that *LF*   90.7 all] on *LF*   91.5 *Thessalians LF*: *rom. Print*   92.1 the]
their *1622*   92.2 In all] all in *LF*

93

For Rhetorick clothing speech in rich aray
In looser numbers teacheth her to range,
With twentie tropes, and turnings every way,
And various figures, and licentious change:
But Poetry with rule and order strange
  So curiously doth move each single pace,
  As all is mard if she one foote misplace.

94

These Arts of speach the guides and Marshals are,
The Logick leadeth Reason in a daunce,
(Reason the Cynosure and bright Load-star
In this worlds Sea t'avoid the rock of Chaunce)
For with close following and continuance
  One reason doth another so ensue,
  As in conclusion still the daunce is true.

95

So Musick to her owne sweet tunes doth trip
With tricks of, 3, 5, 8, 15, and more:
So doth the Art of Numbring seeme to skip
From ev'n to odd in her proportion'd score:
So doe those skils whose quick eyes doe explore
  The just dimension both of earth and heav'n
  In all their rules observe a measure ev'n.

96

Loe this is Dauncings true nobilitie.
Dauncing the child of Musick and of Love,
Dauncing it selfe both love and harmony,
Where all agree, and all in order move;
Dauncing the Art that all Arts doe approve:
  The faire Caracter of the worlds consent,
  The heav'ns true figure, and th'earths ornament.

93.2 her] for *LF*   94.7 conclusion *1622*: conlusion *1596*

97

THE Queene, whose dainty eares had borne too long
  The tedious praise of that she did despise,
Adding once more the musick of the tongue
To the sweet speech of her alluring eyes,
Began to aunswer in such winning wise
  As that forthwith *Antinous* tongue was tyde,
  His eyes fast fixt, his eares were open wide.

98

Forsooth (quoth she) great glory you have won
To your trim Minion Dauncing all this while,
By blazing him Loves first begotten sonne;
Of every ill the hatefull Father vile
That doth the world with sorceries beguile:
  Cunningly mad, religiously prophane,
  Wits monster, Reasons canker, Sences bane.

99

Love taught the mother that unkind desire
To wash her hands in her owne Infants blood;
Love taught the daughter to betray her Sire
Into most base unworthy servitude;
Love taught the brother to prepare such foode
  To feast his brother, that the all-seeing Sun
  Wrapt in a clowd, that wicked sight did shun.

100

And even this selfe same Love hath dauncing taught,
An Art that shewes th'*Idæa* of his mind
With vainesse, frenzie, and misorder fraught;
Sometimes with blood and cruelties unkind:
For in a daunce, *Tereus* mad wife did finde

97.2 that] what *LF*   97.3 the tongue] her tongue *LF*   97.5 winning]
[~~winninge~~] cunninge *LF*   97.6 forthwith] for sooth *LF*   97.7 fast fixt]
fixt fast *LF*   99.2 wash] bath *LF*   99.3 her] the *LF*   99.6 brother
LF, 1622 Errata list: brothers *1596, 1622 Text*   100.2 shewes *1622c, LF*:
sheweth *1596, 1622u*

Fit time and place by murther of her sonne,
T'avenge the wrong his trayterous Sire had done.

101

What meane the Mermayds when they daunce and sing
But certaine death unto the Marriner?
What tydings doe the dauncing Dolphins bring
But that some dangerous storme approcheth nere?
Then sith both Love and Dauncing lyveries beare
    Of such ill hap, unhappy may I prove,
    If sitting free I either daunce or love.

102

Y Et once againe *Antinous* did reply,   *True Love*
    Great Queene, condemne not Love the innocent,   *inventor of*
For this mischeivous Lust, which traiterously   *Daucing.*
Usurps his Name, and steales his ornament:
For that true Love which dauncing did invent,
    Is he that tun'd the worlds whole harmony,
    And linkt all men in sweet societie.

103

He first extracted from th'earth-mingled mind
That heav'nly fire, or quintessence divine,
Which doth such simpathy in beauty find
As is betweene the Elme and fruitfull Vine,
And so to beautie ever doth encline.
    Lives life it is, and cordiall to the hart,
    And of our better part, the better part.

100.6 murther of *1622*: murthering *1596*: murdringe of *LF*   101.3 Dolphins
ed.: Dilphins *Print*: dolphines *LF*   101.5 Then sith . . . lyveries beare] sith
then . . . [~~lovers~~] liveries were *LF*   101.6 may I *1622*: may they *1596*: might
they *LF*   101.7 If sitting free I] That sitting free, will *1596* which sittinge
free will *LF*   102.3 this . . . which] that . . . that *LF*   102.4 steales]
robbes *LF*   102.5 which] that *LF*   102.6 tun'd] made *LF*   103.2 or]
and *LF*   103.3 Which] that *LF* beauty] nature *LF*

104

Thys *is true Love*, by that true *Cupid* got
Which daunceth Galliards in your amorous eyes,
But to your frozen hart approcheth not,
Onely your hart he dares not enterprize.
And yet through every other part he flyes,
   And every where he nimbly daunceth now,
   That in your selfe, your selfe perceive not how.

105

For your sweet beauty daintily transfus'd
With due proportion throughout every part,
What is it but a daunce where Love hath us'd
His finer cunning, and more curious Art?
Where all the Elements themselves impart,
   And turne, and wind, and mingle with such measure,
   That th'eye that sees it, surfeits with the pleasure.

106

Love in the twinckling of your eylids daunceth,
Love daunceth in your pulses and your vaines,
Love when you sew your needles poynt advaunceth,
And makes it daunce a thousand curious straines
Of winding rounds, whereof the forme remaines,
   To shew, that your faire hands can daunce the Hey,
   Which your fine feet would learne as well as they.

107

And when your Ivory fingers touch the strings
Of any silver-sounding instrument,
Love makes them daunce to those sweete murmurings,
With busie skill, and cunning excellent:
O that your feet those tunes would represent
   With artificiall motions to and fro,
   That Love this Art in every part might shoe.

104.1 *is true Love 1622: rom. 1596*   104.6 now, *1622:* ~. *1596*   105.7
That ... with] as ... at *LF*   106.3 sew *ed.:* sow *Print*   106.7 well *1622:*
wel *1596 (full line)*   107.7 this] his *LF*

108

Yet your faire soule which came from heav'n above,
To rule thys house, another heav'n below,
With divers powers in harmony doth move,
And all the vertues that from her doe flow,
In a round measure hand in hand doe goe.
    Could I now see as I conceive thys Daunce,
    Wonder and Love would cast me in a traunce.

109

The richest Jewell in all the heav'nly Treasure
That ever yet unto the Earth was showne,
Is perfect Concord, th'onely perfect pleasure   *Concord.*
That wretched Earth-borne men have ever knowne,
For many harts it doth compound in one:
    That what so one doth will, or speake, or doe,
    With one consent they all agree thereto.

110

Concords true picture shineth in thys Art,
Where divers men and women ranked be,
And every one doth daunce a severall part,
Yet all as one, in measure doe agree,
Observing perfect uniformitie:
    All turne together, all together trace,
    And all together honor and embrace.

III

If they whom sacred Love hath link't in one,
Doe as they daunce, in all theyr course of life,
Never shall burning griefe nor bitter mone,

108.1 Yet ... which] See ... that *LF*   108.4 that] which *LF*   109–26 *These stanzas were not written for the earliest version of the poem, which concluded here with stanzas 127–31. See discussion on Composition in Commentary.*   109.6 that when so one doth speake or will or doe *LF*   109.7 With] when *LF*   110.2 divers] many *LF*   110.3 severall] sun dry *LF*   110.4 yet all in that one measure doth agree *LF*   111.2 Doe∧ ... life, *ed.:* ~, ... ~∧ *Print*

Nor factious difference, nor unkind strife,
Arise betwixt the husband and the wife.
  For whether forth or back, or round he goe,
  As the man doth, so must the woman doe.

112

What if by often enterchange of place
Sometime the woman get the upper hand?
That is but done for more delightfull grace,
For on that part shee doth not ever stand:
But as the Measures law doth her commaund
  Shee wheeles about, and ere the daunce doth end,
  Into her former place shee doth transcend.

113

But not alone this corespondence meet
And uniforme consent doth dauncing praise,
Comlines.   For *Comlines* the chyld of order sweet
Enamels it with her eye-pleasing raies:
Faire Comlines, ten hundred thousand waies
  Through dauncing shedds it selfe, and makes it shine
  With glorious beauty, and with grace divine.

114

For *Comlines* is a disposing faire
Of things and actions in fit time and place,
Which doth in dauncing shew it selfe most cleere,
When troopes confus'd which here and there do trace
Without distinguishment or bounded space,
  By dauncings rule, into such ranks are brought,
  As glads the eye, and ravisheth the thought.

111.5 betwixt] betwine *LF*   112.3 That] This *LF*   112.7 Into . . .
transcend] unto . . . descend *LF*   113.1 But] And *LF*   113.3 *Comlines*
1622: rom. 1596   113.5 ten] an *LF*   114.1 *Comlines 1622: rom. 1596*
114.6 dauncings *1622c, LF*: dauncing *1596, 1622u*   ranks] ranke *LF*
114.7 and] as *1622*

115

Then why should reason judge that reasonles
Which is wits of-spring, and the worke of Art,
Image of concord, and of comlines.
Who sees a clock mooving in every part,
A sayling Pinesse, or a wheeling Cart,
    But thinks that reason ere it came to passe
    The first impulsive cause and mover was?

116

Who sees an Armie all in ranke advaunce
But deemes a wise Commaunder is in place
Which leadeth on that brave victorious daunce?
Much more in dauncings Art, in dauncings grace
Blindnes it selfe may reasons footsteps trace:
    For of Loves Maze it is the curious plot,
    And of mans fellowship the true-love knot.

117

But if these eyes of yours, (Load-starrs of love
Shewing the worlds great daunce to your minds eye)
Cannot with all theyr demonstrations move
Kind apprehension in your fantasie
Of Dauncings vertue, and nobilitie:
    How can my barbarous tongue win you thereto
    Which heav'n and earths faire speech could never do?

118

O Love my King: if all my wit and power
Have done you all the service that they can,
O be you present in this present hower,
And helpe your servant and your true Leige-man
End that perswasion which I earst began:

115.3 and of] and trew *LF*   115.7 impulsive] compassive *LF*   116.1
ranke] rankes *LF*   116.4 in] and *LF*   116.5 footsteps *LF*: footstep *Σ*
116.6–7 *ital. 1622: rom. 1596*   117.3 theyr] these *LF*   117.5 vertue]
virtewes *LF*   117.7 heav'n] heavens *LF*   118.5 End . . . I] in . . . he *LF*

For who in praise of dauncing can perswade
With such sweet force as Love, which dauncing made.

119

A Passiage to
the discription
of Dauncing
in this age.

LOve heard his prayer, and swifter then the wind,
  Like to a Page, in habit, face, and speech,
He came, and stood *Antinous* behind,
And many secrets to his thoughts did teach.
At last, a cristall Mirrour he did reach
  Unto his hands, that he with one rash view,
  All formes therein by Loves revealing knew.

120

And humbly honoring, gave it to the Queene
With this faire speech: See fairest Queene (quoth he)
The fairest sight that ever shall be seene,
And th'onely wonder of posteritie,
The richest worke in Natures treasury;
  Which she disdaines to shew on this worlds stage,
  And thinks it far too good for our rude age.

121

But in another world devided far,
In the great, fortunate, triangled Ile,
Thrise twelve degrees remov'd from the North star,
Shee will this glorious workmanship compile
Which shee hath been conceiving all thys while
  Since the worlds birth, and will bring forth at last,
  When sixe and twenty hundreth yeeres are past.

122

PEnelope the Queene when she had view'd
  The strange-eye-dazeling-admirable sight,
Faine would have praisd the state and pulchritude,

118.7 such ... which] that ... who *LF*   119.1 wind, *ed.:* ~_∧ *Print*
119.2 face] voyce *LF*   119.6 that] and *LF*   121.3 star, *ed.:* ~_∧ *Print* (*full*
line)   121.5 *om. LF*   121.6 will bring] bringinge *LF*

But she was stroken dumbe with wonder quite,
Yet her sweet mind retayn'd her thinking might:
  Her ravisht minde in heav'nly thoughts did dwell,
  But what she thought, no mortall tongue can tell.

123

You Lady Muse, whom *Jove* the Counsellour
Begot on Memorie, wisdoms Treasuresse,
To your divining tongue is given a power
Of uttering secrets large and limitlesse:
You can *Penelopes* strange thoughts expresse
  Which she conceiv'd, and then would faine have told,
  When shee the wondrous Christall did behold.

124

Her winged thoughts bore up her minde so hie
As that shee weend shee saw the glorious throne
Where the bright Moone doth sit in majestie,
A thousand sparkling starres about her shone,
But she herselfe did sparkle more alone
  Then all those thousand beauties would have done
  If they had been confounded all in one.

125

And yet she thought those starrs mov'd in such measure
To doe their Soveraigne honor and delight,
As sooth'd her mind with sweet enchanting pleasure
Although the various change amaz'd her sight,
And her weake judgement dyd entangle quite:
  Beside, theyr moving made them shine more cleere,
  As Diamonds mov'd, more sparkling do appeare.

126

Thys was the Picture of her wondrous thought,
But who can wonder that her thought was so,
Sith *Vulcan* King of Fire, that Mirrour wrought

122.4 wonder] wondringe *LF*   122.6 dwell, *ed.*: dwel‸ *Print* (*full line*)
123.2 on *LF*: of *Σ*   123.5 thoughts] thought *LF*   123.6 then *LF*: thē
Print   125.3 sweet] such *LF*   126.1 her] the *LF*   126.3 Fire *1622*: fire *1596*

(Who things to come, present, and past doth know)
And there did represent in lively show
   Our glorious English Courts divine Image,
   As it should be in this our golden age.

127

Away *Terpsichore*, light Muse away,
And come *Uranie*, Prophetesse divine;
Come Muse of heav'n, my burning thirst allay,
Even now, for want of sacred drinke I tine.
In heav'nly moysture dip thys Pen of mine,
   And let my mouth with Nectar overflow,
   For I must more then mortall glory show.

128

O that I had *Homers* aboundant vaine,
I would heereof another *Ilias* make,
Or els the man of *Mantuas* charmed braine
In whose large throat great *Jove* the Thunderer spake.
O that I could old *Gefferies* Muse awake,
   Or borrow *Colins* fayre heroike stile,
   Or smooth my rimes with *Delias* servants file.

129

O could I sweet Companion, sing like you,
Which of a shadow, under a shadow sing;
Or like fair *Salices* sad lover true,
Or like the Bee, the Marigolds darling,
Whose suddaine verse Love covers with his wing:
   O that your braines were mingled all with mine,
   T'inlarge my wit for this great worke divine.

126.4 Who *Σ*: Which *1596*   126.5 show_∧ *1622*: ∼, *1596*   126.6 Image, *1622*:
∼_∧ *1596*   127–31 *Stanzas om. 1622.*   *128.4 Thunderer *ed.*: thunder
1596: thunderer *LF*   129.1 sweet] deere *LF*   *129.3 *Salices LF*: Salues
1596   *129.4 Bee *ed.*: Bay *1596*: baye *LF*

130

Yet *Astrophell* might one for all suffize,
Whose supple Muse Camelion-like doth change
Into all formes of excellent devise:
So might the Swallow, whose swift Muse doth range
Through rare *Idæas*, and inventions strange,
   And ever doth enjoy her joyfull spring,
   And sweeter then the Nightingale doth sing.

131

O that I might that singing Swallow heare
To whom I owe my service and my love,
His sugred tunes would so enchant mine eare,
And in my mind such sacred fury move,
As I should knock at heav'ns great gate above
   With my proude rimes, while of this heav'nly state
   I doe aspire the shadow to relate.

FINIS.

127[A]

Her brighter dazeling beames of Majestie
Were laid aside, for she vouchsaft awhile
With gracious, cheerefull, and familiar eye
Upon the Revels of her Court to smile,
For so Times Journeis she doth oft beguile,
   Like sight no mortall eye might elsewhere see
   So full of State, Art, and varietie.

128[A]

For of her Barons brave, and Ladies faire,
Who had they been elswhere most faire had been,
Many an incomparable lovely payre,
With hand in hand were inter-linked seene
Making faire Honour to their Soveraigne Queene;

130.2 supple] subtile *LF*   131.1 might] could *LF*   131.6 heav'nly]
dawning *LF*

Forward they pac'd, and did their pace apply
To a most sweet and solemne Melody.

129[A]

So subtile and so curious was the measure,
With such unlookt for chaunge in every straine;
As that *Penelope* rapt with sweet pleasure,
Weend shee beheld the true proportion plaine
Of her owne webb, weavd and unweavd againe,
    But that her Art was somewhat lesse she thought,
    And on a meere ignoble Subject wrought.

130[A]

For here, like to the Silkewormes industry,
Beauty it selfe out of it selfe did weave
So rare a worke, and of such subtilty,
As did all eyes entangle and deceive,
And in all mindes a strange impression leave:
    In this sweet Laborinth did *Cupid* stray,
    And never had the power to passe away.

131[A]

As when the Indians, Neighbours of the morning,
In honour of the Cheerefull rising Sunne,
With Pearle and painted plumes themselves adorning,
A solemne stately measure have begun,
The God well pleasd with that faire honour done
    Sheds foorth his Beames and doth their faces kis
    With that immortall glorious face of his.

132[A]

So &c. &c.

131A.4 begun, *ed.*: ~. *1622*

EPIGRAMMES

Title: Epigrammes and Elegies. By I.D. and C.M. *E1*, *E2*   *For titles in manuscript collections, see Textual Introduction.*

Epigrammes.

Ad Musam. 1

Flie merry Muse unto that merry towne,
Where thou mayst playes, revels, and triumphes see,
The house of fame, and Theatre of renowne,
Where all good wits and spirits love to be.

Fall in betwene their hands, that praise and love thee,   5
And be to them a laughter and a jest:
But as for them which scorning shall reproove thee,
Disdayne their wits, and thinke thyne owne the best.

But if thou finde any so grose and dull,
That thinke I do to privat Taxing leane: 10
Bid him go hang, for he is but a gull,
And knowes not what an Epigramme doth meane:
    Which Taxeth under a particular name,
    A generall vice that merits publique blame.

Of a Gull. 2

Oft in my laughing rimes, I name a gull,
But this new terme will many questions breede;
Therefore at first I will expresse at full,
Who is a true and perfect gull indeede.

Epigrammes. *Printed texts: E1, E2 MSS.: Ca, F, H, LF, R, Ro, Υ Text from E1. The apparatus for each epigram gives initially the sigla of MSS. containing that epigram used to establish the text, but does not repeat there the sigla of the printed texts since they contain the complete collection.*
Ad Musam. 1 *MSS.: LF, Ca, Ro, F, R, H Layout slightly normalized. (E1 precedes title with 'Epigrmmata [sic] prima.')*
  2 see, *ed.*: ~ₐ *Print*   3 and] the *Ro, F, R, H*   5 praise and love *Σ*: love & praise *E1*: sayes to love *R*: seeme to love *H*: so they love *F*   thee, *ed.*: ~ₐ *Print*
7 reproove *Σ*: approve *E1*   12 doth *Σ*: does *E1*   meane: *E2*: ~. *E1*
14 that *Σ*: which *E1, H, F*

Of a Gull. 2 *MSS.: LF, Ca, Ro, F, R, H*
  2 breede; *E2*: ~ₐ *E1 (full line)*   3 expresse] describe *R, F, Ro*: disclose *H*

A gull is he, who feares a velvet gowne,   5
And when a wench is brave, dares not speake to her:
A gull is he which traverseth the towne,
And is for marriage knowne a common wooer.

A gull is he, which while he prowdlie weares
A silver hilted Rapier by his side: 10
Indures the lyes, and Knockes about the eares,
Whilst in his sheath, his sleeping sword doth bide.

A gull is he which weares good hansome cloathes,
And standes in presence stroaking up his hayre:
And filles up his unperfect speech with othes,   15
But speakes not one wise word throughout the yeere:

But to define a gull in termes precise,
A gull is he which semes, and is not wise.

In Rufum. 3

Rufus the Courtier, at the theater,
Leaving the best and most conspicuous place,
Doth eyther to the stage himselfe transferre,
Or through a grate, doth shew his doubtfull face,

For that the clamorous frie of Innes of court,   5
Filles up the privat roomes of greater price:
And such a place where all may have resort,
He in his singularitie doth despise.

Yet doth not his particuler humour shun
The common stewes and brothells of the towne,   10
Though all the worlde in troopes do thither run,
Cleane and uncleane, the gentle and the Clowne.

5 who] that F, R, H, Ro: which Ca   7 which] that Ca, F, R, H, Ro
9 which] that F, R, H, Ro: who LF   while] when R, H, Ca: where F   weares∧
E2: ∼, E1   11 lyes] lye R, H, Ro   15 othes, E2: ∼. E1   16 yeere:
E2: ∼∧ E1 (full line)   18 which] that R, H, Ca, Ro

In Rufum. 3   MSS: LF, Ro, Ca, F, R, H
   2 Leaving] havinge F, R   4 doubtfull Σ: double E1: dolefull Ca   face, ed.:
∼. Print   5 of Innes] of the Innes Ca, F, R, H,   11 run, E2: ∼. E1

Then why shoulde Rufus in his pride abhorre,
A common seate that loves a common whoore.

In Quintum. 4

Quintus the Dauncer useth evermore,
His feete in measure and in rule to move,
Yet on a time he calde his mistresse whoore,
And thought with that sweete worde to win her love.
　　Oh had his tongue like to his feete bin taught,
　　It never woulde have uttered such a thought.

In Plurimos. 5

Faustinus, Sextus, Cinna, Ponticus,
With Gella, Lesbia, Thais, Rodope:
Rode all to Stanes for no cause serious,
But for their mirth, and for their lecherie.

Scarse were they settled in their lodging, when   5
Wenches, with wenches: men with men fell out.
Men with their wenches, wenches with their men,
Which strait dissolved this ill assembled rowt.

But since the Divel brought them thus together,
To my discoursing thoughts it is a wonder,   10
Why presently as soone as they came thither,
The selfe same divel did them part a sunder.

　　Doubtlesse it seemes it was a foolish divel,
　　That thus would part them, ere they did some evill.

In Quintum. 4   *MSS.:* LF, Ro, Ca, F, R, H
　2 move, *E2:* ~. *E1*   4 love: *E2:* ~ʌ *E1*
In Plurimos. 5   *MSS:* LF, Ro, Ca, H
　2 Rodope *E2:* Rodpe *E1*   8 dissolved *MSS.:* dissolves *Print*   9 thus]
first LF, *Ca*, H   10 wonder, *E2:* ~. *E1*   12 did them part] parted them
LF, *Ro:* should them parte *Ca*   14 That thus would part them, ere they did
E2: That thus did ... *E1:* which straight did ... *LF:* which straight would ...
Ca: that straight would ... *H:* to part them straight ere they had done *Ro*

In Titum. 6

Titus the brave and valorous young gallant,
Three yeeres together in this towne hath beene,
Yet my lord Chauncellors tombe he hath not seene:
Nor the New water worke, nor the Elephant.
   I cannot tell the cause without a smile,
   He hath beene in the Counter all this while.

In Faustum. 7

Faustus not lord, nor knight, nor wise, nor olde,
To every place about the towne doth ride,
He rides into the fieldes, Playes to beholde,
He rides to take boate at the water side,
He rides to Powles, he rides to th'ordinarie,
He rides unto the house of bawderie too.
Thither his horse so often doth him carry,
That shortlie he wil quite forget to go.

In Katam. 8

Kate being pleasde, wisht that her pleasure coulde,
Indure as long as a buffe jerkin would.
Content thee Kate, although thy pleasure wasteth,
Thy pleasures place like a buffe jerkin lasteth:
   For no buffe jerkin hath bin oftner worne,
   Nor hath more scrapings or more dressings born.

In Titum. 6   *MSS.: LF, Ro, Ca, F, R, H*
   2 this] the *MSS.*

In Faustum. 7   *MSS.: LF, Ro, Ca, R, H Layout slightly normalized.*
   1 not] nor *Ro, Ca, R, H*

In Katam. 8   *MSS.: LF, Ro, F*
   Title. Katam *ed.:* Katum *Print*   1 coulde] would *LF, Ro:* should *F*   2 Indure] Last *MSS.*   4 like a buffe jerkin lasteth] a buffe Jerkin outlasteth *MSS.*
6 Nor] Or *MSS.* scrapings . . . dressings] scraping . . . dressing *F, Ro*

In Librum. 9

Liber doth vaunt how chastely he hath livde
Since he hath bin in towne, seven yeeres and more,
For that he sweares he hath foure onely swivde,
A maide, a wife, a widow and a whoore:
   Then Liber thou hast swivde all women kinde,
   For a fift sort I know thou canst not finde.

In Medontem. 10

Great Captaine Medon weares a chaine of golde,
Which at five hundred crownes is valued,
For that it was his graundsires chaine of olde,
When great king Henry Bulleigne conquered.
   And weare it Medon, for it may ensue,   5
    That thou by vertue of this Massie chaine,
    A stronger towne then Bulloigne maist subdue,
    Yf wise mens sawes be not reputed vaine.
For what saide Phillip king of Macedon?
There is no Castle so well fortifid,   10
But if an Asse laden with gold come on,
The guarde wil stoope, and gates flie open wide.

In Gellam. 11

Gella, if thou dost love thy selfe, take heede,
Lest thou my rimes, unto thy lover reade,
For straight thou grinst, and then thy lover seeth,
Thy canker-eaten gums, and rotten teeth.

In Librum. 9   *MSS.: LF, Ro, Ca, H*
  1 livde_∧ *E2:* ~, *E1*   2 towne, *E2:* ~_∧ *E1*

In Medontem. 10   *MSS.: LF, Ro, Ca, F, R, H*
  Title. Medontem *Σ:* Medonem *E1, H*   2 valued, *E2:* ~_∧ *E1*   6 vertue
of this] wearinge of that *F, R, H*   8 reputed] reported *LF, Ca:* accounted *H:*
imputed *F*   11 come *MSS.:* comes *Print*

In Gellam. 11   *MSS.: LF, Ro, Ca, R, H*
  3 seeth *MSS.:* reeth *E1*

In Quintum. 12

Quintus his wit infused into his braine,
Misliked the place, and fled into his feete,
And there it wanders up and down the streete,
Dabled in the durt, and soaked in the raine.
　　Doubtlesse his wit intendes not to aspire,
　　Which leaves his head to travell in the mire.

In Severum. 13

The puritane Severus oft doth reade,
This text that doth pronounce vaine speech a sinne,
That thing defiles a man that doth proceede
From out the mouth, not that which enters in.
Hence is it, that we seldome heare him sweare,　　　5
And thereof like a Pharisie he vaunts,
But he devoures more Capons in a yeare,
Then would suffice a hundreth protestants.
And sooth, those sectaries are gluttons all,
Aswell the threedbare Cobler as the knight,　　　10
For those poore slaves which have not wherwithal
Feede on the rich, til they devoure them quite.
　　And so like Pharoes kine, they eate up cleane,
　　Those that be fat, yet still themselves be leane.

In Leucam. 14

Leuca in presence once a fart did let,
Some laught a little, she forsooke the place:

In Quintum. 12　*MSS.: Ro, Ca, F*
　2 Misliked *F*: Mislikes *Print, Ro*: Mistook *Ca*　fled] fell *F*: slides *Ro*　　3 there]
now *Ca, F*　　streete *MSS.*: streetes *Print*　　4 in the durt] in dirt *Ro, Ca, F*
6 Which leaves] That left *Ca*: that lest *F*

In Severum. 13　*MSS.: LF, Ro, Ca, F, R, H*
　9 sooth, *E2*: ∼‿ *E1*　those] these *Ro, Ca, F, R, H*　　11 those] these *LF, Ro,
Ca*　which] that *LF, Ro, Ca, F, R*　　14 be . . . be] are . . . are *MSS.*

In Leucam. 14　*MSS.: LF, Ro, Ca, F*

And mazde with shame, did eke her glove forget,
Which she returnde to fetch with bashfull grace:
 And when she would have said, this is my glove,
 My fart (quoth she) which did more laughter move.

In Macrum. 15

Thou canst not speake yet Macer, for to speake,
Is to distinguish soundes significant,
Thou with harsh noyse the ayre dost rudely breake,
But what thou utterest common sence doth want:
 Halfe English wordes, with fustian tearms among,
 Much like the burthen of a Northerne song.

In Faustum. 16

That youth saith Faustus, hath a Lyon seene,
Who from a Dycing house comes monielesse,
But when he lost his hayre, where had he beene?
I doubt me he had seene a Lyonesse.

In Cosmum. 17

Cosmus hath more discoursing in his head,
Then Jove, when Pallas issued from his braine,
And still he strives to be delivered,
Of all his thoughtes at once, but al in vaine.

---

 3 And mazde with shame *LF, Ca, Ro*: and madde with shame *Print*: but goinge thence *F* did eke] shee did *Ca, F* 4 grace] face *LF, Ro*: shame *F* 5 this is *Σ*: *om. E1*. 6 quoth *E2*: qd *E1*

In Macrum. 15 *MSS.: LF, Ro, Ca, R, H*
 4 doth *E2*: dnth *E1* 5 among, *E2*: ∼ₐ *E1*

In Faustum. 16 *MSS.: LF, Ro, Ca, F, R, H*
 1 a Lyon] the lion *R*: the Lions *Ca, H, F* 2 who] which *F, R, H*
3 beene? *ed.*: ∼, *Print* 4 doubt] feare *F, H* he *Σ*: *om. E1*

In Cosmum. 17 *MSS.: LF, Ro, Ca, R, H*
 2 Jove *Σ*: love *E1* 3 still] often *Ca*: oft *Ro*

For as we see at all the play house dores,   5
When ended is the play, the daunce, and song:
A thousand townsemen, gentlemen, and whores,
Porters and serving-men togither throng,
So thoughts of drinking, thriving, wenching, war,
And borrowing money, raging in his minde,   10
To issue all at once so forwarde are,
As none at all can perfect passage finde.

In Flaccum. 18

The false knave Flaccus once a bribe I gave,
The more foole I to bribe so false a knave,
But he gave back my bribe, the more foole he,
That for my follie, did not cousen me.

In Cineam. 19

Thou dogged Cineas, hated like a dogge,
For still thou grumblest like a Mastie dogge,
Comparst thy selfe to nothing but a dogge:
Thou saist thou art as weary as a dogge,
As angry, sick, and hungry as a dogge,   5
As dull and melancholy as a dogge,
As lazie, sleepie, idle as a dogge.
But why dost thou compare thee to a dogge?
In that, for which all men despise a dogge,
I will compare thee better to a dogge.   10

---

5 at all the] it at the *R*: y^t att the *H*   6 play, *E2*: ∼. *E1*   7 whores
E2: ∼_∧ *E1*   9 drinking, thriving] thriving, drinking *R, H*   11 forwarde]
ready *Ro, Ca*   12 As . . . can perfect passage] That . . . can perfect issue *Ro*:
That . . . may perfect issue *Ca*

In Flaccum. 18   *MSS.: LF, Ro, Ca, F, R, H*
  2 The more foole I] I was a foole *Ro, Ca, F, R, H*   3 my] the *Ro, F, H*

In Cineam. 19   *MSS.: LF, Ro, Ca, H, R*
  1 Cineas, *ed.*: ∼_∧ *Print*   2 dogge, *E2*: ∼: *E1*   3 dogge: *E2*: ∼, *E1*
4 dogge, *E2*: ∼. *E1*   5 and] as *Ro, Ca*   6 and] as *Ro, Ca*   dogge, *E2*: ∼ :*E1*
7 lazie, sleepie, idle *Σ*: lazie, sleepie, & as idle *E1*: idle lazy sleepy *Ca*: lither, and as
idle *Ro*

Thou art as faire and comely as a dogge,
Thou art as true and honest as a dogge,
Thou art as kinde and liberall as a dogge,
Thou art as wise and valiant as a dogge.
    But Cineas, I have often heard thee tell,   15
    Thou art as like thy father as may be,
    Tis like inough, and faith I like it well,
    But I am glad thou art not like to me.

In Gerontem. 20

Geron whose mouldie memorie corrects
Old Holinshed our famous chronicler,
Which morrall rules, and pollicie collects
Out of all actions done thiese fourescore yeere,
    Accounts the time of everie odde event,   5
    Not from Christs birth, nor from the Princes raigne,
    But from some other famous accident,
    Which in mens generall notise doth remaine.
The siege of Bulloigne, and the plaguie sweat,
The going to Saint Quintines and New haven,   10
The rising in the North, The frost so great,
That cart-wheele prints on Thames face were graven,
    The fall of money, and burning of Paules steeple,
    The blasing starre and Spaniardes overthrow:
    By thiese events, notorious to the people,   15
    He measures times, and things forepast doth shew.
But most of all, he chieflie reckons by
A privat chaunce, the death of his curst wife:
This is to him the dearest memorie,
And th'happiest accident of all his life.   20

---

15 often *MSS.*: oft *Print*   16 Thou art as like thy] That th'art as like thy
R: That thou art like thy *H*: Thou art like the *Ca*

In Gerontem. 20   *MS.*: LF   *Layout slightly normalized.*
  1 whose *Σ.*: *om.* E1   corrects∧ *ed.*: ~, *Print*   3 Which *LF*: With *Print*
collects∧ *E2*: ~, *E1*   4 thiese . . . yeere] this . . . yeere *E2*: these . . . yeares
LF   yeere, *E2*: ~. *E1*   5 time] times *E2*   odde *Σ*: olde *E1*   11 great,
E2: ~. *E1*   12 graven *LF*: seene *Print*   16 times] tyme *LF*
17 chieflie] countes and *LF*   by∧ *E2*: ~, *E1*   19 the] of *LF*

In Marcum. 21

When Marcus comes from Mins, he stil doth sweare
By, come on seaven, that all is lost and gone,
But thats not true, for he hath lost his hayre
Onely for that, he came too much on one.

In Ciprium. 22

The fine youth Ciprius is more tierse and neate,
Then the new garden of the'olde Temple is,
And stil the newest fashion he doth get,
And with the time doth chaunge from that to this,
He weares a hat now of the flat crown-block,   5
The treble ruffes, long cloake and doublet French:
He takes Tobacco, and doth weare a locke,
And wastes more time in dressing then a Wench.
    Yet this new-fangled youth, made for these times,
    Doth above al, praise olde George Gascoines rimes.   10

In Cineam. 23

When Cineas comes amongst his friends in morning,
He sliely lookes who first his cap doth move:
Him he salutes, the rest so grimly scorning,
As if for ever they had lost his love.
    I knowing how it doth the humour fit,   5
    Of this fond gull to be saluted first,
    Catch at my cap, but move it not a whit:
    Which he perceiving seemes for spite to burst.

In Marcum. 21   *MSS.: LF, Ro, Ca, F, R, H*
   2 on *MSS.:* a   *Print*   that] *om. LF, Ro, Ca, R, H*   4 on *LF, Ro, Ca, R, H:* at
Print: to *F*

In Ciprium. 22   *MSS.: LF, Ro, Ca, R, H*
   2 the' *ed.:* the *Print*   4 chaunge *ed.:* chaung *E1:* change *E2*   9 times
E2: tims *E1 (full line)*   10 George *MSS.: om. Print*

In Cineam. 23   *MSS.: LF, Ro, Ca, F, R, H*
   1 morning, *E2:* ∼ ∧ *E1 (full line)*   2 lookes] notes *MSS.*   6 first, *E2:* ∼:
E1   8 he perceiving *MSS.:* perceiving he *Print*   for] with *LF, Ro, Ca, R, H:*
in *F*

But Cineas, why expect you more of me,
Then I of you? I am as good a man,   10
And better too by many'a quallitie,
For vault, and daunce, and fence, and rime I can;
　　You keep a whore at your own charge men tel me,
　　Indeede friend (Cineas) therein you excell me.

In Gallum. 24

Gallus hath bin this Sommer in Friesland,
And now returned he speakes such warlike wordes
As if I coulde their English understand,
I feare me they would cut my Throat like swordes.
　　He talkes of counterscarfes and casomates,   5
　　Of parapets, curteynes and Pallizadois,
　　Of flankers, Ravelings, gabions he prates,
　　And of false brayes, and sallies and scaladose:
But to requite such gulling termes as these,
With wordes of my profession I replie: 10
I tel of foorching, vouchers, counterpleas,
Of Withernams, essoynes, and champartie.
　　So neyther of us understanding eyther,
　　We part as wise as when we came together.

In Decium. 25

Audacious Painters have nine worthies made,
But Poet Decius more audacious farre,
Making his mistres march with men of warre,

11 many' *ed.*: many *Print*　　　quallitie, *E2*: ~ ∧ *E1*　　　12 daunce, and fence]
fence and daunce *LF, Ro, H*　　　　fence, *E2*: ~ ∧ *E1*　　　　can; *ed.*: ~, *Print*
13 charge *E2*: charg *E1* (*full line*)　　me, *E2*: ~ ∧ *E1* (*full line*)
[15–16]　　　You keepe a whore att your charge in towne
　　　　　　　in deede frend Ceneas there you put me downe. *H*

In Gallum. 24　*MSS.: LF, Ro, Ca, H*
　1 Sommer *MSS.*: Sommertime *Print*　　　4 swordes. *E2*: ~ ∧ *E1* (*full line*)
6 parapets, curteynes *MSS.*: parapets, of curteneys *Print*　　9 requite *Σ*: require
E1　　　11 vouchers, counterpleas *E2, LF, Ro*: vouchers, and counterpleas *E1*:
vouchers of Counterplies *H*: vouching and counterpleas *Ca*　　　14 as wise as
when we] as wisely as wee *MSS.*

In Decium. 25　*MSS.: LF, Ro, Ca, R, H*

With title of tenth worthie doth her lade;
   Me thinkes that gul did use his termes as fit,
   Which termde his love a Giant for hir wit.

In Gellam. 26

If Gellas beautie be examined
She hath a dull dead eye, a saddle nose,
An ill shapte face, with morpheu overspread,
And rotten Teeth which she in laughing showes.
   Brieflie, she is the filthyest wench in Towne,   5
   Of all that do the art of whooring use:
   But when she hath put on her sattin gowne,
   Her cut lawne apron, and her velvet shooes,
Her greene silk stockings, and her peticoate,
Of Taffatie, with golden frindge a-rounde: 10
And is withall perfumed with civet hot,
Which doth her valiant stinking breath confounde,
   Yet she with these addicions is no more,
   Then a sweete, filthie, fine, ill favored whoore.

In Sillam. 27

Silla is often challenged to the fielde,
To answere like a gentleman his foes,
But then doth he this only answere yeelde,
That he hath livings and faire landes to lose.
   Silla, if none but beggars valiant were,
   The King of Spaine woulde put us all in feare.

---

4 worthie *Σ*: worthlie *Print*: worthies *H*   lade; *ed.*: ~, *E1* ~ₐ *E2*   6 Which]
That *R, H*: Who *Ca*

In Gellam. 26   *MSS.*: *LF, Ro, Ca, F, R, H*
  5 Brieflie, *E2*: ~ₐ *E1*   8 cut *MSS.*: out *Print*   shooes, *E2*: ~. *E1*   12 con-
founde, *ed.*: ~ₐ *E1*: ~. *E2*   14 fine, . . . whoore. *E2*: ~ₐ . . . ~, *E1*

In Sillam. 27   *MSS.*: *LF, Ro, Ca, F, R, H*
  3 But then doth he this *E2*: But when doth he his *E1*: But then he doth this *LF*:
But he doth all this *Σ*

In Sillam. 28

Who dares affirme that Silla dares not fight?
When I dare sweare he dares adventure more,
Then the most brave, and most all daring knight,
That ever armes with resollucion bore.
    He that dares touch the most unholsome whoore,   5
    That ever was retirde into the spittle:
    And dares court wenches standing at a dore,
    The porcion of his wit being passing litle.
He that dares give his deerest friend offences,
Which other valiant fooles do feare to do: 10
And when a fever doth confounde his sences,
Dares eate raw biefe, and drinke strong wine thereto.
    He that dares take Tobacco on the stage,
    Dares man a whore at noon-day throgh the street,
    Dares daunce in Powles, and in this formall age,   15
    Dares say and do what ever is unmeete.
Whom feare of shame coulde never yet affright,
Who dares affirme that Silla dares not fight?

In Haywodum. 29

    Haywood which did in Epigrams excell,
    Is now put down since my light muse arose:
    As buckets are put downe into a well,
    Or as a schoole-boy putteth downe his hose.

In Sillam. 28   *MSS.: LF, Ro, F, H*
   1 dares not *Σ*: dare not *E1, Ro*   3 brave, and most *Σ*: brave, most *E1*:
valiant, and *F, H*   knight *MSS.*: wight *Print (comma after* wight *in E2, colon in E1)*
5 dares *MSS.*: dare **Print**   9 friend *E2, LF*: friendes *Σ*   12 Dares *MSS.*:
Dare **Print**   14 street, *ed.*: ~‸ **Print** *(full line)*

In Haywodum. 29   *MSS.: LF, Ro, Ca, R, H*
   1 which] who *LF*: that *Ro, H*   did in Epigrams *Σ*: in Epigrams did *E1*

In Dacum. 30

Amongst the Poets Dacus numbred is,
Yet could he never make an English rime,
But some prose speeches I have hearde of his,
Which have bin spoken many'a hundreth time.
   The man that keepes the Eliphant hath one,   5
   Wherein he tels the wonders of the beast.
   An other Bankes pronounced long agone,
   When he his curtalls qualities exprest:
He first taught him that keepes the monuments
At Westminster his formall tale to say,   10
And also him which Puppets represents,
And also him which with the Ape doth play:
   Though all his poetrie be like to this,
   Amongst the Poets Dacus numbered is.

In Priscum. 31

When Priscus raisde from low to high estate,
Rode through the streetes in pompous jollitie,
Caius his poore famillier friende of late,
Be-spake him thus, Sir now you know not me:
   Tis likely friende (quoth Priscus) to be so,
   For at this time my selfe I do not know.

In Brunum. 32

Brunus which thinkes him selfe a faire sweet youth
Is nine and Thirtie yeeres of age at least:

In Dacum. 30   *MSS.: LF, Ro, Ca, R, H*
    4 many' *ed.:* many *Print*   hundreth *E2, LF:* dundreth *E1:* thousand *Σ*   7 agone
ed.: agoe *Print*   9 monuments‸ *E2:* ∼, *E1*   10 say, *E2:* ∼. *E1*   11 And]
As *Ro, Ca*   which *Σ:* with *E1:* who *LF:* that *Ro, Ca*   12 And] As *LF, Ro, Ca*
which] that *LF, Ro, Ca, R*   play: *E2:* ∼‸ *E1*   13 poetrie *E2:* poetrre *E1*
14 Dacus *Σ: om. E1*

In Priscum. 31   *MSS.: LF, Ro, Ca, F, R, H*
    1 When *E2:* Whhen *E1*   2 streetes *Σ:* streete *E1, R, Ca*   4 thus, *ed.:*
∼, *E1*

In Brunum. 32   *MSS.: LF, Ro, Ca, R, H*   *Layout normalized.*
    2 nine and Thirtie *MSS.:* Thirtie nine *Print*

Yet was he never, to confesse the truth,
But a dry starveling when he was at best.
   This gull was sick to shew his night cap fine,
   And his wrought Pillow overspred with lawne:
   But hath bin well since his griefes cause hath line,
   At Trollups by Saint Clements church in pawne.

In Francum. 33

When Francus comes to sollace with his whoore
He sends for rods and strips himselfe stark naked:
For his lust sleepes, and will not rise before,
By whipping of the wench it be awaked.
   I envie'him not, but wish I had the powre,
   To make my selfe his wench but one halfe houre.

In Castorem. 34

Of speaking well, why do we learne the skill,
Hoping thereby honor and wealth to gaine.
Sith rayling Castor doth by speaking ill,
Oppinion of much wit, and golde obtaine.

In Septimum. 35

Septimus lives, and is like Garlicke seene,
For though his head be white, his blade is greene.
This olde mad coult deserves a Martires praise,
For he was burned in Queene Maries dayes.

---

3 never, E2: ∼ˌ E1   8 in] at Ca, R, H
In Francum. 33   MSS.: LF, Ro, Ca, R, H
  5 envie' ed.: envie Print   I had Σ: he had E1   6 one halfe] halfe an Ro, Ca
houre. E2: ∼ˌ E1
In Castorem. 34   MSS.: LF, Ro, Ca, R, H
  3 Sith] When Ro, Ca
In Septimum. 35   MSS.· LF, Ro, Ca, F, R, H

Of Tobacco. 36

Homer of Moly, and Nepenthe sings,
Moly, the Gods most soveraigne hearbe divine.
Nepenthe, Hellens drinke which gladnes brings,
Harts griefe expells, and doth the wits refine.
    But this our age an other worlde hath founde,   5
    From whence an hearb of heavenly power is brought,
    Moly is not so soveraigne for a wounde,
    Nor hath Nepenthe so great wonders wrought.
It is Tobacco, whose sweet subtile fume,
The hellish torment of the Teeth doth ease   10
By drawing downe, and drying up the rume,
The mother and the nurs of ech disease.
    It is Tobacco which doth colde expell,
    And cleeres the'obstructions of the arteries,
    And surfets threatning death, digesteth well,   15
    Decocting all the stomacks crudities.
It is Tobacco which hath power to clarifie,
The clowdie mistes before dim eies appearing,
It is Tobacco which hath power to rarefie,
The thick grose humour which doth stop the hearing.   20
    The wasting Hectick and the quartaine fever,
    Which doth of Phisick make a mockerie,
    The gowt it cures, and helps il breaths for ever,
    Whether the cause in Tooth or stomacke be.
And though ill breaths were by it but confounded,   25
Yet that vile Medicine it doth far excell,
Which by sir Thomas Moore hath bin propounded,
For this is thought a gentleman-like smell.
    O that I were one of thiese mountiebankes,
    Which praise their oyles, and pouders which they sel,   30

Of Tobacco. 36   MSS.: LF, Ca, R, H, L (lines 1–12 only).   Layout normalized.
   2 Moly, ed.: ~ʌ Print   3 Nepenthe, ed.: ~ʌ Print   Hellens MSS.: Hekens
E1: Hevens E2   which Σ: with E1: that R, H   9 subtile MSS.: substanciall
Print   14 the' ed.: the Print   15 death, ed.: ~ʌ Print   17 which]
that R, H   18 mistes] mist H, R: lines 18–20 om. LF   19 which] that R,
H, Ca   20 which] that R, H hearing. ed.: ~, E1: ~ʌ E2   22 mockerie,
E2: ~: E1   24 Tooth Σ: Teeth E1, Ca, R, H   25 breathsʌ . . . confounded,
E2: ~, . . . ~ʌ E1   26 vile MSS.: om. Print   27 propounded, E2: ~. E1
28 smell. ed.: ~, Print   29 thiese] those LF: the Ca, H   30 their]
the LF, Ca   sel, E2: ~ʌ E1 (full line)

My customers would give me coyne with thankes,
  I for this ware, so smooth a Tale would tell:
Yet would I use none of those tearmes before,
  I would but say, that it the pox wil cure:
This were inough, without discoursing more,   35
  All our brave gallants in the towne t'alure.

In Crassum. 37

Crassus his lies are not pernitious lies,
  But pleasant fictions, hurtfull unto none:
But to himselfe, for no man counts him wise,
  To tell for truth, that which for false is knowne.
    He sweares that Gaunt is threescore miles about,   5
    And that the bridge at Paris on the Seine,
    Is of such thicknes, length and breadth, throghout
    That sixscore arches can it scarse sustaine.
He sweares he saw so great a dead mans scull,
  At Canterbury digde out of the grounde: 10
That woulde containe of wheat, three bushels ful,
  And that in Kent, are twentie yeomen founde,
    Of which the poorest every yeere dispendes
    Five thousand pound: these and five thousand moe
    So oft he hath recited to his friendes,   15
    That now himselfe, perswades himselfe tis so:
But why doth Crassus tel his lies so rife,
  Of bridges, Townes, and things that have no life?
    He is a lawyer, and doth wel espie,
    That for such lies an action will not lie.   20

---

31 would] should *MSS.*   thankes, *E2*: ~. *E1*   32 so smooth *Σ*: forsooth
E1: so faire *H*   tell: *E2*: ~, *E1*   33 those *Σ*: these *E1, H*   34 but *E2*:
hut *E1*   wil] would *MSS.*   35 This] y^t *R, Ca*: It *H*   36 our] the *Ca, R, H*
gallants in the towne t'alure] English gallants to allure *R, H*   t'alure. *E2*: ~, *E1*

In Crassum. 37   *MSS.*: *LF, Ro, Ca, F, R, H*

 1 not] no *F, R, H*   11 ful, *E2*: ~, *E1* (*full line*)   13 yeere] day *F, R, H*
dispendes‸ *E2*: ~, *E1*   14 moe‸ *E2*: ~, *E1*   15 recited] repeated *F, R:*
reported *H*   17 his] these *F, R:* those *H*   18 life? *E2*: ~. *E1*

In Philonem. 38

Philo the gentleman, the fortune teller,
The schoolemaister, the midwife and the bawde,
The conjurer, the buyer and the seller,
Of painting which with breathing wil be thawde,
    Doth practise Phisicke, and his credite growes,   5
    As doth the ballade-singers auditorie,
    Which hath at Temple Bar his standing chose,
    And to the vulgar sings an ale-house storie.
First standes a Porter, then an Oyster wife
Doth stint her crie and stay her steps to heare him,   10
Then comes a cutpurse ready with his Knife,
And then a cuntrey Client presseth neere him,
    There stands the Cunstable, there stands the whore,
    And harkning to the song mark not ech other.
    There by the Serjeant standes the debtor poore,   15
    And doth no more mistrust him then his brother:
Thus Orpheus to such hearers giveth Musique,
And Philo to such Patients giveth phisicke.

In Fuscum. 39

    Fuscus is free, and hath the worlde at will,
    Yet in the course of life that he doth leade:
    Hees like a horse which turning rounde a mill,
    Doth alwaies in the selfe same circle treade:
        First he doth rise at ten, and at eleven   5
        He goes to Gilles, where he doth eate till one,
        Then sees a play till sixe, and sups at seaven,
        And after supper, straight to bed is gone.

In Philonem. 38   *MSS.*: *LF, Ro, Ca, R, H*
   1 gentleman, the *MSS.*: lawyer and the *E1*: Gentleman and the *E2*   4 thawde,
E2: ~. *E1*   6 auditorie, *E2*: ~. *E1*   7 Bar *E2*: *l.c. E1*   9 standes]
sticks *LF, Ro, Ca, R*: comes *H*   wife∧ *E2*: ~, *E1*   10 crie∧ *ed.*: ~. *Print*
stay] stayes *MSS.*   11 his *Σ*: a *E1, Ca*   12 presseth *Σ*: passeth *E1*
13 whore, *E2*: ~∧ *E1* (*full line*)   17 Thus] This *LF, Ro, Ca, H*

In Fuscum. 39   *MSS.*: *LF, Ro, Ca, F, R, H*
   2 that] which *LF, F, R*   3 which] that *Ro, Ca, F, R, H*   5 ten, *E2*: ~∧
E1   7 Then sees *Σ*: Then sees he *E1*: Hee seeth *H, F*: And sees *R*

And there til tenne next day he doth remaine,
And then he dines, then sees a commedie: 10
And then he suppes, and goes to bed againe,
Thus rounde he runs without varietie:
    Save that sometimes he comes not to the play,
    But falls into a whoore house by the way.

In Afrum. 40

The smell feast Afer Travailes to the Burse
Twice every day the flying newes to heare,
Which when he hath no money in his purse,
To rich mens Tables he doth often beare:
    He tels how Gronigen is taken in,   5
    By the brave conduct of illustrious Vere:
    And how the Spainish forces Brest would win,
    But that they do Victorious Norris feare.
No sooner is a ship at Sea surprisde,
But straight he learnes the newes and doth disclose it, 10
No sooner hath the Turke a plot devisde
To conquer Christendom, but straight he knows it.
    Faire written in a scrowle he hath the names,
    Of all the widowes which the plague hath made,
    And persons, Times and places, still he frames, 15
    To every Tale, the better to perswade:
We cal him Fame, for that the wide-mouth slave
Will eate as fast as he wil utter lies:
For Fame is saide an hundreth mouthes to have,
And he eates more then woulde five score suffice. 20

13 Save] But *MSS.*

In Afrum. 40   *MSS.: LF, Ro, Ca, R, H*
  1 Afer *Σ*: after *E1, Ca*   4 often] ever *MSS.*   11–12 *Lines missing in E1;*
text from E2.   12 conquer *ed.*: conquerie *E2: line om. E1*   it. *ed.:* ~, *E2: line*
om. E1   14 made, *E2:* ~. *E1*   17 slave‸ *E2:* ~, *E1*   18 lies: *ed.:* ~‸
E1: ~, *E2*

In Paulum. 41

By lawfull mart, and by unlawfull stealth,
Paulus, in spite of envie, fortunate,
Derives out of the Ocean so much wealth,
As he may well maintaine a Lordes estate.
    But on the lande a little gulfe there is,
    Wherein he drowneth all that wealth of his.

In Licum. 42

Lycus which lately is to Venice gone,
Shall if he do returne, gaine three for one:
But ten to one, his knowledg and his wit,
Wil not be bettered nor increasde a whit.

In Publium. 43

Publius student at the common law,
Oft leaves his bookes, and for his recreation:
To Paris Garden doth himselfe Withdrawe,
Where he is ravisht with such delectation
As downe amongst the dogges and beares he goes,   5
Where whilst he skipping cries To head, To head,
His Satten doublet and his velvet hose,
Are all with spittle from above be-spread.
Then is he like his Fathers cuntrey hall,
Stinking with dogges, and muted all with haukes.   10

In Paulum. 41   *MSS.: LF, Ro, Ca, F, R, H*
    2 Paulus *E2*: Paules *E1*   Paulus, . . . envie, *ed.*: ~ʌ . . . ~ʌ *Print*   fortunate,
E2: ~: *E1*   3 Ocean so much *LF, Ro, F*: Oceans so much *Print*: Ocean sea
much *R*: Ocean sea so much *Ca*: Ocean much *H*   6 that *LF, Ro, R*: the *Σ*:
this *E2*

In Licum. 42   *MSS.: LF, Ro, Ca, F, R, H*
    1 which] that *Ro, F, R, H*   4 nor *E2, Ca, Ro*: or *Σ*

In Publium. 43   *MSS.: LF, Ro, Ca, R, H*
    3 Garden *ed.*: *l.c. Print*   5 As] That *R, H* dogges and beares *Σ*: Beares and
dogges *E1*   6 Where *Σ*: were *E1* head, ² *E2*: ~. *E1*   9 Then is he like
his *Σ*: When he is like a *E1*   10 with dogges] of doggs *R, H*

And rightly too on him this filth doth fall,
Which for such filthie sports his bookes forsakes,
    Leaving olde Ployden, Dier and Brooke alone,
    To see olde Harry Hunkes and Sacarson.

In Sillam. 44

When I this proposition have defended,
A cowarde cannot be an honest man,
Thou Silla seemest foorthwith to be offended:
And holdes the contrarie and sweres he can.
But when I tel thee that he will forsake   5
His dearest friend, in perill of his life,
Thou then art changde and saist thou didst mistake,
And so we ende our argument and strife.
    Yet I thinke on, and thinke I thinke aright,
    Thy argument argues thou wilt not fight.   10

In Dacum. 45

Dacus with some good collour and pretence,
Tearmes his loves beautie silent eloquence:
For she doth lay more collours on her face,
Then ever Tullie usde his speech to grace.

In Marcum. 46

Why dost thou Marcus in thy miserie,
Raile and blaspheme, and call the heavens un-kinde,

---

11 And rightly too this filth doth on him fall *LF, R*: And rightly to his fitts doth on him fall *Ca*: And rightly doth such filth upon him fall *H*: And rightly so this filth on him doth fall *Ro*   12 Which] who *LF*: that *R, H*   sports *Σ*: spots *E1* forsakes *MSS.*: forsake *Print*   13 Leaving] And leaves *Ca, R, H*

In Sillam. 44   *MSS.: LF, Ro, Ca, H*
   1 have *LF, Ca*: had *Σ*   9 on *Σ*: oft *Print*: om. *H*

In Dacum. 45   *MS.: Ro*
   4 his *E2*: hig *E1*

The heavens do owe no Kindenesse unto thee,
Thou hast the heavens so litle in thy minde:
    For in thy life thou never usest prayer,
    But at primero, to encounter faire.

Meditations of a Gull. 47

See yonder melancholie gentleman,
Which hoode-winked with his hat, alone doth sit,
Thinke what he thinkes and tell me if you can,
What great affaires troubles his litle wit.
    He thinkes not of the war twixt France and Spaine,   5
    Whether it be for Europs good or ill,
    Nor whether the Empire can it selfe maintaine
    Against the Turkish power encroching stil.
Nor what great Towne in all the Netherlandes,
The states determine to besiege this spring,   10
Nor how the Scottish pollicie now standes,
Nor what becomes of th'Irish mutining.
    But he doth seriouslie bethinke him whether
    Of the gull people he be more esteemde,
    For his long cloake, or for his great blacke Feather,   15
    By which each gull is now a gallant deemde.
Or of a Journey he deliberates,
To Paris Garden cocke-pit or the play:
Or how to steale a dogge he meditates,
Or what he shall unto his mistris say: 20
    Yet with these Thoughts he thinks himselfe most fit
    To be of Counsell with a King for wit.

In Marcum. 46   *MS.: Ro*
  3 do owe *Σ*: draw *E1*   4 minde: *E2*: ∼ₐ *E1*

Meditations etc.   *MS.: Υ*   *Layout slightly normalized.*
  5 Spaine, *E2*: ∼ₐ *E1* (*full line*)   9 Netherlandes *ed.*: nether landes *Print*
10 states *Σ*: starres *E1*   spring, *E2*: ∼ₐ *E1*   12 th' *Σ*: ths *E1*   14 gull
Υ: guld *Print*   15 for *Σ*: om. *E1*   Feather, *E2*: ∼. *E1*   18 Garden *ed.: l.c.*
Print   cocke-pit] Cockpittes *Υ*   20 he *Σ*: he he *E1*   22 of] a *Υ*

Ad Musam. 48

Peace idle muse, have done, for it is time,
Since lowsie Ponticus envies my fame,
And sweares the better sort are much to blame
To make me so wel knowne for so ill rime:
    Yet Bankes his horse is better knowne then he,   5
    So are the Cammels and the westerne hog,
    And so is Lepidus his printed dogge:
    Why doth not Ponticus their fames envie?
Besides, this muse of mine, and the blacke fether,
Grew both together fresh in estimation,   10
And both growne stale, were cast away togither:
What fame is this that scarse lasts out a fashion?
    Onely this last in credit doth remaine,
    That from henceforth, ech bastard cast forth rime
    Which doth but savour of a Libel vaine,   15
    Shal call me father, and be thought my crime.
      So dull and with so litle sence endude,
      Is my grose headed judge, the multitude.

FINIS.

J.D.

Ad Musam. 48
  2 envies *E2*: ensues *E1*   4 so² *E2: om. E1*   rime: *ed.*: ∼ₐ *E1*: ∼, *E2*
7 his *E2*: hie *E1*   8 envie? *ed.*: ∼. *E1*: ∼, *E2*   9 Besides, *ed.*: ∼ₐ *Print*
fether, *E2*: ∼. *E1*   12 fashion? *ed.*: ∼. *E1*: ∼: *E2*   14 cast forth *E2*:
castforth *E1*   15 vaine, *E2*: ∼. *E1*   16 crime. *E2*: ∼, *E1*   18 judge,
E2: ∼ₐ *E1*

EPIGRAMS FROM MANUSCRIPT

Epigrams from Manuscript

In Hirum. [49]

Hirus doth pray his tenaunts all may dye
Before old Luscus whome hee deadly hates;
Hirus doth shew witt in his charitye,
For if all dye hee gaineth all their states.

In Meandrum. [50]

Meander is not as hee seemes to bee
In outward shape: a proper, tall, streight youth;
Nor is that his owne face which you doe see,
Nor doe his hands and leggs resemble truth:
   Though among strangers for a man he passe,
   Yet they that knowe him, knowe him for an asse.

In Gallum. [51]

Thou saiest thy daughter understands the Greeke,
And can in Latine and Italian prate;
Gallus, els where a sonne in law goe seeke,
A woman of soe many tongues I hate.

In Crispum. [52]

Crispus loves Musicke, no man more then hee;
And yet hee cares not greatly for the Lute,
Nor for the violls, nor the Symphonye
Of voyces, nor the cyterne, sackbutt, flute,

Epigrams from Manuscript. *Texts of Epigrams 50–9 from R, the only extant witness.*
Texts of Epigrams 49, 60–2 from the first MS. listed in apparatus for these poems. Layout,
enumeration, and punctuation supplied throughout, unless otherwise indicated.

In Hirum. 49   *MSS.:* R, H, Ro, Ca
  Title. 1 Hirum/Hirus] Lyrum/Lyrus *Ro*

Nor yet doth the Orpharion please him much,   5
Nor virginall, nor solemne organ sounde,
Nor yet the harpe, though *Phœbus* should it touch,
Nor yet the Regall, nor the Hoboy round:
    But if a Taber or a Bagpipe playe,
    Hee will admire it a whole summers day.   10

In Crispum. [53]

Crispus, if ever it could well be said
That one is all in beaten sattin cladd,
Of thee it justly may, that being araid
In sattin hast the bastinado had.

In Gellam. [54]

Gella of late is growne a Puritane:
Unlesse she jape, shee will not kisse a man.

In Decium. [55]

Decius is of a gentle disposition,
That in an hower will acquainted bee
With every man, but then note this condition:
Within an hower no man so straunge as hee.

In Bretton. [56]

Bretton, though thou wert vexed with the Rhewme,
Or with the Neopolitan disease,
Or with the cough that doth the lungs consume,
Or with the tickling murre, or all of these,
    Yet Bretton knowe that it were farre unfitt,
    For thee at every woord thou speakst to spitte.

52.7 *Phœbus ed.*: rom. R
56.1 Rhewme *ed.*: Rhewne R

In Mundayum. [57]

Munday I sweare shalbee a hollidaye,
If hee forsweare himselfe but once a daye.

In Floram. [58]

Flora will keepe her vawting house no more?
The queane is madd! How will shee eate and drinke?
How will she pay her honest surgeons skore,
That with his Lotium scoures her filthy sincke?
   You of the parrish, trust not her vaine oathes;
   Shee is preserved by the thinge shee loathes.

[In Floram.] [59]

Who saith that Flora hath the French disease?
Why shee can shake her legg, and stretch her arme,
She can drinke drunke and shee can jape with ease,
And though her breath stinks, it doth no man harme.
   Now I perceave whence this suspicion growes;
   Forsooth she speaks a little through her nose.

In Siderum. [60]

Narbo unto his neighbour Siderus sent,
Invitinge him and his unto his boord:
Thankes was retorned, for he was well content.
The waye to Narboes house laye through a forde.   5
   Siderus gave charge his wife on mule should ride;
   Shee littell knew what would betide that daye,
   And therefore wil'd the mule should have no guide,
   Nor wattred be, but only fedd with haye.

---

59. *Epigram 59 is joined to 58 in MS.*
In Siderum. 60 *MS.*: H
  5 on *ed.*: one *MS.* (On *frequently spelled* one *in H.*)   7 wil'd *ed.*: wild *H*

The mule then drye, his head then hastened downe,
And did his Mistress will, his mistriss drowne: 10
Siderus, then wandringe up the River side,
Mett one and asked if he did see his wife,
  Which through the ford did venture for to ride,
  Where hard misfortune made hir leave her life.
  If shee be drowned, looke down, quoth he, belowe,   15
  Yt is the likelyest waye your wife to finde;
Few thinges doe swime against the streme I know.
Siderus replyed, I am not of your mynde:
For dead shee flottes againste the streame, I feare,
Which in hir life did all against the haire.   20

In Valentem. [61]

Why marvaile you that Valence holds his tong?
Thinck you him wise therefore, you do him wrong:
Hee hath nor witt, nor reason, therefore muse not
If hee the instrument of Reason use not.

In Claium. [62]

Goe to the warrs, yonge gallant Claius, goe,
Thowe canst endure the warres necessities,
For in thy life thowe doest noe weaknes showe,
Nor peevish trickes, nor singularities.
  Thowe canst eate cheese and canst behold a Catt,   5
  And heare a dogg cracke bones and never sweate,
  Looke on a pigges head and not gape thereat,
  And see the salt fall downe and never freet;
Nor when a duck is to the table served
Wilt thowe ducke downe under the table deade,   10
Nor wilt thowe rage as if thowe shouldest be sterved
When he that sitteth next thee takes thy breade.

15 down *ed.*: doth *MS.*   20 haire *ed.*: heare *H*

In Valentem. 61   *MSS.: Ca, F, Ro*
  2 therefore] nay then *Ro*

In Claium. 62   *MSS.: Y, F, H, Ro*
  2 Thowe *Σ*: That *Y*   12–13 thee *ed.*: the *Y*   12 thee takes] doth take
Ro: takes uppe *F*

But like a gallant I have seene thee eate
Egges shells and all, a candle, and a glasse,
The burrs of Artichokes, and such vile meate   15
As never dogg did through his throat let passe.
Others can kill, but thowe canst eat thy foe;
Goe therefore to the warrs, yong Claius, goe.

16 As never dogg did] which scarse a dogge would *F*, *H*: which scarce a dogg
will *Ro*   18 yong Claius] goe Claius *Σ*

GULLINGE SONNETS

Title and text from Ms. Che.

[*Dedication.*]

To his good freinde Sir Anthony Cooke.

Here my Camelion Muse her selfe doth chaunge
To divers shapes of gross absurdities,
And like an Antick mocks with fashion straunge
The fond admirers of lewde gulleries.
Your judgement sees with pitty and with scorne   5
The bastard Sonnetts of these Rymers bace,
Which in this whiskinge age are daily borne
To theire owne shames, and Poetries disgrace.
Yet some praise those, and some perhappes will praise
Even these of myne: and therefore thes I send   10
To you that pass in Courte your glorious dayes,
That if some rich, rash gull these Rimes commend,
Thus you may sett his formall witt to schoole,
Use your owne grace, and begg him for a foole.
                                        J.D.

Gullinge Sonnets.

1

The Lover under burthen of his Mistress love,
Which lyke to *Ætna* did his harte oppresse:
Did give such piteous grones that he did move
The heav'nes at length to pitty his distresse.
But for the fates in theire highe Courte above   5
Forbad to make the grevous burthen lesse,
The gracious powers did all conspire to prove
Yf miracle this mischeife mighte redresse.
Therefore regardinge that the loade was such
As noe man mighte with one mans mighte sustayne,   10
And that mylde patience imported much
To him that shold indure an endles payne,
By their decree he soone transformed was:
Into a patiente burden-bearinge Asse.

2

As when the brighte Cerulian firmament
Hathe not his glory with black cloudes defas'te,
Soe were my thoughts voyde of all discontent
And with noe myste of passions overcast;
They all were pure and cleare, till at the last   5
An ydle, carles thoughte forthe wandringe wente,
And of that poysonous beauty tooke a taste
Which does the harts of lovers so torment.
Then as it chauncethe in a flock of sheepe
When some contagious yll breedes first in one,   10
Daylie it spreedes, and secretly doth creepe
Till all the silly troupe be overgone;
So by close neighbourhood within my brest,
One scurvy thoughte infecteth all the rest.

Gullinge Sonnets. 1.2 *Ætna ed.*: rom. *MS.*   1.6 burthen *ed.*: burhen *MS.* 1.7
gracious *ed.*: gracous *MS.*   1.13 their *ed.*: there *MS.*
  2.8 does *ed.*: doe *MS.*

3

What Eagle can behould her sunbrighte eye,
Her sunbrighte eye that lights the world with love,
The world of Love wherein I live and dye,
I live and dye and divers chaunges prove;
I chaunges prove, yet still the same am I,   5
The same am I and never will remove,
Never remove untill my soule dothe flye,
My soule dothe fly and I surcease to move;
I cease to move which now am mov'd by yow,
Am mov'd by yow that move all mortall hartes,   10
All mortall hartes whose eyes your eyes doth veiwe,
Your eyes doth veiwe whence Cupid shoots his darts,
Whence Cupid shootes his dartes and woundeth those
That honor you, and never weare his foes.

4

The hardnes of her harte and truth of myne
When the all seeinge eyes of heaven did see,
They streight concluded that by powre devine
To other formes our hartes should turned be:
Then hers as hard as flynte, a Flynte became,   5
And myne as true as steele, to steele was turned,
And then betwene our hartes sprunge forthe the flame
Of kindest love which unextinguish'd burned.
And longe the sacred lampe of mutuall love
Incessantlie did burne in glory brighte,   10
Untill my folly did her fury move
To recompence my service with despighte,
And to put out, with snuffers of her pride,
The lampe of love which els had never dyed.

5

Mine Eye, myne eare, my will, my witt, my harte,
Did see, did heare, did like, discerne, did love,
Her face, her speche, her fashion, judgement, arte,
Which did charme, please, delighte, confounde and move.

Then fancie, humor, love, conceipte, and thoughte   5
Did soe drawe, force, intyse, perswade, devise,
That she was wonne, mov'd, caryed, compast, wrought,
To thinck me kinde, true, comelie, valyant, wise.
That heaven, earth, hell, my folly and her pride
Did worke, contrive, labor, conspire and sweare   10
To make me scorn'd, vile, cast off, bace, defyed
With her my love, my lighte, my life, my deare;
So that my harte, my witt, will, eare, and eye
Doth greive, lament, sorrowe, dispaire and dye.

6

The sacred Muse that firste made love devine
Hath made him naked and without attyre;
But I will cloth him with this penn of myne
That all the world his fashion shall admyre:
His hatt of hope, his bande of beautye fine,   5
His cloake of crafte, his doblett of desyre;
Greife for a girdell shall aboute him twyne;
His pointes of Pride, his Iletholes of yre,
His hose of hate, his Codpeece of conceite,
His stockings of sterne strife, his shirte of shame;   10
His garters of vaine glorie, gaye and slyte,
His pantofels of passions I will frame;
Pumpes of presumption shall adorne his feete,
And Socks of sullennes excedinge sweete.

7

Into the Midle Temple of my harte
The wanton Cupid did himselfe admitt,
And gave for pledge your Eagle-sighted witt
That he wold play noe rude uncivill parte.
Longe tyme he cloak'te his nature with his arte,   5
And sadd, and grave, and sober he did sitt;
But at the last he gan to revell it,
To breake good rules, and orders to perverte.
Then love and his yonnge pledge were both convented
Before sadd Reason, that old Bencher grave,   10

5.11 off *ed.*: of *MS.*

Who this sadd sentence unto him presented
By dilligence, that slye and secreate knave:
That love and witt for ever shold departe
Out of the Midle Temple of my harte.

8

My case is this, I love Zepheria brighte.
Of her I hold my harte by fealtye
Which I discharge to her perpetuallye,
Yet she thereof will never me accquite.
For now supposinge I withhold her righte,   5
She hathe distrein'de my harte to satisfie
The duty which I never did denye,
And far away impounds it with despite.
I labor therefore justlie to repleave
My harte which she unjustly doth impounde,   10
But quick conceite which nowe is loves highe Shreife
Retornes it as esloynde, not to be founde;
Then, which the lawe affords, I onely crave
Her harte for myne in withername to have.

9

To Love my lord I doe knightes service owe,
And therefore nowe he hath my witt in warde;
But while it is in his tuition soe
Me thincks he doth intreate it passinge hard.
For thoughe he hathe it marryed longe agoe   5
To Vanytie (a wench of noe regarde)
And nowe to full, and perfect age doth growe,
Yet nowe of freedome, it is most debarde.
But why should love, after minoritye,
When I am past the one and twentith yeare,   10
Perclude my witt of his sweete libertye
And make it still the yoake of wardshippe beare?
I feare he hath an other Title gott,
And holds my witt now for an Ideott.

Mr Davyes.

8.11 Shreife *ed.*: Sheife *MS*.

POEMS
NOT HITHERTO ASCRIBED
TO DAVIES

[On the Marriage of Lady Elizabeth Hatton to Edward Coke.]

[1]

Caecus the pleader hath a lady wedd,
  And swelling steppes into his velvet gowne,
But in her wombe a Timpanye was bredd,
  Which swelling up, doth bring his swelling downe.

His pride thus turnd into an angrye frowne,   5
  He sighes, and brawles, and scratcheth face and head,
And then he weepes to heare men talke and rowne,
  Feareing ech tongue should tell howe he hath spedd.

But why should Caecus so himself torment?
  Brought she the mouth? so did she bring the meate;   10
And he him self doth still increase the rent,
  And every daye doth newe possessions get.

Toyle not so much, resigne her half thy cares;
Buy thou the land, let her provide the heires.

[2]

Upon the Astrian hills the mountayne Mare,
  Impregned by the breath of Westerne winde,
Bringes fourth her colte, not of dull stallions kinde,
  Brave sprighted beast more swifter and more fayre;

[On the Marriage etc.] *MSS.: Υ (poems 1–11); A27, A28 (poems 1–6). For titles of series in manuscript see descriptions of MSS. in Bibliography. Text from Υ for poems 1–11. Layout from Υ, slightly normalized.*
   1.2 velvet *ed.*: vellet Υ   1.4 Which . . . his Σ: That . . . the Υ   1.5 into] to Σ   1.8 tell howe Σ: tell him howe Υ   1.13 Toyle A27: Deale Υ: Tort A28   2.4 sprighted Σ: spighted Υ   swifter and Σ: swift, eke Υ

On Holborne hills behold an acte more rare: 5
    Aeolus him self of late blewe up the skirte
Of fayre Olympia whistling there a spirte,
    To get her future spouse a heavenlye heire.

O happy man, the gods delight full care,
    Brother to Phillip king of Macedon,   10
Well maye thy sonne with greatest kinges compare,
    Yf fates doe prosper what is well begonne.

What Alexander lackt he conquer shall,
Unlesse before his tyme thou purchase all.

[3]

What if thy wife were privement enciente?
    Th'enfant is thine by course of common lawe.
Grosse were thy wittes, yf she were grossement,
    Not to see that which every other sawe.

But love and lucre makes a man a dawe,   5
    Desire of praye did overcome thy sent;
Till after witt did shame and sorrowe drawe,
    Seing thy disgrace made but a meriment.

Learne to be wise, and be noe more so rashe,
    The hastye bitch bringes fourth the blindest whelps; 10
Courage, what though the vulgar laugh a crashe?
    A mischeife done vaine sorrowe never helpes.

Let noe man saye a silly womans tayle
Hath put a laywer to a *Jeofayle*.

[4]

Followe thy booke, and let Primero goe,
    Fond lawyer plye the trade thou knowest best,
That throughly yet the bommecard doest not knowe,
    The packe, the privye marke, the sparrowes nest.

2.5 On *ed.*: One *Υ*   hills *Σ*: hill *Υ*   2.7 Olympia *ed.*: Olympa *Υ* (*as throughout in Υ*).   there *ed.*: their *Υ*   2.11 compare *ed.*: Compare *Υ*   2.13 conquer *ed.*: Conquer *Υ*   3.1 enciente *ed.*: in sent *Υ*   3.2 Th'enfant *ed.*: Thenfant *Υ*   3.8 thy *Σ*: that *Υ*   3.10 The *Σ*: Thy *Υ*   3.12 mischeife *ed.*: misceife *Υ*   3.14 *Jeofayle ed.*: Jeo fayle *Υ*   4.4 sparrowes *Σ*: woodcockes *Υ*

Els shuffle well before thou setst thy rest;   5
　　Looke to the cut of wilye playeing foe,
And have an eye still to the dealing, least
　　A grosse encounter give thy rest a blowe.

Witnes the lucke that thou hast had of late,
　　Which lost it all by one deceiptfull tricke;   10
Too fayre a gamester for so slie a mate,
　　That stoppes a card and playes upon the nicke.

When all was up the vie before was made
And thou neare sawest yt till the game was plaid.

[5]

Madam Olympia rideth in her coach,
　　And goeth to church, and traverseth the towne
Yet greene and pale, to shake off her reproache
　　By takeing witnes of her belly downe.

The people laugh, the wives both blush and frowne,   5
　　Sayeing, what shame is this to weomanhead!
Acteon poutes, and clappes upon his crowne
　　A case of Cappes to hide his velvet head.

All will not help, though he a Turbane weare
　　Bigger then that of *Sulton Solyman*;   10
The best is theirfore patiently to beare
　　The Dianes badg till mewing tyme and then

To geld himself by licence of his wife:
So maye he live a pollard all his life.

4.12 playes *Σ*: playe *Υ*   4.13 vie *A27:* pie *Σ*   5.3 off *ed.*: of *Υ*
5.6 is this to weomanhead *Σ*: is it this to weoman he *Υ*   5.7 poutes *ed.*:
pootes *Υ*   5.8 velvet *ed.*: vellet *Υ*   5.9 Turbane *Σ*: Turface *Υ*
5.12 The Dianes] his *Cynthian A27:* his Scithian *A28*   mewing *ed.*: muing *Υ*
5.14 live *Σ*: prove *Υ*

[6]

Holla my muse, leave Caecus in his greife,
    And turne the force of thy two edged penne
To punishe Meochus as a arrand theife,
    Filcher of ladyes, murtherer of men.

Soone is it said, but first we must him ken,   5
    Then catch him, then demaund of lawe reliefe;
The uncoth fellowe lurketh in his denne,
    Scorning the judge his censure and repriefe.

Let dame Olympia bring him to be tried,
    Or Caecus that can canvas such a case;   10
Find me the fault, convict or not deniede,
    My pen shall damne him for his lacke of grace.

Still to be flyeing and yet never fledd,
    By Eves fayre ofspring till he shalbe dead.

[7]

A widdowe fayre, and fresh, and fat, and full,
Well fed, well taught, well used from her wadle,
Loathing to lye alone, desired a pull,
And wisht a rider for her ritchest saddle.

A Cooke she had that brought her breakfast uppe,   5
His meate or somwhat so well liked was
As she must have him drinke of her owne cuppe.

. . . .

So long he plaid as she was pleased so well,
(Feeding o fat ech morning by her lover)   10
That was the widdowes belly ganne to swell,
And she must have a mate that scape to cover.

Beleeve me Cooke, thou art not much beguild,
Thy Lady trulye sweares its a Cookes childe.

6.8 censure and repriefe *Σ*: censure, sentence and reproofe *Y*   7.8 *MS. lacks*
line 8.

[8]

A Lady meaning with a Cooke to marry,
Though much disparaged by such a match,
Whilest he woed longer then she listes to tarry,
Her hungry appetite gapt for a snatche.

The pregnant guilefull girle stole many a bitt,   5
Yet for names sake, she had it of her Cooke,
Who fedd the calf, who ere must father it,
And gave him puddinge whilest he plied his booke.

Thus lackeing yet for Love she bare the Cooke
She fed her self to the'full with kitchinne stuffe;   10
What though her belly swell, he must it brooke;
Blind busserd, nowe it bootes him not to snuffe.

The faults not foule, ift happe the babe prove fayre:
A young Cookes child to be an old Cokes heire.

[9]

What can she saye? sith all the world hath seene
Her belly being so hugh before her time.
Help to excuse her pleasures, lovely Queene,
For shees undone, and done, and put in rime.

Yf she denies the fact triall reproves her,   5
For its noe tympany, the midwife sware;
Yf she confesst the man, oh he that loves her
Must leave the sport, which she maye not forbeare.

O *Esculapius* help her, great allaye
This naturall, unnaturall high swelling,   10
But girdes her not when men for mothers praye,
Yet Davids helpd her with good councell telling.

8.10 the' *ed.*: the *Y*   9.7 he that *ed.*: that he *MS.*   9.12+ *Final couplet*
missing in *MS.*

[10]

Didst thou ere heare the bargemans merry tale
Of the old lawyer by his wife cornuted?
And howe the elf devisd a prittye tale
To excuse the fault by his more vile reputed?

Then but compare the story to this time,   5
And thou wilt thinke it to be lawiers lucke,
When old and young to beutyes bed they clime,
To chaung their velvet head as doth the bucke.

For all alike, *Cocus* or *Jocus* nowe
Hath found his wife pusht with anothers pinne,   10
Yet feares she not at all his beetle browe,
But beares it boldly out as it went in.

Sweareing sith he was found a case to bugger,
She put her case to one can better tugger.

[11]

A covetous lawier a free Lady wonne;
Ere he began, yet had another donne,
And as all vice contagious is by kinde,
He her infected with a covetous minde.

And nowe though of her owne she had good stoore,   5
Yet seekes she still of others to get more;
Her vessel is full laden with full weight,
Yet though she sinckes theirwith, she seekes more fraight.

O covetous humor, howe strong is thy desire?
Though downe she fall theirby she would mount higher,   10
Which sawe her *Ganimed*, and wisht him to light,
Feareing his weight would hinder his quicke sprit.

In heavy plight and with her burthen charged,
She laid her downe, and laughd, and wisht her paine inlarged.

[Finis]

10.1 bargemans *ed.*: bargaines *MS.*   10.8 velvet *ed.*: vellet *T*

[On the Marriage of Lady Mary Baker to Richard Fletcher, Bishop of London]

[12]

The pride of Prelacy, which now longe since
Was banish't with the Pope, is sayd of late
To have arivd' at Bristowe, and from thence
By Worce'ster into London brought his state,
Wher, puffed up with more then vanity,   5
He quite forgetts his calling and his place;
And like a compound of extremity,
He beares of Lust the hart, of Pride the face.
None but a lady can content his eyes,
None but a whore his wanton lust suffice.   10

[13]

The Romaine Tarquine in his folly blind,
Of faire chast Lucres did a Lais make;
But our proud Tarquin beares a better mind,
And of a Lais doth a Lucrece make;
And she as not confirmed in her fayth,
Will now be truly Bishopped she sayth.

[14]

John London was condemnd for spoiling wood,
And now Dick London Commons doth enclose;

[On the Marriage etc.] *Text of poems 12–16 from Ro. The individual apparatus to each of poems 12–16 lists the witnesses used in constructing the text. Title supplied.*
    12 *MSS.: Ro, A58, Tan–I*   12. 1–2 which now . . . Was] which hath . . . bin
Tan–I   12.5 with more then vanity *Σ*: more with variety *Ro*   12.6 for-
getts *A58*: forgott *Σ*   and his *Σ*: leavd' his *Ro*   12.9 can *ed.*: Can *Ro*   can
content his] for his lordlyke *Tan–I*   13. *MSS.: Ro, A58, Tan–I*   13.2 Did
fayre chast Lucrece for a Lais take *A58*   13.3 our . . . better *Σ*: now . . .
braver *Ro*
13.4 He dothe a Layis for his Lucrece take *Tan–I*:
    He of a *Lays* doth a *Lucrece* make *A58*
13.5 And she as not . . . in *A58*: She being not . . . of *Ro*:
    And she not yet . . . in *Tan–I*
13.[7–8] If Fletcher wedded to amend her misse
    Good Fletcher did an honest deed in this *Ro*: om. *Σ*
14. *MSS.: Ro, A58, Tan–I*

He sought his private, this the publicque good,
And both their Credditt by their gettinges lose.
Now tell me Martin, whethers gaine is more?
He sould the wood, and this hath bought a whore.

[15]

It is a question in Heraldry
What name proud Prelates ladyes now may beare:
Though London like she bee of all trades free,
And longe hath bin a London occupier,
Her Lord of London cannot London give;   5
It is his owne but as he holdes his place:
And that so proud a foole in it doth live,
It was but superfluity of grace.
And lady Fletcher lesse she may be namd;
How can a viccars sonne a Lady make?   10
And yet her ladyshipp weare greatly shamd'
If from her Lord she should no tytle take;
Wherfore they shall devide the name of Fletcher:
He my Llord F, and she my Lady Letcher.

[16]

If any aske why Tarquin ment to marry,
It better is to marry then to burne;
If any why he could no longer tarry,
The devill ought his pride a shamefull turne.
If any why he would a lady wedd,   5
It was because he would a miter weare;
If why a lady of a common bedd,
The match was equall, both had Common geare.

---

15 *MSS.: Ro, A58, LF, R, Tan-I*   15.1 question in *Tan-I, LF*: question doubt-
full in *Ro*: question now in *A58*: question made in *R*   15.4 London] common
R, A58   15.5 cannot *ed.*: Cannot *Ro*   15.6 It is his owne] Its none of
his *R*   15.7 foole] preist *LF*   15.8 was] is *R*   15.9 . . . she may . . .
Σ: . . . may she . . . *Ro, A58*: And Lady Fletcher ought she not be named *Tan-I*
15.10 can *ed.*: Can *Ro*   15.11 greatly] clearly *R*   15.14 Llord F] Lord
Foole *LF (marginal alteration)*   16. *MSS.: Ro, A58, LF, R, Tan-I*   16.6 It
was because he would a *Σ*: By cause he would a double *Ro*

But yet if any will the reason find
Why he, that lookt as lofty as a steeple,   10
Should be soe base as for to come behind
And take the leavinges of the Common people:
Tis playne, for in processions, you know,
The preist must after all the people goe.

[Finis]

[17]
[Love's All.]

I love thee not for sacred chastitie,
Who loves for that? nor for thy sprightly wit:
I love thee not for thy sweete modestie,
Which makes thee in perfections throane to sit.

I love thee not for thy inchaunting eye,   5
Thy beauties ravishing perfection:
I love thee not for unchast luxurie,
Nor for thy bodies faire proportion.

I love thee not for that my soule doth daunce,
And leap with pleasure when those lips of thine   10
Give Musicall and gracefull utterance,
To some (by thee made happie) poets line.

I love thee not for voice or sweet or small,
But wilt thou know wherefore? faire sweet for all.

16.10 lookt] lookes *Tan-I, R*   16.11 come *ed.*: Come *Ro*   16.13 proces-
sions, you] procession yow *Tan-I*: processions as you *R*   17. *Printed texts: E1,*
E2 MS.: Dyce   Text from E1.   Title supplied.   17.1 chastitie *ed.*: chaststie *E1*
17.2 for *ed.*: fot *E1*   17.6 beauties *Dyce*: beautie *Print*   ravishing] ravishing
rare *Dyce*   17.7 for] for thy *Dyce*   17.10 thine‿ *ed.*: ~: *E1*   17.13 sweet
or *Dyce*: slender *Print* (*Dyce reads, with alterations:* I love thee not for voyce [~~or grace~~?]
\both sweet/ or small)

[18]

[A Lover out of Fashion.]

Faith (wench) I cannot court thy sprightly eyes,
With the base Viall placed betweene my Thighes;
I cannot lispe, nor to some Fiddle sing,
Nor run uppon a high strecht Minikin.

I cannot whine in puling Elegies,   5
Intombing Cupid with sad obsequies.
I am not fashioned for these amorous times,
To court thy beutie with lascivious rimes.

I cannot dally, caper, daunce and sing,
Oyling my saint with supple sonneting.   10
I cannot crosse my armes, or sigh ay me,
Ay me Forlorne: egregious Fopperie.

I cannot busse thy fist, play with thy hayre,
Swearing by Jove, Thou are most debonaire.
    Not I by Cock, but shall I tel thee roundly,   15
    Harke in thine eare, zounds I can ( ) thee soundly.

[19]

[No Muskie Courtier.]

Sweet wench I love thee, yet I wil not sue,
Or shew my love as muskie Courtiers doe;
Ile not carouse a health to honor thee,
In this same bezling drunken curtesie,
And when als quafde, eate up my bowsing glasse,   5
In glory that I am thy servile asse.

18. *Printed texts: E1, E2   MSS.: Dyce, Rosb   Text from E1.   Title supplied.   Layout normalized.*
    18.1 sprightly] piercing *Dyce*   18.2 Thighes; *ed.:* ∼∧ *E1*   18.5–8 *Rosb transposes couplets 7–8 and 5–6*   18.9 and] or *Dyce*   18.11–14 *Rosb transposes couplets 11–12 and 13–14*   18.11 or] and *MSS.*   18.13 fist *E2, Rosb:* fill *E1:* cheeks *Dyce*   18.15 I² Σ: *om. E1*   by Cock] by God *E2:* by Jove *Rosb:* in fayth *Dyce*
19. *Printed texts: E1, E2   MSS.: Dyce, Rosb   Text from E1.   Title supplied.*
    10.2 doe; *ed.:* ∼, *E1*   19.4 curtesie, *ed.:* ∼. *E1*   19.5 glasse, *ed.:* ∼. *E1*

Nor wil I weare a rotten burbon locke,
As some sworne pesant to a female smock.
Wel featurde lasse, Thou knowest I love thee deere,
Yet for thy sake I wil not bore mine eare   10
To hang thy durtie silken shootires there.
Nor for thy love wil I once gnash a brick,
Or some pied collours in my bonnet sticke.
    But by the chaps of hell to do thee good,
    Ile freely spend my Thrise decocted bloud.   15

[20]

[On Ben Jonson.]

Put off thy Buskins, Sophocles the great,
And morter tread with thy disarmed shankes,
For this mans head hath had a happier sweat,
For which the world doth con him little thankes;
    Blush *Seneca* to see thy feathers loose,
    Pluckt from a Swan and stuckt upon a goose.
              J. D.

[21]

[A Lady with Two Suitors.]

A Lady faire two suiters had,
A courtier and a cuntry swadd;
The Courtier first came lepping in
And tooke the Lady by the chin,
The cuntry swadd as he was blunt
Came tooke the lady by the elbow.
              J. D.

  19.7 locke, *ed.*: ~. *E1*   19.9 thee deere, *ed.*: the deere, *E1*   19.10 eare,
ed.: ~. *E1*   19.13 sticke *ed.*: stiche *E1*
20. [On Ben Jonson.]   *MSS.*: Ro, Che *Text from Ro. Title supplied.*
  Title. Of on that makinge a play stole much out of Seneca his Tragedies *Ro*: Of
one that had stolne much out of Seneca *Che*   20.1 off *ed.*: of *Ro*   20.3 hap-
pier *Che*: happie *Ro*   20.4 For which] whereof *Che*   little *Che*: double *Ro*
20.6+ J.D.] J.H. *Che*
21. [A Lady etc.] *MS.*: Ro *Title supplied.*

[22]

To his Mistress.

Sweet, what doth he deserve that loves you soe?
At least some litle favour he deserves,
Which you in Justice and in kindnes owe
To him which with such trew devotion serves.
Yet know you this, that he contentes him not   5
With a sweet glove, or an enameld ringe,
A feather of a fan, a trew loves knot,
A Cypresse skarffe, or such a light vaine thinge.
As for such tokens of [trew] love as theis
Children and fooles perhaps they may content,   10
But that which my aspiring thoughtes would please
Is farr more rare and farr more excellent:
Yet which with lesser cost may graunted bee,
For all is but a litle lecherye.

J. D.

[23]

In Curionem.

The great archpapist learned *Curio*
Is nowe perswaded to the Church to goe;
He nowe decernes the jugling fopperies
Wherewith the shaveling antiques bleard his eyes.

He nowe perceives that Romes ambition   5
Is author of Romes superstition:
Thankes be to God, and great *Basilius*,
Whose exhortacions have prevailed thus,
For to his powerfull argumentes alone
Curio attributes his conversion.   10

22. To his Mistress. *MS.: Ro*
    22.9 [trew] *ed.: om. MS.*
23. In Curionem. *MSS.: H39, M23, Ro, Y Text from Y. Title.* Lo. H. Howard
Ro: In Hen Com. North *H39:* Upon Henry Howard Earle of Northampton. 1603.
M23   23.3 decernes] perceaves *Ro, H39*   23.7 Thankes be to God *Ro,*
H39: Tanked be God *Y, M23*

He nought respecteth *Luther*, *Zuinglius*,
Melancthon, *Martyr*, *Oecolampadius*,
Ursinus, *Calvin*, *Buchanan*, nor *Knox*,
Nor English *Juell*, *Whitakers*, nor *Fox*,
Nor any grayebearde prelates of these times,   15
Though we accompt them reverend divines.
He saies their argumentes are sleight and weake,
Basilius only doth to purpose speake.
True *Curio*, true, *Basilius* on this theame
Is able to saye, more then all of them:
For he hath power to saye, recant thine error,
And thowe shalt be a privie counsellor.

[24]

In Cynnam.

Cynna is pleasd to render up againe
Into the handes of his high majestie
An office of inestimable gaine,
Singuler trust, and great authoritie,
Provided that he maye invested be   5
In the kinges grace and good opinion.
Beleeve me, *Cynna*, he deserv'd a fee
Whose Councell added that condicion;
For take you care to winne the princes grace,
And Ile take care you shall not loose your place.   10

[25]

In Milonem.

Since *Milo* travelled, his groundes surcease
To bringe fourth their accustomed encrease;
But *Milos* wife, more fruitefull then his feildes,
Encrease of issue in his absence yeildes.
The reason of this oddes I take to bee,
The groundes want husbanding, soe doth not she.

23.15 graybearde prelates *M23*: graybeardes prelates *Y*: grey beard Prelate *Ro*,
H39   23.16 Which we account our learnedest Devines *Ro, H 39*
24. In Cynnam. *MS.: Y*
25. In Milonem. *MS.: Y*

LOVE POEMS

Ten Sonnets, to Philomel.

Sonnet 1.

Upon Loves entring by his Eares.

Oft did I heare, our Eyes the passage were,
  By which Love entred to assaile our hearts;
  Therefore I guarded them, and voyd of feare
  Neglected the defence of other parts.
Love knowing this, the usuall way forsooke;   5
  And seeking, found a by-way by mine Eare:
  At which hee entring, my Hart pris'ner tooke,
  And unto thee, sweet *Philomel*, did beare.
Yet let my hart, thy hart to pittie move,
  Whose paine is great, although smal fault appeare: 10
  First it lies bound in fettering chaines of Love,
  Then each day it is rackt with hope and feare.
And with loves flames t'is evermore consumed,
Only, because to love thee it presumed.

Sonnet 2.

[*How Fame betrayed his heart.*]

O why did Fame my Hart to Love betray,
  By telling my Deares vertue and perfection?
  Why did my Traytor Eares to it convay
  That Syren-song, cause of my Harts infection?
Had I bene deafe, or Fame her gifts concealed,   5
  Then had my Hart been free from hopeles Love:
  Or were my state likewise by it revealed,
  Well might it *Philomel* to pitty move.

Ten Sonnets, to Philomel.   *Printed texts: A, B, C, D*   *Text from A.*
Sonnet 1. *2 assaile *Σ*: availe *A*   8 thee, . . . Philomel, *ed.*: ~ₐ . . . ~ₐ *A*
Sonnet 2. *Title supplied.*   3 convayₐ *ed.*: ~, *A*   4 song, *ed.*: ~ₐ *A*

Then shold she know how love doth make me languish,
   Distracting mee twixt hope and dreadfull feare: 10
Then shold she know my care, my plaints, and anguish,
   All which for her deere sake I meekely beare.
Yea I could quietly deaths paynes abide,
So that shee knew that for her sake I dide.

Sonnet 3.

Of his owne, and his Mistris sicknes at one time.

Sickenes entending my Love to betray,
   Before I should sight of my Deare obtaine:
Did his pale collours in my face display,
   Lest that my Favour might her favour gaine.
Yet not content herewith, like meanes it wrought,   5
   My *Philomels* bright beauty to deface:
And Natures glory to disgrace it sought,
   That my conceived Love it might displace.
But my firme Love could this assault well beare,
   Which Vertue had, not beauty for his ground: 10
And yet bright beames of beauty did appeare,
   Throgh sicknes vail, which made my love abound.
If sicke (thought I) her beauty so excell,
How matchlesse would it bee if shee were well?

Sonnet 4.

Another of her Sicknes, and Recovery.

Pale Death himselfe did Love my *Philomel*,
   When hee her Vertues and rare beutie saw:
Therefore hee sicknesse sent, which should expell
   His Rivall, life, and my Deere to him draw.
But her bright beauty dazeled so his Eyes,   5
   That his dart life did misse, though her it hitt:
Yet not therewith content, new meanes hee tries,
   To bring her unto Death, and make life flitt.

9, 11 know *ed*.: kno *A* (*full lines*)   11 plaints *Σ*: plants *A* anguish, *ed*.: ∼ₐ *A*
Sonnet 4. 3 expellₐ *ed*.: ∼, *A*   4 Rivall, *ed*.: ∼ₐ *A*

But Nature soone perceiving, that hee meant
 To spoyle her only Phœnix, her chiefe pride: 10
 Assembled all her force, and did prevent
 The greatest mischiefe that could her betide.
So both our lives and loves Nature defended,
For had shee dide, my love and life had ended.

Sonnet 5.

Allusion to Theseus voyage to Crete, against the Minotaure.

My Love is sayl'd, against dislike to fight,
 Which, like vild monster, threatens his decay:
 The ship is Hope, which by Desires great might,
 Is swiftly borne towards the wished Bay:
The company which with my Love doth fare,   5
 (Though met in one) is a dissenting crew;
 They are Joy, Greefe, and never sleeping Care,
 And Doubt, which ne'r beleeves good news for true.
Black Feare the Flag is, which my ship doth beare,
 Which (Deere) take downe, if my Love victor be: 10
 And let white Comfort in his place appeare,
 When Love victoriously returnes to mee,
Lest I from rocke Despayre come tumbling downe,
And in a Sea of Teares bee forc't to drowne.

Sonnet 6.

Upon her looking secretly out of a window as hee passed by.

Once did my *Philomel* reflect on mee
 Her Christall pointed Eyes as I passt by,
 Thinking not to be seene, yet would mee see;
 But soone my hungry Eyes their foode did spie.
Alas, my Deere, couldst thou suppose, that face   5
 Which needs not envy *Phœbus* cheefest pride,

Sonnet 5. *Layout normalized.* 8 Doubt *ed.*: *l.c. A* true. *ed.*: ~‸ *A* 9 Feare
ed.: *l.c. A*

Sonnet 6. *Title. of*] *at B, C, D*

Could secret bee, although in secret place,
  And that transparant glas such beams could hide?
But if I had beene blinde, yet Loves hot flame
  Kindled in my poore heart by thy bright Eye,   10
  Did plainely shew when it so neere thee came,
  By more then usuall heate, the cause was nie:
So though thou hidden wert, my hart and eye
Did turne to thee by mutuall *Sympathy*.

Sonnet 7.

[*Upon her Picture drawn and burning in his Hart.*]

When time nor place would let me often view
  Natures chiefe Mirror, and my sole delight;
  Her lively Picture in my hart I drew,
  That I might it behold both day and night,
But shee, like *Phillips* Son, scorning that I   5
  Should portray her, wanting *Apelles* Art,
  Commaunded Love (who nought dare hir deny)
  To burne the Picture which was in my Hart.
The more Love burn'd, the more her picture shin'd;
  The more it shin'de, the more my hart did burne: 10
  So what to hurt her picture was assign'd,
  To my Harts ruine and decay did turne.
Love could not burne the Saint, it was divine,
And therefore fir'd my hart, the Saints poore shrine.

Sonnet 8.

[*Of his Sun being eclipsed.*]

Whenas the Sun eclipsed is, some say
  It thunder, lightning, raine, and wind portendeth:
  And not unlike but such things happen may,
  Sith like effects my Sun eclipsed sendeth.

Sonnet 7. *Title supplied.*   6 portray her, wanting] portraiture, which wanting
B: portraiture which wanted C, D   her, *ed.*: ~ₐ A   9 burn'd, *ed.*: ~ₐ A
Sonnet 8. *Title supplied.*   *Title: om.* A, B: To the Sun of his mistris beauty
eclipsed with frownes C, D   1 say ₐ *ed.*: ~, A

Witnes my throat made hoars with thundring cries,   5
   And hart with loves hot flashing lightnings fired,
   Witnes the showers which stil fal from mine eies,
   And brest with sighs like stormy winds neare rived.
O Shine then once againe, sweete Sun on mee,
   And with thy beames dissolve clouds of dispaire,   10
   Whereof these raging Meteors framed bee,
   In my poore hart by absence of my faire,
So shalt thou prove thy Beames, thy heate, thy light,
To match the Sun in glory, grace, and might.

Sonnet 9.

Upon sending her a Gold Ring, with this Posie
Pure, and Endlesse.

If you would know the Love which I you beare,
   Compare it with the Ring, which your faire hand
   Shal make more pretious, when you shal it weare;
   So my Loves Nature you shall understand.
Is it of mettall pure? so you shall prove   5
   My Love, which ne're disloyal thought did stain.
   Hath it no end? so endles is my Love,
   Unlesse you it destroy with your disdaine.
Doth it the purer waxe the more tis tride?
   So doth my Love: yet herein they dissent,   10
   That whereas Gold the more tis purifi'd,
   By waxing lesse, doth shew some part is spent,
My Love doth wax more pure by your more trying,
And yet encreaseth in the purifying.

Sonnet 10.

[How she enchayned his Hart.]

My Cruell Deere having captiv'de my hart,
   And bound it fast in Chaynes of restles Love:

8 rived. *ed.*: ∼ₐ *A*   9 O *C, D: om. A, B*

Sonnet 9.   1 I you *Σ*: you I *A*   4 understand. *ed.*: ∼ₐ *A*   6 stain. *ed.*:
∼, *A*   13 your *Σ*: you *A*
Sonnet 10.   *Title supplied.*   *Title: om. A, B*: The Hearts captivitie *C, D*

Requires it out of bondage to depart,
   Yet is shee sure from her it cannot move.
Draw back (sayd shee) your hopelesse love from me,   5
   Your worth requireth a more worthy place:
   Unto your sute though I cannot agree,
   Full many will it lovingly embrace.
It may bee so (my Deere) but as the Sun
   When it appeares doth make the stars to vanish: 10
   So when your selfe into my thoughts do run,
   All others quite out of my Hart you bannish.
The beames of your Perfections shine so bright,
That straightway they dispell all others light.

Melophilus.

Elegies of Love.

[1]

Like as the divers fretchled Butter flye,
When winters frost is fallne upon his winge,
Hath onely left lifes possibility,
And lies halfe dead untill the cherefull Spring:

But then the Sunne, from his all quickning eye,   5
Darts forth a sparkle of the Livinge fire,
Which (with kinde heate) doth warme the frozen flye,
And with newe spirit his little breast Inspire:

Then doth hee lightly rise and spread his winges,
And with the Beames that gave him life doth playe,   10
Tasts every flower that on th'earthes bosoome springs,
And is in busye motion all the day:

6 requireth a more] requires a far more *B, C, D*   *Melophilus.*] I.D. *B, C, D*

Elegies of Love. *MSS.: L, L740 (Elegy 3 only) Text from L. Layout supplied. Elegy 1 is not grouped with the other Elegies in MS.*
Like as etc. 7 Which (with *ed. (Grosart)*: With which *MS.*   10 the *ed. (Grosart)*: they *MS.*   11 th' *ed.*: th *MS.*

Soe my gaye muse, which did my heart possesse,
And in my youthfull fantasie doth raigne,
Which cleard my forehead with her cheerefullnes,   15
And gave a lively warmth unto my Brayne,

With sadder studyes, and with grave conceite,
Which late my'Immagination entertaynd,
Beganne to shrinke, and loose her Active heate,
And dead as in a Læthargy remaynd.   20

Long in that senceles sleepe congeald shee laye,
Untill even now another heavenly eye,
And cleare as that which doth begett the daye,
And of a like revivinge simpathy,

Did cast into my eyes a subtile beame,   25
Which peirceinge deepe, into my fancy went,
And did awake my muse out of her dreame,
And unto her new life and vertue lent:

Soe that shee now begins to raise her eyes,
(Which yett are dazled with her beautyes raye)   30
And to record her wonted melodyes,
Although at first shee bee not full soe gaye.

[2]

. . . . . .
But those Impressions by this forme are staynd,
And blotted out as if they had not beene.

And yet if nothing else in mynde I beare,
[That] makes me not lesse learned then before,
For that in her as in a merrour cleare,   5
I see, and learne, far better things and more.

The students of the world and naturs booke,
Beauty and order in the world doe Noate;
She is my little world, on her I looke,
And doe in her the same perfections quoate: 10

18 my' *ed.*: my *MS.*

But those etc.   4 [That] *ed.*: *om. MS., but space left blank for missing word.*   learned
ed.: learnd *MS.*

For in her eyes the Beames of beauty shine,
And in her sweete beheaviour and her grace,
Order apears and comlines divine,
Befitting every tyme and every place.

3

Unto that sparkling wit, that spirit of fire,
That pointed diomond looke, that Ægles eye
Whose lyghtning makes audacity retire,
And yet drawes on respective modesty,

With wings of feare and love my spirit doth fly,   5
And doth therein a flame of fire resemble;
Which when it burnes most bright, and mounts most high,
Then doth it waver most and most doth tremble.

O that my thoughts were words, or could I speake
The tongue of Angels to expresse my mynd: 10
For mortall speach is far too faint and weeke,
To utter passions of so high a kynde.

You have a beauty of such life and light
As it hath power all wandring eyes to stay:
To move dombe tongues to speake, lame hands to write,   15
Stayd thoughts to run, hard harts to melt a way.

Yet painters can of this draw every line,
And every wittles person that hath eyes
Can see and Judg, and sweare it is divine:
For in those outward formes all fooles are wise.   20

But that which my admireing spirit doth veiw,
In thought whereof it would for ever dwell,
Eie never saw, the Pensill never drew,
Pen never could describe, tongue never tell.

Unto that etc.   2 pointed diomond looke] diamond-like aspect *L740*   6 re-
semble *ed.*: resemple *L*   9 or] O *L740*   10 Angels *ed.*: Angles *L*   19 see
ed.: se *L*   22 In *L740*: I *L*

It is the'invisible beauty of your mynd,   25
Your cleare Immagination, lively witt,
So tund, so temp'rd, of such heavenly kind,
As all mens spirits ar charmd, and rapt with it.

This life within begetts your lively looke,
As fier doth make all Metalls looke like fier;   30
Or your quicke soule by choise this body tooke,
As angells with bright formes themselves attire.

O that my brest might ope, and hart might cleave,
That so you might my silent wondring veiw:
O that you might my serveing spirit perceive,   35
How still with trembling wings it waites on you.

Then should you see of thoughts an endles chaine,
Whose links your beauties and your vertues bee:
Then should you see how your fair forme doth raigne
Through all the Regions of my fantesie.   40

Then should you fynde that I am yours as much
As ar your sharpe conceits borowd of none;
Or as your Native Beautye which is such
As all the world will sweare it is your owne.

                        4

As they that worke in Mines rich vaines beray
By some few garaines of Ore whereon they hit,
And as one letter found is oft a kay,
To many lines that ar in Cipher writt:

So I by your few loveing lines descry   5
Of your long hiden love the golden Mine,
And reade therin, with a true lovers eye,
Of the harts volume every secrett line.

25 the' *ed.*: the *L*   32 formes] Beames *L740*   34 wondring *L740*:
wandring *L*   35 might] could *L740*   37 see *ed.*: se *L*   38 beauties
L740: vertues *L*   39 your *L740*: yᵉ *L*   42 sharpe] quicke *L740*
43 Beautye which is *L740*: Beautyes that are *L*

As they etc. 2 they *ed.* (*Grosart*): the *MS.*

But what availes it now, alas, to know
That once a blessed man I might have beene?   10
Since I have lett, by lookeing downe too low,
My highest fortunes sore away unseene.

And yett if I had raisd my humble eyes
As high as heaven, I could not have discernd
Th'Invisible thoughts, which in your hart did rise,   15
Unles of you I had my lesson learnd.

But all was darke and folden up to me.
As soone might I my selfe, my selfe have tought
To read the blacke records of destiny,
As read the ridles of your silent thought.   20

But whereto may I best resemble this?
Your love was like the springing of a tree:
We cannot see the growing when it is,
But that it hath sprunge up, and growne, we see.

Or it is like to wealth by fairyes brought,   25
Which they bring still while they Invisible goe;
But all doth vanish and doth turne to nought
If once a man enricht, those fairyes know.

But now your love (say you) is dead and gone;
But my strong faith shall give it life againe: 30
By strength of fancy, Miricles are done,
And true beleefe doth seldom hope in vaine.

Your Phœnix love is unto Ashes turnd,
But now the fier of my affection true,
Which long within my hart hath kyndly burnd,   35
Shall spread such heate, as it shall live a new.

Or if the fyer of your Cælestiall love
Be mounted up to heaven and cannot dye,
Another slye *Prometheuse* will I prove,
And play the theife to steale it from the skye.   40

15 Th' *ed.*: Th *MS.*   *20 your *ed.*: the *MS.*   39 slye *Prometheuse ed.*: flye
Prome⸗theuse *MS.*

When you vouchsaft to love unworthy me,
Your love discended like a shower of raine,
Which on the earth, even senceles though she bee,
When once it falls returneth not againe.

Then why should you withdraw the heavenly dew,   45
Which fell sometymes on your dispairing lover?
Though then his earthly spirit full little knew,
How good an Angel did about him hover.

O you the glory of your sex and race,
You that all tymes and places hapie make,   50
You that in beeing verteous, vertue grace,
And make men love it better for your sake:

One sunbeame yet of favour cast on mee,
Let one kinde thought in your cleare fancy rise:
Love but a thought, or if that may not be,   55
Be pleasd that I may love; it shall suffise.

48 Angel *ed.*: Angle *MS.*

OCCASIONAL POEMS
AND
POEMS FROM ENTERTAINMENTS

[To George Chapman on his Ovid.]

Onely that eye which for true love doth weepe,
Onely that hart which tender love doth pierse,
May read and understand this sacred vierse
For other wits too misticall and deepe:

    Betweene these hallowed leaves *Cupid* dooth keepe   5
    The golden lesson of his second Artist,
    For love, till now, hath still a Maister mist
    Since *Ovids* eyes were closd with iron sleepe;

But now his waking soule in *Chapman* lives,
Which showes so well the passions of his soule,   10
And yet this Muse more cause of wonder gives,
And doth more Prophet-like loves art enroule:

    For *Ovids* soule, now growne more old and wise,
    Poures foorth it selfe in deeper misteries.

Another.

Since *Ovid* (loves first gentle Maister) dyed
He hath a most notorious trueant beene,
And hath not once in thrice five ages seene
That same sweete Muse that was his first sweet guide;

    But since *Apollo* who was gratified   5
    Once with a kisse, hunting on *Cynthus* greene,
    By loves fayre Mother tender Beauties Queene,
    This favor unto her hath not envied,

That into whome she will, she may infuse
For the instruction of her tender sonne,   10
The gentle *Ovids* easie supple Muse,
Which unto thee (sweet *Chapman*) she hath doone:

[To George Chapman etc.]   *Text from Chapman.   Layout and title supplied.*
  13 *Ovids* ed.: rom. *Chapman*
Another. *Text from Chapman. Layout supplied.*

Shee makes (in thee) the spirit of *Ovid* move,
And calles thee second Maister of her love.

[To Sir Thomas Egerton,
on the Death of his Second Wife, in 1599.]

You that in Judgment passion never show,
(As still a Judge should without passion bee)
So Judge your self; and make not, in your woë,
Against your self a passionate decree.

    Greef may become so weake a Spirit as mine;   5
    My prop is falne, and quenched is my light;
    But th'Elme may stand when withred is the vine;
    And though the Moone eclipse, the Sunne is bright.

Yet were I senslesse, if I wisht your Mind
In sensible, that nothing might it move;   10
As if a man might not bee wise and kind;
Doubtlesse the God of Wisdome and of Love,

    As Solomons braine he doth to you impart,
    So hath he given you Davids tender hart /

           Your Lordships in all humble Duties
           and condoling with your Lordship most
           affectionatly

           Jo. Davys.

[Epithalamion for the Marriage of Lady Elizabeth Vere
and William Stanley, Earl of Derby.]

Love not that Love that is a child and blynde,
But that Heroicke, honorable Love
Which first the fightinge Elements combinde,
And taught the world in harmony to move:

[To Sir Thomas Egerton etc.]   *Text, punctuation, and layout reproduce Davies's holo-*
graph, MS. TE.   *Title supplied.*
    8 [~~go downe~~] \eclipse/ MS.   11 bee [~~& be~~] \wise/ MS.
[Epithalamion etc.]   *Text:* MS. LF   *Title supplied.*   *Title:* Epithalamion Io: Dauisij
MS.

That God of Love, whose sweet attractive power   5
First founded cityes, and societyes,
Which linkes trewe frendes, and to each paramor
That virtewe loves, a virtewous Love affies.
This Love hath causd the Muses to record
Their sweetest tuens, and most celestiall,   10
To you sweet Lady, and to you great Lorde,
In honor of your joyfull nuptiall.
    And to their tuens this prayer they still apply,
    That with your dayes your joyes maye multiplye.

Clio.

Illustrious Lord, heire of that happy race   15
Which with great Lordshipps doth great Love inherit,
Raysd by the heavens unto that glorious place,
Which your great grawnseirs did by virtewe merit:
    And you sweete Lady, virtewes noble fayre,
    Whom when I name your grandsier, father, mother,   20
    Of all whose excellencies you are heire,
    I then extoll, and prayse above all other:
Your famous Auncestors eternall names
My diamond pen in adamant shall write,
And I will spread your owne younge Loving fames,   25
As far as *Phœbus* spreades his glorious Light.
    Still with my tuens importuninge the skye,
    That with your dayes your Joyes maye multiplye.

Thalia.

And I the merry Muse of Comedyes,
That with a marriage ever end my playe,   30
Will into mirth, and greatest joye arise,
While I applawd this blessed marriage daye.
    Yet will I sadly praye my Father *Jove*,
    That as crosse chaunce fought not agaynst your will
    In the fayre course of your most happy Love,   35
    So with out crosse ye maye continewe still.

20 mother *ed*.: Mother *MS.*   33 *Jove ed.*: *rom. MS.*

That as the voyce and *Echo* doe agree,
So maye you both, both doe, and saye the same,
And as your eyes beinge two, but one thinge see,
So maye ye to one end your actions frame.   40
    So shall your Lyves be a sweete harmonye,
    And with your dayes your Joyes shall multiplye.

Melpomene.

And I which sownd the tragicke tuens of warr,
Have Layd my harsh and fearfull Trumpe aside,
Wherwith I usd to rende the ayre a farr,   45
In service of your cosin, bewtious bride.
    Your most victorious cosin, warlike Vere,
    The glory of your glorious familye;
    A braver spirit the earth did never beare,
    Since first the fyer of lyfe came from the skye: 50
This fyery starre of *Mars* my trumpett tooke,
And put a warblinge lute betwine my handes,
And with a joyfull voyce and joyfull looke,
Sent me to blesse these sacred marriage bandes,
    And to commend his vowes to *Jove* on hie,   55
    That with your dayes your joyes maye multiplye.

Euterpe.

And I betwine whose lipps the ayre doth playe,
Chaunginge her wanton forme ten thousand wayes,
Will not distingwish one halfe note this daye,
Which shall not sownd both to your joye and prayse;   60
    For even your marriage doth sweete musicke make,
    Like two sweete notes matcht in an unisone,
    Where each from other doth full sweetnesse take,
    Where one could make no harmony aloane.
Longe maye you Joye such sympathye of Loves   65
As doth betwine the Elme and Vine remayne,

43 warr *ed.*: ware *MS.*   45 farr *ed.*: fare *MS.*   52 put *ed.*: but *MS.*
55 *Jove ed.: rom. MS.*

Or betwine palme trees, twinns, and turtle doves,
Wher in one Lyfe doth live the Lives of twayne.
   Longe live you in each other mutually,
   That with your dayes your Joyes maye multiplye.   70

Terpsicore.

And I whose cunninge feete with measurd motion
Expresse the musicke which my Sisters singe,
Will nowe in songes expresse my trewe devotion,
To you which to my Arte most honor bringe;
   For who can dawnce with better skill and grace,   75
   Then you great bridgroome, or then you fayr bride?
   Whether a solleme measure ye doe pase,
   Or els with swifter tuens more swiftly slide.
Still maye you dawnce, and keepe that measure still
In all your lyfe which you in dawncinge shewe,   80
Where both the man and woman have one will,
And both at once the selfe same paces goe.
   So shall you never drawe your yoke awry,
   But with your dayes your joyes shall multiply.

Erato.

And I the waytinge mayde of bewtyes Queene,   85
Which oft am wonte to singe of wanton Love,
Since I these sacred nuptials have seene,
An other godhead in my brest doth move;
   For nowe I singe of bewty of the minde,
   Which bewtifies the fayrest outward bewty,   90
   And of a passion which is never blinde,
   But waytes on virtewe with respectfull dutye.
O sacred Love, wher one loves only one,
Where each to other is a mirror fayre
Wherein them selves are each to other shone: 95
Such is your sacred love, illustrious payre,
   Whose fyer like *Vestas* flame shall never dye,
   But with your dayes your joyes shall multiplye.

75 grace *ed.* (*Childs*): dawnce *MS.*

Polyhimnia.

And I which with my gesture seeme to speake,
Will speake indeede, in honor of this daye,   100
And with my sweetest tuens the ayre will breake,
Which shall to *Jove* passe through the milkey waye.
   Even to the eares of *Jove* my tuens shall come,
   And be for you (sweete bride) a zelous praier,
   That as a cherye graft uppon a plumme,   105
   You maye be fruitfull in your isues fayre.
Or that you and your Love be like two streames,
Which meetinge after many windes and crookes,
Doe spread their mingled waves through many realmes,
And from them selves dirive a thousande brookes.   110
   And though the lesser loose her name therby,
   Yet with her dayes her Joyes shall multiplye.

Calliope.

And I which singe th'eroicke Love of Kinges,
Must use like notes whiles I your names rehearse,
For he which your great names in number singes,   115
With names of Princes doth adorne his verse.
   And princly is your match as gold and Pearle,
   Both bewtifull, each other bewtifie;
   So an earls daughter married to an Erle,
   Gives and receaves like honor mutually.   120
And as the purest cullors which alone,
Sett by themselves, imperfect bewty make,
Wher they are mingled and conjoynd in one,
One from an other lyfe and lustre take.
   So you beinge matcht, each other glorifie,   125
   That with your dayes your Joyes maye multiplye.

Urania.

But I the Muse of Heaven, to heaven will rayse ⟨you,⟩
And your fayre names in starry letters write,

113 singe *ed.*: signe *MS.*   127–40 *Bracketed letters, cut away in binding, supplied by editor.*

That they which dwell under both poles maye prayse you
And in rehearsall of your names delight. 130
    And you fayre Bride, shall like fayre *Cynthia* sh⟨ine,⟩
    Which beinge in conjunction with the Sunne,
    Doth seeme her beames and glory to resigne,
    But hath indeede more light and virtewe wonne.
Longe shall you shine on earth, like Lampes of heaven, 135
Which when you Leave, I will you stellifie;
To you sweet bride, shall *Hebes* place be given,
But your Lord shall his *Ganimedes* roome supplye.
    Till when I will invoke each dyetye,
    That with your Dayes your joyes maye multipl⟨ye.⟩ 140

[An Entertainment at Harefield.]

[A Lotterie.]

A Marriner with a Box under his arme, containing all the severall things following, supposed to come from the Carrick, came into the presence singing this Song.

[Song.]

    Cynthia queene of seas and landes,
    Thatt fortune every wher comandes,
    Sent forth fortune to the sea
    To trye her fortune every waye.
Ther did I fortune meete, which makes me now to singe, 5
Ther is no fishing to the sea, nor service to the kinge.

[A Lotterie] *Printed text: B MSS.:* A22, Con, Mann *(Note: B omits marginal notes.* A22 *omits Song.* Mann *omits Song and has only 16 Lots; its readings are to be assumed only where specifically cited.) Text of Song and Lots 1–34 from* Con. *Text of Lots 35–9 from* A22 *(these lots being omitted from* B, Con, Mann*). Prose from* B, *omitted by* A22, Mann. *Main title, layout, and enumeration supplied.*
Titles: The devyses [to] entertayne hir Majesty att Harfielde, the house of Sir Thomas Egerton Lord Keeper and his Wife the Countess of Darbye. In hir Majestys Progresse. 1602. *Con:* A Lotterie presented before the late Queenes Majestie at the Lord Chancellors house. 1601. *B:* Somme of the lotteries which were the last Summer at hir Majesties, being with the Lord Keeper. *Mann:* A Lottery Proposed before Supper at the Lord Chief Justice his House in the First Entrance: to hir Majestie, Ladies, Gentlewomen and Straungers. 1602. A22.
[Song.] 6 *nor* B: noe *Con*

All the nymphes of *Thetis* trayne
Did *Cynthias* fortune intertayne,
Many a Jewell, many a Jemme,
Was to her fortune broughte by them.   10
Hir fortune spedd so well, which makes me now to singe,
Ther is no fishing to the sea, nor service to the kinge.

Fortune thatt itt might be seene,
Thatt she did serve a royall Queene,
A Franke and royal hande did beare,   15
And cast hir fortunes every where.
Some toyes fell to my share, which makes me now to singe,
Ther is no Fishing to the sea, nor service to the kinge.

And the song ended, he uttered this short speech.

*God save you faire Ladies all: and for my part, if ever I be brought to answer
for my sinnes, God forgive me my sharking and lay Usurie to my charge. I am
a Marriner, and am now come from the sea, where I had the fortune to light
upon these few Trifles. I must confesse I came but lightly by them, but I noe
sooner had them, but I made a vow, that as they came to my hands by fortune,
so I would not part with them but by fortune. To that end I have ever since
caried these lots about me, that if I met with fit company I might devide my
booty among them. And now (I thanke my good fortune) I am lighted into the
best company of the world, a company of the fairest Ladies that ever I saw.
Come Ladies try your fortunes, and if any light upon an unfortunate blank,
let her thinke that fortune doth but mock her in these trifles, and meanes to
pleasure her in greater matters.*

The Lots.

Hir Majestye.   [1] *Fortunes Wheeles.*

Fortune must now noe more in tryumphe ride;
The wheeles ar yours thatt did hir chariott guide.

---

10 her *B*: *om. Con*   12, 18 nor *B*: noe *Con*   The Lots. *B*: The Severall Lottes
Con: *om. A22*   1.2 The wheeles ar yours] Yours are the wheeles *A22*

[2] *A Purse.*

The Countess of Derbye Dowager.

You thrive, or woulde, or maye; your lott's a purse:
Fill itt with golde, and you ar ne'r the worse.

[3] *A Ring with this Poesye,
As faithfull as I finde.*

Lo. Derbyes Wife.

Your hande by fortune on this ringe doth lighte,
And yett the word doth fitt your humor righte.

[4] *A Nuttmegg with a Blanke Parchment in itt.*

La. Worcester.

This nuttmegg hath a blanke, butt Chance doth hide itt;
Write you your wishe and fortune will provide itt.

[5] *A Snuffkin.*

La. Warwicke.

Tis sommer, yet a snuffkin is your lott,
But t'will be winter one day, doubte you nott.

[6] *A Maske.*

La. Scroope.

Wante you a maske? heere fortune gives you one;
Yett nature gives the Rose and Lillye none.

[7] *A Necklace.*

Mrs. Nevill.

Fortune gives your faire necke this lace to weare,
God graunte a heavier yoake itt never beare.

[8] *A Fanne.*

Mrs. Thynne.

You love to see, and yett to bee unseene;
Take you a fanne to be your beautyes screene.

3.2 word doth fitt *A22, Mann*: wordes do fit *Con*: words doth hit *B*   4. *Title.*
Parchment B: *om. Con*: *A22 entitles*, a Nuttmegge   4.1 hath] houlds *B*   4.2 you
your] your owne *B*   8.2 a] this *B*

Mrs. Hastinges.   [9] *A Blanke.*

Wott you why fortune gives to you noe prize?
Good fayth she sawe you nott, she wantes hir eyes.

Mrs. Bridges.   [10] *Poyntes.*

You ar in every poynte a lover true,
And therefore fortune gives the poyntes to you.

La. Scuda-   [11] *A Dyall.*
mour.

The dyall's yours; watch tyme leste itt be loste;
Yett they moste lose their time thatt watche itt most.

La. Francis.   [12] *A Playne Ringe.*

Fortune hath sent you, happe itt well or ill,
A playne golde ringe to wedd you to your will.

La. Knevette.   [13] *A Looking Glasse.*

Blinde fortune doth nott see how faire you bee,
Yett gives a glasse thatt you your selfe may see.

La. Susan   [14] *A Blanke.*
Vere.

Nothinge's your lotte; thatt's more then can be tolde;
For nothinge is more pretious then golde.

9m. *Mrs. Hastinges.*] La. Susan Vere *A22*   10. *Title. Poyntes.*] A Dozen of
points. *B*   10.2 the] theis *A22*   11m. *La. Scudamour.*] No Name. *A22*
11.1 The] This *A22*   11.2 Yet they moste lose their time thatt *A22*: Yet
they most loose it that do *B*: And yett they spende itt worste thatt *Con, Mann*
12m. *La. Francis.*] Mres. Southwell. *A22*   12.1 hath sent] hath sent to *Mann*:
doth send *B*   12.2 A] This *B*   13.2 Yett] it *A22*: But *B*   14m. *La.*
Susan Vere.] No name. *A22*

[15] *A Hand kerchefe.*

Mrs.
Vavissour.

Whether you seeme to weepe, or weepe indeede,
This hand kercheff will stand you well in steede.

[16] *A Paire of Gloves.*

La.
Sowthwell.

Fortune these gloves in double challeng sendes,
For you hate fooles and flatterers, her beste frendes.

[17] *A Lace.*

La. *Anne
Clifford.*

Give hir the lace thatt loves to be straite laced;
Soe fortunes little gifte is aptly placed.

[18] *A Paire of Knifes.*

Mrs. *Hyde.*

Fortune doth give these paire of knifes to you,
To cutt the thredd of love if't be nott true.

[19] *A Girdle.*

La. *Kildare.*

By fortunes girdle happie may you bee,
Yett they thatt ar lesse happie ar more Free.

[20] *A Paire of Writing Tables.*

La. *Effing-
ham.*

These tables may contayne your thoughtes in parte,
Butt write not all thatt's written in your harte.

---

16. *Title. A Paire of B, A22: om. Con*   16.1 in double] to you in *B:* to you
in double *A22* 16.2 For that you love not fooles that are her frends. *B* 17.2 aptly
A22, B: fittlye *Con*   18. *Title. A Paire of B, A22: om. Con*   19.1 By *A22,*
B: With *Con, Mann*   19.2 Yett] But *B, Mann*   20. *Title. A Paire of B,*
A22: om. Con

La. Pagette.   [21] *Garters.*

Thoughe you have fortunes garters you wilbe
More staide and constant in your steppes then she.

Mrs.   [22] *A Blanke.*
Kiddermister.

Tis pittye suche a hande should drawe in vayne;
Thoughe itt gaine nought, yet shall itt pittye gaine.

Mrs.   [23] *A Coyfe and Crosscloth.*
Strangwidge.

Frowne in good earnest, or be sicke in jeste,
This coife and crossecloth will become you beste.

Mother of the   [24] *A Scarfe.*
Maydes.

Take you this scarfe, binde Cupid hande and foote;
So love must aske you leave before he shoote.

La.   [25] *A Falling Bande.*
Cumberland.

Fortune would have you rise, yett guides your hande
From other lottes to take a fallinge bande.

La.   [26] *A Stomacher.*
Walsingham.

This stomacher is full of windowes wroughte,
Yett none throughe them can looke into your thoughte.

21. *Title. Garters.*] A paire of garters. *B*   21.1 wilbe] must be *B*   22m.
Mrs. Kiddermister.] No name. *A22*   22.2 nought, yet shall itt *B, A22, Mann*:
nothing itt shall *Con*   23.1 in good *B, A22*: you in *Con*   jeste *ed.*: Jeste *Con*
25.2 to take a *A22*: unto a *Con*: to take the *B*   26. *Title. A Stomacher B,*
A22: Cuttwork Stomacher *Con*   26.2 looke] see *B*

[27] *A Scisser Case.* La. Newton.

These scissers doe your huswiferye bewraye;
You love to worke thoughe you be borne to playe.

[28] *A Chaine.* Mrs. Wharton.

Because you scorne loves captive to remaine,
Fortune hath sworne to leade you in a chaine.

[29] *A Blanke.* La. Digbye.

You faine would have, butt whatt you cannott tell;
If fortune gives you nothing she doth well.

[30] *A Paire of Bracelettes.* Mrs. ⟨Ratc⟩liffe.

Ladye, your handes ar fallen into a snare,
For *Cupids* manacles your bracelettes ar.

[31] *A Bodekin.* La. Dorothye.

Even with this bodkin you may live unharmed,
Your beawtye is with vertue so well armed.

[32] *A Blanke.* [No Name.]

You ar so dayntye to be pleased, God wott,
Chance knowes nott whatt to give you for your lott.

27.2 You . . . be *A22, Mann*: Thatt . . . be *Con*: You . . . were *B*   29m. *La. Digbye.*] Mres. Drury *A22*   29.2 In giving nothing fortune serves you well. *B* 30. *Title. A Paire of B*: om. *Con*: *A22 omits Lot.*   30m. ⟨*Ratc*⟩*liffe ed.* (*Con torn here*): *A22 omits Lot.*   30.2 your] these *B*: *A22 omits Lot.*   32m. [*No Name.*] Mres. Hastinges *A22*

[33] *A Cushionett.*

To hir thatt little cares whatt lott she winnes,
Chance gives a little cushionett for hir pinnes.

*This onely
lefte un-
drawne.*

[34] *A Prayer Booke.*

Your fortune may proove good another daye;
Till fortune come, take you a booke to praye.

*A Country
Wenche.*

[35] *A Pair of Sheres.*

You whisper many tales in many eares;
To clipp your tongue your lot's a paire of sheares.

*A Country
Wenche.*

[36] *An Apron.*

You love to make excuses for all thinges;
An Apron is your lott which hath no stringes.

*A Country
Wenche.*

[37] *A Reele.*

You are high in the'instepp, short in the heele;
Your head is giddy, your lott is a reele.

No name.

[38] *A Blank.*

Fortune is bountifull, and from hir store,
Gives you as muche as you were worth before.

No Name.

[39] *A Blank.*

For all thy witt, fortune might favour thee;
For God forbidd all fooles should happy bee.

33.2 a little] hir this *A22*   for hir] to stick *B*   34m. *This onely lefte un-
drawne.*] La. Digby *A22*   34.1 may proove *B*: may be *Con, Mann*: will
proove *A22*   37.1 the' *ed.*: the *A22*

The Humble Petition of a Guiltlesse Lady,
delivered in writing upon Munday Morninge,
when the robe of rainbowes was presented to
the Queen by the Lady Walsingham.

Beawtyes rose and vertues booke,
Angells mynde and Angells looke,
To all Saintes and Angells deere,
Cleerest Majesty on earth,
Heaven did smile att your faire birth,   5
And since your dayes have bene most cleere.

Onely pore *Saint Swithin* now
Doth heare you blame his clowdy browe,
Butt he, pore Saint, devoutly sweares
It is butt a tradicion vayne   10
Thatt his much weeping causeth rayne,
For Saintes in heaven shed no teares.

Butt this he saith, thatt to his feaste
Comes *Iris* an unbidden gueste
In hir moiste roabe of collors gaye,   15
And when she comes she ever stayes
For the full space of fortye dayes,
And more or lesse Raines every daye.

Butt he, good Saint, when ones he knewe
This rayne was like to fall on you,   20
If Saintes could weepe, had wepte as muche
As when he did the ladye leade
Thatt did on burning Iron treade;
To Ladyes his respecte is suche.

The Humble Petition etc.   *Printed text: Nichols MS.: Con   Text from Con.   Layout
supplied.   Title from Nichols, where 'robe' supplied by editor.*
   Title. The humble peticion of a giltles sainte, wherwith the gowne of rainebowes
was presented to hir majesty in hir progresse 1602. *Con*   5 Heaven *Nichols:*
Heavens *Con*   7 *ital. ed.: rom. Con*   9 he] that *Nichols*   14 Comes]
Commeth *Nichols*   *Iris ed.: rom. Con*   16 when she comes] she cometh
Nichols   19 he] the *Nichols*

He gentlye first bidds *Iris* goe   25
Unto th'antipodes belowe,
Butt she for this more sullen grewe;
When he sawe thatt, with angry looke
From hir hir raynye roabe he toke,
Which heere he doth presente to you.   30

Tis fitt itt shoulde with you remayne,
For you know better how to raigne,
Yett if itt rayne still as before,
Saint Swythen prayes thatt you woulde guesse
That *Iris* doth more Roabes possesse,   35
And thatt you would blame him noe more.

A Contention betwen a Wife, a Widowe and a Maide for Precedence at an Offringe.

Wife: Widowe well met, whether goe you to daye?
               Will you not to this solemne offringe goe?
               You knowe it is *Astreas* holydaye,
               The sainte to whome all hartes devotion owe.

Widowe: Marry, what ells? I purpose soe to doe: 5
               Doe you not marke howe all the wives are fyne?
               And howe they have their presentes ready too,
               To make their offringe at *Astreas* shryne?

               See then the shrine, and tapers burning bright:
               Come frend, and let us first our selves advaunce, 10
               We knowe our place, and if we have our right,
               To all the parish we must lead the daunce.

---

25 *Iris ed.: rom. Con*   27 this] that *Nichols*   34 *ital. ed.: rom. Con*   35 *Iris ed.: rom. Con*

A Contention etc.   *Printed text: B   MSS.: A22, Y.   Text from Y.   Title: om.* for Precedence at an Offringe *B*: A Dialogue betwene the Mayde, the Wife, & the Widow for the defence of their Estates. *A22*

Title. Precedence ed.: Precendence *Y*   1 met *ed.:* meet *Y*   5 purpose] purpos'd *B*   7 their *A22:* sent *Σ*   8 their] the *A22*   9 See then the shrine] Then see the lampes *A22*   10 frend, and] therefore *A22*

But soft, what meanes this bold presumptuous maide
To goe before without respect of us?
Your forwardnes (proude girle) must needes be staide:
Where learnde you to neglect your betters thus?   16

Maide: Elder you are, but not my better here;
This place to maides a priviledg must give:
The goddesse being a maide, holds maidens dere,
And grauntes to them her owne prerogative.   2c

Besides, on all true virgins at their birth
Nature hath set a crowne of excellence,
That all the wives and widowes of the earth
Should geve them place, and doe them reverence.

Wife: If to be borne a maide be such a grace,   25
Soe was I borne, and gracd by nature too,
But seeking more perfection to embrace,
I did become a wife as others doe.

Widowe: And if the maide and wife such honor have,
I have ben both, and hold a third degree: 30
Moste maides are wardes, and every wife a slave,
I have my liverie sued and I am free.

Maide: That is the fault: that you have maidens ben
And were not constant to continewe soe;
The fall of angells did increase their synne,   35
In that they did soe pure a state forgoe.

But wife and widowe, if your wittes can make
Your states and persons of more worth then myne,
Advauntage of this place I will not take;
I will both place and priviledge resigne.   40

15 needes] now *B*: *om. A22*   17 better] betters *B*   19 holds Σ: hold *Υ*
20 grauntes] yeldes *A22*   23 of] on *A22*   33 the] your *A22*   38 states
A22: state Σ

Wife: Why marriage is an honorable state;
Widowe: And widowhoode'is a reverend degree;
Maide: But maidenhead that will admitt noe mate,
                   Like majestie herselfe must sacred bee.

Wife: The wife is mistris of her familie,   45
Widowe: Much more the widowe, for she rules alone,
Maide: But Mistris of myne owne desires am I,
                   When you rule others wills but not your owne.

Wife: Only the wife enjoyes the vertuous pleasure,
Widowe: The widowe can abstaine from pleasures knowne,   50
Maide: But th'incorrupted maide observes such measure
                   As being by pleasures wooed she cares for none.

Wife: The wife is like a fayer supported vine,
Widowe: Soe was the widowe, but nowe standes alone,
                   For being growne stronge, she needes not to inclyne: 55
Maide: Maides, like the earth, supported are of none.

Wife: The wife is as the dyamond richly sett,
Maide: The maid unset doth yet more rich appeare,
Widowe: The widowe a jewell in the Cabinet,
                   Which though not worne, is still esteemd as deare.   60

Wife: The wife doth love and is belovd againe,
Widowe: The widowe is awakt out of that dreame,
Maide: The maides white mynde had never such a staine,
                   Noe passion troubles her cleare vertues streame.

                   Yet if I would be lovde, loved would I bee   65
                   Like her whose vertue in the baye is seene;
                   Love to a wife fades with satietie,
                   When love never enjoyde is ever greene.

41 Why] *om. A22* 42 widowhoode' *ed.*: widowhoode *Υ*   is] *om. A22*   a *Σ*: an *Υ*
44 herselfe] itselfe *B*   51 observes] doth keepe *A22*   52 As . . . pleasures]
that . . . pleasure *A22*   52 wooed *ed.*: woed *Υ*   53 supported *Σ*: unspotted
Υ   57 the] a *B*: *line om. A22*   63 had] hath *A22*   64 vertues *ed.*:
vertueus *Υ*   66 Like her whose vertue] As she whose bewty *A22*   67 satietie
ed.: sacietie *Υ*   68 When] whose *A22*: Where *B*

Widowe: Then whats a vergin but a fruitles baye?
Wife: And whats a widowe but a rose-less bryer?   70
Maide: And what are wives, but woodbynes which decaye
             The statly oakes by which themselves aspire.

             And what is marriage but a tedious yoake?
Widowe: And what virginitie but sweet selfe love?
Wife: And what is widowhood but an'axell brocke?   75
             Whose one part failing neyther part can move.

Widowe: Wives are as birdes in golden cages kept,
Wife: Yet in those cages cherefully they singe:
Widowe: Widowes are birdes out of those cages lept,
             Whose joyfull notes make all the forrest ringe.   80

Maide: But maides are birdes amide the woodes secure,
             Which never hand coulde touch nor net could take,
             Nor whistle could deceyve, nor baite alure,
             But free unto themselves doe musicke make.

Wife: The wife is as the turtle with her mate,   85
Widowe: The widowe as the widowe dove alone,
             Whose truth shines moste in her forsaken state:
Maide: The maid a Phenix, and is still but one.

Wife: The wifes a soule unto her body tyed,
Widowe: The widowe a soule departed into blisse,   90
Maide: The maid an angell which was stellified,
             And nowe to'as fayer a howse descended is.

Wife: Wives are fayer howses kept and furnisht well,
Widowe: Widowes old castles voide, but full of state;
Maide: But maides are temples where the gods doe dwell,   95
             To whome alone themselves they dedicate.

69 vergin] mayden *A22*   69 *A22 assigns speech to Wife.*   70 rose-less *Σ*:
restles *Υ   B assigns speech to Maid.*   71 which *Σ*: that *Υ*   71–2 *A22 assigns
speech to Widow and Maid together.*   73 *A22 assigns speech to Widow.*   74 what]
what is *A22*   75–6 *A22 assigns speech to Wife and Maid together.*   75 what
is widowhood] what's a widow *B*   an' *ed.*: an *Υ*   77 *A22 assigns speech to Wife.*
78 Yet] but *A22*   those *Σ*: these *Υ*   79 those] their *A22*   81 woodes
Σ: woode *Υ*   82 never ... net *Σ*: neyther ... yet *Υ*   88 a *Σ*: as *Υ*
92 to' *ed.*: to *Υ*

But marriage is a prison duringe life,
Where one waye out, but many entries bee:

Wife: The Nunne is kept in cloyster, not the wife;
Wedlocke alone doth make the virgin free.   100

Maide: The maide is ever fresh like morne in Maye,
Wife: The wife with all her beames is beautified,
Like to high noone, the glorie of the daye:
Widowe: The widowe like a mild sweet eventyd.

Wife: An office well supplied is like a wife,   105
Widowe: The widowe like a gainefull office voide,
Maide: But maids are like contentment in this life,
Which all the worlde have sought, but none enjoyde.

Goe wife to Dunmowe, and demaund your flitch,
Widowe: Goe gentle maide, goe lead the apes in hell: 110
Wife: Goe widowe, make some yonger brother rich,
And then take thought and dye, and all is well.

Alas poore maide, that hast noe help nor staye;
Widowe: Alas poore wife, that nothing doest possesse;
Maide: Alas poore widowe, charitie doth saye,   115
Pittie the widowe and the fatherlesse.

Widowe: But happie widowes have the world at will.
Wife: But happier wives whose joyes are ever double.
Maide: But happiest maides whose hartes are calme and still:
Whome feare, nor hope, nor love, nor hate doth trouble.

Wife: Everie true wife hath an indented hart,   121
Wherein the Covenantes of love are writt,
Whereof her husband keeps the Counterpart,
And reades his comfortes and his joyes in it.

---

97 a *Σ: om. Υ*   99 Nunne ... cloyster] Maide ... Closett *A22*   101 ever
fresh like] like to a faire *A22*   105 a] the *B: line om. A22*   109–16 *A22*
assigns lines 109–10 to Widow; 111–12 to Wife & Maid together; 113–14 to Widow;
115–16 to Wife & Maid together.   109 and demaund your flitch] for your
bacon fleche *A22*   110 maide, goe lead the] maydes, &: lead your *A22*
120 feare, nor hope] hope, nor fear *A22*   123 her *B:* the *Υ: line om. A22*

Widowe: But everie widowes harte is like a booke,   125
           Where her joyes past imprinted doe remaine,
           But when her judgmentes eye therein doth looke,
           She doth not wish they were to come againe.

Maide: But the maids harte a fayer white table is:
           Spotles and pure, where noe impressions bee   130
           But the imortall carracters of blisse,
           Which onely God doth write, and angells see.

Wife: But wives have children, what a joye is this?
Widowe: Widowes have children too, but maides have none.
Maide: Noe more have angells, yet they have more blisse   135
           Then ever yet to mortall man was knowne.

Wife: The wife is like a fayer manured feild,
Widowe: The widowe once was such but nowe doth rest;
Maide: The maide like paradice, undrest, untilde,
           Beares cropps of natures vertue in her brest.   140

Wife: Whoe woulde not dye a wife as *Lucrece* did?
Widowe: Or live a widowe as *Penelope*?
Maide: Or be a maide and soe be stellified?
           As all the vertues and the graces bee.

Wife: Wives are warme Clymates well inhabited,   145
           But maides are frozen zones where none maye dwell;
Maide: But fayrest people in the North are bred,
           When *Affrica* breedes monsters blacke as hell.

Wife: I have my husbandes honor and his place.
Widowe: My husbandes fortunes all survive to me.   150
Maide: The moone doth borrowe light, you borrowe grace,
           When Maides by their owne vertues graced bee.

---

126 doe *B*: doth *Υ*: *line om. A22*   129 But the maids harte] The Maydes pure
minde *A22*   135 they have *Σ*: have they *Υ*   136 man] wight *A22*
137 a] t'a *A22*   140 Beares *Σ*: breedes *Υ*   140 natures vertue] natures
vertues *A22*: native vertue *B*   141–2 *ital. ed.*: *rom. Υ*   142 live *B*: like *Υ*:
line om. A22   146 maye] do *A22*   147 bred *ed.*: breed *Υ*   148 When]
Where *B*   151 moone] wife *A22*

White is my coullor, and noe hewe but this
It will receive, noe tincture shall it staine:

Wife: My white hath tooke one coullor, but it is   155
An honorable purple dyed in graine.

Widowe: But it hath ben my fortune to renewe
My coullor twise, from that it was before;
But nowe my blacke will take noe other hewe,
And therefore nowe I meane to chang noe more.   160

Wife: Wives are fayer aples servd in golden dishes,
Widowe: Widowes good wyne which tyme makes better much;
Maide: But maides are grapes desird by many wishes,
But that they growe soe high as none can touch.

Wife: I have a daughter equalls you my girle: 165
Maide: The daughter doth excell the mother then,
As pearles are better then the mother of pearle;
Maides loose their valewe when they match with men.

Widowe: The man with whome I matcht, his worth was such
As nowe I skorne a maide should be my peere: 170
Maide: But I will skorne the man you praise soe much,
For maides are matchles, and noe mate can beare.

Hence is it that the virgine never loves,
Because her like she findes not any where:
For likenes evermore affeccion moves,   175
Therefore the maide hath neyther love nor peere.

Wife: Yet many virgins married wives would be:
Widowe: And many'a wife woulde be a widowe faine:
Maide: There is noe widowe but desires to see,
If soe she might, her maiden dayes againe.   180

---

153 White is my coullor] My coolor is white *A22*   154–5 I mean to take no mixture shal it staine/But I have changd my coolor & it is *A22*   161 fayer] as *A22*   164 that] yet *A22*   166 excell] exceed *A22*   167 pearles are] pearle is *A22*   170 As nowe I] that I do *A22*   171 will] do *A22* 173 is] comes *A22*   175 likenes evermore] ever likenes more *A22*   177 Yet many virgins] Ther's many Maides that *A22*   178 many' *ed.*: many *Y* a wife] wifes *A22*   180 might, her maiden dayes] may her maiden head *A22*

There never was a wife that likt her lott,
Nor widowe but was clad in mourning weedes.
Doe what you will, marry or marrie not.
Both this estate and that repentaunce breeds.

Wife: But she that this estate and that hath seene   185
        Doth finde great odds betwixt the wife and girle.
Maide: Indeed she doth, as much as is betweene
        The melting hailestone and the solid pearle.

Wife: If I were widowe my merrie dayes were past.
Widowe: Naye then you first become sweet pleasures guest: 190
Wife: For maidenheade is a continuall faste,
        And marriage is a continuall feast.

Maide: Wedlocke indeed hath oft compared ben
        To publique feastes where meet a publique rout,
        Where they that are without would faine goe in,   195
        And they that are within would faine goe out.

        Or to the jewell which this virtue had,
        That men were madd till they might it obtaine:
        But when they had it they were twise as madd,
        Till they were dispossest of it againe.   200

Wife: Maides cannot judge, because they cannot tell
        What comfortes and what joyes in marriag be:
Maide: Yes, yes, though blessed spirites in heaven doe dwell
        They doe the soules in purgatorie see.

Widowe: If everie wife doe live in purgatorie,   205
        Then sure it is that widowes live in blisse,
        And are translated to a state of glorie,
        But maides as yet have not attainde to this.

---

181 Ther's never wife was pleased with her lott *A22*   *B assigns speech to Wife,*
A22 to Widow.   182 *B assigns speech to Widow, A22 to Wife.*   *189–92 A22*
assigns speech to Wife; B, Y to Widow. See Commentary for Davies's revisions.   193 Wed-
locke] Marriage *A22*   194 publique . . . meet] Comunion . . . meets *A22*
197 to the jewell] like this flower *A22*   198 they might it] it thei might
A22   202 comfortes] pleasures *A22*   203 spirites] Saints *B*   doe] *om.*
A22

Maide: Not maides? to spotles maides this grace is geven,
           To live in incorruption from their birth: 210
           And what is that but to inherite heaven,
           Even whilest they dwell upon the spotted earth.

           The perfectest of all created thinges,
           The purest gold that suffers noe alaye,   214
           The sweetest flower that on earthes bosome springes,
           The pearle unbord whose price noe prince can paye.

           The Christall glasse that will noe venome hold,
           The mirror wherein angells love to looke,
           Dianaes bathinge fountaine clere and cold,
           Beauties fresh rose and virtues livinge booke.   220

           Of love and fortune both the mistris borne,
           The soveraigne spirit that wilbe thrall to none,
           The spotles garment that was never worne,
           The princely eagle that still flies alone.

           She sees the world, yet her cleare thought doth take
           Noe such deep print as to be changd thereby;   226
           As when we see the burninge fyer doth make
           Noe such impression as doth burne the eye.

Wife: Noe more sweet maide, our strife is at an end:
           Cease nowe, I feare we shall transformed be   230
           To chattring pyes, as they that did contende
           To match the muses in their harmonie.

Widowe: Then let us yeeld the honor and the place,
           And let us both be sutors to the maide,
           That since the goddesse geves her speciall grace,   235
           By her cleare handes this offringe be convaied.

Maide: Your speech I doubt hath some displeasure moved,
           Yet let me have the offringe, I will see:
           I knowe she hath both wives and widowes loved,
           Though she woulde never wife nor widowe bee.   240

209 grace] gift *B*: *line om. A22*   218 mirror . . . to] Booke . . . doth *A22*
219 *Dianaes ed.*: rom. *Y*   220 virtues livinge] bewties lovinge *A22*
221 mistris] Sov'raigne *A22*   224 that] which *A22*   236 this] the *B*:
line om. A22   240 never] neither *B*: *line om. A22*

Verses given to the Lord Treasurer upon Newyeares Day upon a Dosen of Trenchers, by Mr. Davis.

The Courtier. 1

Longe have I servd in Court, yet learned not all this while,
To sell poore suitors smoke, nor where I hate to smile,
Superiors to adore, inferiors to dispise,
To fly from them that fall, to followe them that rise,
To Cloake a poore desire under my riche araye,
Nor to aspire by vice, though twere the quicker waye.

The Divine. 2

My Callinge is divine, one Cure doth me content,
I will no Chop-churche be, nor paye my Patron rent
Nor yeld to sacrilege, but like the kinde true mother
Rather loose all the child, then part it with another.
Nor followe Princes Courtes, nor worldly maisters serve,
So to growe riche and fatt, while my poore flock doth starve.

The Souldier. 3

My occupation is the noble trade of kinges,
The tryall that decides the highest right of thinges;
Though *Mars* my Master be I do not *Venus* love,
Nor honor *Bacchus* oft, nor often sweare by *Jove*.
Of speaking of my selfe I all occasions shunne,
And rather love to doe then bragge what I have donne.

The Lawyer. 4

My practise is the lawe; my robe, my tongue, my pen
Wealth and opinion gaine, and make me Judge of men.

Verses . . . upon . . . Trenchers. *Printed text: B MSS.: Dow, A22 Text from A22*
Title from Dow: Yet other 12. Wonders of the World never yet published *B*: om.
A22 Sequence of Stanzas as indicated in textual introduction. 1.1 servd] liv'd *B*
1.2 to *B, Dow*: I *A22* 1.4 them that . . . them that] such as . . . such as *B*
1.5 my] a *B* 2.1 one Cure doth me content] and I from God am sent *B*
2.3 kinde true] true kinde *Dow* 2.5 Nor followe Princes Courtes] Much
wealth I will not seeke *B* 3.3–4 ital. ed.: rom. *A22* 3.5 speaking *B,*
Dow: talkinge *A22* 3.6 bragge] boast *B* 4.1 My practise is the lawe]
The Law my calling is *B*

The knowne dishonest Cause I never did defende,
Nor spunn out suites at length, but wisht and sought an ende,
Nor Counsell did bewray, nor of both parties take,
Nor ever tooke I fee for which I never spake.

The Phisition. 5

I studye to uphold the slippery life of man,
Who dyes when I have don the best and all I can,
From practise and from bookes I draw my learned skill,
Not from the knowne receipts or Pothecaries bill.
The Earth my faultes doth hide; the world my cures doth see,
What youth and time effects is ofte ascrib'd to mee.

The Merchaunt. 6

My trade doth every thinge to every land supply,
Discover unknowne worldes, straunge Countries doth ally,
I never did for stall, I never did engross,
Nor Custome did withdrawe, though I retourn'd with loss.
I thrive by faire exchaunge, by sellinge and by buyinge,
And not by Jewish use, reprisall, fraude, or lyinge.

The Country Gentleman. 7

Though straunge outlandish spirits praise Townes and Country
scorne,
The Country is my home, I dwell where I was borne;
There profitt and comaunde with pleasure I partake,
Yet do not Hawkes and Doggs my sole Companions make.
I rule but not oppress, end quarrels not mayntaine,
See Townes but dwell not there t'abridge my charge or traine.

4.3 The] A *Dow*   4.4 spunn out] spinnd my *Dow*   an] theire *Dow*
4.5–6 nor of . . . tooke B: whereof . . . kept *A22*:
              Some say I have good giftes, and love where I doe take/
              Yet never tooke I fee, but I advisd or spake. *Dow*
5.1 uphold] prolonge *Dow*   life] state B   5.2 Who *Dow*, B: Which *A22*
I . . . I *Dow*: we . . . we *A22*, B   6.2 worldes] costs B   Countries] kingdomes
Dow   6.6 And] But *Dow*   7.2 dwell] live *Dow*   7.4 and B, *Dow*:
nor *A22*   7.5 not² B, *Dow*: and *A22*

The Batchelour. 8

How manie thinges as yet are deare alike to me,
The Horse, the dogge, the field, Love, armes, or libertie,
I have no wife as yet whome I may call mine owne,
I have no Children yet that by my name are knowne,
Yet if I married were I would not wish to thrive,
If that I could not tame the veriest shrewe alive.

The Married Man. 9

I only am the man amongest all married men,
That would not wish the Priest to be unlinkt agen,
And though my shoo did wringe, I would not make my moane,
Nor thinke my neighbours chaunce more happie then mine owne.
Yet curse I not my Wife but yeld observance due
Beinge neither fonde nor cross, nor Jealous nor untrue.

The Wyfe. 10

The first of all our Sex came from the side of man,
I thither am retournd, whence first our Sex began.
I do not visite muche, nor many when I doe,
I tell my minde to fewe, and that in Counsell too:
I seeme not sick in health, nor sulleyn but in sorrowe,
I care for somewhat els then what to weare to morrowe.

The Widowe. 11

My dyinge husband knew howe much his death would grieve me,
And therefore lefte me wealth to Comforte and relieve me,
Though I no more will love, I moste not love disdaine,
Penelope hir selfe did Suitors intertaine,

8.2 The Horse . . . the field] The field, the Horse, the Dog *B*   8.3 I . . . yet
B, Dow: As yet I have no wife *A22*   8.6 tame *B, Dow*: rule *A22*
9.2 would] do *B*   wish *B, Dow*: seeke *A22*   9.3 And] Yea *Dow*   9.4
chaunce] choise *Dow*   9.5 curse *ed.*: Court *A22*, B: Courst *Dow*   10.2
whence first our] from whence our *B*: where first my *Dow*   10. 3-4 muche:
oft *B*:
        I goe not maskd abroad to visit when I do
        My secretes I bewray to none but one or two *Dow*
10.6 I] And *Dow*   11.3 love] have *B*   11.4 *Penelope ed.: rom. A22*

And yet to drawe on such as are of best esteeme,
Nor richer then I am nor yonger will I seeme.

The Mayde. 12

I marriage would forsweare but that I heare men tell,
That shee that dyes a maide must leade an Ape in hell,
Therefore if fortune comme, I will not mocke and play,
Nor drive the bargaine on till it be driven away.
Titles and landes I like, yet rather fancie can,
A man that wanteth golde, then gold that wants a man.

The Kinges Welcome.

O nowe or never gentle muse, be gaye,
And mount up higher on thy paper winges
Then doth the larke, when he salutes the daye,
And to the morne a merrie welcome singes.

Fly swifter then the egle sent by art   5
From Noremberg to the'Almaine emperor;
A hand lesse cuning, but as true a hart,
Sends thee to'a prince of greater worth and power.

Rencounter him thowe shalt upon the waye,
Like *Phebus* midst of all his golden trayne;   10
And knowe him too thow shalt at first survaye,
By proper notes, and by distinctions plaine.

By his faire outward formes and princely port,
By honors done to him with capp and knee,
He is decyphred by the vulgar sorte,   15
But truer caracters will rise to thee.

11.6 richer . . . yonger] yonger . . . richer *B*   will *B*: then *A22*: woulde *Dow*
12.3 Therefore] Wherefore *Dow*   12.4 till *B*, *Dow*: while *A22*   12.5 yet]
but *Dow*

The Kinges Welcome. *MSS.: Y, L   Text from Y.*
    Title: To the kinge. upon his Majesties first comming into England. *L*   2 on]
with *L*   5–8 *om. L*   6 the' *ed.*: the *Y*   8 to' *ed.*: to *Y*   9–10 Thou
must goe meete King James upon the way/Advanceing Southward with his golden
trayne *L*   10 *Phebus ed.*: *rom. Y*   11 shalt] maist *L*   14 honors]
honour *L*   15 decyphred by] distinguist to *L*   16 thee *ed.*: the *Y*

Thy sight had once an influence devine
Which gave it power the soule of man to viewe;
Wipe and make cleare that dazeled eye of thine,
And thowe shalt see his reall markes and true.   20

Looke over all that divers troope, and finde
Whoe hath his spirites most Joviall and free,
Whose bodie is best tempred, and whose minde
Is ever best in tune, and that is hee.

See who it is, whose actions doe bewraye   25
That threefold power, which rarely mixt we see:
A judgment grave, and yet a fancie gaye,
Joynd with a ritch remembrance, that is hee.

Marke who it is, that hath all noble skill
Which maye to publique good referred bee;   30
The quickest witt, and best affected will,
Whence flowes a streame of vertues, that is hee.

If any more then other clearely wise,
Or wisely just, or justly valiant be,
If any doe fainte pleasures more despise,   35
Or be more maister of himselfe, tis hee.

But soft, thine Egletes eye will soone be dym,
If thow this rising sunne directly viewe;
Looke syde waies on the beames that spread from him,
Faire peace, rich plentie, and religion true.   40

Besides a guard of blessed angells hover
About his sacred person, day and night,
And with invisible winges his head doe cover,
That dangers dartes thereon may never light.

19 cleare *L*: cleane *Y*   20 shalt *L*: shall Y   31 quickest] sharpest *L*
35 pleasures] pleasure *L*   36 tis] its *L*   37 thine *L*: thie *T*   Egletes]
Eagles *L*   39 him] them *L*   40 rich] with *L*   41 With that strong
gard of Angells which doe hover *L*

When by these proper notes thowe shalt him ken,   45
Fly towardes him with winges of Love and feare;
Like fire which most doth wave and tremble then,
When it doth mount most high, and burne most cleare.

Yet on; for winged time with thee goes on,
Which like old *Æson* hath his youth renewd;   50
His hower glase turned, and his sickle gone,
And all his graye and broken fethers mewd.

On, for the brave yong sonn above his head
Comes Northward, that he may his glorie meete,
Whilest the fresh earth in all her pride doth spread   55
Greene velvit carpettes under neath his feete.

On, for the birds will help to fill thie songe,
Whereto all English hart-stringes doe agree;
And th'Irish harpe stringes that did jarre soe long,
To make the musicke full, nowe tuned be.   60

There is noe eye cast downe, there is noe voice
That to pronounce the hartes assent is dombe;
The world of thinges doth everie where rejoyce,
In certaine hope of blessed times to come.

Thousandes while they possesse and fill the waies,   65
Doth both desire, and hinder his repaire;
They fill the emptie heaven with praier and praise,
Which he requites with demonstrations faire.

Then what hast thowe to doe, and what remaines?
Praie as the people doth, and add but this,   70
This litle wish: that whiles he lives and raignes,
He maye be still the same, that nowe he is.

45-8 *om.* L   47 wave] *Y unclear whether* waue *or* wane.   49 Yet] Now L
49 thee *ed.*: the *Y*   50 *Æson ed.*: *rom. Y*   55 Whilest] While L   57 the
L: thee *Y*   thie] the L   58 doe] will L   59 th' *ed.*: the *Y*   did jarre] have
jarrd L   62 That to pronounce] Which to expresse L   65 Thousandes
while they] While thousands doe L   66 Doth] The [*i.e. They*] L   67 heaven]
aire L   69-72 *om.* L

To the Queene at the Same Time.

If wee in peace had not received the Kinge,
Wee see wee had beene conquered, since wee see
The Queene such Armyes doth of beauties bringe,
As all our eyes and hearts her vassals bee.

    The Danish Armyes once great honnour wonne   5
    Upon this land, yett conquered but a part:
    But you Great Lady, more alone have done,
    For at first sight you conquerd every heart.

Starre of the North, upon these Northerne Realmes
Long may your vertues, and your beauties raigne: 10
Beyond our *Cinthiaes* yeares, whose golden Beames
Ar sett with us, and cannot shine againe.

    Well may it bee, though sunne and Moone goe downe,
    Seas have noe power the North pole starre to drowne.

Mira Loquor Sol Occubuit Nox Nulla Secuta Est.

    By that Eclipse which darkned our *Apollo*,
    Our sunne did sett, and yett noe night did follow;
    For his successors vertues shone soe bright
    As they continued still their former light,
    And gave the world a farther expectation,
    To adde a greater splendor to our nation.

Charles his Waine.

Brittaine doth under those bright starres remaine
Which English sheapheards *Charles his waine* doe name;

To the Queene etc. *Text: MS. L Layout supplied.*   11 *Cinthiaes ed.: rom. MS.*
Mira Loquor etc. *Text: MS. L*
  1 *Apollo ed.: rom. MS.*
Charles his Waine. *Text: MS. L.*
  2 *ital. ed.: rom. MS.*

But more this Ile is Charles his waine,
Since Charles her Royall wagoner became:
For Charles, which now in Arthures seate doth raigne,
Is our Arcturus and doth guide the waine.

Of the Name of Charolus,
Being the Diminative of Charus.

The name of Charles, *darlinge* signifies;
A name most fitte, for hee was ever such.
Never was Prince soe deare in all mens eyes,
Soe highly valued, or esteemd soe much;
Edgar was Englands darlinge once, wee find,
But Charles the Darlinge is of all mankind.

Verses Sent to the Kinge with Figges
By Sir John Davis.

To add unto the first mans happiness,
His maker did for him a garden make,
And plac'd him there, that hee the same might dresse,
And pleasure great with little labour take.

And this with nature stands, and reason right: 5
That man, who first was formed of the earth,
In trimminge of the earth should take delight,
And her adorne from whom hee tooke his birth.

Nor her for this doth hee ungratefull finde,
For shee in gardens her best fruites doeth yealde;   10
The Earth in gardens is a mother kinde,
When shee is but a steepdame in the feild.

Sir, in your service God hath mee soe blest,
As I have beene enabled to acquire
A garden ready planted, trim'd and drest,   15
Whereto in vacant times I doe retire.

Of the Name etc.   *Text: MS. L*
  1 *darlinge ed.: rom. MS.*

Verses Sent etc.   *Text: MS. L   Layout supplied.*

This garden and the fruite thereof indeede,
Are fruites of your great favour unto mee,
And therefore all the fruites which thence proceed,
A proper offeringe to your Highnes bee.   20

But if this verse or boldnes meritt blame,
Those figge leaves, Sir, I hope shall hide the same.

[To the Ladyes of Founthill.]

Ladyes of Founthill, I am come to seeke
My hart amongst you, which I late did leese;
But many harts may be perhaps alike,
Therefore of mine, the proper markes are theise:

It is not hard, though true as steele it be,   5
And like the Diomond cleare from any spot;
Transfixt with many darts you shall it se,
But all by vertue, not by Cupid shot.

It hath no wings because it needeth none,
Being now arived and settled where it would;   10
Winged desires and hopes from it are gon,
But it is full of Joyes as it can hold.

Faine would I find it where it doth remaine,
But would not have it though I might againe.

Upon a Paire of Garters.

Go loveinge woode-bynd, clip with lowly grace
Those two sweete plants, which beare the flowers of love;
Go silken vines, those tender Elmes embrace
Which flourish still, although their roots doe move.

[To the Ladyes etc.]   *Text: MS. L   Title and layout supplied.*
  7 Transfixt *ed.*: Transmixt *MS.*   11 are gon *ed.*: gon are *MS.*
Upon a Paire etc.   *Text: MS. L   Layout supplied.*

As soone as you possesse your blessed places,   5
You are advanced, and enobled more
Then Dyodemes, which were white silken laces
That Ancient kings about their forehead wore.

Sweete bands take heed, lest you ungently bynd,
Or with your stricktnes make too deepe a print;   10
Was never tree had such a tinder rynd,
Although her Inward hart be hard as flynt:

And let your knots be fast, and loose at will;
She must be free, though I stand bounden still.

[A Sonnet sent with a Booke.]

In this sweete booke, the treasury of witt,
All virtues, beautyes, passions written be;
And with such life they are sett forth in it
As still methinkes that which I read, I see.

But this bookes Mistris is a liveing booke,   5
Which hath Indeed those vertues in her mynde;
And in whose face, though envyes selfe do looke,
Even envyes eye shall all those beautyes fynd.

Onely the passions that are printed here
In her calme thoughts can no Impression make;   10
She will not love, nor hate, nor hope, nor feare,
Though others seeke theise passions for her sake.

So in the sonne, some say, there is noe heate,
Though his reflecting beames doe fire begett.

8 their *ed.*: there *MS.*   9 ungently *ed.*: ungetly *MS.*   11 tree *ed.*:
free *MS.*

[A Sonnet etc.] *Text: MS. L   Title and layout supplied.*
  1 this *ed. (Grosart):* his *MS.*

OTHER POEMS

Title of section supplied by editor.

A Hymne in Prayse of Musicke.

Prayse, Pleasure, Profit, is that three-fold band,
Which ties mens minds more fast then Gardions knot:
Each one some drawes, al three none can withstand,
Of force conjoyn'd, Conquest is hardly got.
   Then Musicke may of harts a Monarke bee,   5
   Wherein Praise, Pleasure, Profit, so agree.

Praise-worthy Musicke is, for God it prayseth,
And pleasant, for brute beasts therein delight:
Great profit from it flowes, for why it raiseth
The minde overwhelmed with rude passions might.   10
   When against reason passions fond rebell,
   Musicke doth that confirme, and these expell.

If Musicke did not merit endlesse prayse,
Would heav'nly Spheres delight in silver round?
If joyous pleasure were not in sweet layes,   15
Would they in Court and Country so abound?
   And profitable needs wee must that call,
   Which pleasure linkt with praise doth bring to al.

Heroicke minds with praises most incited,
Seeke praise in Musicke, and therein excell: 20
God, man, beasts, birds, with Musicke are delighted;
And pleasant t'is, which pleaseth all so well.
   No greater profit is then selfe content,
   And this doth Musick bring, and care prevent.

When Antique Poets Musicks praises tell,   25
They say it beasts did please, and stones did move:
To prove more dul then stones, then beasts more fel,
Those men, which pleasing Musick did not Love.

A Hymne in Prayse of Musicke. *Printed texts: A, B, C, D*   *Text from A*
  2 knot: *ed.:* ~, *A*   12 these] those *B, C, D*

They fain'd, it Cities built, and States defended,
To shew the profit great on it depended.   30

Sweet birds (poore mens Musitians) never slake
To sing sweet Musicks prayses day and night:
The dying Swans in Musicke pleasure take,
To shew, that it the dying can delight;
    In sicknes, health, peace, war, wee do it need,   35
    Which proves, sweet Musicks profit doth exceed.

But I, by niggard praysing, do disprayse
Prayse-worthy Musicke in my worthles Ryme:
Ne can the pleasing profit of sweet layes,
Any save learned Muses well define.   40
    Yet all by these rude lines may clearly see,
    Prayse, Pleasure, Profit, in sweet Musicke bee.
                          I.D.

Of Faith the First Theologicall Vertue.

Faith is a sunbeame of th'Æternall light
That in mans soule infusd by grace doth shine,
Which gives her dazled eye soe cleare a sight,
As evidently sees the truith divine.
This beame that cleares our eyes, inflames our hearts,   5
And Charities kind fire doth there begett;
For sunlike it both light and heate Imparts:
Faith is the light, and Charitie the heate.
This light of faith the noblest wisdome is,
For it the onely truith Allowes, and aplyes: 10
The virgins Lamp, that lights the soule to blisse,
The Jacobs scales, whereby shee clymes the skyes:
    The eye that sees, the hand that apprehends
    The cause of causes, and the end of ends.

Of Faith etc.   *Text: MS. L*
  1 th' *ed.*: th *MS.*

A Songe of Contention
betweene Fowre Maids Concerninge that which Addeth Most Perfection to that Sexe.

The First for Beautye.

Our fairest Garland, made of beautyes flowers,
Doth of it selfe supplye all other dowers;
Women excell the perfects' men in this,
And therefore herein theire perfection is:
For beautye wee the glorious heavens admire,   5
Faire feilds, faire howses, gold and pearle desire:
Beautye doth alwayes health and youth Imploy,
    And doth delight the noblest sense, the eye.

The Second for Witte.

Beautye delights the soule, but witte the Reason;
Witte lasts an age, and beautye but a season: 10
The sense is quickly cloyd with beautyes tast
When witts delight still quicke and fresh doth last.
Beautye weake eyes with her illusion blindes;
Witte Conquers spirits, and triumphes over minds.
Deade things have beautye onely; man hath witte,   15
    And mans perfection doth consist in it.

The Third for Wealth.

Wealth is a power that passeth nature farre,
Makes every goose a swanne and sparke a starre;
Queene money bringes and gives with royall handes
Freinds, kindred, honour, husband, house, and landes;   20
Not a faire face, but fortune faire I crave:
    Lett mee want witte, soe I fooles fortune have.

A Songe of Contention etc. *Text: MS. L*
   3 perfects' *ed.*: perfec'ts *MS.*
   20 *The MS. is missing a couplet about Wealth; probably it followed line 20.*

The Fourth for Vertue.

Yet those perfections most Imperfect bee
If there bee wantinge vertuous modestye:
Vertues aspect would have the sweetest grace,   25
If wee could see, as wee conceave her face.
Vertue guids witte with well affected will,
Which if witte want, it proves a dangerous ill:
Vertue gaines wealth with her good goverment;
    If not, sh'is rich because shee is contente.   30

A Maids Hymne in Praise of Virginity.

Sacred virginity, unconquered Queene,
Whose kingdome never hath Invaded beene;
Of whose sweete Rosy Crowne, noe hand hath power
    Once but to touch, much lesse to plucke a flower;

Gainst whome proud love which on the world doth raigne,   5
With Armies of his passions fights in vaine;
To whome graye winter never doth appeare,
    To whome greene springtide lasteth all the yeare;

O fresh Immortall baye, untroubled well,
Or violett which untouch't doest sweetest smell,   10
Faire vine which without prop doest safely stand,
    Pure gold new coynd which never past a hand;

O temperance in the supreame degree,
And highest pitch that vertues winges can flee,
O more then humane spirit, of Angells kind,   15
    O white unspotted garment of the mind,

Which first cloathd man before hee was forlorne,
And wherein God himselfe choase to bee borne;
Within my soule, O heavenly vertue, rest,
    Untill my soule with heaven it selfe bee blest.   20

A Maids Hymne etc.   *Text: MS. L*
11 prop *ed. (Grosart)*: drop *MS.*   14 highest *ed.*: higest *MS.*

Part of an Elegie in Praise of Marriage.

When the first man from Paradice was driven
Hee did from thence his onely comfort beare:
Hee still enjoyes his wife, which God had given,
Though hee from other Joyes devorced were.

This Cordiall Comfort of societye,   5
This truelove knott that tyes the heart and will,
When man was in th'extremest miserye,
To keepe his hart from breakinge, rested still.

There is a tale that when the world beganne
Both sexes in one body did remaine,   10
Till *Jove*, offended with that double man,
Causd *Vulcan* to divide him into twayne.

In this division hee the hart did sever,
But cunningly hee did Indent the heart,
That if they should be reunited ever,   15
Each part might knowe which was the Counterpart.

Since when all men and women thinke it longe,
[Till] each of them their other part have mett;
Sometimes they meete the right, sometimes the wrong:
This discontent, and that doth joy begett.   20

It joye begetts in their indented harts
When like indentures, they are matcht aright;
Each part to other mutuall Joy imparts,

. . . .

And thus the man which *Vulcan* did devide   25
Is nowe againe by *Hymen* made entire,
And all the ruine is reædified,
Two beeinge made one by this divine desire.

Part of an Elegie etc.   *Text: MS. L*
   7 th' *ed.*: the *MS.*   9 that when *ed.*: then *MS.*   10 sexes *ed.*: sex *MS.*
11–12 *ital. ed.: rom. MS.*   17 women *ed.*: woman *MS.*   18 [Till] *ed.: om.*
MS.   19 they *ed.*: the *MS.*   21 their *ed.*: there *MS.*   24 *Line om. in*
MS.   25–6 *ital. ed.: rom. MS.*   27 reædified *ed.*: raeedified *MS.*

Sweete marriage is the honny never cloyinge,
The tune which being still plaid doth ever please;   30
The pleasure which is vertues in Injoyinge,
It is the band of peace and yoake of ease.

It is a yoake, but sweete [and] light it is;
The fellowship doth take a way the trouble;
For every greife is made halfe lesse by this,   35
And every joy is by reflection double.

It is a band, but one of loves sweete Bands,
Such as hee binds the worldes great parts withall,
Whose wonderous frame by their Connvention stands,
But beinge disbanded would to ruine fall.   40

To the Queen.

What Musicke shall we make to you,
To whome the stringes of all mens harts
Make musicke of ten thousand parts
        In tune and measure true,
        With straines and changes new?   5

How shall wee fraime a harmony
Worthie your eares, whose princely hands
Keepe harmony in sundry lands,
    Whose people divers be
    In faction and degree?   10
        Heavens tunes may onely please,
        And not such aires as theise.

For you which downe from heaven are sent
Such peace upon the earth to bring,
Have hard the quire of Angells sing,   15
        And all the sphæres consent,
        Like a sweete Instrument.

33 [and] *ed.* (*Grosart*): *om. MS.*
To the Queen.   *Text: MS.* L
    7 [~~heavenly~~] princely *MS.*

How then should theise harsh tunes you heare,
(Created of the trubled Ayer)
Breed but distast, when they repaire   20
   To your Cælestiall eare?
   So that this Center here
     For you no Musicke fynds,
     But harmony of mynds.

Upon a Coffin by S.I.D.

There was a man bespake a thing,
Which when the owner home did bring,
He that made it, did refuse it,
He that bought it would not use it,
And he that hath it doth not know,
Whether he hath it, ay or no.

Upon a Coffin etc.   *Printed texts: Parkes, PB   MSS.: S14, RP172   Text from Parkes.*
  Title. A Riddle *RP172*: A Riddle upon a Coffin *PB*: A Riddle *(title), but subscribed*
A Coffin. *S14*   2 owner] maker *S14*   3–4 *S14 inverts these lines.*   4 He
MSS.: And he *Print*

THE PSALMES

Title: The Psalmes translated into verse Anno dni. 1624.

The Psalmes.

Psalm 1

That man is blest which hath not walkt aside,
Takeinge ungodly Counsell for his guide;
Nor in the way of Synners stood and staied,
Nor in the Couch of Scorners downe him layed;
But in Gods Lawe hath plac't his whole delight,   5
And studieth to performe it day and night.
Hee, like a plant which by a Streame doth growe,
His timely fruite shall in due season showe,
Whose leafe shall not decay but flourish ever,
And all things prosper which hee doth endeavour.   10
But with th'ungodly it shall not bee soe:
But as the dust which whirlewindes to and fro
Uppon the surface of the earth doth drive,
They shall a restless liffe, and fruitles live,
Nor shall they stand upright when they are tride,   15
Nor in the'assembly of the just abide:
But in his way God doth the good man cherish,
When wicked men in their bad way shall perish.

Psalm 2

Why doe the nations thus in furie rise?
Why doe the people such vaine plottes devise?
Monarches stand up, and *Princes* doe conspire
Against the *Lord* and his Annoynted Heire:
Let us in sunder breake their Bandes, say they,   5
And let us lightly cast their *Yokes* away.
But hee that sittes in Heaven shall them deride,
And laugh to scorne their follie and their pride;
And in his wrath he shall *reprove* them sore,
And vex them in his Anger more and more,

The Psalmes.   *Text: MS. L*

Sayinge, I sett on *Sion* hill My *Kinge*,
To preache my *Lawe*, and shew this heavenly thinge;
Thou art my *Sonne*, this day I thee begott:
Aske, and I will assigne thee for Thy Lott
Of heritage the landes and nations all,   15
Betweene the *Sunnes* uprisinge and his fall.
Thou with an *Iron* rodd shalt keepe them under,
And breake them like an earthen pott in sunder.
Bee wise, yee *Monarches*, and yee *Princes* then,
Bee learned yee that judge the Sonnes of men: 20
Serve yee the *Lord*, with humble feare him serve;
Rejoyce in him, yet tremblinge him observe;
Kisse yee the *Sonne*, lest yee him angrie make,
And perish while his just wayes yee forsake.
If his just wrath but once enkindled bee,   25
Who trustes in him a blessed man is hee.

Psalm 3

Lord, how my foes in number doe encrease,
That rise against mee to disturbe my peace.
Many there are which to my Soule have said,
His *God* to him noe safety yeildes nor aid.
But God is my defence, my *Succour* nigh;   5
My glory and my head hee lifteth high:
To him with earnest praier appealed I,
And from his holy *Hill* hee heard my crie.
I layed mee downe and slept, and rose againe,
For mee the *Lord* doth evermore sustaine;   10
Though Thousand of my foes besett mee round,
Noe feare of them my courage shall confound:
Rise *Lord*, and save mee: thou hast given a stroke
On my foes cheeke, that all his teeth are broke:
Salvation commeth from this *Lord* of ours,   15
Who blessinges on his people daily powers.

Psalm 4

O God, whose righteousness by grace is mine,
A gracious eare unto my voyce encline:

Thou that hast set mee free when I was thrall,
Bee mercifull and heare my prayer withall.
Vaine, wordly men how long will yee dispise   5
Gods honnour, and his truth, and trust in lies?
God for himselfe the good man doth select,
And when I crie, hee doth not mee reject.
Bee angrie, but bee angrie without synne,
Try your owne hearts in silence close within: 10
To *God* of godly workes an offeringe make,
Then trust in him, that will not his forsake.
For that which good is, many seeke, and pray;
And who shall shew the same to us, say they.
Lord, shew to us thy countenance divine,   15
And cause the *Beames* thereof on us to shyne;
Soe shall my heart more joyfull bee and glad
Then if encrease of Corne and wine I had:
In peace therefore lye downe will I and sleepe,
For God alone doth mee in safetie keepe.   20

Psalm 5

Lord weigh my words, and take consideracion
Of my sad thoughts, and silent meditation:
My *God*, my *Kinge*, bowe downe thine eare to mee,
While I send up mine humble prayer to thee.
Early before the morne doth bringe the day   5
I will, O *Lord*, looke up to thee and pray;
For thou with Synne art never pleased well,
Nor any ill may with thy goodnes dwell:
The foole may not before thy wisdome stand,
Nor shall the impious scape thy wrathfull hand;   10
Thou wilt destroy all such as utter lies;
Blood and deceit are odious in thine eyes;
But trustinge in thy manie mercies deare,
I will approch thy house with holy feare.
Teach mee thy plaine and righteous way to goe,   15
That I may never fall before my foe,
Whose flatteringe tongue is falce, and heart impure,
And throat an open place of *Sepulcure*:

Destroy them Lord, and frustrate their devices,
Cast out those *Rebells* for their manie vices,   20
But all that trust in thee, and love thy name,
Make them rejoyce, and rescue them from shame.
Thou wilt thy blessinge to the righteous yeild,
And guard them with thy grace as with a *Shield*.

Psalm 6

To judge mee, *Lord*, in thy just wrath forbeare,
To punish mee in thy displeasure spare:
O I am weake, have mercie Lord therefore,
And heale my brused Bones which payne mee sore.
My *Soule* is alsoe trubled and dismayed,   5
But *Lord* how long shall I expect thine aid?
Turne thee, O *Lord*, my *Soule* from death deliver,
Even for thy mercies sake, which lasteth ever:
They which are dead remember not thy name,
Nor doth the silent *Grave* thy praise proclaime.   10
I faint and melt away with greifes and feares,
And every night my Bed doth swymme with teares;
Myne eyes are suncke, and weakned is my sight,
My foes have vexed mee with such dispight.
Away from mee, yee sinfull men away;   15
The *Lord* of *Heaven* doth heare mee when I pray:
The Lord hath my petition heard indeed,
Receave my prayer and I shall surely speed;
But shame and sorrow on my foes shall light,
They shall bee turn'd and put to suddaine flight.   20

Psalm 7

O *Lord* my *God*, I put my trust in thee.
From all my *Persecutors* rescue mee,
Lest my proud foe doth like a *Lyon* rend mee,
While there is non to succour and defend mee:
Lord God, if I bee guilty found in this   5
Wherewith my foes have charged mee amisse,

If I did use my freind unfreindly soe,
Nay, if I did not helpe my causlesse foe,
Let him prevaile, although my cause bee just,
And lay my life and honnour in the dust.   10
Up Lord, and stand against my furious foes.
Thy *judgement* against them for mee disclose:
Soe shall thy *People* flocke about thee nigh;
For their sakes therefore lift thy selfe on high.
Judge of the world, give sentence on my parte,   15
According to the cleanes of my heart;
Let wickenes be brought unto an end,
And guide the Just that they may not offend:
Thou *God* art just, and Thou [the] searcher art
Of hart and Raynes, and every inward part;   20
My helpe proceedeth from the Lord of *Might*,
Who saveth those which are of hart upright;
A powerfull and a patient *Judge* is hee,
Though every day his wrath provoked bee.
But if men will not turne, his sword hee whets,   25
And bends his Bowe, and to the stringe hee setts
The *Instrumentes* of death (his Arrowes keene)
Gainst such as Rebells to his will have beene.
The impious man conceaves iniquity,
Travailes with mischeife, and brings forth a ly;   30
The *Righteous* to entrapp hee diggs a pitt,
But hee himselfe first falls and sinkes in it:
The wicked plotts his workinge braine doth cast
Light with a mischeife on himselfe at last.
My thankes with Gods great justice shall accord,   35
And I will highly praise the highest Lord.

Psalm 8

O God our Lord, how large is the extent
Of thy great name and glorie excellent:
It fills this world, but it doth shyne most bright
Above the heavens in th'unapproched light.

7.19 [the] *ed.: om. MS.*

By Suckinge Babes thou do'st thy strength disclose,　5
And by their mouth to silence put thy foes.
When I see *Heaven* wrought by thy mighty hand,
And all those glorious lights in order stand,
Lord, what is man that thou on him do'st looke,
Or of the *Sonne of Man* such care hast tooke?　10
Next *Angells* in degree thou hast him plac't,
And with a Crowne of honnour hast him grac't:
Thou hast him made *Lord* of thy *Creatures* all,
Subjectinge them to his commaund and call:
All Birds and Aiery Fowles are under him,　15
And fishes all which in the Sea doe swymme.
O *Lord* our *God*, how large is the extent
Of thy great name and glorie excellent.

Psalm 9

Thee will I thanke ever with my hart entire,
And make the world thy wondrous workes admire:
In thee rejoyce, in thee trihumph will I,
My songs shall praise thy name, O *God*, most high,
While my proud foes are put to shamefull flight,　5
And fall and perish at thy dreadfull sight.
Thou, righteous *Judge*, dost sitt upon thy *Throne*,
And do'st maintaine my rightfull cause alone:
Thou check'st the *Heathen*, and the wicked race
Thou dost destroy, and all their names deface.　10
O *Enemy*, behould thy finall fall:
Thy *Citties* perish, and their names withall;
But *God* our *Lord* for ever shall endure,
His judgement *Seate* hee hath establisht sure,
Where hee judges the *World* with equall right,　15
And measures *Justice* unto every wight:
Hee likewise will become a *Bulwarke* strong,
And tymely aide to them that suffer wrong.
Who knowes thy name, in thee his trust will place,
Who never failest them that seeke thy face.　20

8.17 extent *ed.*: entent *MS.*　　9.16 wight *ed.*: weight *MS.*

O praise the *Lord*, you that in *Sion* dwell,
His *Noble* Acts among the *Nations* tell;
When of oppression hee enquiry makes,
Of every poore mans plaint hee notice takes.
Have mercy *Lord*, and take into thy thought   25
My trubles, which my hatefull foes have wrought:
Thou from the gates of death my *Soule* dost raise,
That I in *Sions Gates* may sing thy praise;
The sweet salvation which thou dost impart,
Shall bee the joy and comfort of my hart.   30
The *Infidells* make pitts, and sinke therein;
Their feet are caught in their owne proper synne:
Thy judgement Lord, Thou hast thereby declar'd,
When wicked men in their owne workes are snar'd;
Hell is a place for impious men assign'd,   35
And such as doe cast *God* out of their minde;
But poore men shall not bee forgotten ever,
Nor meeke mens patience if they doe persever.
Rise Lord, and let [not] man above thee rise;
And judge the Infidells with angrie eyes: 40
Strike them with feare, that though they know not thee,
Yet they may know that mortall men they bee.

Psalm 10

Why standest thou O *Lord*, soe farr away?
And hid'st thy face when trubles mee dismay?
The wicked for his lust the poore man spoyles;
Lord take him in the trap of his owne wiles:
Hee makes his boasts of his profane desires,   5
Contemninge God while hee himselfe admires;
He is soe proud that *God* hee setts at naught;
Nay rather God comes never in his thought.
Thy judgements Lord, are farr above his sight;
This makes him to esteeme his foes soe light,   10
And in his hart to say, I cannot fall,
Nor can misfortune light on mee at all.
His mouth is full of execracions vile;
Under his tongue doth sit ungodly guile:

9.39 [not] *ed.*: *om. MS.*   10.1 O *ed.*: *l.c. MS.*

Close in the corners of the waies hee lies,   15
And lurkes and waits, the simple to surprize.
Even as a lyon lurkinge in his den
To'assault and murther innocent poore men;
Gainst whome his eyes maliciously are sett,
To catch them when they fall into his nett.   20
Himselfe hee humbles, bowes, and crouchinge stands,
Till poore men fall into his powerfull hands;
Then in his heart hee sayth God hath forgott,
Hee turnes away his face and sees it not.
Arise O Lord, and lift thy hand on high!   25
The poore forgett not which oppressed ly.
For why should wicked men blaspheme thee thus:
Tush, God is carelesse, and regards not us.
Surely thou seest the wronge which they have done,
And all oppressions under neath the Sunne;   30
To thee alone the poore his cause commends
As th'only freind of him that wanteth freinds.
Lord breake the power of the malicious minde,
Take ill away, and thou noe ill shalt finde.
The Lord is kinge and doth for ever raigne;   35
Nor miscreants shall within his land remaine.
Hee hearkeneth to the poore, but first prepareth
Their hearts to pray, then their peticion heareth;
That hee poore Orphans may both helpe and save,
That worldly men on them noe power may have.   40

Psalm 11

I trust in *God*; to mee why should you say,
Fly like a Bird to Mountaines farr away.
Their Bowes and Arrowes wicked men prepare
To peirce the hearts of them that faithfull are:
Even him whome *God* hath made a corner stone   5
They have cast downe; but what hath hee misdone?
God in his holy temple doth remaine,
The heav'n of *Heavens*, where hee doth sitt and raigne.

10.18 To' *ed.*: To *MS*.

Upon the poore hee casteth downe his eye,
The Sonns of *Men* hee doth discerne and trie.   10
The just and righteous men hee doth approve,
But hateth Synners which their sinns doe love:
On them hee rayneth snares, brimstone and fire;
This is their cup, their wages and their hire.
The righteous *God* loves him whose way is right,   15
And on the just his gracious eye doth light.

Psalm 12

Helpe, Lord, for all the godly men are gon,
And of the faythfull fewe there are or non;
Each man to other doth vaine things impart,
With lipps deceiptfull and with double hart.
The Lord will soone cutt off the lipps that lie,   5
And root out tongues that speake proud words and hi⟨gh⟩;
With mighty words wee will prevale, say they,
What Lord is hee that dareth us gainesay?
Now for the trubles and oppressions sore,
The gronings and the sighings of the poore,   10
I will arise, sayth *God*, and quell their foes
That swell with pride, and them in rest repose.
Gods words are pure and chaste, like silver tride
Which hath with seaven fires bene purified.
Thou wilt preserve them Lord, and guard them still   15
From this vile race of men which wish them ill;
The'ungodly walke in circles, yet goe free,
When such as feare not God exalted bee.

Psalm 13

How long O Lord, shall I forgotten bee?
How long wilt thou thy bright face hide from mee?
How long shall I my thoughts tosse to and fro,
And bee thus vext by my insultinge foe?

12.5 off *ed.*: of *MS.*   12.6 *Bracketed letters, supplied by editor, cut off in binding.*
12.17 The' *ed.*: The *MS.*

Give eare O Lord, give light unto mine eyes,   5
Lest death in endlesse sleepe doth mee surprise;
Lest my proud foe vaunt that hee doth prevaile,
And laugh at mee when I shall faint or faile.
But in thy mercie all my trust is pight,
And thy salvation is my hearts delight;   10
Of thy sweet kindnes therefore sing will I,
And highly praise the name of *God* most high.

Psalm 14

There is noe God, the foole sayth in his heart,
Yet dares not with his tongue his thought impart;
All are corrupt and odious in *Gods* sight,
Not one doth good, not one doth well upright.
God cast his eyes from heaven on all mankinde   5
And lookt if hee one righteous man could finde;
But all were wicked, all from God were gone;
Not one did good in all the world, not one.
Their throat an open grave, their flattering tongue
And lyinge lips like stinge of Aspes have stung;   10
With bitter cursing they their mouthes doe fill,
Their feet are swift the guiltles blood to spill.
Sad, wretched mischeife in their wayes doth lye,
But for the wayes of peace, they passe them by;
Noe feare of *God* have they before their eyes,   15
Nor knowledge while these mischeifes they devise,
While they *Gods* people doe with might oppresse,
And eat them up like bread with greedines.
And since on *God* they never use to call
They fear'd where cause of feare was non at all.   20
But to the righteous man, and to his race,
God present is with his protectinge grace;
Though fooles doe mocke the Counsell of the poore,
Because in God hee trusted evermore.
Who shall salvation out of *Sion* give   25
To *Israell* but God, Who shall releive
His people, and of *Captives* make them free.
Then *Jacob* joyfull, Israell glad shallbee.

Psalm 15

Lord, who shall dwell in thy bright Tent with thee?
And of thy rest in heaven pertaker bee?
Even hee that is upright in all his wayes,
And from his hart speakes truth in all hee sayes;
Who hath forborne to doe his neighbour wrong,   5
Nor him deceav'd or slaundered with his tong;
Who of himselfe an humble thought doth beare,
But highly valewes them which *God* doe feare;
Who of his promis doth himselfe acquitt,
Though losse hee suffer by performinge it;   10
Nor hath for bitinge use his monie lent,
Nor tooke reward against the innocent:
Who shall observe these poynts and doe them all,
Assuredly that man can never fall.

Psalm 16

Mee thy poore Servant, Lord, preserve and save,
For all my trust in thee repos'd I have.
Lord, said my Soule, thou art my *God*, to thee
My goods are nothinge when they offered bee;
But my delights are in those *Saints* of thine,   5
Which live on earth, and doe in vertue shine;
But they which runn to worshipp Idolls vaine
Shall multiply their sorrow and their paine.
Of their blood offerings will I not pertake,
Nor of their names shall my lipps mencion make;   10
The portion of mine heritage and cupp
Is God himselfe, who houlds and keepes mee upp;
In a faire ground to mee my lott did chance,
Soe I possesse a rich Inheritance.
Thankes bee to *God*, his warninge gives mee light;   15
My Raynes with paine doe chasten mee by night.
I looke to *God* in my endeavours all,
Hee stands soe neare mee that I cannot fall;
This hath my heart and tongue with joyes possest,
And now my flesh in hope to rise shall rest.   20

16.5 delights *ed.*: delight *MS*.

My soule shall not bee buryed in the grave,
Nor shall thy holy one corruption have:
Shew mee the path of life, for in thy sight
Doth endles pleasure rest, and full delight.

Psalm 17

Heare my just cause Lord, heare my prayer and crie,
Which come from lipps not us'd to faine or lie:
Lord let my sentence from thy mouth proceed,
For thou regards't things just and right indeed.
In the darke night of my adversitie   5
Thou dids't my hart examine, prove and trie;
And yet upon this triall did'st not finde
My heart or tongue to any ill enclin'de:
For that their workes against thy word are done,
I doe their wayes which tend to ruine shunn.   10
Lord, in thy pathes doe thou my goings guide,
Lest in this slippery life my footstepps slide;
Thy name have I invok't, thou shalt mee heare,
And to my humble words incline thy eare.
O Saviour of all those that trust in thee,   15
Thy mercies full of wonder shew to mee,
Preserve mee as the apple of thine eye,
Under thy winges in safetie let mee lie;
Save mee from them which thy right hand oppose,
And from my'ungodly circumventing foes.   20
Their fatt estates doe them soe fortifie
As they presume to speake proud words and high;
In all my wayes, in wait for mee hee lies,
To cast mee downe hee downewards casts his eyes;
Even like a Lyon watchinge for his pray,   25
Or Lyons whelpes which lurke beside the way.
Up Lord, defeat, defeat this foe of mine,
That wicked man who is a sword of thyne:

17.3–4 *The above text follows marginal alterations by a later hand, possibly that of Davies.*
Before alteration the lines read:
        Lord let my sentence from thy mouth bee given
        For thou regards't things only just and even.
17.20 my' *ed.*: my *MS.*   17.26 lurke *ed.*: lurkes *MS.*

From worldly men vouchsafe my soule to save,
Who in this mortall life their portion have,   30
Whose Bellies with thy treasure thou dost fill,
Who children have, and leave them wealth at will.
But I thy face in righteousnes shall see,
And with thy presence shall contented bee.

Psalm 18

Thou art my strength, O Lord, thee will I love;
Thou art my Rocke, which nothinge can remove:
My God, in whome my trust I will repose,
My Saviour, sheild and horne against my foes.
Lord most praise worthy, pray will I to thee,   5
Soe shall I from my foes protected bee
When deadly sorrowes did besett mee round,
And floods of wickednes did mee surhound,
When paines of hell I felt in my desease,
And pangs of death upon my Soule did sease.   10
On *God* I called in that instant truble,
And my complaints unto the Lord did dubble;
But when his wrath and vengeance kindled were,
The earth did quake and mountaines shooke for feare,
And coles grew redd with his inflaminge ire;   15
His presence smoke, his mouth sent wastinge fire:
Hee bowed the heavens, and did descend withall,
And shadowes darke beneath his feet did fall;
Hee ridinge on the *Cherubins* did fly,
And with the winged windes was borne on high;   20
Darkenes his clossett, his pavilion wide,
Made of blacke clouds his face a while did hide.
But at his presence bright away they flew
When haile and coles of fire abroad hee threwe:
The Lord from heaven did send his thunder loud,   25
With fire and haile from out the broken cloud;
A shower of Arrowes on his foes did fall,
His thunderboults and lightenings slewe them all:
Fountaines were dride, and the earthes foundation mov'd
When Synners in his wrath the Lord reprov'd.   30

18.8 surhound *ed.*: surbound *MS.*

But hee from heaven shall send His Angells downe,
And take mee up when waters would mee drowne;
Hee from my foe too mightie and too strong
Shall save mee when hee doth mee mightie wrong,
Preventinge mee [in] my disastrous day,   35
But then the Lord was my support and stay.
When I was captive hee did sett mee free,
And brought mee forth, because hee favoured mee;
He shall reward mee as my dayes bee right,
And hands bee cleane; soe shall hee mee requite.   40
For I still kept his pathes, and did not shunn
To walke therein, as other men have done,
But ever sett his lawes before mine eyes,
And never did his holy words dispise.
My heart was uncorrupt before him still,   45
Pursuinge goodnes and escheweinge ill;
Hee shall reward mee as my deeds bee right,
And hands bee cleane; soe shall hee mee requite.
Unto the good thou wilt thy goodnes show,
And righteous men thy righteousnes shall know,   50
The pure of heart shall thee behould most pure,
But froward men thy crosses shall endure.
Them will *God* raise, which under pressures ly,
And proud men humble, which doe looke soe high;
Hee shall sett up for mee a candle bright,   55
My *God* shall turne my darknes unto light.
Through thee an host of men I conquere shall,
And with thy helpe transcend the highest wal:
Gods way is pure, his word is tride with fire,
Hee heales all them which unto him retire;   60
For who is God? or who hath strength and power
Except our Lord, our *God* and only our?
Hee girdeth mee with furniture to fight,
And guideth mee, and houldeth mee upright;
My feet as swift as *Harts* feet hee doth make,   65
And up to honnors tower hee doth mee take;
Hee gives such strength unto my fingers weake
As that my Arme a Bowe of steele shall breake.

18.35 [in] *ed.: om. MS.*   18.40 cleane *ed. (cf. line 48)*: cleare *MS.*   *18.59+ All
those that trust in him will hee uphould *MS. (variant line)*

Thy hands shall bee my safety and protection,
Thou shalt advance mee with thy sweet correction,   70
Thou for my feet shalt make a passage wide
Soe as my steps shall never goe aside.
I shall pursue, and in pursuite outgoe,
And never turne till I have quelld my foe;
When I him smite, hee shall not rise at all,   75
If once at my victorious feet hee fall.
Thou hast mee girded with a sword of strength
Wherewith I shall subdue my foes at length;
For thou shalt turne the stubburne necke about
Of them that hate mee till I root them out: 80
Then shall they crie (but helpe there shall bee non)
Even to the Lord who shall not heare their mone.
My foes to powder I shall breake and bray,
And tread them downe like mire amid the way;
Thou my rebellious Subjects shalt accord,   85
And over Heathen Nations make mee Lord:
A people whome I knowe not shall mee serve,
And with base adulation mee observe;
These Aliens all shall faint and bee dismaid,
And in their strongest Castles bee afraid.   90
Live, Lord my strength, and blessed bee therefore,
And praised bee my Saviour evermore,
Who doth repay my foes with vengeance due,
And unto mee my Vassalls doth subdue;
Who doth not only save but sett mee high   95
Above my foes, and their feirce crueltie.
For this, both of my thankes and praise to thee,
The Heathen Nations witnesses shall bee;
For wealth and power and blessings manie moe,
On David and his race thou dost bestowe.   100

Psalm 19

The workmanship of heaven soe bright and faire,
Thy power O Lord, and glorie doth declare;
One day thy praise doth to another preach,
One night another doth in order teach:

18.75 smite *ed.*: sute *MS.*   18.98 Heathen *ed.*: Heathe *MS.*

Where ever any tongue or voyce doth sound,   5
In all the world their speech is heard around.
In middest of heaven the hand of God hath pight
For the Sunns lodgeinge a pavilion bright,
Who as a Bridegroome from his chamber goes,
Or *Giant* marchinge forth against his foes,   10
Hee issues, and from *East to West* doth runne;
His peircinge heat noe liveinge wight can shun.
Gods lawe is perfect, and mans soule renues,
And simple mindes with knowledge it endues;
Right are his Statutes, and rejoyce the heart,   15
Light to the eyes his precepts pure impart;
His feare is cleane and soe endures for aye,
His judgements true and righteous every way:
More sweet then honie, to bee valewed more
Then many heapes of finest goulden oare.   20
They rectifie withall thy servants minde,
And who soe keepes them, great reward shall finde.
But Lord, who knowes how oft hee doth transgresse?
O clense mee from my secret wickednes,
Nor let presumptuous sinns beare rule in mee: 25
Soe shall I from the great offence bee free.
And Lord, my strength and Saviour, soe direct
My words and thoughts as thou maiest them accept.

Psalm 20

The Lord give eare to thee in thy distresse,
And bee thy Sheild when trubles thee oppresse,
And let his helpe come downe from heaven for thee,
And strength from Syon hill imparted bee;
Let him remember and accept withall   5
Thine offerings, and thy sacrifices all,
And of his Bountie evermore fullfill
Thy hearts desire, and satisfie thy will.
But wee will glory in our great Gods name,
And joy in our salvation through the same,   10

19.9 [~~Whence~~] Who *MS.*   19.12 wight] weigh *altered by later hand to* weight;
then wight *written above by same later hand.*

And pray unto the Lord our *God* that hee
The'effect of all thy prayers will graunt to thee.
Hee now I know will heare, and helpe will bringe,
With his strong hand to his annoynted *Kinge*;
On Chariots some, on horses some rely,   15
But wee invoke the name of God most high.
Those others are bowed downe, and fall full lowe,
When wee are risen and upright doe goe;
Save us O Lord of heaven, and heare us thence,
When wee invoke thy name for our defence.   20

Psalm 21

Glad is the kinge, and joyfull is his hart,
That thou O Lord, his strength and safety art;
That thou hast given him what his heart desired,
And not denied him what his lipps required;
Preventinge him with blessings manifould,   5
And crowninge him with pure refined gould.
Hee askt thee life, thou gavest him length of daies,
Even endlesse life to give thee endlesse praise:
His safety through thy providence devine,
With honour great, and glorie makes him shine;   10
Blisse without end thou wilt to him impart,
The Sunn Beams of thy face shall cheare his hart,
For in thy mercy hee doth trust with all,
Which stayes his stepps, that hee shall never fall.
But thy long hand shall reach thy flyinge foe,   15
And finde him when hee most secure doth goe:
Thine enimies shall (when kindled is thine Ire)
As in a furnace bee consumed with fire;
Their ofspringe from the earth shall rotted bee,
Their second generation non shall see.   20
For against thee and thine, their Councell was,
Yet could not bringe their wicked plott to passe:
But turn'd their Backes, and put themselves to chase,
When thou hadst bent thy bowe against their face.
Bee pleased in thine owne strength thyselfe to raise,   25
Soe shall wee, Lord, thy power and mercie praise.

20.12 The' *ed.*: The *MS.*

Psalm 22

My God, my God, why leavest thou mee? and why
Dost thou soe farr withdraw thee from my crie?
I cry all day, but thou dost not give eare;
At night I cease not, yet thou wilt not heare:
Yet thou art holy still, thou God of might,   5
Thy peoples great renowne and glory bright.
When our forefathers plac't their hope in thee,
From cruell Bondage thou didst sett them free:
In thee they trusted, and to thee they prayed,
And never failed of thy cælestiall aid.   10
But as for mee, a worme, noe man am I;
A scorne to every man that passeth by:
They laugh and mocke my poore estate to see,
They draw their mouth and shake their heads at mee,
And say, hee hop't in God that hee should save him,   15
Now let God rescue him if hee will have him.
But thou Lord from my mothers wombe didst take mee,
And when I suckt her brest didst not forsake mee;
Even from my birth I was to thee bequeathed,
And thou hast bene my *God* since first I breathed.   20
O Leave mee not, when trubles doe mee presse,
And there is non to helpe mee in distresse:
Many strong Beasts have mee invironed,
As fatt and faire as Bulls in *Bashan* fedd:
They runne on mee with open mouthes and wide,   25
Like hungry Lyons rampinge in their pride.
My Soule like water on the earth is spilt,
My joynts are loosed, my heart like wax doth melt,
My Synewes shrunke are like a potsheard drie,
My tongue cleaves to my jawes, dead dust am I.   30
For many doggs have compast mee about,
I am besett with a malitious rout;
They peirce my hands and feet, and stare on mee,
And every ribb of my leane bodie see;
They spoyle mee of my *Garments*, and beside,   35
The parts thereof by lotts they doe devide.
Lord bee not farr, when I thy help shall need:
Thou art my strength, O succour mee with speed,

And sheild mee from the sword, and from the power
Of doggs which would my dearest *Soule* devoure;   40
And from the *Lyons* mouth, and from the hornes
Of many fearce insultinge Unicornes:
Among my kinn will I declare thy name,
And in the great assembly spread the same.
Yee that feare him, his praise and glory tell,   45
And honnour him yee seed of *Israell*;
Hee scorneth not the poore, nor hides his face,
But heares his crie when hee laments his case:
When all thy faithfull Folke assembled bee,
I sound thy praise and pay my vowes to thee;   50
The *Lord* shall fully satisfie the meeke,
Their soule shall live which his light face doe seeke.
Both *East and West* shall turne to their right minde,
And to the true *Gods* worshipp bee inclinde,
Who doth of all the world the *Scepter* beare,   55
Rules and commaunds the nations every where.
The fatt shall eate and worshipp him therefore,
And they that lye in dust shall him adore:
Even hee which cannot his owne life preserve,
Nor quicken his own Soule, the Lord shall serve.   60
Their seed O Lord shall serve to worshipp thee,
And with thy chosen people numbred bee,
And to their childrens children shall expresse
Thine everlasting truth and righteousnes.

Psalm 23

The *Lord* my *Sheaperd* is, hee doth mee feed;
His bounty evermore supplies my need.
When I in pastures greene my fill have tooke,
He leads mee forth into the silver Brooke;
Hee turnes my Soule when it is gon astray,   5
For His names glory, to his righteous way:
Therefore although my Soule detruded were
Even to Hell gates, yet I noe ill should feare.
When thou art with mee, what should mee dismay?
Thy Crooke my comfort is, thy Staffe my stay.   10

23.6 righteous *ed.* (*Grosart*): right *MS.*

My Table thou hast spread and furnisht soe
As glads my heart, and greives my envious foe;
Thy Balme powr'd on my head doth sweetly smell,
Thou makst my cup above the brimms to swell;
Thy mercy, while I breath, shal follow mee,   15
And in thy house my dwellinge place shallbee.

Psalm 24

The Earth, and all things which on the'earth remaine,
Even all the world doth to the *Lord* pertaine;
Amid the Sea hee founded hath the land,
And made this *Globe* above the floods to stand.
Who shall unto *Jehovahs Mount* assend?   5
Or who shall in his holy place attend?
Even hee whose hands are cleane, whose heart is pure,
Whose tongue is true, whose oath is just and sure.
Hee shall receave both righteousnes and Blisse
From *God*, whose mercy his salvation is: 10
Such are the seed of *Jacobs* faithfull race,
Which seeke the *Lord*, and long to see his face.
Yee everlastinge *Gates*, your heads upreare,
And let the king of glory enter there.
That glorious name, to whome doth it belong?   15
To God most mightie and in warr most stronge.
Eternall dores, lift [up] your heads I say,
That there the king of glorie enter may;
The king of glory enters, what is hee?
The lord of Hosts is knowne that kinge to bee.   20

Psalm 25

Mine humble Soule, O Lord, I lift to thee,
On whome my trust shall ever fixed bee.
O suffer not my cheekes with shame to glowe,
Nor make mee slave to my insultinge foe;
For they which hope in thee incurr noe blame,   5

23.14 brimms *ed.*: brimns *MS.*   24.1 the' *ed.*: the *MS.*   24.17 [up] *ed.*
(*Grosart*): om. *MS.*

But willfull synners shallbee cloth'd with shame.
To mee, O *Lord*, vouchsafe thy wayes to show,
And thy right pathes, that I therein may goe:
Teach mee the way of truth, direct my will;
Thou art my *Saviour*, I attend thee still.   10
Receave mee Lord, and to remembrance call
Thy ould compassions, and thy mercies all;
But of thy wonted grace to mee, O *Lord*,
O'the errours of my youth keepe noe record.
The Lord is good, and for his goodnes sake   15
Hee teaches Sinners godly wayes to take;
Yet hee his learninge doth to non impart,
But to the meeke and to the humble hart:
His pathes are grace and truth: that only way
Hee leads all those which doe his will obey.   20
For thy names glorie I doe thee intreat,
To my great sinns extend thy mercie great;
To him which feares the *Lord*, the Lord doth showe
How in his callinge hee may safely goe;
His soule shall bee at ease, and all his race   25
Shall in the land possesse a blessed place.
His covenant and his Councells neare,
God shewes to them in whome hee plants his feare;
My looke to him shall ever raised bee
Who from the nett, my captive feet doth free.   30
Have mercy Lord on mee, and turne thy face
To see my desolate and witherd case:
Enlarged is my greife and heavines,
But Lord, enlarge thou mee from my distresse.
Looke on the wofull *State* that I am in,   35
Remitt the cause thereof which is my synne;
My foes consider, and their multitude
Which mee with deadly hatred hath pursude;
And keepe my soule from sinne, my face from shame,
Who trust in thee and call upon thy name.   40
Let truth and righteousnes without deceipt
Still wait on mee, because on thee I wait;
And sett thy faithfull *Israell* at rest
From all the trubles which doe him molest.

25.14 O' *ed.*: O *MS.*   25.39 my [~~face~~] soule from [~~shame~~] sinne *MS.*

Psalm 26

Bee thou my *Judge, O Lord,* my cause is just:
I shall not stagger while in thee I trust.
Weigh and examine mee, search all my vaines,
The bottome of my heart and inward raines.
I sett thy goodnes ever in my sight,   5
Which in thy truth doth guide my stepps aright;
I use not to converse with persons vaine,
Nor with dissemblers, fellowship retaine;
My soule the'assembly of the wicked hates,
Nor will I sitt among ungodly *Mates.*   10
Repentance haveinge made my conscience cleare,
Then will I, Lord, approch thine *Alter* neare,
That I may thanke [thee] both with harte and voyce,
And tellinge of thy wondrous workes rejoyce.
Thy temple, *Lord,* I love exceeding well,   15
Wherein thy *Majestie and glorie* dwell;
O let not sinfull men my soule enclose,
Nor of my life let sinfull men dispose,
Whose hands are foule (their sinns them foule doe make)
And full of guifts which they corruptly take.   20
But I to leade a blamelesse life entend;
O *Lord* therein with mercie mee defend;
My foot stands right, and therefore all my dayes
In all assemblies I the Lord will praise.

Psalm 27

God is my light, salvation, strength and aid:
Of whome and what shall I then bee afraid?
The wicked came to have devour'd mee quite,
But stumbled in their way, and fell downe right;
Though mighty Armies in my wayes were laid,   5
I stand secure, I cannot bee dismaid.
One thinge I wish, even while I live to dwell
In *Gods* faire house, whose beauty doth excell;

26.9 the' *ed.:* the *MS.*   26.13 [thee] *ed. (Grosart): om. MS.*   26.18 my
[~~Soule~~] life *MS.*   26.21 leade *ed.:* leave *MS.*

His tent in time of truble shall mee hide,
And I shall on his rocke of safety bide: 10
Now shall hee lift my head above my foes,
Which mee with armed multitudes enclose;
And now will I his praise in trihumph singe,
And joyfull offerings to his temple bringe;
And let my cries approch thy gracious eare,   15
Vouchsafe in mercie my complaints to heare;
My heart doth tell, that thou biddest mee still
Thy face to seeke: Lord, seek thy face I will.
Then doe not hide from mee thy face soe bright,
Nor in thy wrath exclude mee from thy sight;   20
Thou ever wert mine aid since I was borne:
God of my safety, leave mee not forlorne.
My father and my mother both forsooke mee,
But then the *Lord* to his tuition tooke mee:
Teach mee the way, that I therein may goe;   25
Soe shall I never fall before my foe,
Nor fall into their power which doe mee hate,
And brought false oathes against mee in the gate.
My heart had fail'd, but that my hope to see
Gods endlesse blisse in heaven did comfort mee: 30
Then stay *Gods* time, hee shall thee stay at length;
And hee till then shall arme thy heart with strength.

Psalm 28

Heare (Lord my strength) the cries I make to thee;
I am but dead if thou seeme deafe to mee.
Heare when with humble prayer I thee entreat,
With lifted hands before thy mercy seate;
But rancke mee not with those which wicked are,   5
Whose lipps speake peace, whose hearts are full of warr;
Accordinge to their Actions let them speed,
And as their merrit is, soe make their meed.
For that they see thy workes, and yet neglect them,
Thou shalt destroy and never more erect them;   10

27.10 on *ed.*: in *MS.*   27.17 biddest *ed.*: bidst *MS.*   28.4 hands *ed.*
(*Grosart*): hand *MS.*

The Lord bee praisd, who hath vouchsaft to heare,
And lend unto my prayer a gracious eare.
His sheild protects, his strength doth mee advance;
My tongue shall singe his praise, my heart shall dance:
Hee to his Servants force and vertue gives,   15
Through him in safetie his annoynted lives.
Save thy peculier people Lord, and blesse them,
And lift their heads above them that oppresse them.

Psalm 29

Yee kings, since by *Gods* power and grace yee raigne,
Glory and power ascribe to him againe;
Yeild him the honnour due to his great name,
And in his glorious *Courts* his praise proclaime.
His voyce doth cause the Seas to swell and slake,   5
And in the heavens the dreadfull thunder make;
Jehovahs voice effects of power doth breed,
It is a stronge and glorious voyce indeed:
His voyce the Cedars doth in sunder teare,
The *Cedars* which *Mount Lebanus* doth beare;   10
Makes *Lebanus* and *Hermon* hill to tremble,
And skippinge *Calves* and *Unicornes* resemble,
Doth breake the Clouds, and flames of fire devide,
The deserts shake, even *Cades* desert wide;
Makes *Hindes* to calve, for feare, makes forrests bare,   15
While in his temple wee his praise declare.
The Lord upon the water floods doth raigne;
The *Lord* a *Kinge* for ever doth remaine:
The Lord shall still his peoples strength encrease,
And give to them the blessinge of his peace.

Psalm 30

Highly the *Lord* I praise who setts mee high,
Above my proud insultinge enimie;
Sicke to the death, I cried to *God* for ease,
And hee hath cur'd my dangerous desease;

Hee from the grave hath lifted up my head,   5
And hath reduc't mee from among the dead.
Yee *Saints* of his, in Songs his praise expresse,
With thanks make mention of his holines;
For momentarie his displeasure is,
When in his favour there is life and blisse;   10
Sad sorrow may continue for a night,
But joy returneth with the morninge light.
When my estate did prosper, then said I,
I shall not fall, my Seat is fixt on high;
But when thou, Lord, didst turne thy face aside,   15
Then was I trubled, and to thee I cride;
To thee began I then againe to pray,
And in my humble prayer thus did say,
What profitt can there by my death arise,
When buried in the grave my bodie lies?   20
Shall dust and ashes celebrate thy name?
Or shall the silent *Toombe* thy truth proclaime?
Lord heare my prayer, and then thy mercie show,
In aidinge mee against my cruell foe;
Loe now to dancinge thou hast turnd my sadnes,   25
Put off my sackloth, girded mee with gladnes.
For this shall everie good man singe thy praise,
And I shall thanke and blesse thee all my dayes.

Psalm 31

In thee, O Lord, have I put all my trust;
Then rescue mee from shame, as thou art just.
Give eare, and soone from perill sett mee free;
Bee thou a *Rocke* and stronge defence to mee:
Thou art my Rocke and *Castle* when I stray,   5
Bee thou my Guide, and lead mee in the way.
Thou art my strength, O cleare mee from that net
Which privily my foes for mee have sett;
Into thy handes my Soule I doe committ,
Lord God of truth, thou hast redemed it.   10

30.26 girded *ed.*: guarded *MS.*

I hate all those which in vaine lies delight,
For all my trust is in the lord of might:
Thy mercies glad my heart; for in my woe
Thou hast vouchsaft my [trubled] Soule to knowe.
Thou hast not left mee prisoner with my foe,   15
But sett mee free, that I at large may goe.
Yeild to my trubles mercifull releife;
My eares wax deafe, my heart doth melt with greife.
Few are my yeares in number to bee tould,
Yet sorrow, care, and greife hath made mee ould;   20
My strength with prayer and anguish doth decay,
My joints growe weake, my Bones consume away:
I am a scorne to all my enimies,
But specially my *Neighbours* mee dispise;
My very presence did my freinds affright,   25
And all my ould acquaintance shun my sight.
I am forgott as if I buried lay,
And viler then a broken pott of *Clay*.
I heard the raylings of the multitude,
And trembled while they did my death conclude;   30
But all my hope hath bene, O *Lord*, in thee,
Whome I professe my only *Lord* to bee.
My tyme is in thy hand; O doe not leave
Mee in their hands which would my life bereve:
O turne to mee the brightnes of thy face,   35
And save mee through thy mercie and thy grace;
Make not mee blush, who did invoke thy name,
But put my foes to silence and to shame,
And let the lipps bee dumbe which utter lyes,
Against the righteous in spightfull wise.   40
O what rich blessings dost thou keepe in store
For them that feare and love thee evermore;
Thou shalt protect them from the great mens pride,
And in thy Tent from storme of tongues them hide.
Blest bee the *Lord*, whose mercies manifold   45
Doe keepe mee safer then the strongest hold;
When I with passion was transported quite,
I said I was sequesterd from his sight,
And yet (for all my weaknes) heard was I,

31.14 [trubled] *ed.: om. MS.*

When to my *Maker* I did make my crie. 50
Love Him, yee *Saints* of his, who guardeth those
Who trust in him, and pay'st their proudest foes.
Yee that rely on him be strong of hart,
And hee to you shall heavenly strength impart.

Psalm 32

Happie indeed, and truly blest is hee
Whose Sinns remitted, and faults covered bee;
To whome the *Lord* doth not impute his sinne,
Whose single heart hath not deceipt therein.
When I was silent I consum'd away, 5
And pyninge greife did waste mee day by day;
Thy hand on mee was heavy still, whereby
My moisture grewe like draught in Summer drie.
My sinne I will acknowledge, *Lord*, to thee;
My secret faults shall not concealed bee: 10
I said I will my synnes to God confesse,
And God forthwith forgave my wickednesse.
If good men seeke him when hee may bee found,
The worlds high waves shall never them surround.
Thou hid'st mee close, and savest mee from annoy, 15
And do'st environe mee with songs of joy;
When thou hast sett mee in thyne owne right way,
Thine eye doth guide mee that I doe not stray.
Then must I not bee Brute, as horse and Mule
Which men with bitt and bridle only rule: 20
With many whipps God doth the wicked chase,
But doth with mercies faithfull men embrace.
Bee glad, rejoyce, and glory in the *Lord*,
All yee whose hearts doth with his will accord.

Psalm 33

Rejoyce yee Righteous in the *Lord*, and singe;
To give *God* thankes, it is a comely thinge:
Singe prayses unto him, and sett your songs
To harpe and *Lute* that speaketh with ten tongues;
Singe to the *Lord* a new composed songe, 5

With chearfull heart and with affection stronge;
For his most holy word is ever true,
And all his workes his constancie doe shew.
Hee loveth right and justice evermore,
And with his blessinge hee the earth doth store;   10
For by his word the heavens created were;
His breath made every *Starr* and every *Sphare.*
The Seas as in a *Storehouse* hee doth keepe,
And heapes them up as treasures in the deepe;
The earth before the *Lord* shall quake for feare,   15
And all that dwell on his round *Center* here:
Hee spake, and they were made at his commaund;
The heavens began to move, the earth to stand.
Councells of princes and of *Nations* great,
And peoples plotts his wisdome doth defeat;   20
But Gods owne Counsell, purpose and decree
Eternall stand and cannot frustrate bee.
That *Nation* hath true happines and Blisse
Whose *God* and *Lord* the *Lord Jehovah* is;
Downe from the highest *heaven* the *Lord* did looke,   25
And of all men a full survay hee tooke:
From heaven above the *Lord* did cast his eye,
And all mens wayes and wanderings did espie.
Hee formed all their hearts and understands
Their thoughts, their words, and workes of all their hands. 30
The greatest Armies cannot save a *Kinge*,
Nor strength unto a stronge man safety bringe;
His trust is vaine who trusteth in his horse,
And seekes deliverance by soe small a force.
With gracious eye the *Lord* behoulds the just,   35
Which him doe feare and in his mercie trust
In tyme of dearth their hungrie soules to feed,
And from deathes jawes to rescue them with speed.
Our soules with patience for the *Lord* have staid,
Who is our only sheild, support and aid: 40
Our hearts shall him as our true joy embrace,
For wee our only trust in him doe place;
Thy mercie *Lord*, to us exceeded bee,
According to the hope wee have in thee.

33.12 *Sphare ed.: Spare MS.*

Psalm 34

Lord evermore will I give thankes to thee,
And in my mouth thy praise shall ever bee;
My Soule shall boast that shee thy servant is;
The humble shall bee glad to heare of this.
Come then, *O come* and let us praise the *Lord*,   5
And magnifie his name with sweet accord.
I sought the *Lord* by prayer, which hee did heare,
And saved mee from that ill my Soule did feare.
Looke towardes God, thou shalt enlightened bee,
And noe foule shame shall ever light on thee: 10
The poor mans crie the *Lord* doth quickly heare,
And doth from all his trubles quitt him cleare;
Such as feare God, his Angell guards them all
From every mischeife that may them befall.
O taste the *Lord*, and see how sweet hee is: 15
The man that trusts in him lives still in Blis.
O feare the *Lord*, yee that are *saints* of his:
Who feare the *Lord* noe needfull thinge shall misse.
Rich become poore, and lyons hungrie bee,
But such as feare the *Lord* noe want shall see.   20
Come then yee *Children*, listen and give eare,
And I will teach you this religious feare:
What man art thou that longest long to live,
And wouldst that *God* to thee good dayes should give?
Refraine thy tongue from speakeing ill the while,   25
And from thy lipps let there proceed noe guile;
Doe that is good, decline from that is ill;
Seeke peace with God and men, and hould it still:
Upon good men God casts a gentle eye,
And lends a gentle eare unto their crye.   30
But to the wicked shewes an angrie browe,
Till they bee quite exterped root and bough;
But when the righteous cry, the *Lord* doth heare them,
And from all trubles absolutely cleare them.
Gods present helpe the [contrite heart] doth finde,   35
And such hee saves as are of humble minde;

34.32 bough *ed.*: bow *MS.*   *34.35 [contrite heart] *ed.*: Lord *MS.*: Lord['s
own folk] *Grosart*

The righteous into many trubles fall,
But Gods sweet mercy brings them out of all:
Their very Bones so keepe and count doth hee,
As not one broken nor one lost shall bee: 40
But some foule death shall on the wicked light,
And they which hate the just shall perish quite;
But of his servants *God the Saviour* is:
They trust in him, their hope they cannot misse.

Psalm 35

Plead Thou my cause, O *Lord* my Advocate,
Against all those with whome I have debate;
Fight against them that doe against mee fight,
Take up thy sheild, and helpe mee with thy might;
Lift up thy *Launce*, stopp them which mee pursue: 5
Say to my *Soule*, I am thy *Saviour* true.
Let shame on them which seeke my ruin light,
And with confusion turne them all to flight:
Let them bee like the dust before the winde,
With *Gods* feirce Angell followinge them behinde;   10
Set them in slipperie wayes, and darke withall,
And let Gods Angell smite them as they fall:
For they have spred a nett, and dig'd a pitt,
Even without cause, to catch my soule in it.
But in that pitt let them fall unawares,   15
And bee entangled in their proper snares;
But thou my Soule, whome God thus guids from ill,
Rejoyce in him and his salvation still:
My bones shall say, *Lord* who is like to thee,
Who poore weake men from their strong foe dost free?   20
Falce witnesses arose with oathes untrue,
And charged mee with things I never knew:
They (to my greife) did ill for good requite,
And recompenc't my kindnes with dispight;
Yet in their sicknes I did sackcloth weare,   25
And fast and pray with many'a secret teare:

35.12 they *ed.*: the *MS.*   35.26 many' *ed.*: many *MS.*

I could not more for freind or brother mourne
Or if my mother to her grave were borne.
But in my woe they made great mirth and glee,
The very Abjects mockt and mowde at mee: 30
Base flatterers, and *Jesters* came withall,
[And] gnasht their teeth to show their bitter gall:
How long shall this bee *Lord*? my soule withdraw
From these mens wrongs, and from the lyons jaw:
Soe in thy *Church* shall I my thankes proclame, 35
And in our great assembly praise thy name.
Let not my foes trihumph on mee againe,
Nor with their mockinge eyes shew their disdaine;
They meet and parte, but peace they doe not seeke,
But to supplant the peaceable and meeke: 40
They gape and drawe their mouthes in scornefull wise,
And cry *fie, fie*, wee sawe it with our eyes.
But thou their deeds, O *Lord*, dost alsoe see:
Then bee not silent; goe not farr from mee.
Awake, stand up O *God and Lord of might:* 45
Avenge my quarrell, judge my cause aright.
To thy *doome* rather lett mee fall or stand,
Then subject bee to their insultinge hand.
Then they should say, soe, soe, these things goe right,
We have our will, and have devour'd him quite. 50
Shame bee to them that joy in my mischance,
And which to cast mee downe themselves advance;
Let them bee glad that my wellwishers bee,
And blesse the Lord that hath soe blessed mee:
As for my tongue, it shall sett forth thy praise, 55
And celebrate thy justice all my dayes.

Psalm 36

The wicked mans bould sinns my heart doe tell,
Noe feare of God before his eyes doth dwell;
Yet flattereth hee himselfe in his owne sight,
Untill his hatefull deeds bee brought to light;
His words are lies, and most deceiptfull too; 5
He leaves off quite all honest deeds to doe.

35.32 [And] *ed.* (*Grosart*): *om. MS.*   36.6 off *ed.*: of *MS.*

Hee on his Bed doth nought but mischeife muse;
Hee shunns noe ill, and noe good way doth choose.
Thy mercie, *Lord*, doth to the heavens extend;
Thy faithfullnes doth to the *Cloudes* assend;   10
Thy justice stedfast as a *Mountaine* is,
Thy *judgements* deepe, as is the great *Abisse*;
Thy *Noble* mercies save all liveinge things;
The sonnes of men creepe underneath thy winges.
With thy great plenty they are fedd at will,   15
And of thy pleasures streame they drinke their fill;
For even the well of life remaines with thee,
And in thy glorious light wee light shall see:
To them that know thee, *Lord*, bee loveinge still,
And just to them whose heart intends noe ill;   20
Let not the foot of pride tread on my *Crowne*,
Nor the'hand of the ungodly cast mee downe:
Fallne are the wicked in their slippery wayes,
And have noe power againe themselves to raise.

Psalm 37

If ill men prosper, doe not thou repine,
Nor envy them though they in glory shyne;
For as the grasse they shall bee mowen away,
And as greene hearbes shall turne to withered hay:
Trust thou in God, and still bee doinge good,   5
And thou shalt never want nor house nor food.
Delight in him, hee shall to thee imparte
The full desires and wishes of thy heart;
On him rely, to him thy way commend,
And hee shall bringe it to a blessed end.   10
Thine upright light shall shine like morninge light,
And thy just dealinge, like the *Noone*-day bright:
Bee still, and frett not, but *Gods* leasure stay,
Though wicked men doe prosper in their way.
Suppresse thine Anger, let offences die,   15
Lest thou bee moved to offend thereby:
Expect a while, observe what will befall;
Th'ungodly shallbee gon, their place and all:

37.2 they *ed.* (*Grosart*): thou *MS.*   37.18 Th'ungodly *ed.*: Thungodly *MS.*

The *Lord* shall root out Sinners out of hand
When good men and their heires shall hould their land.   20
Meeke persons shall enjoy the earthes encrease,
And shall abound in plentie and in peace;
Against the just the wicked have combin'd,
And in dispight their teeth at them they grinde;
But God with scorne behoulds them from the *Skie*,   25
For that hee sees their day of ruin nigh:
The'ungodly drawes his sword, and bends his Bowe,
To slay the just, the weake to overthrowe:
But his bent Bowe shall breake, and make him start,
And his owne sword shall peirce his wicked heart.   30
That little which the just enjoyes with peace
Is better then th'ungodlies great encrease;
For th'armes of impious men the *Lord* will breake,
And give the righteous strength when they are weake.
The just mans dayes the *Lord* doth know and see,   35
That his inheritance shall endlesse bee;
The tymes of danger shall not him confound,
And in the dayes of dearth hee shall abound.
Thy foes, O *Lord*, shall perish and consume
Like fatt of *Lambes*, and vanish into fume: 40
Th'ungodly want and borrow, but repay not,
The good men frankly give, yet [they] decay not;
Their seat is firme whom God hath best belov'd,
But such as hee doth curse shall bee remov'd.
The good mans goings soe directeth hee   45
As it most pleasing to himselfe may bee;
Oft falls the just, yet is not cast away,
For Gods owne hand is his support and stay.
Though I am ould, the just man or his seed,
I never sawe forsaken or in need: 50
Hee doth give daily Almes, and frankly lend
Which makes his offspringe blessed in the end.
Shun to doe ill, bee ever doinge well,
And evermore thou shalt in safety dwell;
The *Lord* (who loveth right) forsaketh never   55
Those that are his, but keepeth them for ever:

37.27 The' *ed.*: The *MS.*   37.32 th'ungodlies *ed.*: thungodlies *MS.*
37.42 yet [they] *ed.*: yet *MS.*: [and] yet *Grosart*

His children hee correcteth now and then,
But roots out quite the race of wicked men.
As long as *Heaven* shall move, and earth shall stand,
The righteous men inherit shall the land; 60
The just mans mouth is wisdomes flowinge well,
His tongue of truth and judgement loves to tell;
And in his heart the lawe of *God* doth bide,
Which makes him walke upright and never slide.
The wicked sees the just with envious eye, 65
And lies in waite to wound him mortally;
But God will never leave him to his hands,
Nor him condemne when hee in judgement stands:
Then wait thou on the *Lord*, and keepe his way;
Hee shall thy patience with promotion pay: 70
Thy dwellinge in the *Land* shall stablisht bee,
When thou the fall shalt of the wicked see.
The'ungodly in great power myselfe have seene,
Soe that hee florish't like a Bay tree greene;
Eft soones I passed by, and gon was hee, 75
His place I sought, but noe where could it see.
Keepe a cleare conscience, right and truth intend,
For that brings peace and comfort in the end;
When Sinners shall at once togeather fall,
And in the end shallbee exterped all. 80
But good mens safety doth from God proceed,
Who is their strength in truble, helpe at need;
Against the wicked hee assists the just,
And rescues them because in him they trust.

Psalm 38

If for my Sinns thine Anger kindled bee,
Lord, let not then thy justice chastice mee;
Thine Arrowes fixed in my fleshe doe stand,
I feele the pressure of thy heavie hand:
I have noe health, thine Anger is soe much; 5
My bones noe rest, my greivous synne is such:

37.73 The' *ed.*: The *MS.*

My wickednes doth mount above my head,
And fallinge presse mee like a load of lead;
My ulcers are corrupted and doe smell,
Caus'd by my folly, which I blush to tell.   10
I am with greife soe broken and soe torne,
As I all day in heart and habit mourne.
My *loynes* are filled with a sore desease,
Noe parte of all my bodie feeleth ease;
I am soe faint, soe feeble and soe sore,   15
As paine and anguish make mee crie and roare.
Thou, *Lord*, the longings of my heart dost see,
My sighes and groanings are not hidd from thee;
My heart doth pant, my sinewes faile mee quite,
My weepinge eyes have lost their power of sight: 20
Meane while my freinds and Neighbours they looke on,
My nearest kinsmen farthest off are gon;
And they which seeke my life have layed their snares,
And sett their trapps to catch mee unawares.
They that to doe mee mischeife lye in wait,   25
Doe plott and practise nothinge but deceit.
But as for mee, in silent patience
I seemed deafe and dumbe, and voyd of sence;
As one whose eare admitts not any sound,
And in whose mouth there is noe answeare found.   30
For on the *Lord* I evermore rely,
Though I stand mute thou shalt for mee replie;
My Suite is that my foes may not prevaile,
Who greatly joy to see my footinge faile;
For in a place of stumblinge sett am I,   35
My sad estate is still before mine eye.
But I with sorrow will confesse my synne,
And greive that I offend my God therein,
And yet my foes do live and grow in might;
They grow in number which do beare mee spight.   40
They which doe ill for good doe hate mee too,
Because I love good turnes for ill to doe;
Lord leave mee not, ne from mee farr depart,
Save mee with speed; for thou my safety art.

38.22 off *ed.*: of *MS.*   38.30 there *ed.*: their *MS.*

Psalm 39

I said I will bee wary in my way,
Lest I offend in that my tongue should say:
I will my mouth as with a Bridle hould,
While wicked men with envy mee behould.
I dumbe did stand, and from all speech refraine,   5
Even from good words, which was to mee a paine:
My heart was hott, while I such doubts did cast;
The fire brake out, and thus I spake at last:
Lord of my life, reveale to mee the end;
The period showe to which my dayes doe tend.   10
My life is but the measure of a spann;
Nought as to thee: soe vaine a thinge is man,
Who dreaminge walkes and toyles for wealth in vaine,
And doth not know to whome it shall remaine.
But what doe I expect? what is my hope?   15
Of my desires thou art the only scope.
Lord, from my Synnes thine indignation turne,
And make mee not to wicked fooles a scorne;
When thou didst strike, I silent was and dum,
Because I knew the blowe from thee did come.   20
Remove thy hand; withdrawe thy plague from me,
Wherewith my vitall spirrits consumed bee.
Thy plagues for sinne doth like a moth consume
Mans beauty vaine, which is nought else but fume.
Lord heare my prayer, and listen to my cries;   25
Let not thy gracious eye my teares dispise;
For I am but thy guest, and sojourne here:
On earth a pilgrim as my fathers were.
O spare a little, and my strength restore,
Before I goe from hence to come noe more.   30

Psalm 40

Long on the Lord I waited patiently,
Till hee enclin'd his eare, and heard my cry;
Drew mee from out the pitt of mire and clay,
Did sett mee on firme ground, and guide my way:

39.10 showe *ed.*: showes *MS*.   39.27 here *ed.*: heare *MS*.

Put in my mouth a new and joyfull song,   5
Of thankes and praise, that to himselfe belong:
Of this great mercie many shall have sence,
And of the *Lord* have feare and confidence.
Blest is the man who hath on God reli'de,
Not turninge unto lies or wordly pride;   10
O Lord, thy workes of wonder, they are such,
Thy care and love to usward is soe much;
They are soe great, they are soe numberlesse,
As if I would I could not them expresse.
My sacrifice of meates thou would'st not take,   15
But thou mine eare didst peirce and open make;
Thou didst not aske burnt offerings at my hand,
Then *Lord*, said I, I come at thy commaund:
Thy Booke eternall doth of mee record
That I should come to doe thy will, O Lord: 20
To doe thy will my heart is pleased well,
For in my heart thy lawe doth ever dwell.
Thy truth I have to all thy people tould,
Therein thou knowest my tongue I cannot hould;
Thy justice in my heart is not conceal'd,   25
Thy mercy to the world I have reveal'd;
I have not spar'd to make thy Bounty knowne,
But in the great assembly have it showne.
Take not thy wonted mercy *Lord* from mee,
But let thy goodnes still my safety bee: 30
My trubles numberlesse such hould have tooke
On my weake soule as up I cannot looke:
My sinns beinge more than haires upon my head,
Make my heart faint and vitall spirrits dead.
But bee it, Lord, thy pleasure and thy will,   35
With speed to save and rescue mee from ill:
Bringe them to shame that would my life destroy,
Reprove them *Lord*, that wish my soules annoy.
Let them bee left to scorne and pride with blame,
Which scorninge say to mee, fie, fie for shame;   40
But let all those that seeke their blisse in thee,
Rejoyce and say, the *Lords* name praised bee.
For mee, who am contemtible and poore,
The *Lord* takes care and feeds mee evermore;

Thou, *Lord*, art my protection and my aid;   45
Let not thy gracious helpe bee long delay'd.

Psalm 41

That man is blest who doth the poore regard;
In tymes of trouble God shall him reward,
Prolong his life, and blesse him in the land,
And free him from his foes oppressinge hand;
Shall comfort him when sicke and weake hee lies,   5
And make his bedd till hee in health doe rise.
My synne hath given my soule a greivous wound;
Apply thy mercy Lord, and make it sound.
Thus speakes my foe of mee, to show his spight,
When shall his life and honnour perish quite?   10
Hee vissitts mee but with falce heart and tongue,
And thereof vaunts his complices amonge;
Even all my foes against mee doe conspire,
And with one minde my ruin doe desire:
Let him (say they of mee) in judgement fall,   15
And when hee once is downe, not rise at all.
The freind I trusted, which did eat my bread,
Hath lifted up his heele against my head;
Thy mercies winges on mee, O Lord display,
Raise mee againe, and I shall them repay: 20
By this I doe thy gracious favour see,
In that my foe doth not trihumph on mee.
Thou in my health uphouldst mee with thy hand,
And in thy presence I shall ever stand:
The name of *Jacobs God* bee blessed then,   25
From age to age for evermore: amen.

Psalm 42

As for the streames the hunted *Hart* doth bray,
Soe for Gods grace my heart doth pant and pray.
My soule doth thirst (O God of life) for thee,
When shall I come thy blessed face to see?

My teares are all my food both night and day,   5
While, where is now thy God? the wicked say.
I powred out my hart while thus I thought,
And to Gods house the multitude I brought,
With songs of praise and thankfullnes withall,
To celebrate the lords great festivall.   10
Then why art thou, my soule, soe full of woe?
Unquiet in thy selfe, and vexed soe?
O put thy trust in God, and thankfull bee,
For his sweet helpe his presence yeilds to thee.
My soule is greiv'd, remembringe all the ill   15
I felt in *Jordans* vale, and *Hermon* hill:
One depth of sorrow doth to'another call,
Thy waves, O God, have overgon mee all:
I prais'd at night Gods bounty of the day,
And unto him that gives mee life did pray.   20
God of my strength, why hast thou left mee soe,
With heavy heart oppressed by my foe?
My foe doth cutt my bones as with a sword,
While hee in scorne repeates this bitter word,
Where is thy God? (his speech to mee is such)   25
Where is thy God of which thou talk'st soe much?
But why art thou, my soule, dejected soe?
Why art thou trubled and soe full of woe?
Trust thou in God, and give him thankfull praise,
Who is thy present helpe in all thy wayes.   30

Psalm 43

Judge thou mee, [plead my] cause, and right mee then
Against ungodly and deceiptfull men.
O God my strength, why settst thou mee aside,
And leav'st mee to my foes oppressinge pride?
Send forth thy light and truth, and guide mee still   5
In the right way to thy most holy hill:
God of my joy, before thine Alter high
My thankfull harte my harpe shall justifie.

42.17 to' *ed.*: to *MS.*   42.29 [O put thy trust in God and thankfull bee] *MS.*
43.1 mee, [plead my] cause *ed.*: mee cause *MS.*

Then why art thou, my Soule, dejected soe?
Why art thou trubled and soe full of woe?　　　　10
O put thy trust in God, and thankfull bee,
For that sweete aide his presence gives to thee.

Psalm 44

Lord, of thy workes our fathers have us tould,
Donne in their dayes and former times of ould,
How thou hast rooted out the *Pagan* race,
And thy choice people planted in their place,
Who did not with their owne sword winne the land,　　5
Nor make the conquest with their proper hand,
But by thine Arme, thy favour and thy grace,
Thy countenance and brightenes of thy face.
Thou art my *Kinge* O God, and royal Guide,
And thou for *Jacobs* safety dost provide.　　　　10
Wee through thine aid our foes doe bouldly meet,
And by thy vertue cast them at our feet;
Therefore my trust I place not in my Bowe,
Nor in my sword to save mee from my foe:
Thou only sav'st us from our enimies,　　　　15
Confoundinge them that doe against us rise.
Wee boast and glory in our strength therefore,
And to thy name singe praises evermore.
But now thou standest off, and leav'st us quite,
And dost not lead our Armies out to fight;　　　20
Thou makst us fly before our foes with feare,
While they from us rich spoyles away doe beare:
Like *sheepe* to feed them, thy poore flocke is given,
Or scattered into severall *Nations* driven.
Thyne owne deare people thou dost sell for naught,　25
And setts on them noe price when they are bought;
Thou hast us made unto our *Neighbours* all
An object of reproch, and scorne withall;
To *Nations* which doe worship *Idolls* dumbe
Wee are a byword of contempt become.　　　　30

44.19 off *ed.*: of *MS.*

All the day long my shame is in my sight,
Which makes mee hide my face and shunn the light,
Not able to endure the blasphemies
And scornes of my revengefull enimies.
For all these ills wee doe not thee forgett,   35
Thy blessed *Covenant* wee renounce not yet;
Our hearts recede not from the *Lawe* devine,
Nor doe our footsteps from thy pathes declyne;
Though wee in denns of dragons have bene plac't,
And with deaths fearfull shadowes overcast.   40
If wee the name of our true *God* forgett,
And Idolls falce wee in his place doe sett,
Shall not hee search [this] out, whose eye doth see
The heart of man, whose thoughts most trubled bee?
But for thy cause, *Lord*, wee are martird still,   45
Like *sheep* which *slaughter men* cull out to kill.
Up Lord, why dost thou seeme to slumber thus?
Awake and bee not alwayse farr from us:
Why hidest thou from us thy blessed face,
Forgettinge our distresse and wretched case?   50
Our soules even to the dust are humbled lowe,
Our prostrate bodies to the ground doe growe;
Arise, and helpe us *Lord*; defend us still,
And save us for thy mercies sake from ill.

Psalm 45

My heart is mov'd to utter some good thinge,
Which I entend to offer to the kinge:
My tongue shall bee the pen, and swiftly write
What in my heart devotion doth endite.
Fairest of men, whose lipps with grace abound,   5
Whom with eternall blessings God hath crown'd,
Gird thy sharp sword upon thine Armed thigh,
And shew thy selfe in power and *Majestie*:
Ride on with thy great honnour prosperously;
Raigne and trihumph, and bee thou mounted high,   10

44.43 [this] *ed.*: *om. MS.*

Borne up with justice, truth and meeknes wings,
And thy right hand shall teach thee dreadfull things;
Thine Arrowes sharpe shall make thy foes to fall,
Which thou shalt shoote, and peirce their hearts withall.
Eternall is thy judgement seat, O *God*;   15
Thy scepter is a true directinge rod:
Right hast thou lov'd, and loth'd unrighteousnes,
And therefore *God*, thy *God* who doth thee blesse,
Hath powr'd on thee, O *Prince of Princes* best,
More oyle of gladnes then on all the rest.   20
Thy garments which thy person shall aray,
Brought out of *Ivory* wardropes where they lay,
Of *Myrrh*, of *Alloes* and of *Casha* smell;
Which odours doe refresh and please thee well.
The queene all cladd in gould at thy right hand,   25
Daughters of Kings attendinge her shall stand.
Attend faire daughter, listen and give eare:
Forgett thy fathers house and *Cuntry* deare.
Soe shall the kinge take pleasure in thy beautie,
Hee is thy lord, yeild him both love and duty;   30
The *Tyrian* virgins shall bringe guifts to thee,
And *Merchants* rich thy suppliants shall bee.
The daughter of the kinge is rich without,
Her gownes embroidered all with gould about,
And yet within shee is more glorious farr,   35
The jewells of her minde more precious are.
In finest dressings with the *Needle* wrought,
Shee with her fellow virgins shallbee brought.
They shall with joy, O kinge, bee brought to thee,
And in thy princely *Courte* receaved bee: 40
Thou in thy fathers stead, O Bride, shalt gaine
Sonns which in sundry *Provinces* shall raigne.
Thee, Lord, will I remember all my dayes,
And all the world shall give Thee endlesse praise.

Psalm 46

God is our hope and strength, which never failes,
Our present helpe when mischeife us assailes.

Though the earth removed, and the mountaines were
Amid the Ocean cast, wee would not feare:
Though raginge Seas a dreadfull noise doe make,   5
Though floods and tempestes [roar, though] hills doe shake,
There is a streame, which though it bee not great,
Makes glad Gods *Cittie* and his holy Seate.
God in her *Center* dwells, and makes his place
Unmoveable by his preventinge grace: 10
They warr enrag'd which heathen kingdomes sway,
But when *God* spake, the earth did melt away.
The *Lord* of Hosts assists us with his power,
And *Jacobs God* to us becomes a Tower.
Come and behould what workes the *Lord* hath wrought
How hee his foes hath to distruction brought;   16
In all the world hee warr to peace doth turne,
The Bowe and Speare doe breake, and Chariotts burne.
Bee quiett then, and still, and know that I
Am lord of [all] the world, and *God* Most High.   20
The *Lord* of *Hosts* assists us with his power,
And *Jacobs God* to us becomes a Tower.

Psalm 47

Clap handes yee people, with applause rejoyce;
Singe to the *Lord* with loud and chearfull voyce:
His throne is high, his judgement breedeth feare,
On all the earth hee doth the *Scepter* beare.
Hee makes much people our commaund obay,   5
And many *Nations* at our feet doth lay,
And hath for us an heritage in store,
Even *Jacobs* portion, whom hee lov'd before.
In glorious trihumph *God* is mounted high,
The *Lord* with trumpets sound ascends the *Skie*,   10
Singe, singe unto our *God*, unto our *Kinge*;
All praises due, even all due praises singe.

46.6 Though *ed.* (*Grosart*): Thou *MS.*   [roar, though] *ed.: om. MS.*   **46.20** [all]
ed.: om. MS.

[All] *Kingdomes* of the earth to him belonge,
Singe wisely then, and understand your song.
In all the Heathen hee doth raigne alone,   15
And sitts in *judgement* in his holy throne.
The Heathen *Princes* which were severd farr,
To Abrahams faithfull seed now joyned are;
And God, whose highnes doth the heavens transcend,
As with a Buckler doth the earth defend.   20

Psalm 48

Great is the *Lord*, and highly to bee praised,
In Gods owne *Cittie*, *Syon* hill is rays'd,
The Beautie and the joy of all the land,
The great kings *Cittie* on the *North* doth stand;
In her faire *Pallaces* Gods name is knowne,   5
Where hee doth cherish and protect his owne.
Though manie kings against her gathered bee,
They stand astonisht her great strength to see:
As when a woman doth in travell fall,
A suddaine feare and tremblinge takes them all;   10
And God shall breake them, though they bee combin'd,
As *Shipps* are broken with an *Easterne* winde.
What wee have heard, wee see thou dost fullfill:
Thou *God of Hosts* uphouldst thy *Cittie* still.
Amidd thy temple *Lord*, wee doe attend,   15
Till thou to us thy grace and favour send.
Great is thy name O *God*, thy praise noe lesse,
And thy right hand is full of righteousness.
Rejoyce O *Sion*, and your joyes renew
Daughters of *Judah*, for his judgements true.   20
About the walls of *Sion* walke yee round,
And tell the Towres wherewith that forte is crownd;
Observe her Bulwarkes and her Turrets high,
And tell the same to your posterity.
This ever liveinge God, our *God* is hee,   25
And shall our Guide while wee have liveinge bee.

47.13 [All] *ed.* (Grosart): *om. MS.*   48.26+ And while we live, our only
guide shal be (*Follows last line, in later hand.*) *MS.*

Psalm 49

Heare this yee people, all yee people heare;
Listen to mee and give attentive eare,
All yee that in the world residinge bee,
Both rich and poore of high and low degree;
My mouth shall utter, and my heart devise   5
Matters of greatest skill, profound and wise:
Mine eares to parables will I encline,
And singe unto my harpe of things devine.
Then why should I in ill times fearfull bee,
When mischeife at my heeles doth follow mee?   10
Howbeit some doe in their riches trust,
And glory in their wealth which is but dust;
Yet non from death his brothers life can stay,
Nor unto *God* for him a ransome pay.
For it cost more the soule of man to save,   15
Then all the wealth is worth which worldlyngs have.
Nor may men hope to live on earth for ever,
Though long they last ere soule and body sever:
That fooles and wise men die alike, they finde,
And unto strangers leave their wealth behinde: 20
Their houses yet they thinke shall ever stand;
They give their proper names unto their land.
Yet noe man can in honnor ever bee,
But as the Brute beast dies, even soe dies hee:
This is their follie, theis their stumblinge wayes,   25
And yet the children doe their fathers praise.
They are shut up in graves as sheepe in folde,
And hungry death feeds on their bodies cold;
The just shall rule them when the Sunne doth rise,
With them their pride and beauty buried lies: 30
But God shall from deathes power my soule deliver,
When hee shall take it to himselfe for ever.
Then let not feare and envy thee surprize,
When thou seest men in wealth and honnour rise;
For to their graves they naught away shall beare,   35
Nor shall their glory waite upon them there.
Yet they themselves thought happie all their dayes,

49.10 *MS. smeared; possibly reads* heele *not* heeles.   49.27 [And] They *MS.*

For him who helpes himselfe others will praise.
As his forefathers all are gon before,
Soe shall hee die, and see the light noe more.   40
Soe man on honnour little doth foresee,
But as Brute Beasts doe perrish, soe dies hee.

Psalm 50

The *Lord*, the God of Gods, the world doth call,
Even from the Sunns uprisinge to his fall;
From out of *Sion* doth the *Lord* appeare,
And shewes the brightnes of his beauty cleare.
In trihumph, not in silence, come shall hee;   5
His Usher fire, his guard a storme shallbee:
Hee (by his summons) heaven and earth will call,
That hee [may] judge at once his creatures all.
To mee, saith hee, let all my Saints repaire
Which worship mee with sacrifice an prayer.   10
Gods justice shall from heaven declared bee,
For who is judge of all the world but hee?
Harke *Israell*, I am thy God, give eare;
I will against thee speake and witnes beare:
Not for the dailie taske of sacrifice,   15
Or that burnt offerings shine not in mine eyes.
I want them not, nor will I take at all,
Goat from thy fould, or Bullocke from thy stall;
All Beasts are mine within the forrest wide,
And cattle on a thousand hills beside,   20
I know all fowles which in the aire doe fly,
And see all Beastes which in the feild doe lye.
If I were hungrie, would I begg of thee,
When all things in the world belong to mee?
Art thou, O man, soe simple as to thinke   25
That Bulls flesh is my meat, goats blood my drinke?

.   .   .   .   .

50.8 *The present edition follows Grosart in adding* may. *A hand later than the scribe's
inserted* will *and supplied* for *for* That.   50.25 [⚹] O *MS.*

Psalm 67

Show us thy mercy, Lord, and grace divine;
Turne thy bright face, that it on us may shine,
That all the men on earth enlight'ned so,
Theire owne salvation, and thy wayes may know.
O let thy people praise thy blessed name,   5
And let all tongues and nations doe the same,
And let all mortall men rejoyce in this,
That God their Judge and just his judgment is.
O let thy people praise thy blessed name,
And let all tongues and nations doe the same,   10
Then shall the earth bringe forth a rich encrease,
And God shall blesse us with a fruitfull peace;
Even God shall bless us and his holy feare,
Possesse the harts of all men every where.

Psalm 91

Who under the most high himselfe doth hide,
In most assured safety shall abide.
Thou art, O Lord, my hope and my defence;
My God, in thee is all my confidence.
Hee shall preserve thee from the hunters snare,   5
And from the pestilent contagious aier;
His winges shall both protect and cherish thee;
His faithfull promise shall thy buckler bee.
Noe terror of the night shall thee dismay,
Nor Satans arrow flyinge in the day,   10
Nor mortall plague which in the darke annoyes,
Nor that ill angell which at noone destroyes.
Thousands, ten thousands shall about thee fall,
Yet noe such ill shall thee approach at all.
Yea, with thine eyes thou shalt behould and see,   15
The just reward of such as impious bee;
Thou art my hope, I will on thee rely:
Thy tower of safety, Lord, is sett soe high

67.11 [nations] earth *MS.*   67.13 [w th] and *MS.*   91.1 *MS. numbers*
1–16 the alternate lines of Psalm 91.   91.3 O *ed.:* o *MS.*   91.4 My *added*
later, possibly in different hand.   91.12 noone *ed.:* none *MS.*

Noe mischeefe, noe mischance shall thee betide,
Nor plague come near the place where Thou shalt bide.
The Lord his Angells will thy keepers make,   21
In all thy righteous wayes which thou shalte take;
They in their hands shall thee sustaine and stay,
That thou shalt never stumble in thy way:
Uppon the Basilisk and Adders head,   25
Dragon and Lyon, thou shalt safely tread.
Thy love to mee shall save thee from mischance,
Thy knowledge of my name shall thee advance.
I will him hear and help him in his trouble,
I will protect him and his honour double;   30
With length of dayes hee satisfied shall bee,
And hee at last shall my salvation see.

Psalm 95

Come let us hartily rejoyce and singe,
To God our mightie saviour and our kinge;
Present the prayse which doth to him belonge,
And show our gladnes in a cheerfull songe;
For God our Lord, the greatest God is hee,   5
And Monarch of all gods that worshipt bee.
The earths round globe hee holdeth in his hand,
And the highest mountaynes are at his command;
The sea is his, hee hath it made of old,
And the dry land his blessed hands did mould.   10
Come, let us worship then, and humbly fall
Before our mightie God, which made us all.
Hee is our Lord and wee his people bee,
Our shepheard and his proper sheepe are wee:
This day, yf you his holy voice will hear,   15
Let not your hearts bee hardned as they were
When in the desert you his wrath did move,
And temptinge him, his mightie power did prove.
Full forty yeares this nation greevd mee so;
Their erringe harts my wayes would never know: 20
Therefore displeas'd, by oath I did protest,
They never should possesse my land of rest.

91.26 [~~thy~~] thou (*corrected by later hand*) MS.

Psalm 100

Bee joyfull in the Lord, yee nations all;
Cheer up your harts in mirth, and songs withall:
The lord is God: not wee, but hee alone
Hath made us all, and feeds us every one.
Then enter yee his gates and courts with prayse,
And strive with hart and voice his name to raise.
For why? the Lord is sweet, his mercy sure,
His truth for ever constant shall endure.

Psalm 103

My soule, with all thy powers thy maker praise;
Forget not all his benefits to thee,
Who pardons all thy sinnes, and doth thee rayse
When thou art fal'n through any infirmitie;
Who doth thee save from mischeefs that would kill thee,   5
And crowneth thee with mercies ever more;
And with the best of thinges doth feed and fill thee,
And Egle-like thy youth and strength restore.
When men oppressed doe to him appeale,
Hee righteth every one against his foe: 10
Hee unto Moses did his lawes reveale,
And unto Jacobs race his workes did show.
Hee is more full of grace then wee of sinne;
To Anger slow, compassionate and kind;
Hee doth not ever chide, and never linne,   15
Nor keepes displeasure alwayes in his minde;
Nor after our misdeedes doth hee us charge,
Nor takes hee of our faults a strict account:
But as the space from earth to heaven is large,
Soe farr his mercy doth our sinnes surmount.   20
As east from west is distant farr away,
Soe farr doth hee from us our sinnes remove;
As fathers kindnes to their sonnes bewray,
Soe God, to them that feare him, showes his love.

Psalm 103.   *Layout supplied.*

For hee that made us, and knowes all, doth know   25
The matter whereof man was made of old:
That wee were formed heer on earth below
Of Dust and clay, and of noe better mold.
Mans age doth wither as the fadinge grasse,
He flourisheth but as the flower in May,   30
Which when the Southwind over it doth passe,
Is gone, and where it grew noe man can say.
But Gods sweet kindnes ever doth consist,
His truth from age to age continew shall
To them that in his righteous lawes persist,   35
And thinke uppon them to performe them all.
Heaven is Gods seat, there doth his glorie dwell;
But over all his Empire doth extend:
Praise him yee Angells which in strength excell,
And his command doe evermore attend.   40
Praise him yee Hosts of heaven, which serve him there,
Whose service with his pleasure doth accord;
And praise him all his creatures every where,
And thou, my soule, for thy part praise the Lord.

Psalm 150

To him with Trumpets and with flutes,
With cornets, clarions, and with lutes,
With Harpes, with organs, and with shawmes,
With holy Anthems and with psalmes,
With voice of Angells and of men,
Sing Aleluyia: amen, amen.

103.33–5 *Before alteration by a later hand, possibly that of Davies, lines 33 and 35 read:*
          But Gods sweet kindnes to mankind for ever
          To them that in his righteous lawes persever
150.6 Aleluyia *ed.*: Alelugia *MS.*

LATIN POEMS

Title of section supplied by editor.

[Epitaph on his Son.]

Qui iacet hic fuit ille aliquid, fuit et nihil ille.
Spe fuit ille aliquid, re fuit ille nihil.

Mr Davies.

[Anagram on his Daughter Lucy Davis.]

LUCIDA VIS oculos teneri perstrinxit amantis,
Nec tamen erravit, nam VIA DULCIS erat.

[Epitaph on his Son.] *Text from MS. Che. Title supplied. MS. entitles:* **Epitap.**
[Anagram etc.] *Text from Wood. Title supplied.*

POEMS
POSSIBLY BY DAVIES

I. Poems Ascribed to Davies in Manuscripts.

II. Poems Appearing Among Davies's Works.

I

Poems Ascribed to Davies in Manuscripts.

[1]

On the Deputy of Ireland his child Sir John Davis.

As carefull mothers doe to sleepinge lay
Their babes which would too longe the wanton's play,
So to prevent my youthes approchinge crymes,
Nature, my nurse, had me to bedd betymes.

Finis.

[2]

Davis beinge committed to prison for a quarrell
betweene him and Martin, wrote as ensueth.

Now Davis for a birde is in,
But yet it is but for a Martin.

[3]

An Epitaph.

Here lieth Kitt Craker, the kinge of good fellowes;
Who was his craftes maister in makinge of Bellowes:
But yet for all that, in the tyme of death,
He that made Bellowes, could not make breath.

finis. q^d D.

1. On the Deputy etc.   *Text: MS. RP117*
   1.2 too *ed.*: to *MS.*

2. Davis etc.   *Text: MS. RP148*

3. An Epitaph.   *Text: MS. RP148*

[4]

An other Epitaph: of one who died with the Maple Buttons.

Heere lieth *Dick Dobson* iwrapped in molde,
Which never gave peny to have his head polde:
A plague and a pox of such a device,
That grubd up the heare to sterve up the lice.

finis. q^d D.

II

Poems Appearing Among Davies's Works.

[5]

In Hircum.

Hircus incountring with hott Mistres Franke,
Did burne his [Priapus] by mischaunce of fire,
But since he gave her whoreshipp many a thanke,
By cause this chaunce hath made his fortune hier,
For begging almes he sweares most cunninglye,
He was consumd by fier and tis no lye.

[6]

In Macerum.

Macer doth hould that all our womenkind
Must by the forelock (as occation)
Be surely held, or else they chaunge their mind,
And plott deceite and meere illution.
It is not trewe in every comon whore,
For if you feele them, they are bald before.

4. An other Epitaph etc.　*Text: MS. RP148*
　　4.3 pestilence *erased*; pox *inserted.*　　4.4 and *erased*; to *inserted.*
5. In Hircum.　*Text: MS. Ro*
　　5.2 [Priapus] *An illegible word resembling* Priores *appears here.*
6. In Macerum.　*Text: MS. Ro*

[7]

In Marcum.

Marcus, a student at the lawe,
  When wealth he might have wonne,
Would needes bee maried all in hast,
  By which he is undonne.
Who ever saw so pritty a tricke
  Since juggling first begonne?
By tying of him selfe so fast,
  Him selfe he hath undonne.

[8]

[In Neream.]

Sweet Mistres Nerea, let it not thee greive
That I did take a pinn from off thy headgeare,
For I to thee a greater pin will give,
Which shall doe better service to thy beadgeare,
So that thou'lt graunt that I shall choose the pin,
And stick it wheare I will, and wheare it will runne in.

[9]

[In Meieam.]

Meiea being angry that I would not stay
Straight tould Cornella she had donne with mee.
Fye, Meiea, fye, wilt thou thy selfe bewray?
I would not tell if I had done with thee.

[10]

[To a woman Fallen from Horseback.]

Madam, what needs this care to make it knowne
You caught a bruise from horsebacke latelie throwne?

7. In Marcum.   *Text: MS. Ro*

8. [In Neream.]   *MS.: Ro   Title supplied.*
   8.2 off *ed.:* of *MS.*

9. [In Meieam.]   *MS.: Ro   Title supplied.*

That cast you were is clearer then the skies;
Had you not fallne, youre bellie could not rise:
The onlye scruple is, that men doe scan,
Whether youre gelding threw you or youre man.

[11]

[On his Love.]

My Love doth flye with winges of feare
And doth a flame of fyer resemble,
Which mounting high and burning cleare
Yet evermore doth wave and tremble.

My love doth see, and doth admire,   5
Admiring breedeth humblenes;
Blinde love is bold, but my desire
The more it loves presumes the lesse.

My love seekes not reward nor glorie,
But with it selfe, it selfe contentinge,   10
Is never sullen, never sorry,
Never repyning not repentinge.

O who the sunne beames can behold
But hath some passion, feeles some heate?
For though the sunne himselfe be cold,   15
His beames reflecting fire beget.

O that myne eye, o that myne hart
Were both enlarged to contayne,
The beames and joyes she doth impart
While she this bowre doth not disdaine.   20

10. *Text: MS. Dyce.   Title supplied.*

11. *MSS.: Υ, Don, Burley   Text from Υ, except for lines 21–4, found in Burley only.   Υ, Burley omit titles. Don entitles:* Of the last Queene by the Earle of Clanrickard.   *Title supplied.*

11.4 wave] weane *Burley*: move *Don*   11.5 doth[(2)] still *Burley*   11.8 presumes *Σ*: presume *Υ*   11.9 not . . . nor] no . . . or *Burley*   11.10 contentinge] contenteth *Burley*   11.12 repyning nor repentinge] repyneth nor repenteth *Burley*   11.13 O *Burley*: But *Σ*   11.17 eye] eyes *Burley*   11.20 bowre *Burley*: love *Σ*

This bowre unfit for such a gueste,
But since she makes it now her Inn,
Would God twere like her sacred breast
Most faire without, most rich within.

[12]

Verses of the Queene.

A virgin once a glorious starre did beare,
Like to the Sunne inclosd in globe of glasse;
A virgins hart is nowe the golden Sphere
Whence to this earth that influence doth passe.
He shynes on her, and she on him againe,   5
Reflecting Love all earthly starres doth staine.

He whylome tooke a stable for his Cell,
Thrise happie Cell in which a god hath ben,
But he will nowe in princes pallace dwell,
And wedds himselfe to rare *Eliza* queene.   10
Come wise men come, present your giftes devine,
Here standes the starr that makes your starr to shine.

This Sacred Nimphe, because noe mortall wight
Deserved to Lincke with her in chaines of Love,
Unto the god of soules her faith hath plight,   15
And vowde her selfe to him without remove.
Thus doth this brid tenn thowsand children breed,
And virgins milke the Church of god doth feed.

To see this birth did Angells sweetly singe,
Nowe singes that nest of nightingalls againe,   20
Joye, peace, goodwill [on earth] to men they bringe,
Of fortie five yeares thus tuninge they remaine.
Long maye they tune that sweete and pleasant songe,
And longe maye she our angell singe amonge.

For Syons sake preserve from death:
Our noble queene *Elizabeth*: Amen.

11.21–4 *om. Y, Don*

12. Verses of the Queene.   *Text: MS. Y*
    12.21 [on earth] *ed.: om.* MS.

[13]

The Complaint of the Five Satyres against the Nymphes.

Tell me, O Nymphes, why do you
Shune us that your loves pursue?
What doe the Satyres notes retaine
That should merite your disdaine?

On our browes if hornes doe growe,   5
Was not Bacchus armed soe?
Yet of him the Candean maid
Held no scorne, nor was affraid.

Say our colours tawny bee
Phoebus was not faire to see   10
Yet faire Clymen did not shunn
To be Mother of his Sonne.

If our beards be rough and long,
So had Hercules the strong
Yet Deianeir with many a kisse   15
Joyn'd her tender lipps to his.

If our bodies hayry bee
Mars as rugged was as wee:
Yet did Ilia think her grac'd
For to be by Mars imbrac'd.   20

Say our feet ill-favored are
Cripples leggs are worse by farre
Yet faire Venus during life
Was the lymping Vulcans wife.

13. The Complaint etc.   *Printed text: Nichols.*   MS: H39.   *Text from Nichols.*
    Title: Satires H39
    13.15 Deianeir   H39: Deianier *Nichols.*

Breefly if by nature we 25
But imperfect creatures be
Thinke not our defects so much
Since Celestial Powers be such.

But you Nymphes, whose veniall love
Love of gold alone doth move 30
Though you scorne us, yet for gold
Your base love is bought and sold.

POEMS
WRONGLY ATTRIBUTED
TO DAVIES

1. Grosart's 'Appendix to Epigrams' in *Poems*, ii. 47–9. Grosart had no reason to include these epigrams, which have nothing to do with Davies's epigrams appearing in the same manuscript. For the authorship of most of them, all of which were copied from W. B.'s *A Helpe to Discourse*, see David C. Redding and Bernard Harris, 'Some Epigrams Attributed to Sir John Davies', and 'Replies', *N. & Q.* ccvi (1961), 426–7; ccvii (1962), 31, 40.

2. 'Tityrus to his faire Phillis' in Grosart's *Poems*, ii. 114. The poem, by John Dickenson, appears in *The Shepheardes Complaint* (*S.T.C.* 6820).

3. 'Reason's Moane', in Grosart, *Poems*, ii. 108. The poem appears in *A New Post* (1620), a prose work with the title-page reading 'By Sir I. D. Knight' (*S.T.C.* 6354). The title-page is a printer's deception: *A New Post* consists of a new title-page on the old leaves of Robert Mason's *Reasons Academie* (1605) (*S.T.C.* 17619).

4. 'Stay lovely boy, why flyest thou me' and 'Black maid, complain not that I fly' in Grosart, *Poems*, ii. 239–40. These are answering poems by Henry King and Henry Reynolds.

5. *Sir Martin Mar-People, his Coller of Esses* (1590) (*S.T.C.* 6363). Although the title-page bears the name of 'John Davies', there were many people with that name. The work is not by a poet, but by a pious person with the ability to form a couplet-rhyme every 28 syllables. He attacks the wickedness of the world, the corruption of the clergy, and the vices of the age. None of these things ever finds expression in Davies's writings. It is not impossible that it is by the author of a similar pious work, *O Utinam* (*S.T.C.* 6328), printed the following year, but it is not possible that it is by the poet of the present edition.

COMMENTARY

Nosce Teipsum

Textual Introduction

Although the extant textual witnesses reveal little of the artistic develop-ment of *Nosce Teipsum*, they show Davies's corrections at numerous points, and thereby ensure a critical text almost entirely free from corruption.

The poem appears in three closely related manuscripts prepared by pro-fessional scribes for Davies. Probably the manuscripts are contemporaneous with the first printing in 1599, although they may date slightly before it, since they lack one stanza found in *1599*, and Davies almost always lengthened, rather than shortened, his poems. At most, months rather than years separate the first edition from the manuscripts. MS. *AC* was a gift from the author to the Earl of Northumberland, and *HH* a gift to Edward Coke; both manu-scripts contain corrections and dedicatory verses, addressed to the recipients, in Davies's own hand. *H573*, with its identical paper and generally similar appearance, seems to have been written at about the same time. Nevertheless, one can recognize a clear progression in the three manuscripts: *H573* is earliest and least corrected, *AC* intermediate, and *HH* latest, as selected readings reveal. In the following table brackets around material struck through indicate erasure, while two slanting rules indicate corrections in Davies's own hand in *AC*.

	H573	*AC*	*HH*
line 462	Complexions	Complexion[s]	Complexion
1599	play slepe	play \or/ sleepe	play or sleepe
1672	his	[his] \her/	her
1734	to kill	[to] \do/ kill	do kill
1827	in all ages	\hath/ in all ages	hath in all ages
	hath byn	[hath] beene	bene

This evidence of revision helps to clarify the circumstances surrounding the printing of the first edition of *Nosce Teipsum* in 1599. Professor Gerald J. Eberle in 'Sir John Davies' *Nosce Teipsum*, 1599: A Bibliographical Puzzle', *Studies in Bibliography*, i (1948), 135–47 demonstrated that outer formes B and C of *1599* were entirely reset and corrected, while the inner formes were extensively corrected but not reset. Most of the corrections consist simply of altering roman type to italic to bring the type-face into general conformity with the script found in MSS. *AC* and *H573* (*HH* has few italics). Since Davies himself later altered roman type to italic in the second edition of *Orchestra*, he is presumably responsible for such changes in *1599*. He must also be responsible for the substantive corrections: several are too difficult for a printer to have made on his own judgement, and all are supported by *AC* and *HH*.

A comparison of *1599* with the manuscripts reveals that five of the twenty substantive errors in uncorrected formes B and C are conjunctive with *H573*, the least-corrected manuscript, but are not found in *AC*, *HH*, and corrected formes of *1599*: *the* for *th'* (line 12), *how* for *haue* (line 90), *Sense* for *Soule* (line 199), *Doctrine* for *Doctrines* (line 230), and *and in eternall* for *and eternall* (line 256). The text of *1599* then improves. Whereas sheets B and C had some seventy alterations in spelling, italics, and punctuation, sheets D–M show only a few spelling alterations and one pair of altered substantive readings: the rhyming words *Sensualities/Vanities* at lines 1902–4. At this point the manuscripts show the following readings, with alterations in Davies's holograph:

H573	*AC*	*HH*
sensuality	sensuallitie\s/	sensuallityes
vanity	vanitye\s/	vanityes

Evidently Davies corrected sheets B and C and required their resetting; at that point, he either provided a better manuscript or corrected the printer's copy with considerable care, for, after sheet C, *1599* has few manifest errors.

Although the three extant manuscripts show different states of revision, no one descends from another; each has separative errors. *H573*, however, shares conjunctive errors with *1599* even after sheet C; therefore they share a textual tradition distinct from *AC* and *HH*. Similarly, *AC* and *HH* share conjunctive errors not found in *H573* and *1599*. A stemma suggests their interrelationship.

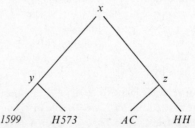

The stemma oversimplifies, in that it implies a single, fixed archetype from which other texts descend. In fact, Davies corrected *AC* in his own hand; he was responsible for corrections in formes B and C of *1599* and for further alterations in the printer's copy that differentiate *1599* from conjunctive readings in the three extant manuscripts; and he altered the copy for *HH* some time after *AC* had been transcribed. Therefore *z*, or a witness between *z* and *HH*, should be understood to have received authorial correction. The four witnesses do not represent imperfect copies of a single, fixed text, but various copies of a text undergoing slight authorial revision during the period in which the different copies were made. Among variant readings, one is not necessarily wrong and another correct, but sometimes one is earlier, the other later. Moreover, it is most unlikely that Davies could have corrected the poem identically each time; consistency is the hobgoblin of textual critics, not poets.

Five editions followed *1599* during Davies's lifetime. The first appeared in the same year: *1599(2)* is a letter-by-letter and word-by-word reprint of *1599*. It twice corrects the first edition: 'of emptie Raine' becomes 'emptie of Raine' in line 45, and 'these' becomes 'those' in line 67; both corrections evidently come from the printer. Otherwise, *1599(2)* follows the uncorrected formes of *1599* in its errors; it shows no indication of recourse to manuscript or authorial correction.

The next edition, published in 1602, is misleadingly advertised on its title-page as '*Newly corrected and amended*'. Conjunctive errors and spelling show sheets G–L to have been set up from *1599(2)*, while similar evidence shows sheets B–F to have been set up from a copy of *1599* containing un-corrected outer formes B and C. Of corrections in outer formes B and C of *1602*, only one ('Mortall' to 'Morall' in line 77) is not found in *1599(2)*; it may have come from the compositor's consulting a copy of *1599* containing corrected formes B and C. Most errors in uncorrected *1599* are continued. Since Davies had earlier taken care to correct these errors in *1599*, the edition of *1602*, which repeats them, cannot have had his direct supervision. Except for the identification of Sir Thomas Egerton in a marginal gloss at line 345, for which Davies might have been responsible, there is no evidence of authorial attention.

The next two editions have no authority whatever: *1608* derives from a mixed copy which had sheet B from *1599* and sheets C–M from *1599(2)*; *1619* was set up from *1608*. Neither received authorial attention; in each instance, errors multiplied.

1622 was set up from *1619*. Evidently Davies corrected the printer's copy, for the text and the errata list found in some copies both contain correct readings found in the manuscripts, but not in other printed texts. The few readings peculiar to *1622* are limited to isolated words.

I have adopted *1599* in its corrected formes as my copy-text. It contains an additional stanza and a few minor alterations not found in the manuscripts. Because Davies normally added to his poems but took nothing away, *1599* is evidently later than the manuscripts and is therefore the last text to have undergone his thorough revision. I generally follow its wording, but make some corrections:

  (i) where *1622* and the MSS. agree against *1599*;
  (ii) where the MSS. agree against *1599* and I cannot suppose Davies to
      have altered their reading to that of the printed text;

(iii) where Davies's holograph corrections differ from *1599*;
(iv) where *1622*, in differing from other texts, seems to offer an authorial correction;
(v) where *AC* and *HH* agree against *H573* and *1599*, and I think their reading superior.

On the whole, however, there are few departures.

Punctuation in the present text is from *AC*, a manuscript initially lightly punctuated by the scribe, and then corrected in a different ink by Davies, who provided about four-fifths of the punctuation, occasionally erasing or altering the scribe's pointing, but usually allowing it to stand and simply adding to it. Because Elizabethan printers did not faithfully follow the pointing of their copy, *AC*, even with its occasional scribal punctuation, is a more accurate guide to Davies's practice than *1599*. I have altered its punctuation only where it seemed misleading or inconsistent with Davies's own methods. These emendations are usually supported by *1599*. The apparatus records, for emendations to punctuation, the readings of *AC* and *1599*, but omits citation of other textual witnesses.

The apparatus includes readings of possible authenticity from the manuscripts and from *1599* and *1622*, the only printed texts to receive Davies's correction. Readings from *1602–1619* are excluded, with two exceptions: one marginal note from 1602 is given; occasionally an error in *1619* is given to explain why Davies altered *1622* to a reading not found elsewhere. In several instances I emended capitalization or typeface, usually because the agreement of two different manuscript traditions suggests that such emendations are closer to Davies's intent than is the copy-text. The apparatus includes the readings of all textual witnesses in these instances.

Spelling and Italics

Nosce Teipsum alone affords the opportunity to observe Davies altering a scribe's spelling. Apart from alterations for metre, he made twelve changes:

92	therto	*to*	thertoo
311	marrynge	*to*	marryinge
857	be	*to*	bee
939	Æconamick	*to*	Œconamick
995	to	*to*	too
1003	mases	*to*	mazes
1245	thre	*to*	three
1332	therto	*to*	thertoo
1701	be	*to*	bee
1752	fare	*to*	feare
1764	litle	*to*	little
1818	agre	*to*	agree

The inclusions and omissions are both interesting. Davies was not concerned whether his scribes spelled *floodes*, *fluddes*, or *flouds; hoate*, *hott*, or *hote; yeald*, *yeld*, or *yeeld*. He may not even have considered pronunciation in making his changes. He probably altered *marrynge* to *marryinge*, *to* to *too*, *thre* to *three*, and *fare* to *feare* for clarity. *Æconamick* became *Œconamick* because of its Latin source, and *mases* became *mazes* probably because the latter spelling was more common. The alteration from *litle* to *little* is puzzling, since elsewhere Davies let *litle* stand.

The remaining alterations show Davies's attention to sight-rhyme and metrical stress. The scribe of *AC* spells *fluddes* and *Fludd* at lines 94 and 1224 where the words are unrhymed, but *flood* at line 1894 to rhyme with *good*. Lines 1890–2 reveal the spellings *brest/chest*, *breste/cheste*, and *breast/cheast* in *HH*, *AC*, and *1599* respectively; and in Davies's thirteenth Hymn of Astræa the compositor spelled *write* as *wright* when it rhymed with *light*.

Davies sometimes added a vowel to words in stressed positions when they were rhymed or when stressed within a line, such as at lines 857 and 1701, 'Love must free hearted *bee*, and voluntarie. . . . For though the body wasted *bee* and weake' (italics mine), and at lines 92, 1332, and 1818. Probably he wished to indicate heavier stress or quantitative lengthening; some scholars hold that Milton followed this practice. In the text of *1599*, *he*, *she*, *we*, *be*, and similar words seldom have double final vowels unless they are rhymed or stressed or lengthened.

1599 uses italics abundantly, apparently by Davies's intent, not the compositor's whim, since their appearance in *AC* and *H573* often parallels that of *1599*. They serve several purposes: to set off proper names, unusual terms, and a few words which Davies emphasized regardless of content— *sun*, *soul*, and *sense*, for example. He also used italics to indicate quotations from known authors, as when quoting Socrates and Democritus:

> For this, the wisest of all Morall men,
> Said *he knew nought, but that he nought did know;*
> And the great mocking Maister, mockt not then,
> When he said, *Truth was buried deepe below.* (*N.T.* 77–80)

(In *1599*, *sententiae* and common tags without recognizable authors, as at lines 1597–1600 and 1860, are generally placed in quotation marks.) Perhaps most often, Davies used italics as a rhetorical device to emphasize particular words, or to highlight a balance or antithesis:

> *I know* my life's a paine, and but a span,
> *I know* my *Sense* is mockt with every thing;
> And to conclude, *I know* my selfe a *Man*,
> Which is a *proud* and yet a *wretched* thing. (*N.T.* 177–80)

Although sometimes annoying to the eye unaccustomed to them, italics are an integral part of Davies's text.

Date and Composition

Nosce Teipsum was registered on 14 April 1599 and printed the same year; the manuscripts seem to date from about the same time. The date of poetical composition, however, is uncertain.

The year 1592 has frequently been mentioned: Nahum Tate in his editions of 1697–1715 popularized it, and from there it was copied into British Museum Add. MS. 25304, an eighteenth-century transcript of Tate's text. It originated with the edition prepared by 'W. R.', identified as William Ravenhill by G. A. Wilkes in 'William Ravenhill and *Nosce Teipsum*', *T.L.S.*, 20 October 1961, p. 753. His edition appears in two issues: one in 1688, another in 1689. An example of *1688*, the rarer of the two, is the British Museum copy bearing the pressmark 695.k.9.

The title-page of *1688*, which bears the imprimatur 10 April 1688, refers to *Nosce Teipsum* as a work 'Written Eighty Years since'. This issue omits Davies's dedication to Queen Elizabeth, found in *1599* and the early manuscripts, and offers no date of composition. *1689* consists of sheets with the poetical text printed for *1688*, but replaces the title-page and its conjugate leaf with a cancellans of two leaves that omits the phrase 'Written Eighty Years since' but adds Davies's dedication to Queen Elizabeth and follows it with the subscription 'July 11. 1592'. *1689* also adds new prefatory matter and an additional title-page, in which it refers to the poem as having been 'Composed . . . nigh One Hundred Years since'.

The second issue bears the imprimatur 'Aug. 14. 1689', and is dedicated by Ravenhill to Queen Mary, who arrived in England in February 1689:

This small *Treatise* (herewith now reprinted) was Composed and Presented (nigh One Hundred Years since) to Queen *Elizabeth* (of Blessed Memory,) then the great *Guardian* of the *Protestant Religion*, as a subject suitable to the Noble Genius of Her Royal Mind. . . . It was Published when there was a general defect of Learning in this Kingdom: And such was its Fate, that it might have perished in Oblivion, had not I (casually) met with One of the Impression (so long after) whereby to preserve it to Posterity.

I measure its Worth, by the Benefit I have received, in reading, and digesting it . . . And that it might have the same Influence upon Others, I judged it my duty to make it publick, with some weak Endeavors of my own, (by way of Preface and Introduction;) Omitting therein, the Author's Dedication to the Queen, whose precious Name, together with the Holy Religion she defended, were of late become equally obnoxious to the Enemies of Truth, who have so long industriously laboured to blemish the Memory of Both.

But before the Impression was quite finished, it pleased Almighty God, to send Your Majesty's most Heroick Consort . . . to be a Mighty Deliverer of his Church and People in these Kingdoms. . . .

From whence, I take confidence to prefix the Author's Dedication to his Sovereign, most humbly praying, it may go abroad under Your Majesty's most Royal Patronage.

Ravenhill claims that Queen Mary's arrival 'before the Impression was quite finished' encouraged him to print Davies's dedication to Queen

Elizabeth. The cancellandum of *1688*, however, shows that the printing had already been finished on an earlier occasion.

If his statements are misleading, what authority have Ravenhill's dates for *Nosce Teipsum*? Little, to judge from his altering 'Eighty' to 'nigh One Hundred Years'. He may not have known when *Nosce Teipsum* first appeared, for a collation shows his text to derive throughout from *1622*, with no recourse to earlier printed or manuscript copy. He obviously wanted to draw a parallel between Elizabeth and Mary as defenders of Protestantism. Having invented the number 'Eighty' in 1688, he seems to have checked his sums and realized that in 1608 Elizabeth had already been dead five years. Therefore he chose a new number, one that by conveniently implying a centenary, helped to justify reprinting the poem. The date 'July 11. 1592' was invented for his centenary and is pure fabrication.

Another reference must, however, be considered. On 12 January 1593 Thomas Nashe entered *Strange Newes of the intercepting certaine Letters*, in which he says,

By what soever thy visage holdeth most pretious I beseech thee, by *John Davies* soule and by the blew Bore in the Spittle I conjure thee, to draw out thy purse, and give me nothing for the dedication of my Pamphlet. (*Works*, ed. Ronald B. McKerrow (1958), iv. 157, i. 258.)

McKerrow (iv. 157) thought the reference must be to *Nosce Teipsum*, but it might well refer to another John Davies. Writers of that name wrote *O Utinam* (1590) and *Sir Martin Mar-People, his Coller of Esses* (1590), a Marprelate tract. Both are pious works, though they do not treat the nature of the soul as extensively as does *Nosce Teipsum*. Of course, it is possible that the reference is not to a literary work at all, and that its meaning is irrecoverable today.

A third reference supporting an early date of composition comes from Bodleian MS. Carte 62, fols. 590–1, notes toward a life of Davies made in 1674 by Theophilus Hastings, Earl of Huntingdon and son of Davies's daughter and sole heir, Lucy. As Huntingdon was born in 1650 and Davies died in 1626, most of his information must have come from his mother, from family gossip, and whatever of Davies's papers he might once have seen. His own marginal queries indicate that he was writing from recollection rather than research. One entry records of Davies,

A.D. 1593 when Prince Hen: was born to whom Q. Eliz was Godmother hee went in the Company of that Ambassye & when hee Kisst the King of Scots hand hee was owned by him with the name of *Nosce teipsum Davys*.

Huntingdon appears to have confused two incidents, however, for Antony Wood, in *Athenæ Oxonienses* (1818), i. 402, reports that James called Davies '*Nosce Teipsum*' upon meeting him in 1603, when Davies was among the first to bring news of Elizabeth's death to the new monarch in Scotland.

Wood's account is probably correct. Whereas Huntingdon's notes show him to have jotted down stories as he remembered them in 1674, Wood had begun gathering information about Davies from Lucy, John Aubrey, and others some years earlier. An antiquarian's research is more reliable than a grandson's memory. Further, King James is known to have taken an interest in Davies upon his arrival in Scotland in 1603, and Davies alludes to *Nosce Teipsum* in his poem *The Kinges Welcome*, 1603, as he might well have done if James had recently approved of the poem. External evidence is against Huntingdon's date of 1593.

Moreover, Huntingdon's notes themselves contradict the date. In a passage that he entered immediately above the lines already quoted, he gives the background of the composition of the poem.

Upon a quarrell between him & Mr Martin before the Judges where Hee strooke Mr Martin hee was Confined & made a prisoner; after which in discontent hee retired into the Country & writt that Excellent poeme of his *Nosce teipsum* which was so well aprooved on by [him] The Lord Mountjoy after Ld Deputy of Irland & Earle of Devonshire that by his advise hee publisht it & dedicated itt to Queen Elizabeth to whom Hee presented it being introduced by the aforesaid Ld his pattron & this first Essay of his pen was so well rellisht that the Queen encouraged him in his Studdys promising him preferment & had him sworn her servant in Ordinary.

This account, since it places the composition of the poem after Davies's quarrel with Martin in 1598, contradicts Huntingdon's own account of James bestowing the name '*Nosce teipsum Davys*' in 1593.

There remains Huntingdon's reference to *Nosce Teipsum* as 'this first Essay of his pen'. A grandchild and a daughter would of course know of the didactic poem on the immortality of the soul that had often been printed; but Davies the judge and father may have kept from his daughter the knowledge of the licentious *Epigrammes* of his youth, published before *Nosce Teipsum*, and her son might not have known of them either, nor, perhaps, of *Orchestra*, written in 1594 and published in 1596. The phrase 'this first Essay' cannot weigh very heavily in establishing a chronology.

A fourth indication of its date occurs in the text of *Nosce Teipsum*, where the man referred to in lines 345–8 is undoubtedly 'Sir Thomas Egerton Lord Keeper of the great Seale', as he is identified in the marginal gloss in *1602*. Egerton became Lord Keeper in 1596. Although the stanza might have been added to a poem essentially written in 1592, there are no textual witnesses which omit the stanza and thereby support such a hypothesis.

A fifth clue comes in lines 149–56, where Davies says of Affliction:

> This *Mistresse* lately pluckt me by the Eare;
> And many' a golden lesson hath me taught.

These lines generally (and rightly) have been taken to refer to Davies's banishment from the Middle Temple. They are almost the only lines in his poetry that show him writing directly about his own emotional experience, but they could not have been written before 9 February 1598, when Davies attacked Martin and incurred immediate expulsion.

On examination, then, the indications that *Nosce Teipsum* might have been written before 1598–9 are unconvincing. There are various references to Davies's poems in the 1590s: Benjamin Rudyerd refers to *Orchestra* in an epigram attacking Davies (see Introduction, p. xxxiii); Frances Meres in *Palladis Tamia* (1598), and Sir John Harington and Edward Guilpin in their epigrams, all refer to Davies's skill as an epigrammatist. Yet no indisputable references to *Nosce Teipsum* appear before 1599.

Nothing is so consistent about Davies's attitude toward his poetry as his willingness to use it to gain advancement. In his epigrams, he puts down others; in his entertainments written for Egerton, Sackville, and Cecil, he provided verse and speeches for powerful statesmen entertaining Elizabeth. He sent libels to fellow lawyers attacking Edward Coke's unfortunate marriage, but within a year sent a dedicatory copy of *Nosce Teipsum* to Coke and included special verses celebrating his character and accomplishments.

Once banished from the Temple, Davies had to rely primarily on his muse for his restoration. He was not handsome, perhaps ugly; nor was he gracious in movement or manners, if we may judge by the statements of his contemporaries. By attacking Martin he had lost friends, gained imprisonment, and found himself in disgrace after he regained his freedom. His literary reputation rested largely on his scurrilous epigrams, which were burned publicly by the order of the Archbishop of Canterbury and the Bishop of London on 1 June 1599. Being disbarred, he had lost his chance for advancement through his profession; he therefore sought to recover his reputation and to be restored to the Temple. What better way than to set in clear verse the generally accepted philosophic notions of those in authority in a poem of moral rectitude, satisfying orthodoxy, and varied and judicious learning? The poem is not a public confession of error, but it would have suggested to its audience a new-found sobriety in its author.

Sources

Twentieth-century scholarship has shown that the 'deep and original thinking' that Grosart admired in *Nosce Teipsum* is not there. Nor should this surprise us. Verse is not an easy medium in which to be convincing if one wishes to break new theological or philosophical ground. Philosophic verse is more often orthodox than original.

The ideas in *Nosce Teipsum* do not derive directly from classical philosophers and church fathers, as some scholars have thought.[1] Although passages in *Nosce Teipsum* may sound as though they come from Aristotle, Nemesius, Augustine, Aquinas, or Calvin, there is no clear evidence that Davies knew any of these authors directly. He usually found his ideas in the late classical

---

[1] John Nichols, *Illustrations of the Literary History of the Eighteenth Century* (1822), iv. 549–50; E. Hershey Sneath, *Philosophy in Poetry* (1903); Margarete Seemann, *Sir John Davies, sein Leben und seine Werke*, in *Wiener Beiträge zur Englischen Philologie*, xli (1913).

texts used in the schoolroom or in contemporary popular writing.[1] The subject of *Nosce Teipsum* had been widely covered for two thousand years in a scholarly system in which every author cited most of his predecessors. Like most laymen of his time, Davies came upon this knowledge through the compendia, handbooks of mythology, encyclopedias, and popular works of theology that largely restated earlier positions. He was not unusual in using such works; he is unusual in that he so often has a direct source for the supposed commonplaces of his age.

Four authors left distinct marks on the poem. The first is Cicero, whose *Academica* and *Tusculan Disputations* provided material for *Nosce Teipsum*. The small number of the passages borrowed, and the verbal exactness with which they reappear in Davies's poem, suggest that the quotations may have been copied in a commonplace-book, perhaps during his schooldays, for Cicero was included in his reading at Winchester.

The second author is Montaigne, whom Davies called 'a French writer (whom I love well)' in the subscription of his sonnet 'To Sir Thomas Egerton'. Davies's discussion of the sense of smell (*N.T.* 1045–56) obviously derives from Montaigne's essay 'Of Smels and Odors'. More important to Davies was 'An Apologie of Raymond Sebond'; in that sceptical manifesto, Montaigne asserts the vanity of human learning on the grounds that it has not made man happy or virtuous, and that in spite of centuries of study man knows nothing certain about God, the world, or the nature, location, origin, or end of his own soul. Although Davies's tone and emphasis are more hopeful than those of Montaigne, he drew upon Montaigne for his discussion of learned disagreement about the nature and location of the soul, and for several 'Erronious opinions of the creation of soules'.

Two lesser-known French contemporaries of Montaigne, however, account for almost all the ideas and most of the images in *Nosce Teipsum*. Pierre de La Primaudaye wrote a rambling compendium in 1580 that was translated into English in 1594 under the title *The Second Part of the French Academie*; Philippe de Mornay in 1581 wrote a religious tract translated by Arthur Golding and Sir Philip Sidney into English in 1587 as *A Woorke concerning the Trewnesse of the Christian Religion*. Davies could have read these works in French, as he did Montaigne, or in their English translations. Although the ideas found in La Primaudaye's work recur frequently elsewhere, Davies clearly relied on *The French Academie* for much of his general information about psychology and the soul. He used it like a student faithfully consulting a single encyclopedia: he read in it, or perhaps looked up topics in it, and went away with its broad ideas and occasionally its phrases in his memory. Davies's reliance on Mornay is more exact. The similarity in ideas, attitudes, and poetical figures

[1] See Louis I. Bredvold's 'The Sources Used by Davies in *Nosce Teipsum*', *PMLA* xxxviii (1923), which points out Davies's use of La Primaudaye; and George T. Buckley's 'The Indebtedness of Sir John Davies' *Nosce Teipsum* to Philip Mornay's *Trunesse of the Christian Religion*', *Modern Philology*, xxv (1927).

is so close in the two works that Davies must either have copied a number of passages from Mornay, or, more likely, referred directly to Mornay while composing the poem.

La Primaudaye calls his compendium 'a naturall history of man'. Here Davies found a full, if disorganized, discussion of the workings of the soul and its relationship to the body. The senses, the threefold division of the soul, several arguments for immortality, and a diffuse examination of the origin of souls all appear here, and reappear in Davies. Yet the differences are as significant as the many parallels. La Primaudaye lists four requirements for sight, Davies nine. La Primaudaye regards the inner senses as part of the rational soul, Davies as part of the body. La Primaudaye locates will in the heart, and reason, as one of the internal senses, in the middle cell of the brain; Davies gives no fixed location.

More important is a basic difference in attitude. Although they agree that self-knowledge is essential, its purpose for La Primaudaye is to lead man to know God. While the end of *Nosce Teipsum* (based on Mornay) affirms this purpose, *Nosce Teipsum* concentrates on the excellent nature of man, not that of the Creator. For Davies, the soul's ability to overcome the defects of the body is a manifestation of its greatness; La Primaudaye asserts—this is the epitome of his theocentricity—that lip-reading by a deaf man must be acknowledged as a divine miracle.

The way in which Davies has used material from *The French Academie* is clearest in his discussion of traducianism. La Primaudaye treats this subject at length, explaining the question as seen by traducianists (*F.A.*, pp. 492–4; *N.T.* 629–51, 657–60), and providing the solution that Davies uses (*F.A.*, p. 519; *N.T.* 765–84), namely, that God creates souls

pure and entire, yet they keepe not that puritie stil, neither can they be the soules of men and joyned unto their bodies, and so become members of mankinde in them with any other condition, then with that into which the first Father brought all his children by his sinne.

Although Davies takes the statement and the solution of the problem from *The French Academie*, he actually contradicts La Primaudaye, who maintains that the soul is 'naturally created, but yet of God by a certaine order appointed for that ende by him' (*F.A.*, p. 539), and envisages a single decree by which all human souls came to be:

For he created us all in *Adam* and *Eve*, and shut us up as it were in a store-house, or in a spring or fountaine, or as in one stocke of mankinde, out of which hee produceth men continually. (*F.A.*, pp. 385–6.)

Davies denies (*N.T.* 593–600) that there is any storehouse of souls, or any need for one; he denies also that God 'in this doth *Natures* service use' (*N.T.* 621). He adopts instead the theory that La Primaudaye twice denies:

that God by his divine power and vertue createth [the soul] of nothing, after that the body of the infant is made perfect in the wombe of the mother (*F.A.*, p. 518; *N.T.* 613–16.)

The disagreement arises from the differences in focus. La Primaudaye's theories are designed to extol God the Creator, those of Davies to proclaim the excellence of the creation. His departures from the source show his rationalist and humanist bias.

This bias was well served by Mornay, his main source. Davies uses almost all of Mornay's chapter xiv, on the immortality of the soul, from which he takes most of the discussion of the nature of the soul, at least parts of four proofs of immortality, and the refutation of three objections to immortality, often complete with examples and figures of speech. Mornay provides the mixture of Augustinianism and Scholasticism that appears in *Nosce Teipsum*, as well as the habit of casting material into the form of argument.

Mornay's aim is to defend Christian doctrine against the enemies mentioned on his title-page: atheists, epicures, pagans, Jews, etc. For this purpose he argues from common ground, by alleging the Old Testament against Jewish objections, Greek philosophers against 'pagans', arguments from nature against materialists. The resulting combination may well have inspired Davies's blend of natural, classical, and Christian material.

While his chapter on the immortality of the soul supplies the basis for most of *Nosce Teipsum*, echoes of other parts of the book appear frequently in the poem. Although Davies does more than simply versify Mornay, he seldom changes Mornay's material, and never alters it radically. He moderates Mornay's theism, but not as thoroughly as he ignores La Primaudaye's teleology. He reduces Mornay's wordiness, and he changes the order of presentation: for example, the definition of the soul comes largely from evidence that Mornay used to prove immortality. The changes do not reflect disagreement; they merely subordinate Mornay's material to Davies's greater mental orderliness and to his own purpose, which is to expound the nature of the soul, not to defend Christianity.

Most important, Davies's major principle, his rationalism, is found in Mornay, who frequently speaks of 'the soule or mynde'. Davies adopts completely this identification of the soul with reason.

Nosce Teipsum. The title, 'know thyself', comes from the ancient Greek maxim inscribed over the entry to the temple of Apollo at Delphi. This message is the 'oracle', or revelation that the poem will expound in two 'elegies' or poems, neither heroic nor lyrical, written in pentameter. The phrase was taken from Plato by Augustine, who adopted the injunction for all Christianity: for a man, to know himself is to know his soul, his source, and his end. The words became a Renaissance catchphrase.

To . . . Northumberland. These verses appear in a manuscript copy of *Nosce Teipsum*, *AC*, given by Davies to Henry Percy (1564–1632), ninth Earl of Northumberland, a book-collector, scholar, minor author, and patron of scholars, though his family is famous for its fighting men. Davies compares him advantageously in line 23 with Hotspur, or Henry Percy (1364–1402), son of the first Earl. 'Great Charles', line 24, is probably Charles Percy, a brother of the ninth Earl who was distinguishing himself in Ireland in the battles of Blackwater, Cahin Castle, and Dundalk in 1598–9, about the time the manuscript was probably presented.

1–4. These lines summarize Davies's second and longest argument for the immortality of the soul, *N.T.* 1334–1432.

9. *Prince*: In the fourteenth century a Percy ancestor married a great-granddaughter of Henry III. This remote claim to the throne was mentioned in some pamphlets on the royal succession circulating in 1594–1600, but Northumberland early declared for James.

24. *Brabants Lion*: major element of the Percy Arms, symbol of the extinct duchy of Brabant and Louvain.

28. Cf. Introduction, p. xxxvii.

To ... Ed. Cooke. The career of Edward Coke, and his connections with Davies are discussed in the notes to NHA 1–11.

1. *Procurator*: 'an attorney or solicitor in courts of equity or canon law'— *O.E.D.*

1–4. Similar phrasing is found in *N.T.* 339–40.

To my ... Soveraigne.
1. *cleare*: light-giving.

Of Humane Knowledge. The first elegy contains elements of two attacks on human learning. One is a traditional Christian argument that cites the serpent's promise to Adam and Eve and maintains that learning is likely to lead man away from God; it asserts also that because human reason has been degraded by the Fall, its ability to acquire any knowledge is reduced so that it cannot perceive ultimate truth, the only worthwhile human knowledge. This first argument is supported by a second: that man cannot attain certain knowledge in any circumstances, a view current in the last third of the sixteenth century because of the revival of Greek scepticism. The conclusion of the elegy, in spite of these arguments, sets against man's weakness in attaining knowledge his capacity for greatness and dignity.

1–52. The opening section sees the result of the fall of man, as described in Genesis, as the clouding of his reason. Satan, 'the *Spirit of lies*' (*N.T.* 13), tempted Eve with the forbidden fruit, promising, 'when ye shal eate thereof, your eyes shalbe opened, & ye shalbe as gods, knowing good & evill' (Gen. 3: 5). Upon tasting it, they 'knew that they were naked' (Gen. 3: 7), hid themselves in '*Shame*' and '*Miserie*', and suffered pain in toil and in childbirth as punishment (Gen. 3: 10–19; *N.T.* 29–32).

5–6. 'Thy law is written in the hearts of men, which iniquity itself effaceth not'—Augustine, *Confessions*, I. iv. 9. T. J. Childs's B.Litt. thesis (Oxford, 1939), p. 288 cites a passage in Davies's *Discourse of Common Law*:

The Lawe of Nature, which the Schoolemen call *Ius commune*, and which is also *Ius non scriptum*, being written onely in the heart of man, is better than all the written lawes in the world to make men honest and happy in this life (*Works*, ii. 253).

10. It was a commonplace that eagles could look directly into the sun.

18. The central Christian tradition in Davies's time, as developed by Augustine and accepted by Aquinas, is that evil has no real existence but is only an absence of good. Mornay writes that evil 'is nothing els but a fayling of goodnesse' (p. 213).

41-4. Prometheus, enchained by Zeus for stealing fire to give to man, is often considered the personification of reason, as in Plutarch, *De Fortuna*, 98C, and Robert Greene, *Alcida* (1617), sig. E4. A popular story in classical and Renaissance literature is that when Prometheus brought fire to man, a satyr who did not know what fire was kissed it and was burnt. See Plutarch *De capienda ex inimicis utilitate*, 86F; Lyly, *Euphues and his England* (ed. Bond, p. 42), and *Campaspe*, III. v. 18, and Sir Edward Dyer's poem 'Prometheus when first from heaven high'.

46. *Joves Guest*. Ixion, having conceived a passion for Hera, was deceived by Zeus into making love to her image in a cloud, from which union the centaurs were born. The story was allegorically interpreted as an example of blasphemy by Comes, 'De Ixione', *Mythologiae* (1584), sig. Rr, and of the search for forbidden knowledge by Fulgentius, 'Fabula Ixionis', *Christiani Philosophi Mythologiarum libri tres* (1543), ii. D8ᵛ.

47-8. To a number of Renaissance writers, including Boccaccio and Mornay, the punishment of the Danaides was an image of tedious labour leading nowhere. In Hades 'forbicause they did their cousins kill, /[they] Drew water into running tubbes which evermore did spill' (Ovid, *Met.* trans. Golding, ed. W. H. D. Rouse (1961), iv. 573-4).

50. *Youth*. Phaethon, son of Apollo, insisted on driving the chariot of the sun, although his father warned him that its control was beyond mortal power. Zeus killed him after his recklessness endangered the earth and the heavens.

51-2. Icarus escaped from Crete on wings of wax and feathers constructed by his father, Dædalus. As he flew too near the sun, the wax melted and he fell to his death.

73-80. Though the statement 'Art is long, life short' is proverbial (Tilley, A332), Davies probably drew his lines 75-6, 79-80 from Cicero (*Academica*, I. xii. 44) who, in discussing scepticism, referred to the obscurity of truth which

had led Socrates to a confession of ignorance, as also previously . . . almost all the old philosophers, who utterly denied all possibility of cognition or perception or knowledge, and maintained that the senses are limited, the mind feeble, the span of life short, and that truth (in Democritus's phrase) is sunk in an abyss.

Socrates' statement that he knew only that he knew nothing (*N. T.* 78) was widely known from Plato, *Apology*, 21A; Diogenes Laertius, *Lives*: 'Socrates', ii. 32; and Cicero, *Academica*, I. iv. 6. Two Renaissance writers whom Davies knew well cite the statement: Montaigne, *Essays*, II. xii. 202, and La Primaudaye, p. 188. Davies refers again to Democritus, the 'mocking Maister' in his *Discourse of Common Law*: '*Si veritas sit in profundo demersa, as Democritus* was wont to say' (*Works*, ii. 277).

83–4. The Delphic oracle in Renaissance tradition was an agent of the devil, as were the pagan gods. Cf. Milton's 'On the Morning of Christ's Nativity', stanza 19, *Paradise Lost*, book ii, Burton, *Anatomy of Melancholy*, pt. i, sec. 2, mem. 1, subs. 2. The title of Mornay's chapter xxiii is 'That the spirites which made themselves to be worshipped . . . were feends, that is to say, Divels or wicked Spirites'.

91. *reason, live, and be.* Aristotle says 'the soul is that whereby we live and feel and think' in *De Anima*, II. ii. 414ª.

93–104. Davies largely invents his own illustrations of ideas that he found in Mornay; Mornay criticizes men as Davies does for engaging in external activities so that they remain 'strangers to their owne nature, to their owne Soules, and to the things which concerne them most neerelie' (sig. **4). In *A Discourse of Life and Death* Mornay charges scholars with failing to apply their learning to their own nature and to the proper conduct of their lives:

Some are ever learning to correct their speach, and never thinke of correcting their life. . . . Another by Geometry can measure fields, and townes, and countries: but can not measure himselfe. . . .The Astrologer lookes up on high, and falles in the next ditch: . . . hath often his eie on the heavens, his heart long before buried in the earth. . . . The Lawyer will make lawes for all the world, and not one for himselfe. The Physition will cure others, and be blinde in his own disease (sig. C4).

105–10. Davies here denies the essential part of a Ciceronian statement about self-knowledge: 'The soul has not the power of itself to see itself, but, like the eye, the soul, though it does not see itself, yet discerns other things' (*Tusc.* I. xxvii. 67). Davies's lines are sometimes thought to have influenced a speech by Cassius in *Julius Caesar*, written in 1599:

> And since you know you cannot see yourself
> So well as by reflection, I your glass
> Will modestly discover to yourself
> That of yourself which you yet know not of (I. ii. 67–70).

113–28. Davies's language follows Ovid's description of Io, *Met.* i. 637–41. She was ravished by Zeus, who to protect himself from Hera's jealousy transformed her into a cow. Mornay supplied the general idea for the passage:

Let [a man] but set downe in writing, all the thoughts and imaginations that come in his head by the space of one day, and at night let hym review them and take the account of them; And I dare undertake he shall fynd in them so many vanities, so many crymes, so many Hobgoblins, and so many Monsters; so straunge, so fond, so foule, and so ougly; that he shalbe afraid of himselfe like the beast that starkleth at the sodeine sight of himself in a lookingglasse; and that he shal not stand gasing, enamored at his owne beautie as *Narcissus* did; but ronne away ashamed of his foule deformitie, to seeke where to wash away the myre that he hath wallowed in (p. 302).

Davies reserves his comparison of the soul to Narcissus for the conclusion of *Nosce Teipsum* (*N.T.* 1893–4) where, unlike Mornay, he emphasizes the beauty within the soul.

129–30. *Sprites*. In Davies's time fairies were believed to molest those who lived in slovenly ('sluttish') quarters (M. W. Latham, *The Elizabethan Fairies* (1930), pp. 129–30).

153–6. The idea that suffering instructs was proverbial in Davies's time 'Adversity makes men wise', 'Afflictions are sent us by God for our good'. Tilley, A42, A53). Compare the phrasing of line 153 with Virgil, Eclogue vi. 3–4: 'Cynthius aurem/vellit et admonuit'.

158. Wine was sometimes placed in the holds of ships so that the rocking motion at sea would settle the wine.

161. *Minerva*: goddess of wisdom; *learned Muse*: possibly Urania, or perhaps simply the muses.

165–6. *Listes . . . list*: boundaries . . . choose (to.)

175–6. 'He for whome the highest thinges are made, is become a bond-slave to the basest and vilest thinges' (Mornay, sig. **1ᵛ).

Of the Soule of Man, and the Immortalitie thereof. The second elegy initially continues the scepticism of the first as the poet despairs of unaided reason and declares that to understand the soul one needs illumination by faith (*N.T.* 181–264). Admiration replaces scepticism, however, as the poet's description of the soul exalts reason and innate knowledge, in the manner of the philosophers who were condemned by Calvin and La Primaudaye for urging man to know himself and then expounding only his excellence. In considering the capacities of natural man, the second elegy mirrors a long-standing debate among Christian thinkers over the extent of the damage wrought in human nature by the Fall. Extreme pessimists maintained that human nature was completely changed, and that man can neither learn any-thing nor act virtuously without grace: in Luther's view all man's acts are sinful. While Augustine had considered such a view possibly correct, he held that God never leaves man in this state: the fact that pagans performed acts of heroic virtue proves that God gave grace to them as well as to Christians. Pelagian writers, at another extreme, denied that original sin had any important effects. The Thomist position, adopted by Davies, is that the Fall has cost man whatever he originally possessed by grace, including the unfailing subjection of the body to the soul. Yet man's natural gifts and natural virtue remain, and, though useless for salvation, are valuable in themselves. As Aquinas says, grace presupposes nature just as faith pre-supposes reason, or perfection the perfectible (*S.T.* I. i. 1 ad 1ᵘᵐ). It is his account of nature and grace that underlies the balanced Christian humanism of *Nosce Teipsum*.

Davies implies that his discussion of the soul rests on faith illuminated by scriptural revelation, but his discussion leaves wide scope for the exercise of nature and natural reason. To show that the soul is superior to sense, he cites several examples of pagan virtue (*N.T.* 409–16), and indicates that in men without grace, reason can dominate the body, though only with difficulty. Further, he indicates that man's inborn capacity for knowledge, though reduced by sin to a spark, increases naturally (*N.T.* 1193–6) as well as by grace (*N.T.* 1197–1200).

Davies follows the Pauline conception that part of man's natural endowment is innate knowledge, including information and standards of behaviour upon which man acts instinctively. St. Paul says that the Gentiles have the law written in their hearts, so that in the absence of revealed law their own thoughts nevertheless accuse or excuse their acts (Rom. 2: 14–15; see note to *N.T.* 1185–92). Calvin interprets the Pauline text (*Inst.* I. v. 13) to mean that because of the Fall, man's natural knowledge deprives him of all excuse, since he knows the good yet does not do it. Hooker, on the other side, identifies the innate law with the light of reason 'wherewith God illuminateth every one which cometh into the world, [by which] men being enabled to know truth from falsehood, and good from evil, do thereby learn in many things what the will of God is' (*Laws*, I. viii. 3). Davies's language clearly places him with Hooker, not Calvin; the lawyer-poet puts his faith in reason to comprehend divine law.

181. As in *Orchestra*, Davies uses the Ptolemaic model of the universe with the earth as the centre about which the heavens revolve.

193–208. La Primaudaye compares the requirement of light for physical vision with the need of divine illumination for the acquisition of truth. He proceeds to say that, lacking divine illumination,

many great wits discoursing philosophically of the originall and beginning of things, and looking on every side, yea doubting and fearing many things, which they found contrary to humane reason, have bin caried hither and thither with divers opinions but could never come neere to the knowledge of the trueth (*F.A.*, p. 22).

207–32. Philosophical works treating the nature and substance of the soul characteristically began by surveying the opinions (always erroneous) of earlier writers. Moreover, sceptical logicians in their arguments listed conflicting opinions to show that certainty in knowledge did not exist and was not possible. One can find lists like that of Davies in Aristotle's *De Anima*, I. ii, Agrippa's *De Incertitudine et vanitate scientarum*, and even in a contemporary play, Marston's *What You Will* (II. ii. 183–9). Davies himself found such lists in works we know he read. Although no list identical in sequence to his has been found, those bearing nearest resemblance are Cicero's *Tusculan Disputations*, I. ix. 18–23, and Montaigne's essay, 'Apologie of Raymond Sebond':

There is no lesse dissention nor disputing about the place, where she should be seated. *Hypocrates* and *Herophilus* place it in the ventricle of the braine: *Democritus* and *Aristotle*, through all the body . . . *Epicurus* in the stomacke . . . The Stoickes, within and about the heart: *Erasistratus*, joyning the membrane of the Epicranium: *Empedocles*, in the bloud . . . *Galen* thought that every part of the body had his soule: *Strato* hath placed it betweene the two upper eyelids (*Essays*, ii. 252–3).

Those who compiled lists to indicate the uncertainty of knowledge illustrated their thesis by their inability to agree on who said what.

214. *Complexions*: 'the combination of qualities or of "humours" in a certain proportion'—*O.E.D.* 'Complexion', and 'temperature' at *N.T.* 453m, are nearly synonymous.

215. *Epicures . . . Atomies.* See notes to *Orchestra*, stanzas 20–1.

218. 'But though Starres have lyght of their owne: yet to perfection of their light, they receive supplyment and helpe of the Sunne' (Batman, fol. 136).

219–20. According to Cicero, Pherecrates argues

that the soul is wholly non-existent and the name quite meaningless, and that the terms 'animalia' and 'animantes' denoting 'creatures and plants possessed of soul' are applied without reason . . . and that there is nothing apart from one single body fashioned in such a way that its activity and power of sensation are due to the natural combination of the parts (*Tusc.* I. x. 21).

230. *Hazard*: a game of dice.

233–40. God disrupted the building of the Tower of Babel, designed to 'reach unto the heaven', by introducing a diversity of languages among its builders. The Geneva Bible interprets this event in a marginal note: 'By this great plague of the confusion of tongues, appeareth Gods horrible judgement against mans pride and vaine glory.' Although there are passages in La Primaudaye resembling Davies's statement, the likeliest source of these lines is Montaigne's 'Apologie of Raymond Sebond':

[Philosophy] hath so many faces, and so much varietie, and hath said so much, that all our dreames and devises are found in her. The fantasie of man can conceive or imagine nothing, be it good or evill, that is not to be found in her . . . *Nothing may be spoken so absurdly, but that it is spoken by some of the Philosophers* (ii. 256).
    All things produced by our owne discourse and sufficiencie, as well true as false, are subject to uncertaintie and disputation. It is for the punishment of our temeritie, and instruction of our miserie and incapacitie, that God caused the trouble, downefall and confusion of *Babels* Tower . . . The diversitie of tongues and languages, wherewith he disturbed that worke, and overthrew that proudly-raisd Pile; what else is it, but this infinit altercation and perpetuall discordance of opinions and reasons, which accompanieth and entangleth the frivolous frame of mans learning, or vaine building of humane science? (ii. 264–5).

For a similar use of the story, see Fulke Greville, *A Treatie of Humane Learning*, stanza 46.

247–8. Cf. La Primaudaye:

For in deede wee can not pronounce anie thing certaine of so high a nature as is that of the soule, except it bee by his testimonie who hath created it, and who onelie knoweth it, as the workeman knoweth his worke (*F.A.*, p. 491).

249–52. Davies's pun on *comprehend* and his image of fetters come from Mornay, p. 230:

No thing can comprehend the thing that is greater than it selfe. Now, our Soule is after a sort lesse than it selfe, inasmuch as it is wrapped up in this body, in like wise as the man that hath gyves and fetters on his feete, is after a sort weaker than himselfe.

257–8. Cf.

> The selfsame sun that shines upon his court
> Hides not his visage from our cottage, but
> Looks on alike (*Winter's Tale*, IV. iv. 438–40).

The idea and phrasing are Biblical (Matt. 5: 45) and proverbial (Tilley, S985).

260–5. *Oracles*. Either *oracle*, the reading of the printed texts, or *oracles*, the reading of the manuscripts, is possible, but it is more likely that an *s* was overlooked in printing than that all manuscripts should be in error. Since there is no obvious reason for Davies to have altered the plural to singular, *oracles* is adopted in the present text.

Contemporary works referred to the Holy Scriptures as lamps and oracles. Montaigne ('Apologie of Raymond Sebond', ii. 225) speaks of illuminating nature 'with the holy lampe of that truth, which God hath beene pleased to impart unto us'. Hooker calls the Scriptures 'those oracles of the true and living God' (*Laws*, I. xv. 4). Davies is not claiming that the remainder of the poem is divinely inspired, but that it is the work of reason illuminated by faith in revelation.

267–71. Mornay says that the soul 'is properly the very man', united by God to the body which it uses as an instrument (p. 226).

273–6. Davies takes the definition of the soul as a substance from Mornay, pp. 232–3.

297. *Pegasus*: a winged horse that carried the thunderbolt of Zeus. For the earthbound Elizabethans who travelled on horseback, the idea of a flying horse that moved with the speed of light was their nearest approximation to the speed of the soul, which could survey many places from a superior vantage point.

297–306. This material is taken from Mornay, who, to show that the soul acts independently of the body, describes it as moving

from the one side of the earth to the other without shifting of place; descending downe to the centre of the world, and mounting up above the outtermost circle of it both at once . . . It seeth when the eyes be shut, and sometymes seeth not when the eyes be wyde open: It traveleth while the body resteth, and resteth when the body traveleth (p. 226).

317–20. The image of the body as a prison originates in Plato, *Phaedo*, 64, 82, and is repeated frequently, as in Cicero, *Tusc.* I. xxx. 74; Calvin, *Inst.* III. ix. 4; and Mornay, *passim*.

329–30.

The soule hath this propertie, like a busie woorkeman to bee in the bodie, having all her instrumentes therein. Nowe when a woorkeman woorketh with his tooles, hee must have within himselfe the vertue and skill to doe that which hee doeth, because it is not in the instrumentes whereby he worketh (*F.A.*, p. 435).

337–56. Cf. La Primaudaye:

After [Reason] hath well considered and debated of the whole matter brought and laide before it by the former senses, it giveth sentence as Judge, and judgeth finally without appeale. For there is no other judgement after that (*F.A.*, p. 160).

345–57. In 1596 Queen Elizabeth advanced Egerton, Davies's patron, to the double office of Lord Keeper of the Great Seal and Lord Chancellor. Egerton thereby presided over the Court of Chancery, the highest judicial authority below the House of Lords. In this position he had power to hear all petitions for grace and favour, and to temper the justice of the law with the mercy of equity. Davies's use of the term *mercy seate* (*N.T.* 346) for Egerton's office is therefore apt. For Davies's relations with Egerton, see note to his poem 'To Sir Thomas Egerton', p. 202, and the biography, p. xxxvii–ix.

353. *Gods Angell.* 'My lord the King is even as an Angel of God in hearing of good & bad' (2 Sam. 14: 17). A marginal note in the Geneva Bible reads: 'Is of great wisedome to discerne right from wrong.'

354. *milke and honie.* 'Thy lippes, my spouse, droppe as hony combes: honie and milke are under thy tongue' (S. of S. 4: 11).

357–68. Davies's image of the soul as a monarch commanding the senses probably comes from La Primaudaye, who says reason is

to raigne amiddest all the other senses, as Prince and Lord over them all. For it is he that discourseth and judgeth of trueth from falshoode (*F.A.* p. 159).

369–72.

[The soul] standeth in argument against the Sences, and reproveth them of falshoode, and concludeth contrary to their information (Mornay, p. 229).

373–6. La Primaudaye distinguishes imagination and fantasy, which are 'neerer to the corporall senses', from reason, which leads to higher things:

For the spirite (which the Philosophers expresse by *Understanding*) mounteth up unto those things that cannot be knowen nor comprehended of imagination and fantasie, nor of any other sense (*F.A.*, p. 172).

381–2. The sweetness of the music of Amphion, king of Thebes, caused the stones to move into place to form the walls of Thebes, which city, however, was founded by Cadmus, not Amphion.

385. *selfe being Nature.* 'Selfe being' acts as an adjective modifying 'Nature'; the stanza summarizes the first argument for the soul's independent subsistence, which began at *N.T.* 281.

387–8. Although La Primaudaye has a similar passage (*F.A.* p. 140), the idea is proverbial—'The workman is known by his work' (Tilley, W860).

389–452. In sub-section 2 Davies wants to refute the assertion that human knowledge and action arise from a corporeal and sensory source. He argues (*N.T.* 394) that there are two kinds of knowledge, or '*judgements*', and two kinds of volition, or '*appetites*', one spiritual ('soule') and the other physical ('*Sense*'). His language may need clarification: he uses 'soule' where he means 'reason', the term used by his source, Mornay; he uses '*Sense*' for both sensory perception and what Mornay calls 'sensuall appetyte'.

393–421. Davies follows Mornay (pp. 249–50), who points out that 'as reason doth oftentymes overrule sence . . . so will correcteth the sensuall appetyte or lust' and that while the senses of animals surpass human senses, men 'which have their sences most quicke and lyvely, be not of the greatest wisdum and understanding', so that man's superiority to animals consists in 'some other power than sence'. Davies changes some of Mornay's examples: e.g.

Our eye perchance telleth us that a Tower which we see afarre of is round, whereas our reason deemeth it to be square: or that a thing is small, which our reason telleth us is greate.

On the other hand he simply versifies others:

For our hearing telleth us that the thunderclappe is after the lyghtening: but skill assureth us that they be both togither. . . . Also the tong of him that hath an Agew, beareth him on hand that even sugre is bitter, which thing he knoweth by his reason to be untrew.

Mornay refers to Scaevola, and his statement that 'Sence biddeth us shun and eschew greef; whereas Reason willeth us to profer our leg sometyme to the Surgion' probably suggested to Davies the example of Marius.

405–8. Torn between filial duty and passion for Jason who has come to take the Golden Fleece from her father, Medea (Ovid, *Met.* vii. 20–1) speaks the lines which Davies paraphrases: 'Video meliora proboque,/Deteriora sequor' (I see the better course, and approve it, but follow the worse). The lines are repeatedly quoted during the Renaissance to express the opposition of reason and appetite: see Marston, *Dutch Courtesan*, II. ii. 102; Bacon, *Advancement of Learning*, ed. G. W. Kitchin (Everyman's Library), p. 147; Fulke Greville, *Treatie of Religion*, stanza 13.

409–12. In Homer, Ulysses listened safely to the Sirens by a clever device: he made his companions bind him to the mast and stop their own ears with wax, so that they would neither hear the Sirens nor heed his pleas to be released. Davies's version, which originated in Erasmus's *Similia*, appears frequently in the Renaissance; see Morris P. Tilley, 'A Variant of Homer's Story of Ulysses and the Sirens', *Classical Philology*, xxi (1926), 162–4.

413. *Romane.* C. Mucius Scaevola, having failed in an attempt to assassinate Lars Porsenna, was threatened with death by burning unless he would reveal the names of his fellow conspirators; to show his love for honour above the flesh, he thrust his right hand into the fire (Livy, *Ab Urbe Condita*, II. xii).

415. *Marius.* C. Marius, Roman consul, refused to be bound during an operation for varicose veins. Both Plutarch (*Life of Gaius Marius*, vi) and Cicero (*Tusc.* II. xxii. 53) point out that he did not offer the other leg.

432. A story told by Pliny of a painting by Zeuxis (xxxv. xxxvi. 65–6).

433–6. Mornay provides the idea that the soul infers general and spiritual truth from sensory phenomena; he remarks that a beast can hear music as well as a man, 'but his hearing of it is but as of a bare sound; whereas our hearing therof is as of an harmony, and we discerne the cause of the concords and discords' (pp. 248–9).

441–8. Davies adopts Mornay's statement that we do not receive double impressions of sights and sounds because 'it is the Soule . . . that seeth and heareth' (pp. 236–7).

457–60.

Albeit it seemeth that the natural heate, the humors and the spirits woorke in the body, and effect something therein, yet . . . they doe nothing there of themselves, but that they receive of the soule whatsoever they have. As when a Paynter draweth a picture, his pensill and colours have it not of themselves to doe that which is done by them, but of the Painter (*F.A.*, pp. 435–6).

465–8.

For they judge very well, that the understanding and reason with the discourses thereof, that the judgement and such memory as it hath, that the discerning of good and evill, of thinges honest and dishonest, of vertues and vices, with the knowledge of humane and divine thinges whereof it is partaker, are woorkes and actions, which cannot proceede from such matter as the elements are (*F.A.*, p. 499).

466. *Or aire.* For *or*, read *either*.

467–8. *Quintessence*: a fifth element, held by Aristotle to be the matter of which the soul consisted.

469–72. Mornay denies that the four elements can 'give life, having no life of themselves' or 'understanding, having no sence' (p. 235).

473–80. Davies follows Mornay very closely:

If the Soule were the body, it should lose her strength and soundnesse with the body, so as the maimed in bodie should therewith feele also a mayme in his understanding as well as in his members: whosoever were sick of any disease, should also bee sicke in his reason: he that limpeth or halteth, should therewith halt in Soule also: the blynd mans Soule should bee blynd, and the lame mans Soule should be lame. But we see contrariwise, that the maymed and the sicke, the Cripples and the blynd, have their Soule whole and sound, and their understanding perfect and cleeresighted in it selfe (p. 231).

Mornay also says that 'the Soule is seene to be full of livelinesse in a languisshing body, and to growe the more in force, by the decay of the bodie' (p. 231).

481. *accident*: a non-essential attribute.

485–8. According to Mornay, 'the body without the presence of the Soule, hath neither sence, moving, life, no nor continewance of beeing' (p. 226).

497–504. La Primaudaye argues that the soul is not the vital spirits (cf. *N.T.* 498), and that its 'effectes are such as cannot agree to a corruptible and mortall nature, nor to any other then to a celestiall and immortall nature, like to that of the Angels and blessed spirits' (*F.A.*, p. 499).

497. *spirit.* (1) When Davies defines the soul as a 'spirit', he means it is an incorporeal, rational entity not subject to time and space. (2) He refers to *aire* and *wind* as different kinds of spirit from the soul. Since the words *spiritus* and *anima* each mean both 'wind' and 'spirit', Davies wished to clarify that the soul is not simply a moving, refined physical substance like air. (3) The '*spirits* about the *heart* or *braine*' are rarefied intermediaries between body and soul that circulate in the blood or nervous system. See the discussion of Davies's psychology at lines 937 ff. (4) The *spirits* which alchemists find are either an 'extract from some substance, esp. one obtained by distillation', or the 'four substances so named by the mediaeval alchemists', one of them being mercury (*O.E.D.*).

503–4. Mornay calls the soul 'an Image or rather a shadowe (for the Image is defaced by our sinne) of the Godhead it selfe' (p. 226).

505. *formes*: in philosophy, the immaterial principles that make one body different from another, as distinct from matter, which a body shares with all things. At line 958, it means the image or likeness.

509–80. The argument that the soul cannot be a body is taken, with only slight rearrangement, from Mornay, pp. 233–5, as is seen in the relationship of lines 555–60 and 573–80 to these two passages:

So in a Glasse a thousand shapes are seene: but if the cleere of the Glasse had any peculiar shape of it owne, the Glasse could yeeld none of those shapes at all. Also all visible things are imprinted in the eye; but if the sight of the eye had any peculiar colour of it owne, it would be a blemish to the sight, so as it should eyther not see at all, or els all things should seeme like to that blemish. Likewise, whereas the Tongue is the discerner of all tastes; if it bee not cleere but combered with humours, all things are of tast like to the humour, so as if it be bitter, they also be bitter.

* * * *

Bid thy Soule or Mynd goe to *Constantinople*, and foorthwith to turne backe agayne to *Rome*, and straight way to be at *Paris* or *Lyons*: Bid it passe thorowe *America*, or to go about *Affricke*; and it dispatcheth all these journeys at a trice.

545–8. 'Reason draweth out and concludeth invisible things of visible, of corporall things it concludeth things without bodies, and secret things of plaine and evident matters, and generalles of particulars' (*F.A.*, p. 162).

567–8. Wind is perceived as moving sideways, the motion of its particles ('*Atomies*') being felt, not seen; tongues of flame, lighter than air, are seen as rising in pyramidal shapes.

572. *In point of time*: in a single point of time.

583m. Zech. 12: 1, 'The burden of the worde of the Lorde upon Israel, sayth the Lorde, which spread the heavens, and layd the foundation of the earth, and formed the spirite of man within him.'

585. *Prometheus*: According to some late traditions Prometheus both brought fire to man and created him.

589: *Minerva*: the goddess of wisdom who sprang full-grown and fully armed from the head of her father Jove.

593–648. There were three main theories of the creation of souls in the early Christian tradition. Davies espouses the most widely held, that God creates each soul out of nothing and infuses it into the embryo (creationism). The other two theories were designed to avoid any hint that God created the sin that infects human souls. One, condemned by the Council of Alexandria in 399, was Origen's theory of pre-existence, which omits transmigration, but is nevertheless a survival of the Platonic view. The other theory was traducianism, which held that the soul was transmitted from parent to child by the organic process of generation, or that it originated from the parental soul by some analogous spiritual generation. Originating with Tertullian, traducianism won many adherents in western Christendom, including St. Augustine. In the Renaissance, Lutheranism was traducianist and Calvinism creationist.

Davies follows La Primaudaye, p. 493, in outlining the 'principall objection' of the traducianists. His discussion and illustration of errors about the origin of the soul, lines 593–620, are indebted to both La Primaudaye, p. 507, and Montaigne, II. xii. 258, 267.

623. *traduce*: 'to transmit, esp. by generation'—*O.E.D.*

626. *lampe of God*: Holy Scripture; see note to lines 260–5.

627. *Fathers*: Tertullian, Apollinarius, Gregory of Nyssa.

631. *sinne of kind*: inherited (i.e. original) sin.

639. *spill*: spoil, destroy.

682–3. To Davies, generation implies change and motion, which in turn, necessarily, imply corruption; but corruption is inconsistent with immortality. Cf. *S.T.* I. xc. 2, I. cxviii. 2 ad 2um; *F.Q.* VII. vii. 55.

688. *speed*: succeed.

689–92. Cf. Nemesius: 'All things which depend upon successive procreation for their existence are thereby shown to be mortal. For that is the reason that they beget and are begotten, namely that a race of corruptible creatures may be preserved' (p. 285; see also *N.T.* 1513–14).

693–4. Cf. Mark 12: 25.

697–700. A note in the Geneva Bible on Gen. 1: 26 says: 'God commanded the water and the earth to bring forth other creatures: but of man hee saith, Let us make: signifying that God taketh counsell with his wisedome and vertue, purposing to make an excellent worke above all the rest of his creation.' Davies could have found the same idea in La Primaudaye, *F.A.*, p. 518.

704. Davies is quoting Genesis 2: 23.

706. The phrasing is similar to Hebrews 4: 5.

711. Davies may be quoting from Mornay, who treats pagan testimonies

about the soul in chapter xv. Mornay cites Plato as one who 'termeth [the soul] . . . *kin unto God*', and Seneca who calls it both '*kin to the Gods*' and '*sparkes of holy things shining upon the earth*' (pp. 264, 268).

717. 'Surely hee createth them no otherwise then hee did all other creatures, which hee created good' (*F.A.*, p. 492).

729–48. That is, since it was God's purpose in the beginning to pursue a certain order in the creation of man, namely, to infuse each soul into the newly formed body, can we expect God to change this order and cause souls to combine with bodies in some other way, only because of man's sin?

746. *Adamantine chaine*. 'Adamantine' was originally an adjective meaning hard, or unbreakable; later it designated various specific substances that were regarded as having those qualities. The golden chain mentioned in book viii of the *Iliad* became symbolic of the divinely maintained order of the world, and appears frequently in Renaissance writing. Cf. *F.Q.* IV. x. 35; Bacon, *Advancement of Learning* (Everyman), p. 8; and Commentary on *Orchestra*, p. 362.

765–84. Davies's refutation of traducianism follows La Primaudaye, p. 519.

781–2. *personall/But reall*: i.e. not contingent and applicable to only one person, but absolute and applying to all.

789–824. Davies follows Mornay in defending divine justice by comparing it with the practices of human justice. Mornay gives as his example a rebellious city stripped of its privileges,

and this punishment of their Insurrection extendeth to all their posteritie, albeit they were but fewe at the beginning, and grewe to bee mightily multiplyed afterward (p. 320).

But Davies expands the legal argument in terms that recall Hooker's:

the act of a public society of men done five hundred years sithence standeth as theirs who presently are of the same societies, because corporations are immortal; we were then alive in our predecessors, and they in their successors do live still (*Laws*, I. x. 8).

825–8. Mornay says that God

hath left a certeyne inclination in his Creatures, whereby they tend naturally to nothing, that is to say, to chaunge and corruption, unlesse they bee uphild by his power (p. 26).

833–6. Mornay points out 'that of this rebellious race [God] causeth the partie to bee borne, which can appease his Justice' (p. 321).

834. *guiltie*. The reading of the manuscripts here, *guiltlesse*, points out more sharply the antithesis between man's inheriting Adam's sin but also receiving Christ's grace, and is in keeping with the general argument to line 828. Lines 829–32, however, are not found in the manuscripts, and seem to have been written for *1599*. They emphasize that Adam's race cannot inherit only his good without his sin; thus, man becomes 'guiltie' as well as good by inheritance.

837–40. 'And it is better for the soul to be thus, according to its nature, than not to be at all, especially since it can avoid damnation, by means of grace' (*S. T.* I–II. lxxxiii. 1 ad 5um).

845–60. Mornay and La Primaudaye (p. 207) agree that free will is essential to man, and that without free will, human nature would be 'marred' (Mornay, p. 220) and human worship ungratifying to God. Davies's words strikingly echo Mornay's:

Now, love delighteth to bee frecharted; neither would God bee loved of us as inchaunted to it, but freely and utterly unconstreined. Therfore it behoved this will to be free (p. 319).

Davies's reference to Circe, like the earlier one to the story of Ulysses and the Sirens (*N.T.* 409–12) suggests that his knowledge of Homer was imperfect. Ulysses was not carried by love to Circe's island; once there, he (though not his crew) resisted her charms, which turned men to beasts.

865–8.

Thou wouldest have bin created unchaungeable; howbeit, not as a Rock or a Mountayne, but as a Man. . . . Thou wouldest peradventure have bin an Angel: but there are even of the Angels that are falne; and as thei were farre higher than thou, so was their fall more daungerous than thyne (Mornay, pp. 319–20).

869–76. Davies follows La Primaudaye, pp. 518–19, in concluding his discussion of traducianism with a caution against curiosity and probing too deeply into the mysterious ways of God.

877–96. The reasons for the creation of man come from both Mornay and La Primaudaye. Mornay supplied the idea of man as the union of matter and spirit: 'In man wee have an abridgement of . . . God in respect of Spirit, and of the World in composition of body' (p. 225). La Primaudaye mentions the need for a rational creature to govern the earth, and 'to know and glorifie God on earth as the angels do in heaven' (p. 17).

897–900. *vertue*: 'The power or operative influence inherent in a supernatural or divine being'—*O.E.D.* Cf. Batman:

And heereby it appeareth, that the soule is not streighted, neither spread in length, neither in bredth in the bodie, that he ruleth and governeth; but by the vertue of the soule the body all about is ruled and moved (fol. 12^v).

901–20. The similes for the relationship of the soul to the body that Davies rejects as inappropriate in lines 901–8 have in common the notion of accidental rather than intrinsic union. The list is probably compiled from several sources: Montaigne mentions the pilot (II. xii. 257); Batman, fol. 12^v, citing Chalcidius's commentary on *Timaeus*, mentions the spider; the ideas of wax and a vessel are mentioned and rejected by Cicero (*Tusc.* I. xxv. 61). The analogy of the soul and the sun is commonplace, and appears as early as Nemesius (*Of the Nature of Man*, p. 298) and as late as Montaigne (II. xii. 257) and La Primaudaye, whom Davies probably followed:

Now the soule is joyned to the body as light is unto the aire. For by reason of the conjunction of the aire and light together, the aire is made cleare and lightsome:

and yet the aire and light remaine whole and perfect, without any mixture or confusion of the one with the other (p. 429).

918.

Now as every forme of each body is in the whole body, so the soule is wholly in the whole body, in which the true forme & principall essence of man consisteth (*F.A.*, p. 428).

925–36. Mornay draws an analogy between God and the sun, which Davies adapts:

If they consider the Sunne . . . he giveth Sommer, Daylight, & fayre weather to some, and Winter, night, and fowle wether unto othersome: Hee maketh some folkes whyte, some blacke, some read, and some Tawny; and yet is hee but one selfesame Sunne, and one selfesame Creature, which at one selfesame instant, by one selfesame course, and with one selfesame qualitie of heate, doth all the sayd things, not onely divers, but also contrarie. And hee that should say that it is any other than one selfesame Sunne that maketh the Ethyopian blacke, and the Scotte yellowish, were not worthy to be answered (pp. 21–2).

937–1256. Davies's account of the soul is simplified, conventionally Elizabethan, and probably close to the general ideas that the educated layman had about his own nature. Full discussions of Elizabethan psychology are found in Ruth Leila Anderson, *Elizabethan Psychology and Shakespeare's Plays* (1927), J. B. Bamborough, *The Little World of Man* (1952), and Herschel Baker, *The Dignity of Man* (1947).

937m. The *vegetative . . . power* has three functions: nutrition, growth, and reproduction. Davies discusses only the first.

939. *Œconomicke*: domestic

942. *decocts*: digests, breaks down food into usable substances.

945. *Martha.* See Luke 10: 40–1.

947. *Dryas.* In Greek mythology the Dryad personifies the life of the tree.

957–60. Davies expresses the fundamental theory held about sensory perception, that the brain perceives a mental picture of an object. The simile of the seal in wax is commonplace, apparently originating with Aristotle: 'Sensation is the reception of the form of sensible things without the matter, just as the wax receives the impression of the signet-ring without the iron or the gold' (*De Anima*, II. xii, 424ª).

969–84. Davies and La Primaudaye agree that sight is man's principal sense, and Davies's statements about sight resemble La Primaudaye's on several points: the eyes are 'watch-towers & sentinels, the guides & leaders of the whole body' and the instruments whereby man learns many subjects 'impossible to bee learned and knowen certainly unless they may be seene with the eie' (p. 68).

985–92. Davies maintains one side of a debate still current in his time about the process of vision. The theory of extramission is used by Donne in 'The Extasie', lines 7–8:

> Our eye-beams twisted, and did thred
> Our eyes, upon one double string.

Davies himself uses it in 'Elegies of Love', 1. 22–6.

993–6. Batman gives an almost identical list on fol. 18.

1000. *ingenious*. The printed texts have *all gentle*, a misreading.

1001–24. The commonplace explanation of the functional structure of the ear comes from La Primaudaye, who also mentions that hearing is especially important so that man may 'heare and understand [God's] voyce and worde' (p. 84).

1027. *our Eares unmoved*. 'Amongst all living creatures God hath given unmoveable eares to none, but only to man, and to an ape: for the rest can move them up and downe' (*F.A.*, p. 80).

1049–56. Davies borrows extensively from Montaigne's essay, 'Of Smels and Odors':

Therefore saith *Plautus; Mulier tum bene, olet, ubi nihil olet.* . . . The most exquisit and sweetest savour of a woman, it is to smell of nothing; and sweet, well-smelling, strange savours, may rightly be held suspicious in such as use them . . . For, my selfe have often perceived, that according unto their strength and qualitie, they change and alter, and move my spirits, and worke strange effects in me: which makes me approve the common saying, that the invention of incense and perfumes in Churches, so ancient and so far-dispersed throughout all nations and religions, had an especiall regard to rejoyce, to comfort, to quicken, to rowze, and to purifie our senses, that so we might be the apter and readier unto contemplation (I. lv. 355–7).

1051. *Aire*. Although the reading of the printed texts, *Art*, makes sense, it was probably carried over erroneously from line 1049. *Aire*, meaning 'odour' or 'fragrance' is the reading of all manuscripts and is preferable.

1057–68. Davies's discussion of the sense of touch, including his list of primary qualities (*N.T.* 1066) and secondary qualities (*N.T.* 1067) is parallel to that in La Primaudaye, p. 65. The sensitivity of the spider is a common idea; cf. Batman, fol. 345^v.

1073–96. Davies's terminology was unusual for an Elizabethan. Ordinarily the first of the three internal senses was called simply 'common sense', the second 'imagination or fantasy', and the third 'memory'. Common sense receives separate impressions from the external senses and unites them to form an image corresponding to the object perceived, which image it immediately conveys to fantasy. Fantasy deals with the images produced by the common sense, comparing them to previously held images, and combining or separating images. It possesses an elementary judging power (*N.T.* 1089–92), sometimes regarded as a separate faculty called estimation or sensible reason, and also has a creative power (*N.T.* 1093–6).

1077. *Nerves*: a set of hollow tubes which carry spirits (see below, line 1122) to and from the brain. The liver is similarly served by veins (*N.T.* 943) and the heart by arteries (*N.T.* 1139).

1097–1104. Davies follows La Primaudaye, who terms memory a 'Register' (cf. Davies's '*Lidger Booke*'); La Primaudaye places memory in 'the hindermost part of the braine' and provides Davies with the allusion to Janus (pp. 161–2).

1102. *poll*: the part of the head where the hair grows.

1111. *passions*: emotional responses and impulses to action, arising involuntarily in accordance with the judgements delivered by fantasy. Four or six in number (some authors omit love and hate), they automatically pursue good and are repelled by evil. Since they are natural ('*Natures* passions'), they are good, but in fallen man they are a source of danger: by initiating action in defiance of reason or without waiting for rational judgement, they undermine the dominion of the soul over the body.

1122. *spirits*: refined physical substances in constant motion. Natural spirits are formed in the liver and distilled by the heart into vital spirits (Davies's '*spirits* of life'); they are further refined into animal spirits in the brain (Davies's '*spirits* of *Sense*'). The spirits are the crucial link between the soul and the body. All messages to and from the brain—impressions from the organs of sense to the common sense, images to fantasy, the reports from fantasy to the heart that arouse the passions—and all commands from the soul to the body are carried by the spirits.

1141–4. La Primaudaye is the source of these similes; he compares the brain to a 'Waggonner that guydeth his Waggon' and the sinews to 'the reynes and leathers fastened to the bridles, to holde them in, or to let them loose, and to turne them' (p. 50).

1149m. The rational soul, though entirely different in nature, parallels the sensitive soul in having separate powers of apprehension, motion, and memory.

1157. *wit*. The ultimate goals of reason are to acquire general knowledge freed from particular phenomena, to learn universal truths, and to behold God. Its activities take various forms. Discursive reason gathers sensory information from imagination, compares and combines it with previous knowledge, and makes generalizations and abstractions. As judgement, reason uses acquired and innate standards to distinguish true from false and good from evil. Tentative judgement, when there is not sufficient evidence for certainty, is called 'opinion', while the contemplation of an acquired intelligible idea is called 'understanding' (Lat. *intelligere*).

1164. That is, the wit forms a unified perception of the impressions gathered in the fantasy.

1177–84. Like La Primaudaye, Davies here follows a Platonic ladder of knowledge progressing from sensory knowledge, about which agreement may not be possible, to pure knowledge, such as that of mathematics or first principles. Discursive reason knows by steps; angels, like God, know intuitively, that is, simultaneously and totally.

1185–92. Davies evidently is indebted to La Primaudaye here:

When Saint *Paul* sayeth, that the Gentiles . . . have notwithstanding *a Law written in their hearts that doeth accuse or excuse them* . . . by this Lawe hee understandeth that naturall knowledge which men have both of God, and of good, and evil . . . which every one hath for a schoolemistresse within himself (*F.A.*, p. 153).

Cf. Rom. 2: 14–15; Hooker, *Laws*, I. viii. 3; Calvin, *Inst.* I. v. 13.

1193–6.

This Sunbeame of reason . . . is increased and augmented by all the things which it seeth, heareth, or lighteth uppon, like fire, which gathereth increase of strength by the abundance of the fewell that is put unto it, and becommeth after a short infinite (Mornay, p. 285).

1200. *widowes oyle*: See 2 Kings 4: 1–7.

1201–20.

For the will hath no light of it selfe, but is lightned by the minde, that is to say, by reason and judgement, which are joyned with it, not to governe and turne it from one side to another by commandement and authoritie, either by force or violence, as a Prince or Magistrate, but as a counsailer or directer, to admonish and to conduct it (*F.A.*, pp. 204–5).

1201–16. The motive power, will, is designed to choose the right course of action and to direct the body, through the sensitive motion, to perform it. Davies gives here (lines 1203–4) only one explanation of moral failure: that will is misinformed by reason. Elsewhere in the poem he points to the conflict between reason and passion, and the possibility that will, infected and weakened by original sin, may yield to the passions which it ought to command (cf. *N.T.* 407–8, 1215–16), and incline to immediate sensual gratification instead of choosing the greater, spiritual good.

1217–20. Will is free in that nothing can force a choice upon it; most Christian writers agree, however, that it is genuinely free only when it chooses the true good advised by reason.

1221–4. Montaigne quotes Cicero, '*Assuredly memorie alone, of all other things, compriseth not onely Philosophy, but the use of our whole life, and all the sciences*' (II. xvii. 377). Mornay cites Plotinus as saying 'that they which are passed into another world, have their memorie still' and defines '*the Memorie of understanding*' as 'an abundance of Reason, and as it were a hoorder up of the continuall influences of the Mynd' (pp. 273, 285).

1224. *Lethæan Flud*. In the classical underworld the dead drank of the River Lethe to forget their past lives.

1236.

To be short, the noblest creatures have neede of the bacest, and the bacest are served by the noblest; and all are so linked together from the highest to the lowest, that the ring thereof cannot bee broken without confusion (Mornay, p. 20).

1241–4.

So the Soule vegetative desireth to be, the sensible desireth to be wel, and the resonable soule desireth to be best: and therefore it resteth never, till it be joyned with the best. For the place of the reasonable soule is God, to whom warde it is moved, that it may rest in him (Batman, fol. 16ʳ).

1245–50, 1253–4. Although the notion of the threefold division of the soul is commonplace, Davies's treatment in these lines is indebted to Mornay, who defines 'three sorts of men, according to the three powers or abilities of the inwarde man' which he describes as Davies does (pp. 229–30). Mornay also denies that man has three souls:

not that he hath three Soules but onely one Soule; that is to wit, that like as in the brute Beast the sensitive Soule comprehendeth the quickening Soule; so in man the reasonable Soule comprehendeth both the sensitive and the quickening, and executeth the offices of them all three (p. 227).

1257–60, 1269–72. Davies's language follows Psalm 8: 4–6 in lines 1257–60, and Hebrews 1: 5–6 in lines 1269–72.

1281–1300. Mornay (p. 244) and La Primaudaye (p. 528) both suggest that those who deny immortality are sinners who fear to be judged after death; Davies follows La Primaudaye who quotes the Book of Wisdom (2: 1–7) at length (*N.T.* 1285–91).

1294. *Epicures*: not only the disciples of Epicurus, but anyone 'who disbelieves in the divine government of the world and in a future life', or 'who gives himself up to sensual pleasures'—*O.E.D.*

1305–32. The argument based on the desire for knowledge is drawn from La Primaudaye, who calls the desire 'naturall'; pointing out that in this life men can learn 'as it were nothing' commensurable with their desire, he concludes that another time and place must be appointed to fulfil the longing for knowledge. He commends the 'wisest . . . Philosophers' for basing their argument on the 'common saying, that God and Nature the minister of God doe nothing without cause' (pp. 556–7).

1313–16. Cf. Job 9: 25–6: 'My dayes have bene more swift then a poste: they have fled, and have seene no good thing. They are passed as with the most swift shippes, and as the eagle that fleeth to the pray'.

1337–1432. Davies's long discussion conflates two arguments 'taken from the motion and rest of the soule' (*F.A.*, p. 552). The first, taken from La Primaudaye (p. 538), is that nothing can rise higher than its source; since man's spirit, 'not content with the sight and knowledge of the heavens, starres and Angels themselves mounteth up to God', then God must be its source and end. The second argument, from the aim of motion, rests on a theory formulated by the Stoics from the writings of Aristotle: heavy, gross things (like earth and water) fall, while light and refined ones (like air and fire) rise. Cicero uses this law of motion in proving the immortality of the soul (*Tusc.* I. xvii. 40). He describes the soul as moving upward constantly until it reaches its like in both lightness and heat; in its natural home it rests and fulfils its insatiable longing for truth (*Tusc.* I. xix. 43–5).

That these two arguments can be treated as one is due to the Christian paradox expressed in *N.T.* 1385–8 and Revelations 22: 13: God is both 'Alpha & Omega, the beginning and the ende, the first and the last'. Augustine

(*De Beata Vita*, iv. 34–5) states that, in progressing towards perfection, man returns to his Creator and in him fulfils his desire for truth and good; reason is perfected in possessing God as wisdom, while will is perfected in possessing God as love. The double argument from motion recurs throughout this section; Davies expands it by adding the long similes and by describing the frustration of earthly limitations in juxtaposition to the bliss of heavenly perfection. Most of the expansion is based on Mornay, whose discussion of riches, honour, power, beauty, health, bodily pleasure, virtue, policy, and wisdom (pp. 329–35) supplies Davies's list of the false goals in which men seek happiness. Davies follows Mornay in concluding from the inadequacy of these goals 'that as the worlde cannot be mans ende, so can it not also be his contention' (p. 325). Mornay also identifies the goal of life as God (p. 337) and defines that goal in terms of reason and will:

In respect that his witte looketh thereat, [it] is called his amingpoynt, and in respect that his will resteth thereon, [it] is called his welfare, both of them together being the restingpoint of the whole man (p. 323).

Mornay does not, however, describe even as little as Davies does 'what that felicitie of man shalbe', taking caution from St. Paul's statement (1 Cor. 2: 9) 'that neither eye hath seene it nor hart can conceyve it' (p. 337). Davies's references to heavenly bliss are conventional.

1345–56. Cf. *Orchestra*, stanza 63.

1433–92. The outline of the complementary third and fourth reasons comes mainly from La Primaudaye, who makes the same three points as Davies. First, the death of the spirit is abhorrent because it 'is contrary to the nature of it', a statement that implies an innate knowledge that the soul is immortal. Second, virtuous men, 'resolutely perswaded and assured of a better life', do not fear death. Finally, those who fear death are 'carnall and ledde most by their senses', men who have devoted their energies to the life of sense and are terrified by the loss of that life (*F.A.*, pp. 545–6). La Primaudaye supports his thesis about virtuous men as Davies does, by pointing out that noble persons have killed themselves to avoid shame and infamy, clearly manifesting a belief in immortality (*F.A.*, pp. 564–5).

Davies adopts from Mornay the point (made differently at *N.T.* 1283–1300) that wicked men demonstrate their belief in immortality by their fear of death. Mornay says that at the point of death a man's 'owne nature waketh, and . . . painteth againe before his eyes, the selfsame thing which he tooke so much paynes to deface'. He cites those who 'having bene despisers of all Religion, have at the hower of death bin glad to vow their Soules to any Sainct for releefe'. He considers it valuable evidence to

see an *Atheist* or an *Epicure* witnessing the immortalitie of the Soule, and willingly taking an honorable farewell of nature upon a Scaffold . . . For whatsoever the *Epicures* say there, they speake it . . . fresh and fasting; whereas all that ever they have spoken all their life afore, is to bee accounted but as the wordes of Drunkards

. . . of men besotted and falne asleepe in the delights and pleasures of this world (pp. 244-5).

1455. *Meleagers*. When Meleager was born, the Fates granted him a life-span equal to that of a piece of wood then burning in the fire. His mother preserved the stick for years, but burnt it upon learning that Meleager had killed her brothers (Ovid, *Met.* viii. 451–525).

1493–1520. The idea that the voice of the people is the voice of God, i.e. that widespread agreement among most men indicates the truth of a doctrine, is a Stoic teaching that was extremely popular in the Renaissance. It appears as early as Cicero as a proof of immortality (*Tusc.* I. xv. 35), and is repeated by Hooker (*Laws*, I. viii. 3), La Primaudaye, and Mornay, the source of Davies's argument:

as there have at al tymes bene men, so . . . men have at all tymes beleeved . . . the immortalitie of the Soule; I say not some one man or some one Nation, but the whole world with generall consent, because all men universally and perticularly have learned it in one Schoole, and at the mouth of one Teacher, namely even their owne knowledge in themselves (p. 257).

Mornay also supplies the statement that the desire for immortality is so widespread that even if 'we looke not for it by nature, we seeke to obteyne it by skill and pollicie, some by bookes, some by Images, and some by other devices' (p. 243).

1509–16. Fame and offspring are only poor substitutes for personal immortality. Hooker (*Laws*, I. v. 2) speaks of perpetual life as part of the 'general perfection which all things do seek'; those who cannot have personal immortality try to perpetuate themselves 'by offspring and propagation'. The fruitless efforts of men to preserve their names are discussed by Browne in *Hydriotaphia*.

1513–16. As a proof of immortality, Cicero refers to Statius:

'Trees does he sow to be of service to the coming age', as *Statius* says in the *Synephebi*, and what notion is in his mind except that even succeeding ages are his concern? Shall then a farmer industriously sow trees, no berry of which his eyes will ever see? (*Tusc.* I. xiv. 31.)

1521–52. Mornay states the general idea:

Man can skill to discerne the mortall natures from the immortall; And therefore we may well say he is immortall. For hee that should dispute to the contrarie, shalbe driven to bring such reasons, as shall of themselves make him to proove himselfe immortall (p. 243).

He also provides the analogy for lines 1537–40: we call a man reasonable if he can 'discerne the difference betweene that which is reason, and that which is not'.

The argument of lines 1529–36, that the soul must be an immortal mirror to reflect immortal ideas, comes from La Primaudaye: 'a looking glasse cannot represent the image . . . of a spirituall thing, because it selfe . . . hath no agreement in nature with that which is spirituall' (p. 536).

1553–1608. The very definition of the soul as spiritual precludes its being destroyed. That *'Her cause ceaseth not'* is argued from La Primaudaye:

If it be so then, that our soule is not begotten or produced by this nature, which is the handmaide of God . . . but by God alone, it followeth . . . that nothing in nature can extinguish it, but God onely (p. 540).

The remainder of these statements are taken point by point from Mornay's proof that the soul is a spirit, not a body (pp. 235–43). Although Davies uses this material in a different context, he is often extremely close to Mornay in language, as this example shows:

There is not that step which we set downe in this life, which dooth not continewally step foreward unto death . . . tyme perfecteth, accomplisheth, and increaseth our mynd, and after a sort reneweth and refressheth it from day to day, whereas contrarywise it forweareth, wassheth away and quight consumeth, both it self, and the body with the life thereof (pp. 241–2).

1559–60. Cf. Mark 13: 31: 'Heaven and earth shall passe away, but my wordes shall not passe away.'

1576. *tree of life*. In Gen. 3: 22, man is cast out of Eden 'lest he put foorth his hande, and take also of the tree of life and eate and live for ever'. Denied physical immortality, man still has the means of living forever by the spirit.

1591. *Saturne*: The Greek *Kronos*, identified with *chronos*, 'time', who ate his children to prevent their destroying him.

1597–1600. This stanza reflects contemporary proverbs: 'As soon as man is born he begins to die'; 'Time hath wings' (Tilley, M73, T327).

1604. *her*: Hebe, goddess of youth and cup-bearer to the gods.

1610. *false*. Apparently the scribe of *AC* had difficulty in reading his copy here, for he left blank a space where Davies himself supplied *false*. *Safe*, the reading of other witnesses, might easily be mistaken for *false* in Elizabethan hand.

1613–1704. By identifying the soul with reason Davies must reply to the objection that as intelligence fades, the soul itself decays, and hence is mortal. The objection and refutation follow the arguments and illustrations of Mornay, who, replying to the assertion that the soul 'if corrupted . . . may also dye' (p. 254), says the reason does not decline, but may receive false reports from the senses: 'like as the wisest men being deceyved by false Spyes, do make wrong deliberations . . . So the reason . . . gathereth wrong conclusions, uppon the false reports of the imaginations' (p. 255). Mornay supplied Davies with the image of the sun and the 'cunning of a Luteplaier [which] is not diminished by the moystnesse or slacknesse of his Lute strings' though it may be 'by the nimblenes of his fingars which are perchaunce knotted with the gout' (pp. 231–2). The sources of lines 1613–20 and 1693–1704 are Mornay, pp. 254 and 237–8.

The physiological notions on which the passage rests, especially the idea that the brains of infants suffered excessive moisture, and those of the aged excessive dryness, are commonplace; see, for example, John Huarte, *Examen de Ingenios: The Examination of mens wits*, tr. Richard Carew (1594), sig. E7ᵛ.

1671. *Apollo*: god of music and healing.

1683. *Aesons youth*. Aeson, Jason's aged father, was restored to youth by Medea (Ovid, *Met.* vii. 251–93).

1687. *Crochets*: musical notes.

1705–36. This argument resembles the preceding. Here, however, the issue is not whether the soul can exist without external evidence of its action but whether it can exist even in heaven without the instruments supplied by the body. Like his source, Mornay (pp. 253–4), Davies largely repeats what he has said before.

1737–80. The analogy between prenatal life and this life was often used by writers on the soul; e.g. La Primaudaye (*F.A.*, pp. 403–4) and William Drummond (*A Cypresse Grove*, in *Poetical Works*, ed. Kastner (1913), ii. 97). Davies, however, takes his figures from Mornay, who says that to argue that

because our mynd conceyveth not any thing here, but by helpe of Imagination; therfore when the Imagination is gone [after death] . . . the Soule cannot worke alone . . . is al one as if they should say, that because the Child being in his moothers wombe taketh nourishment of her blud by his navill; therfore he cannot live when he is come out of her womb, if his navillstrings be cut off (p. 256).

The imagined response of children still in the womb overhearing their mothers' conversation is Davies's extension of the simile provided by Mornay. Mornay, however, provided some of the details and the general idea:

To bee short, it shall live, but not in prison; it shall see, but not through Spectacles; it shall understand, but not by reports (p. 256).

1779–80. In heaven man will perceive intuitively instead of discursively as on earth. Cf. 1 Cor. 13: 12: 'For nowe wee see through a glasse darkely: but then *shall wee see* face to face'; also above, *N.T.* 763–4, 1181–4.

1781–1804. The fourth objection and answer resemble ideas in La Primaudaye (p. 532), but are taken primarily from Mornay, pp. 251–2. To Mornay, the question 'If dead mens Soules live still, why come they not to tell us so?' is no better argument against immortality than saying 'There hath not come any man unto us from the Indies of a long tyme: ergo there be no Indies'. He continues,

May not the same argument serve as well to prove that wee our selves are not, because wee never went thether? . . . the Soule that is lodged in the lappe of his God, and come home into his native soyle, forgoeth the desire of these lower things . . . the Soule which is in the Jayle of his sovereine Lord God, hath no respit or sporting-tyme to come tell us what is done there.

1805–24. Much of Davies's fifth objection and answer are found in La Primaudaye, pp. 566–7, who, like Davies, concludes,

Nowe then, when they woulde have men to bee perswaded to vertue, and to doe their duetie by lying and errour, namely, by intertayning in them an opinion of religion, and of a second life, although there bee no such thing, is not this, a very proper meanes to call all trueth into question, and to trample all vertue under foote?

1807–8. *Politique men*: either politicians, or political theorists (used pejoratively). The use of religion in statecraft is referred to in one of Davies's sources for *Orchestra*, Cicero's *De nat. deor.* i. xlii. 118; it was propounded by Machiavelli in the *Discourses*, i. xi–xii.

1825–60. Davies's argument follows La Primaudaye, pp. 553–4, and Mornay, from whom he took several of his illustrations. For example, 1829–36.

Let us runne at this day from East to West, and from North to South, I say not among the *Turkes*, *Arabians*, or *Persians*, (for their *Alcoran* teacheth them that mans Soule was breathed into him of God, and consequently that it is uncorruptible) but even among the most barbarous, ignorant & beastly people of the Wo[r]ld, I meane the very *Caribies* and *Cannibals;* and we shall find this beleefe received and imbraced of them all . . . it is not a doctrine invented by speculations of some Philosophers, conveyed from Countrie to Countrie by their disciples, perswaded by likelyhods of reasons, or . . . entered into mans wit by his eares: but a native knowledge, which every man findeth and readeth in himself (Mornay, p. 275).

1833. *Assirian drugge.*

And that which *Virgill* sayth in his [fourth] Eglog concerning the Drug or Spice of *Assyria*, and the growing thereof everywhere, is interpreted of some men to bee ment of the Immortalitie of the Soule . . . namely, that it should be understood everywhere throughout the whole world (Mornay, p. 261).

1841–52.

If the soule of man be mortall, all that hee hath to doe is in this life, as it is with beasts: and then also it followeth, that hee was created in vaine and without cause. For God created nothing, but hee propounded to himselfe the ende for which hee created it . . . the religion of God, his providence, and the immortalitie of our soule are . . . fast lincked and joyned together . . . if our soules be not immortall, there is neither punishment nor reward, either for vertue or vice . . . Which if it were so, then shoulde God have no care of men: and if hee have no care of them, howe shall hee be their GOD and Creator, and why shoulde they rather then beasts call upon him and honor him? (*F.A.*, pp. 553–4.)

With reference to the simile in *N.T.* 1843–4, cf. Psalms 37: 1–2, Isa. 40: 6–7.

1860. This common saying is similarly used by Donne in *The Second Anniversary*, lines 183–4, and was suggested to Davies by Mornay, p. 238, 'Now, when a man sees so lively a Soule in so weake and wretched a body, may he not say as is said of the hatching of Chickens, that the shell is broken, but there commeth forth a Chicken?'

1861–88. Although Davies shortens Mornay's discussion (pp. 245–7), he follows it very closely, and often only versifies Mornay's statements. Mornay says that a man

commeth out of the first world into the second, as it were fayling in nourishment, but growing in strength unto moving and sence: and he goeth out of the second into the third, fayling in sences and moving, but growing in reason and understanding (p. 247).

He asks 'what child . . . if he had . . . knowledge & speech, would not call that death, which we call birth?' (p. 246).

1889–1924. The closing acclamation unites the two parts of the poem by language and references that combine the ideas of both elegies, and go beyond them to point not only to man's nature, but to his relationship to the rest of the universe. Line 1892 parallels the statement in the closing lines of the first elegy about man's duality. The next two lines recall but contradict the allusion to Io in lines 111–28.

'That God did meane ,/ This worthy mind, should worthy things embrace' expresses a doctrine of Platonic origin: that the soul is degraded when it chooses as its goal or sovereign good an object lower than itself. Devoting one's life to wealth, or earthly power, or sensual pleasure is more than a disastrous error of judgement; it debases the spiritual nature which man shares with the angels and which, by nature, is inferior only to God.

1893–4. Cf. *N.T.* 113–28 and note. In Ovid, Narcissus fell in love with his reflection in a pool and wasted away (*Met.* iii. 407–510); the story of his drowning is a tradition common in the Middle Ages and the Renaissance.

1897–1904. While this is a conventional peroration, it echoes passages in La Primaudaye, who says that since God intends reason to rule the passions, 'Let us not then suffer the spirite to bee brought into bondage by the perturbations of the affections' (pp. 599–600). La Primaudaye refers also to Socrates' advice that everyone look at himself in a mirror, so that the beautiful 'shoulde bee the more afraide to blotte their beautie with vices' (p. 280).

1908. The tradition that the swan, ordinarily mute, sings before it dies is used by Plato (*Phaedo*, 84E) and Cicero (*Tusc.* I. xxx. 73) in discussing the immortality of the soul:

Just as the swans—[which] . . . have a foretaste of the blessing death brings—die with a song of rapture, so must all good and learned men do likewise.

1909–10. Cf. Bacon, 'Of Death': 'Men fear death, as children fear to go in the dark.'

1917–24. The peacock's pride was proverbial as was the detail about his ugly feet. Davies borrows from Mornay:

Yet for all this, let not man bee proude of the excellencie or immortalitie of his Soule: for the more he hath receyved of his maker, the more is he indebted to him; and the more excellent that his nature is, the more lothsome and daungerous is the corruption therof. The Peacocke is sayd to be proud of his gay fethers, when he sets up his tayle round about him: but when he hath once stretched out his wings, he falles into a dump, and as soone as he lookes upon his feete, he casts mee downe his tayle and is ashamed (pp. 287–8).

Hymnes of Astræa

Text and Composition

The first edition, *HA1599*, serves as copy-text. It is well printed, and probably derives from a scribal manuscript given to the printer by Davies. *1619* was set up from *HA1599*, and *1622* from a copy of *1619* that had been slightly corrected by Davies. I emend once from *1622* and adopt its use of italics three times; in a second emendation I follow both *1619* and *1622*. Otherwise, no changes are necessary, except for a few emendations of accidentals—all are purely editorial, but for three that derive from *1622*. Accidentals in *1619* are omitted, and those of *1622* are to be assumed only where specifically cited. Only one hymn has been found in manuscript: a late, corrupt version which the compiler failed to recognize as an acrostic. It is of no textual importance.

The *Hymnes* were entered in the Stationers' Register on Accession Day, 17 November 1599. Six months earlier Davies had dedicated *Nosce Teipsum* to Elizabeth who reportedly liked it so well that she promised him preferment. His next published work, the *Hymnes*, seem written to further that aim. Their near-complete omission from manuscript collections suggests that they did not circulate widely, and may indicate that they were written primarily to gain royal favour. In 1599 Davies was writing verses for people who might assist him in being restored to the Middle Temple. The language and images of many of the *Hymnes* closely parallel those of *Nosce Teipsum* and its accompanying dedication to Elizabeth. The poems themselves imply that they were written in spring, though this implication may be a poetic fiction. The weight of evidence, internal and external, however, points to 1599, probably spring, as the time of composition.

Background

Astraea is a name for the constellation Virgo, an autumnal sign of the zodiac. Virgo-Astraea was identified by the Greek writer Aratus, in his astronomical poem *Phaenomena*, with Hesiod's *Dike* ('Justice'; see *Theogony*, 900), one of the *Horae* or Hours, goddesses of the seasons. Aratus and Ovid both stated that she was the last of the gods to abandon the earth during the Bronze (Aratus) or Iron (Ovid) Age, when men had brought bloodshed and turmoil to human life. Following her departure she became revered by men. In Ovid's *Metamorphoses* she was a symbol of the Golden Age of the past, while in Virgil's fourth Eclogue she symbolized the Golden Age of the future: 'Now the Virgin returns, the reign of Saturn returns' (iv. 6). Since the

Golden Age included spring and autumn simultaneously, Astraea became identified with spring; hence Davies's emphasis upon this season. He celebrates her in twenty-six hymns because, according to Ptolemy, the constellation Virgo had twenty-six stars (see Alastair Fowler, *Spenser and the Numbers of Time* (1962), pp. 198–9).

It is not surprising that Elizabeth should have been addressed as Astraea by many poets, including Peele, Spenser, and Davies (see Elkin Calhoun Wilson, *England's Eliza* (1939), and Frances A. Yates, 'Queen Elizabeth as Astraea', *Journal of the Warburg and Courtauld Institutes*, x (1947), 27–82, for extensive discussions of Elizabeth as Astraea). Davies is not attempting originality of thought but freshness and grace of statement; the poems are intended not as actual portrayals but as compliments to an ideal figure called 'Queen'. The pride of sixteenth-century Englishmen in their country was vested in the monarch, the source of stability, security, and peace. In other poems, Elizabeth is Queen Gloriana as ruler of the seas, or God's elect as the leader of the Church. When she is seen in her role as the preserver of justice, or as the head of a nation with a mild climate, fertile soil, and great prosperity corresponding to the Golden Age or the Fortunate Isles (see Commentary on *Orchestra*, stanza 121), she is addressed as Astraea or Virgo.

IV. 15. *Majestie.* May is said in Ovid's *Fasti* (v. 11–52) to be named after Majesty, daughter of Honour and Reverence.

IV. 16. *clearenesse*: eminence (Lat. *clarus*).

VII. *Rose.* E. C. Wilson points out the manifold symbolism of the rose that was applicable to Elizabeth: beauty, transience, virginity, and its use by the royal houses of York and Tudor; see *England's Eliza* (1939), pp. 133–5.

IX. 3. *Greenewich*: a royal residence.

X. 12. *birth day.* Elizabeth was born on 7 September 1533.

XV. This hymn repeats several ideas from *Nosce Teipsum*; cf. lines 1157–8, 433, 1193–6, 193–200.

XVII. 6–11. Cf. *N.T.* 1101–4.

XIX. 1. *she*: Elizabeth's mind.

XX. 6–11. Cf. *N.T.* 1133–6.

XXI. 15. *begge for*: set down as.

XXII–XXV. In these hymns Davies praises Queen Elizabeth for her pre-eminence in the four natural virtues identified by the Greeks: wisdom or prudence, justice, fortitude or magnanimity, and temperance or moderation.

XXII. 1. *Wisedome* consists in judgement or discernment of truth and of the relative merits of means and ends.

XXII. 3. *daughter*: Pallas Athene (Minerva), daughter of Jove and goddess of wisdom.

XXIII. *Justice* is a public rather than a private virtue, since its object is the proper balance of the differing elements that make up a community. It deals out reward and punishment, apportioning goods and honours to each man according to his merit. As a principle of balance and adjustment, it maintains stable order in the state and in the universe (lines 2–3); cf. *F.Q.* V, Proem x:

> Most sacred vertue she of all the rest,
> Resembling God in his imperiall might;
> Whose soveraine powre is herein most exprest,
> That both to good and bad he dealeth right,
> And all his workes with Justice hath bedight.
> That powre he also doth to Princes lend,
> And makes them like himselfe in glorious sight,
> To sit in his owne seate, his cause to end,
> And rule his people right, as he doth recommend.

While love and human sympathy are always associated with justice, the compliment to the Queen's clemency is more Christian than classical, since mercy mitigates and often runs counter to strict justice.

XXIV. *Magnanimitie* is equated by Cicero with fortitude or courage (*De Officiis*, I. xix. 63); Davies may, however, include some of the characteristics of Aristotle's magnanimous man, who is marked by a sense of his superiority to the common run of men. Macrobius associates with fortitude confidence, composure, and constancy; its possessor 'must exalt his mind above all dread of danger, fear nothing except disgrace, and bear manfully both adversity and prosperity' (*Commentary on The Dream of Scipio*, I. viii. 7).

XXV. *Moderation*, or temperance, is order in the individual, the state achieved when the body is properly subordinated to the soul and the lower powers to reason.

XXV. 16. *no alteration*. Elizabeth's motto was *Semper Eadem* 'always the same'.

XXVI. I. *Envie*: the vice of weeping at another's good fortune. Davies asserts that his poems arouse envy but are exalted above its capacity to harm them.

Orchestra

Textual Introduction

There are three textual witnesses: *LF*, a manuscript copied in 1595 by Leweston Fitzjames, one of Davies's associates at the Middle Temple, which preserves the poem in its earliest form; *1596*, the first printed edition; and *1622*, the second printed edition, which was set up from a copy of *1596* corrected by Davies. The work was entered in the Stationers' Register on 25 June 1594; had it been pirated, the Middle Templar who became a barrister in 1595 could have prevented its printing. Moreover, *Orchestra* is too long to have been copied often, and its circulation was surely very limited before it was printed. Probably the printer of *1596* received from Davies a scribal manuscript containing authorial corrections. Davies's own hand, for which he apologizes in a letter written some years later, was always very bad; it is therefore unlikely that he would have sent the printer a manuscript in his holograph.

1596 is the witness closest to the author's final manuscript, and therefore serves as copy-text. In general, it is well printed and requires little improvement. Davies made a few corrections for the printing of *1622*, and these are adopted in the present text. *LF* allows a few additional corrections, but its main value is to indicate what Davies first wrote. While some of its variants are doubtless Fitzjames's slips or perhaps his efforts at improvement, most of them must be Davies's first attempts. These, except for obvious errors, which are excluded, appear in the apparatus.

Davies in *1622* frequently altered roman type to italic. Such emended accidentals are introduced into the present text from *1622*, as are a few alterations in punctuation and capitalization, but the accidentals of *LF* are not to be assumed unless specifically cited.

Composition and Occasion

Orchestra was copied in *LF* in 1595. Probably the safest assumption is that it was composed early in 1594, not long before its entry in the Stationers' Register on 25 June of that year.

It existed in three versions. The earliest, preserved in *LF*, was complete in 113 stanzas, numbered 1–108, 127–131 by the present numbering (see the present editor's 'Sir John Davies: *Orchestra* complete, *Epigrams*, Unpublished Poems', *R.E.S.* xiii (1962), 18–29). Davies then wrote the stanzas now numbered 109–126: these were sewn into MS. *LF* and were printed in both *1596* and *1622*. Finally, in *1622*, stanzas 127–131 were replaced by stanzas 127A–131A.

The initial version is structurally the most satisfactory. The opening

stanzas give the legendary background, stanza 6 the invocation, and stanzas
7–11 the setting. Antinous then invites Penelope to dance (12–13). Her
refusal (14–15), on the grounds that dancing is an unseemly modern inven-
tion that violates custom and established order, prompts Antinous' defence
of its antiquity, as he shows it to have been Love's agent in ordering the ma-
terial of creation and establishing the empyrean heaven (17–24). Penelope is
partially convinced, but wants to learn more of its origin (25–26). Antinous'
reply, the lengthy 'pedigree' of dancing, constitutes the body of the poem.
Penelope interrupts to argue against Love, thereby suspending the argument
to prepare for Antinous' climactic example: the Queen's beauty itself most
perfectly embodies the cosmic dance (104–107); only her soul has a more
perfect motion (108). Could he picture its angelic beauty, he would be
transported:

> Could I now see as I conceive thys Daunce,
> Wonder and Love would cast me in a traunce (108.6–7).

The stanzas that followed (127–131) concluded the poem with an invocation
to the muse of prophecy as Antinous called on the great poets of past and
present to aid him in picturing the heavenly beauty of the Queen's mind.

At the climax of the poem, Davies inserted eighteen new stanzas that
disrupt its direction. They honour Queen Elizabeth, by making unmis-
takable the identification of 'chast *Penelope, Ulisses* Queene' as a forerunner of
the virgin queen of England, and by treating qualities particularly satisfying
to a monarch: Concord, 'Where divers men and women ranked be' (110.2),
and Decorum, or '*Comlines* the chyld of order sweet' (113.3). Moreover, they
seem to have been written so that the poem might be used as an entertain-
ment for Elizabeth and her court. It could have been read aloud (it is not
half as long as a Shakespearian play), and some of its story could have been
acted. Love might have been dressed as a page, as in stanza 119. The mirror
he brings to Antinous might actually, as described in stanzas 119–120, have
been presented to Elizabeth, in order to show

> The fairest sight that ever shall be seene . . .
> Our glorious English Courts divine Image,
> As it should be in this our golden age (120.3, 126.6–7).

That *Orchestra* was used as an entertainment has been independently
proposed by P. J. Finkelpearl, in *John Marston of the Middle Temple* (1969),
pp. 76–9; he suggests that *Orchestra* was written for the revels of an Inn of
Court. He observes that the sub-title in *1596* is 'A Poeme of Dauncing:
Judicially prooving the true observation of time and measure, in the Authen-
ticall and laudable use of Dauncing', and continues,

The basic action of the poem is, as Tillyard says, a disputation, and with its origin
in the Middle Temple, the poem may be read as a law school tour de force 'judicially'
proving that everything dances. It is the sort of exercise which might have enter-
tained an audience at revels, particularly the Prince d'Amour's revels, for the major
argument is that 'Dauncing' (the prime activity at revels) is 'Loves proper excercise'.

Disputation was a principal source of entertainment and instruction at the Inns of Court; cases and points of law were argued in the hall before the assembled members of the Inn. Such activities were parodied by the mock Grammar Lecture at the Inner Temple revels of 1602, and the recitation of paradoxes at the Gray's Inn revels of 1617, as Mr. Finkelpearl has pointed out in private correspondence. A poem combining the activities of dancing and argument, both part of life at an Inn of Court, may well have been written for a public entertainment there.

Mr. Finkelpearl believes that Richard Martin was 'at a later date the perpetual Prince d'Amour' in revels at the Middle Temple, and suggests that Davies's dedication to him as 'first mover and sole cause' of *Orchestra* may imply it was written at Martin's request for a performance in which he recited the speech of Love. The dedication to Martin in *LF*, by its position in the manuscript and the colour of its ink, appears to have been added by the copyist when he entered the additional stanzas, 109–126, so that the dedication and insertion may well have been written by Davies at the same time. The hypothesis regarding Martin is plausible. More certain is that the poem was written for an audience of lawyers, either as a public entertainment or for their private amusement, and altered to appeal to the Queen and her court.

The poem was complete in 113 stanzas in *LF* in 1595, extended to 131 stanzas in *1596*, but altered by Davies in *1622* to give the appearance of being incomplete. His reason was pique.

In *LF* and *1596* Davies dedicated the poem to Richard Martin in an affectionate sonnet, and in the final stanza of *Orchestra* he placed Martin at the culmination of a group of poets to whom Antinous looks for inspiration. Martin thus begins and concludes the poem. Davies later broke violently with Martin, however, and the two were never genuinely reconciled. Davies wanted to remove all traces of Martin when republishing the poem in *1622*; to do so, he replaced the dedicatory sonnet to Martin with one 'To the Prince'. The five concluding stanzas of *Orchestra* were withdrawn, and on the title-page, to conceal their withdrawal, Davies termed the poem 'Not finished'. In addition, he removed from the title the lines 'Judicially prooving the true observation of time and measure', perhaps to conceal the connection of the poem with the Inns of Court, from which he was banished for three years after attacking Martin. Five new stanzas were written, preceded by the statement 'Here are wanting some Stanzaes describing Queene Elizabeth. Then follow these.' The statement is entirely false; the stanzas removed do not describe Elizabeth. The new stanzas, however, picture her among her court, and thereby strengthen the notion that the poem may have been used as an entertainment for Elizabeth, who may indeed have

> ... vouchsaft awhile
> With gracious, cheerefull, and familiar eye

Upon the Revels of her Court to smile,
For so Times Journeis she doth oft beguile (127[A].2–5).

Sources

Like *Nosce Teipsum*, *Orchestra* is a derivative poem, but Davies allows his
imagination freer play in describing the cosmic dance than he did in treating
the immortality of the soul. The idea that the universal order is a dance
began as a metaphor used occasionally by writers on astronomy such as the
Roman Manilius, who mentions it once in the five books of *Astronomicon*, and
was taken up by defenders of dancing, including Lucian and Thenot Arbeau,
author of the dancing-manual *Orchésographie* (1588). Neither of them, however,
makes much use of it. Davies so expands the metaphor that John Hoskyns
cites *Orchestra* as an example of the rhetorical device of amplification by
division:

This only tricke made upp J: Ds poeme of dauncing, All daunceth, the heavens, the
elements, mens myndes, commonwealths, & soe by parts all daunceth (*Life, Letters,
and Writings*, ed. Louise Brown Osborn (1937), p. 136).

The first source of *Orchestra*, pointed out by A. H. Bullen in *An English
Garner: Some Longer Elizabethan Poems* (1903), pp. viii–ix, is Lucian's *Peri
Orcheseos*, 'The Dance'. Lucian's dialogues were read in Latin translation by
the third form at Winchester, which probably used the selection edited by
Erasmus and More. That edition omits *The Dance*, but all the dialogues were
available in Latin after 1546. Some of the contents were circulated widely in
defences of dancing; for example, Sir Thomas Elyot, accepting the role of
social dancing in the life of a courtier, uses some of Lucian's material in
defending it against attacks on the grounds of immorality and frivolity (*The
Book of the Governor*, I. xx). Davies uses far more of Lucian than Elyot does. He
may even have taken his title from Lucian; in Davies's time 'orchestra' was
still a foreign word used only for the place where the chorus sang and danced
in Greek theatre. Davies's evident borrowings include the references to the
antiquity and respectability of dancing, and the suggestions that various
stories of transformation were corrupted legends about certain skilful dancers
like Proteus and Tiresias.

The cosmological details with which Antinous supports the thesis that
order is dancing come from Book II of Cicero's *De natura deorum*; there the
speaker outlines the natural theology of the Stoics, who proved the existence
of a divine intelligence from the beauty and order of the universe. Almost all
of Love's speech (stanzas 32–58) is based on this book.

The characters, setting, and background derive from Homer's *Odyssey*, but
the slender incident that constitutes the plot is Davies's invention. Davies
uses Homer's story as a backdrop, and to provide details, not substance. For
example, in both works Athene gives Penelope a balm that enhances her
beauty so that each of the suitors feels increased desire for her (*Odyssey*, xviii;
Orchestra, stanza 10). On the other hand, Homer's Antinous is a ruthless,

dangerous man who leads Penelope's suitors in consuming Ulysses' livestock and wine and in plotting to murder her son Telemachus.

In view of these allusions one might assume that Davies had read Homer, yet his three references to Homer in *Nosce Teipsum* are all incorrect. Students in school were often made to read and memorize only selections from classical writings, and possibly he had read only passages of Homer. It is impossible to say whether his reading would have been from Greek or Latin texts (see Introduction, p. xxv), but the Latin translations and bilingual editions of the sixteenth century have excellent indexes, and he could have used these to supply some details without having read the complete work.

The World of 'Orchestra'

The so-called Ptolemaic astronomy maintained its hold on the educated layman long after the publication of Copernicus's *De Revolutionibus*. It was in fact a layman's astronomy, a rather corrupt and unscientific version of the work of Ptolemy, popularized and propagated by Cicero in the portion of his *Republic* called *The Dream of Scipio*, which survived throughout the Middle Ages with the commentary by Macrobius, and was undoubtedly one of the most influential pagan books.

The astronomical model which Davies uses is a system of spheres revolving around an immobile centre, the earth. These fall into two domains, the heavenly spheres and the sublunary ones. The world below the moon is the realm of transience and mutability; it consists of the spheres of the four elements, the sphere of fire enveloping the sphere of air, enclosing in its turn the sphere of water, which envelops the sphere of earth. Thus the earth is not simply the centre of the universe; it is the gravitational bottom.

Above the sphere of fire are the celestial spheres, thought by many to be composed of a fifth element, ether, which Aristotle considered to be the material of the human mind as well. Moving outward, the wandering stars or planets are Moon, Sun, Mercury, Venus, Mars, Jupiter, and Saturn, surrounded by the sphere of the 'fixed' stars, those that do not change their positions relative to one another. All these revolve from east to west, impelled by the contrary spin of the outermost sphere, the *Primum Mobile* or first mover (stanza 13). From the different lengths of their orbits two phenomena arise. The first is a musical note produced by the movement of each sphere, the total harmony being the music of the spheres (stanza 19). The second is the variation in position; as Davies points out, the moon revolves around the earth thirteen times during a solar year. Many writers gave the name 'great year' to the period at the end of which all the spheres would simultaneously complete their orbits and return to their starting-points. This period is variously fixed at anything from 10,000 to 60,000 solar years (Davies's 6,000, in stanza 35, is an unusually low number, and may be an error), after which the system will begin again or the world will end.

In this universe one adamantine law prevails: everything finds its natural place by a kind of gravity, whereby what is heavy—i.e. gross or material—sinks, and what is light—i.e. ethereal or spiritual—rises. The suppositions of physics are supported by the analogy of biology, which presents a clear hierarchy of increasing spiritual complexity: minerals exist, plants exist and vegetate (i.e. grow and reproduce), animals exist and live and feel, and man exists, lives, feels, and reasons. In *Tusculan Disputations* Cicero argues for immortality on the basis of gravity: the ethereal soul, once freed from the body, will ascend until it finds its like in the heavenly spheres.

The law of the natural world is extended analogically to the social world both descriptively and prescriptively; that is, the hierarchical order already manifest in society is justified on the grounds that 'degree' is natural and therefore right, so that it is seen also as an ideal that man should strive for consciously. The achievement, maintenance, and improvement of hierarchical order is the message of political and moral writing for many centuries: the dominion of the soul in the body, of the father in the family, of the ruler in a kingdom.

The pagan Macrobius bestowed on the Middle Ages the image of order that we have come to associate with the Ptolemaic universe:

The close observer will find that from the Supreme God even to the bottommost dregs of the universe there is one tie, binding at every link and never broken. This is the golden chain of Homer, which, he tells us, God ordered to hang down from the sky to the earth (I. xiv. 15).

Certainly the great chain of being engaged the hearts of generations of philosophers, statesmen, and poets. It was their bulwark against the inchoate forces by which men have always known themselves to be menaced, the bright symbol of their assurance that nothing walks with aimless feet.

It is thus with the most fundamental ideas of 'the setled order of the world' that Davies plays in *Orchestra*. The very merriness of the jest depends on his absolute certainty that nature will not 'intermit her course'—an assurance manifest in Antinous' blithe dismissal of heliocentricity (stanza 51). Antinous' argument is effective because it cleverly refutes the most important of Penelope's objections to dancing, her assertion that it is 'disorder and misrule' (stanaz 15). He rebuts this by defining the celebrated order of things as a dance. Since any equation is reversible, the statement 'dancing is order' is implicit as soon as Antinous has proposed his thesis that order is dancing.

Dedications. See discussion under 'Composition', above.

To his very Friend. Richard Martin is identified in the Introduction, pp. xxxii–xxxv.

   2. *halfe-capreol*: a frivolous leap or caper.

   7. *Suada*: the Roman goddess of eloquence.

To the Prince: Prince Charles, later Charles I, who was a noted dancer (see Clare Howard, *The Poems of Sir John Davies* (1941), p. 230).

8. *Saint George his Band*: the Order of the Garter.

1.1. Drummond of Hawthornden reports that Ben Jonson 'scorned such verses as could be transposed

> wher is the man that never yett did hear
> of faire Penelope Ulisses Queene—
> of faire Penelope Ulisses Queen
> wher is the man that never yett did hear.'
> (Jonson, *Works*, i. 143.)

1.5. A paraphrase of the *Odyssey*, i. 3.

1.7. *Midland-sea*: a literal translation of the *Mediterranean Sea*.

2.1. *carouse*: drink a toast to, usually by draining the cup at a draught.

3.2. *Man*: the first word of the *Odyssey*. Greek syntax depends on inflexional endings, not word-order, and thus a writer can, more easily than in English, place a word in an emphatic position. On this point Chapman remarks:

The first word of his *Iliads* is μῆνιν, *wrath*; the first word of his *Odysses* ἄνδρα, *Man*—contracting in either word his each worke's Proposition. (*Chapman's Homer*, ed. Allardyce Nicoll (London, 1957), ii. 4.)

3.4. *illudes*. Davies intends a double meaning: Penelope evades or eludes the suitors by deceiving or illuding them (cf. 'illusion'). She promised to choose a new husband when she finished weaving a shroud for her father-in-law; but every night she undid the day's work.

3.5. *ungratefull*: unwanted.

3.7. *Neptunes*. The enmity of the god of the sea was the major cause of Ulysses' misfortunes.

4.7. *burden*: load; and, in music, the bass or accompanying song.

5.1. *Antinous*: in Homer, the leading suitor to Penelope, and thus a principal enemy to the hero, Ulysses. He little resembles Davies's courtier.

6.1. *Terpsichore*: the Muse of dancing, daughter of Jove and Mnemnosyne (memory).

6.6. *meane*: intermediate musical range, e.g. alto or tenor.

ground: melody. Davies is asking the muse to sing in the middle range, that is, to grant him a moderate degree of inspiration. He is not attempting to 'sing Things unattempted yet in prose or rhyme'; his invocation is to the 'light Muse' of Dancing, not the epic or heavenly muse.

7.1–4. Davies invents this incident; mythology does not record any 'revels' involving Apollo and Tethys, the wife of Oceanus.

7.4. *all alone*: an implied macaronic pun, probably prompted by Davies's reading of Cicero:

The word *sol* [sun] [is] from *solus* [alone], either because the sun 'alone' of all the heavenly bodies is of that magnitude, or because when the sun rises all the stars are dimmed and it 'alone' is visible (*De nat. deor.* II. xxvii. 68).

12.1. Here, and at stanzas 14, 26, 97, 102, and 119 the present edition follows *1596* in using enlarged capitals to indicate a change of speaker.

12.6. *continuall motion.* To Platonists, including Cicero, motion means life. That which causes motion is more excellent than that which is moved; whatever moves continually is immortal.

13.1. *mover*: her partner in dancing; the *primum mobile* to her if she will 'Imitate heav'n' by joining the dance.

15–17. Davies follows Lucian in beginning his defence of dancing by denying that it is a modern innovation:

Those historians of dancing who are the most veracious can tell you that Dance came into being contemporaneously with the primal origin of the universe, making her appearance together with Love—the love that is age-old. In fact, the concord of the heavenly spheres, the interlacing of the errant planets with the fixed stars, their rhythmic agreement and timed harmony, are proofs that Dance was primordial (*The Dance*, par. 7).

15.2. Penelope refers to the common notion that the world has been declining since the Golden Age, as in Ovid, *Met.* i. 1–150; Spenser, *F.Q.* V, Proem i–ii.

17. 1–5. The idea that Love reconciled the warring elements is implicit in Hesiod's *Theogony*, where Eros is said to be among the oldest of the gods. After quoting from Hesiod and Parmenides, Aristotle (*Metaphysics*, I. iv) attributes to Empedocles the notion that love and strife were the causes of motion: strife is the tendency of opposites to repel one another, and love the affinity that draws opposites together; thus, fire is repelled by earth, whereas iron 'loves' the loadstone. The strife of the elements is described in Ovid's *Metamorphoses*, i. 5–20; the role of Love is found in Plato's *Timaeus* (31B–32B) and his *Symposium* (178) and Ficino's commentary on it. Cf. Davies's *Epithalamion*, 2–4, and Spenser's *Hymne in Honour of Love*, 78–91.

18.
Again the continuum of the world's nature is constituted by the cyclic transmutations of the four kinds of matter. For earth turns into water, water into air, air into aether, and then the process is reversed, and aether becomes air, air water, and water earth, the lowest of the four. Thus the parts of the world are held in union by the constant passage up and down, to and fro, of these four elements of which all things are composed (Cicero, *De nat. deor.* II. xxxiii. 84).

19.3. *through-piercing and digesting.* By 'digesting power' Davies means the ability to arrange in order; therefore the line concerns Love's power of intellectual penetration of the 'confused masse'.

20.1. *All*: a translation of the Greek *to pan* and Latin *cuncta*, meaning 'the whole "body" of the universe' (Macrobius, I. xvii. 5).

20.2. *Morpheus*: god of dreams.

20.2–3. *sicke braines . . . Motes.* In *N.T.* 215–16 Davies rejects the Epicurean atomic theory that everything is formed by the haphazard conjunction of atoms floating freely in space. Although a somewhat similar denial of this theory appears in Montaigne's 'Apologie of Raymond Sebond' (*Essays*, II. xii. 254), Davies's passage seems more clearly indebted to Cicero's *De nat. deor.* (II. xxxvii. 93–4):

At this point must I not marvel that there should be anyone who can persuade himself that there are certain solid and indivisible particles of matter borne along by the force of gravity, and that the fortuitous collision of those particles produces this elaborate and beautiful world . . . colliding together at haphazard and by chance . . . The fact is, they indulge in such random babbling about the world that for my part I cannot think that they have ever looked up at this marvellously beautiful sky.

21.1. *Amphion*: see *N.T.* 381–2 and note.

21.6–7. *motes . . . joyn'd hands*. The atoms in Epicurean theory were regarded as tiny round bodies with hooks; as the bodies floated about, the hooks linked with one another by chance. In Davies's story, the attractive force of Love, through music, directs the atoms to join together purposively, as in a dance.

22. Dancing is almost coeval with Time, which came 'into being along with the heaven' (Plato, *Timaeus*, 38B).

23.2. *Time the measure of all moving is*: Aristotle, *Physics*, IV. xi, 220a.

24.2. *lustie*: robust.

24.3–4. Love is called the eldest of the gods in Plato's *Symposium* 178, and the youngest in *Symposium* 195. Cf. Spenser, *Hymne in Honour of Love*, lines 52–6.

25.2. *subtile*: rarefied.

25.6. *doublings*: turns.

27.5. *Gentry*: 'rank by birth'—*O.E.D.*

27.7. *blaze*: blazon, i.e. describe in proper heraldic language (*O.E.D.*).

29–30. In these stanzas Davies draws from notions of the creation found in Plato's *Timaeus*, 43A. Plato describes chaos, or pre-existing matter, as having moved in confused disorder in six linear directions: up and down, side to side, forward and back. In the act whereby the creator imposes form on matter, the matter acquires a seventh, ordered motion, which is circular.

Davies lists the seven motions at *Orchestra*, 62. 3–4. In stanzas 29 and 30 he identifies the creative force of the universe as Love. On seeing men bunched together confusedly, Love resolves to set them in order ('Another shapelesse *Chaos* to digest'), and so extends perfect motion to them by forming them into a ring.

31.1. *rarifie*: refine or purify, by making it less gross and material.

32.7. *mans chiefe pleasure is societie*. A commonplace; see Hooker, *Laws*, I. x. 12; Shakespeare, *Love's Labour's Lost*, IV. ii. 167; Seneca, *De Beneficiis*, VII. i. 7.

33.6. *modell*: copy. Human gatherings are to imitate the order of the dancing universe.

35.1. *mirrour*: 'that which exhibits something to be imitated; an exemplar' —*O.E.D.*

35. Davies draws from Cicero for his discussion:

Moreover the so-called fixed stars also indicate . . . intelligence and wisdom. Their revolutions recur daily with exact regularity. . . . Now the continual and unceasing revolutions of these stars, marvellously and incredibly regular as they are, clearly show that these are endowed with divine power and intelligence (*De nat. deor.* II. xxi. 54–5).

He changes his source, however, in connecting the motion of both the fixed stars and the planets with the Great Year:

On the diverse motions of the planets the mathematicians have based what they call the Great Year, which is completed when the sun, moon and five planets having all finished their courses have returned to the same positions relative to one another. The length of this period is hotly debated, but it must necessarily be a fixed and definite time (*De nat. deor.* II. xx. 51–2).

36.
Again, the consciousness and intelligence of the stars is most clearly evinced by their order and regularity; for regular and rhythmical motion is impossible without design, which contains no trace of casual or accidental variation; now the order and eternal regularity of the constellations indicates neither a process of nature, for it is highly rational, nor chance, for chance loves variation and abhors regularity; it follows therefore that the stars move of their own free-will and because of their intelligence and divinity (*De nat. deor.* II. xvi. 43).

36.7. *Axeltree of Heav'n.* In Davies's time one common notion was that the earth was moulded like a ball of clay around an axle, which remained immobile while the heavenly spheres turned like wheels on the axle.

37.
Most marvellous are the motions of the five stars, falsely called planets or wandering stars—for a thing cannot be said to wander if it preserves for all eternity fixed and regular motions, forward, backward and in other directions. And this regularity is all the more marvellous in the case of the stars we speak of, because at one time they are hidden and at another they are uncovered again; now they approach, now retire; now precede, now follow; now move faster, now slower, now do not move at all but remain for a time stationary (*De nat. deor.* II. xx. 51).

37.7. *Galliard.* See note to stanzas 67–68.

38.
Lowest of the five planets and nearest to the earth is the star of Venus, called in Greek *Phosphoros* (the light-bringer) and in Latin Lucifer when it precedes the sun, but when it follows it *Hesperos*; this planet completes its orbit in a year, traversing the zodiac with a zigzag movement as do the planets above it, and never distant more than the space of two signs from the sun, though sometimes in front of it and sometimes behind it (*De nat. deor.* II. xx. 53).

38.1. *bastard Love.* Davies uses Pausanias' suggestion (*Symposium*, 180–1) that as there are two Aphrodites, a heavenly and an earthly, so there are two Loves, pure love and lust.

38.6. *passages*. This word evidently results from a minor revision by Davies. His first thought is suggested by *LF*, where 'traver fer' is probably Fitzjames's misreading of *traverses*, a movement in the pavan, a dance mentioned in stanza 41.

38.7. *respecting . . . respects*. Both times the word has two meanings: 'to look back at' and 'to have regard for'.

39.1–2.

Take first of all the sun, which is the chief of the celestial bodies. Its motion is such that it first fills the countries of the earth with a flood of light, and then leaves them in darkness now on one side and now on the other; for night is caused merely by the shadow of the earth, which intercepts the light of the sun (*De nat. deor.* II. xix. 49).

39.4. *Lemmans*: sweetheart's.

39.6. *Princely*. This reading was undoubtedly substituted in *1622* for 'gallant', the reading of *LF* and *1596*, because in *1622* Davies dedicated *Orchestra* 'To the Prince'.

39–41.

Of these the sun, which many times surpasses the earth in magnitude, revolves about her, and by his rising and setting causes day and night, and now approaching, then again retiring, twice each year makes returns in opposite directions from his farthest point, and in the period of those returns at one time causes the face of the earth as it were to contract with a gloomy frown, and at another restores her to gladness till she seems to smile in sympathy with the sky. Again the moon . . . roams in the same courses as the sun, but at one time converging with the sun and at another diverging from it, both bestows upon the earth the light that it has borrowed from the sun and itself undergoes divers changes of its light (*De nat. deor.* II. xl. 102–3).

Again the moon in her monthly paths overtakes the yearly course of the sun; and her light wanes to its minimum when she approaches nearest to the sun, and waxes to its maximum each time that she recedes farthest from him. And not only is her shape and outline altered by her alternate waxing and waning or returning to her starting-point, but also her position in the sky (ibid. II. xix. 50).

41.3. *pavine*: 'pavan', a slow, stately processional dance in which the man and woman regularly turn away from, and again toward, each other.

42.3–7. *Vulcan*: god of fire. The two kinds of fire are discussed in Cicero's *De nat. deor.* II. xv. 40–1:

that fire which we employ in ordinary life [and] that which is contained in the bodies of living creatures. Now our ordinary fire that serves the needs of daily life is a destructive agency, consuming everything, and also wherever it spreads it routs and scatters everything. On the other hand the fire of the body is the glow of life and health; it is the universal preservative, giving nourishment, fostering growth, sustaining, bestowing sensation.

43–4.

Animals are sustained by breathing air, and the air itself is our partner in seeing, hearing and uttering sounds, since none of these actions can be performed without its aid; nay, it even moves as we move, for wherever we go or move our limbs, it seems as it were to give place and retire before us (*De nat. deor.* II. xxxiii. 83).

47.2. *hayes*: country dances with a serpentine movement.

49. Coleridge uses this image in *The Ancient Mariner*, lines 414–7:

> Still as a slave before his lord,
> The ocean hath no blast;
> His great bright eye most silently
> Up to the Moon is cast— . . .

49.2. *clips*: embraces.

50–60. The following passage of Cicero is used by Davies in various stanzas, the numbers of which are given in square brackets after the sentences from which they borrow:

And first let us behold the whole earth, situated in the centre of the world, a solid spherical mass gathered into a globe by the natural gravitation of all its parts [51], clothed with flowers and grass and trees and corn, forms of vegetation all of them incredibly numerous and inexhaustibly varied and diverse [55]. Add to these cool fountains ever flowing, transparent streams and rivers, their banks clad in brightest verdure, deep vaulted caverns, craggy rocks, sheer mountain heights and plains of immeasurable extent [51–2] . . . think of the flights and songs of birds! [57] . . . Then why need I speak of the race of men? who are as it were the appointed tillers of the soil, and who suffer it not to become a savage haunt of monstrous beasts of prey nor a barren waste of thickets and brambles, and whose industry diversifies and adorns the lands and islands and coasts with houses and cities [60] . . . Then how great is the beauty of the sea! . . . And the sea itself, yearning for the earth, sports against her shores in such a fashion that the two elements appear to be fused into one [50] (*De nat. deor.* II. xxxix. 98–100).

51.1–5. Like most poets, Davies rejected the Copernican notion of the earth's rotation, which, however, was well known and widely discussed in England in his time. See Francis R. Johnson, *Astronomical Thought in Renaissance England* (Baltimore, 1937), pp. 181–2.

52.5. *wide*. The printed texts read 'wild'; *LF* reads 'Longe', evidently Davies's first thought. Although Davies might have altered *long* to *wild*, it seems more likely that he altered to *wide*, a word easily mistaken for *wild* in Elizabethan hand. *Wide* provides alliteration, as *long* does not, and emphasizes, as *long* does, the extent of the earth covered by the rivers.

53.1–2. Meander, a river in Phrygia, is noted for its winding course. Davies seems indebted for his figure to Ovid, *Heroides*, vii. 1–2:

> Sic ubi fata vocant, udis abiectus in herbis
> ad vada Maeandri concinit albus olor.

53.4. *Creekes*: windings. *wrenches*: sharp turns.

54.1–4.

A running river can almost or quite entirely escape pollution, whereas an enclosed pool is easily sullied (*De nat. deor.* II. vii. 20).

56.1–2. *Vine . . . Elme*: a common figure indicating sympathetic attraction; usually used as an emblem for the love between men and women. Cf. *Epith.* 66; Tilley, V61.

57–8.

Another fact (observed by Aristotle, from whom most of these cases are cited) cannot but awaken our surprise, namely that cranes when crossing the seas on the way to warmer climates fly in a triangular formation. With the apex of the triangle they force aside the air in front of them, and then gradually on either side by means of their wings acting as oars the birds' onward flight is sustained, while the base of the triangle formed by the cranes gets the assistance of the wind when it is so to speak astern. The birds rest their necks and heads on the backs of those flying in front of them; and the leader, being himself unable to do this as he has no one to lean on, flies to the rear that he himself also may have a rest, while one of those already rested takes his place, and so they keep turns throughout the journey (*De nat. deor.* II. xlix. 125).

57.2. *Jumpe*: in exact time with.

59.5–6. *Chaunce . . . On a round slipperie wheele*. Tillyard, in his edition of *Orchestra* (1945), suggested that Davies may have altered 'Chaunce', the reading of LF and *1596* to 'Chaunge' in *1622* after reading Spenser's *Mutability Cantos*. More likely, however, *1622* reveals a printer's error, for Chance or Fortune was traditionally associated with a wheel or ball.

60.6. *vitall twist*: the thread of life spun, measured, and cut by the Fates. Cf. Spenser, *The Ruines of Time*, 181: 'So soone as fates their vitall thred have shorne'.

61.1. *crowne*: the ring (Lat. *corona*, 'crown') into which Love cast men in stanza 30.

61.4. *base*: bass.

62.2. *motions seaven*. Plato identifies these in *Timaeus* 43B; see note to stanzas 29–30.

62.5. *brawles*: the *branle*, a dance distinguished by movement from side to side.

63.6. *traverses*: crossings, movements.

64.5–6. *Beares . . . heavens Axeltree*: the constellations Ursa Major and Ursa Minor, which appear above the north pole: 'The furthest tip of either axle-end is called the pole. Round the pole circle the two Bears, which never set'. (*De nat. deor.* II. xli. 105.)

65–70. *Measures*. These stanzas describe several courtly dances and the *tempi* ('measures' in music and verse) to which they are danced.

66.1. *young*. LF and *1596* both read *old*, which very likely represents Davies's first thought. *1622* reads 'youg', which may be explained as a printers' slip for a marginal alteration by Davies, 'yo~g' or 'yong' in the edition of *1596* used as printer's copy for *1622*. If not, it is an unconscious slip by the compositor of a kind that appears nowhere else in the *1622* text of *Orchestra*. Atlas and Prometheus are 'young Students' in the sense that they were the originators of astronomy.

66.2. *Atlas . . . Promethius*. Comes ('De Prometheo', and 'De Atlante', *Mythologiae* (1584)) says that Atlas was the first Egyptian astronomer, and that the legend of Prometheus bringing fire to mankind arose because he was the first person to raise men's eyes to the study of the heavenly bodies. Cf. Ovid, *Met.* i. 84–5; Cicero, *Tusc.* v. iii. 8.

67–70. Davies's descriptions in the following four stanzas accurately portray the movements of the Elizabethan dances he mentions; see Mabel Dolmetsch, *Dances of England and France from 1450 to 1600* (London, 1949).

67–8. The *galliard* is a lively dance in which the basic step is the cinque-pace, consisting of four hopping steps and a leap. Davies does not mention that its rhythm is trochaic, but its inclusion is appropriate here in his progression from the spondee to the dactyl and anapest in stanzas 66–70.

68.6. *capriols*: leaps.

69. The *coranto* is a dance in triple time with a gliding step.

70. In the *lavolta*, the man and woman dance facing each other, as in a waltz, and make frequent high leaps into the air.

71.1–4. *twinns*: Castor and Pollux, the constellation Gemini. Davies finds them as teachers of dancing in Lucian, who says, 'The Spartans, who are considered the bravest of the Greeks, learned from Pollux and Castor to do the Caryatic' (*The Dance*, par. 10). Sparta is on the banks of the Eurotas.

72. The *Odyssey*, book viii, describes how Vulcan, informed by Apollo of the infidelity of his wife, Venus, with Mars, cast an exceedingly fine net in the lovers' bed, in which they became entangled. He then called the other gods to mock the couple. Lucian praises a dancer who

danced the amours of Aphrodite and Ares, Helius tattling, Hephaestus laying his plot and trapping both of them with his entangling bonds, the gods who came in on them, portrayed individually, Aphrodite ashamed, Ares seeking cover and begging for mercy, and everything that belongs to this story (*The Dance*, par. 63).

72.3. *imply*: enfold.

74.2–3. The Errata list in *1622* incorrectly substitutes 'Doe' for 'Did' at 74.2. Perhaps the alteration was intended for 74.3, and the compositor misread 'Doe' for 'doth', which is the reading of *LF* adopted in the present text in preference to 'did', which is the reading of the printed texts at 74.3.

76. For discussions of Love as the oldest of the gods, see the notes to stanzas 15–17 and 24. Rhea, to protect her son Jove from being devoured by her husband Saturn, hid him on the island of Crete, where the sound of his crying was covered by the noises of the Curetes:

In the beginning, they say, Rhea, charmed with the art, ordered dances to be performed not only in Phrygia by the Corybantes but in Crete by the Curetes, from whose skill she derived uncommon benefit, since they saved Zeus for her by dancing about him; Zeus, therefore, might well admit that he owes them a thank-offering, since it was through their dancing that he escaped his father's teeth. They danced under arms, clashing their swords upon their shields as they did so and leaping in a frantic, warlike manner (*The Dance*, par. 8).

76.6. *that*. *1622* misread ẏ as ẏ because of the minute print in *1596*.

77–80. *Orchestra* has hitherto shown that the universe is involved in a dance, and has depicted man being brought into conformity with the divine order by learning to dance. From this point, the organization becomes looser as the poem asserts that any orderly arrangement is a dance, and that anything that can be called dancing is orderly and therefore laudable. The remainder of the poem redefines all systems as dance, and praises dancing as a worthy exercise always associated with solemn occasions like weddings, funerals, battles, and worship. For his examples Davies has the authority of Lucian and Macrobius.

Orchestra 'substitutes a vision of cosmic dance for universal music' (John Hollander, *The Untuning of the Sky* (1961), p. 121), and Davies relies on the tradition that music is a civilizing force to make his point about dancing. His allegorical interpretations of the archetypal poet-musicians of Greek legend (stanzas 78–9) were current even in classical times:

> While men still roamed the woods, Orpheus, the holy prophet of the gods, made them shrink from bloodshed and brutal living; hence the fable that he tamed tigers and ravening lions; hence too the fable that Amphion, builder of Thebes's citadel, moved stones by the sound of his lyre (Horace, *Ars Poetica*, 391–6).

The Renaissance adopted the allegory, as Golding indicates:

> So in the sixth booke afterward Amphions harp is sayd
> The first foundation of the walles of Thebee to have layd,
> Bycause that by his eloquence and justice (which are ment
> By true accord of harmonie and musicall consent)
> He gathered intoo Thebee towne, and in due order knit
> The people that disperst and rude in hilles and rocks did sit.
> So Orphey in the tenth booke is reported too delight
> The savage beasts, and for too hold the fleeting birds from flyght,
> Too move the senselesse stones, and stay swift rivers, and too make
> The trees too follow after him and for his musick sake
> Too yeeld him shadowe where he went. By which is signifyde
> That in his doctrine such a force and sweetenesse was implyde,
> That such as were most wyld, stowre, feerce, hard, witlesse,
>   rude, and bent
> Ageinst good order, were by him perswaded too relent,
> And for too bee conformable too live in reverent awe
> Like neybours in a common weale by justyce under law.
>   ('Epistle', *Shakespeare's Ovid: The Metamorphoses*, ed. W. H. D. Rouse
>   (1961), lines 511–26.)

Finally, by an illogical but understandable leap, Davies proceeds from the musician-civilizers to the political ones: Hercules, who extirpated savagery by killing monsters, and Theseus, who consolidated the greatest civilization of antiquity.

77.1–2.

> I forbear to say that not a single ancient mystery-cult can be found that is without dancing, since they were established, of course, by Orpheus and Musaeus, the best dancers of that time, who included it in their prescriptions as something exceptionally beautiful to be initiated with rhythm and dancing (*The Dance*, par. 15).

78.1. *he . . . ten-tong'd Lute*. Orpheus' lyre is the constellation Lyra. Davies follows Ptolemy in assigning it ten stars. He alludes also to a tradition, mentioned in the *Mythologia Musarum* usually appended to Comes's *Mythologiae*, that identified the classical cithara with the ten-stringed *asor* of the Hebrews; cf. Davies's *Psalmes*, 33.4.

79.1. *Musæus*: son of Orpheus, and therefore the first human poet.

79.2. *Linus*: the musical teacher of Orpheus and Hercules. His parents, according to Comes, were either Amphimarus and Urania, Mercury and Urania, or Apollo and Terpsichore. Hercules is said to have killed him by striking him with a harp or lyre (Comes, *Mythologiae*, s.v. 'De Apolline').

79.3. *he*: Hercules, whose twelve labours included the slaying of the Lernean hydra, the Nemean lion, *et al.*; he was made a constellation after he died. In *The Arte of Rhetorique*, Thomas Wilson cites the story that Hercules 'had all men lincked together by the eares in a chaine' as an allegory of the power of eloquence (*The Arte of Rhetorique* (1553), sig. A2^v).

79.5. *Theseus*: said to have unified the towns around Athens into a single state with its centre and citadel at Athens. According to Plutarch, at Delos Theseus invented a dance as part of a service of thanksgiving for deliverance from the Minotaur (*Lives*, trans. North (1579), p. 11).

80.5. *Ganimede*: a cupbearer to Jove; the constellation Aquarius, the water-bearer.

80.6. *Hebe*: cupbearer to the gods, later replaced by Ganymede; also, goddess of youth and wife of Hercules after his stellification.

81. The story of Proteus comes from the *Odyssey*, book iv, but Davies's description is from Lucian:

> For it seems to me that the ancient myth about Proteus the Egyptian means nothing else than that he was a dancer, an imitative fellow, able to shape himself and change himself into anything, so that he could imitate even the liquidity of water and the sharpness of fire in the liveliness of his movement; yes, the fierceness of a lion, the rage of a leopard, the quivering of a tree, and in a word whatever he wished (*The Dance*, par. 19).

82.1. *Cæneus*. Davies reverses the usual order of Caenis' sexual change. In most versions of the story, she began as a woman, was changed into a man, and at death again became a woman (cf. *Aeneid*, vi. 448). Lucian says, 'He [a dancer] will not fail to know all the fabulous transformations . . . Caeneus, I mean, and Tiresias, and their like' (par. 57).

83.1. *Tiresias*. Tiresias struck two copulating serpents sacred to Apollo and as a punishment was changed into a woman. Seven years later he was restored to his original form. When Juno and Jove disagreed over whether men or women derive more pleasure from sexual intercourse, he resolved the dispute by replying that women receive the greater pleasure. Cf. *Met*. iii. 316–38.

84.1. *Venus*. At one point during the war between the gods and the giants, the gods escaped only by changing themselves into various animals; Venus changed herself into a fish (Ovid, *Met.* v. 331). In a Latin translation of Lucian's *The Dance*, her daintiness is described as 'Veneris teneram & delicatam . . . molliciem' (1546, sig. d3ᵛ).

85.1. *Bacchus*. Davies takes his figure from Lucian:

As to the Dionysiac and Bacchic rites . . . every bit of them was dancing . . . and it was by the exercise of this art, they say, that Dionysus subdued the Tyrrhenians, the Indians, and the Lydians, dancing into subjection with his bands of revellers a multitude so warlike (*The Dance*, par. 22).

87.2. *war*. Lucian says that 'The Ethiopians . . . even in waging war, do it dancing' (par. 18), and that the Spartans

do everything with the aid of the Muses, to the extent of going into battle to the accompaniment of flute and rhythm and well-timed step in marching. . . . That is how they managed to conquer everybody, with music and rhythm to lead them (*The Dance*, par. 10).

90.3–4. The ultimate source of this image is the *Iliad*, iv. 141, where Menelaos' wound produces an effect compared by Homer to ivory dyed with φοῖνιξ. This word is usually translated by 'Tyrian purple', actually dark red. Cf. *Aeneid*, xii. 67–9; Ovid, *Met.* ii. 607. A similar passage is found in Spenser's *Epithalamion*, lines 204, 226–8:

> Open the temple gates unto my love . . .
> How the red roses flush up in her cheekes,
> And the pure snow with goodly vermill stayne,
> Like crimsin dyde in grayne.

91.5. *Thessalians*.

In Thessaly the cultivation of dancing made such progress that they used to call their front-rank men and champions 'fore-dancers' (*The Dance*, par. 14).

92.1. *liberall Arts*: grammar, rhetoric, logic (trivium), music, arithmetic, geometry, and astronomy (quadrivium). Poetry is usually included in rhetoric. The inspiration for this passage, though not its details, comes from Lucian:

Dance is not one of the facile arts that can be plied without pains, but reaches to the very summit of all culture, not only in music but in rhythm and metre, and especially in . . . philosophy, both physics and ethics. To be sure, Dance accounts philosophy's inordinate interest in dialectics inappropriate to herself. From rhetoric, however, she has not held aloof (*The Dance*, par. 35).

95.2. *3, 5, 8, 15*: the perfect concords or musical intervals, i.e. *mi*, *sol*, *do*, and the double octave.

96.6. *Character*: character, i.e. emblem or symbol.

98–9. Penelope's attack on love is conventional, but its general outlines resemble a passage in Comes's *Mythologiae* (s.v. 'De Cupidine'):

On that account, Apollonius Rhodius thought Cupid the source and beginning of all evils, because by reason of wantonness justice is despised and all wrongs arise . . Many cities, many realms, many provinces are laid waste through this god of madmen and lunatics. For how many states have taken up arms for kidnapped women? How many women have betrayed their countries and parents to the enemy by reason of this frenzy? How many husbands have laid plots against their wives, and *vice versa*, because of this same famous god? How many children have been killed by their mothers? And to put it in a word, there is almost nothing criminal, wicked, or rash, of which Cupid is not the author.

99.1. *mother*: Medea, who killed her children because their father Jason intended to marry someone else.

99.3. *daughter*: perhaps Scylla, daughter of Nisus. Having fallen in love with Minos, who was besieging her father's city, she betrayed her father by cutting off a lock of purple hair that preserved his life. Medea and Scylla are referred to in Octavianus Mirandula, *Illustrium Poetarum Flores* (Lyons, 1582), where, under the heading of Love, the following quotation appears:

> *Saevus amor docuit natorum sanguine matrem*
> *Commaculare manus* [Virgil, Eclogue viii. 47–8].

Ut de Medea legitur. Sic et Scylla Nisi regis filia amoris impatiens patrem interemit.

99.5–7. *brother*: Atreus, king of Mycenae. Thyestes, by seducing his brother Atreus' wife, succeeded in obtaining the golden lamb that entitled its owner to be king. In retribution, Atreus killed Thyestes' sons and served them to him in a feast. The story is told in *De nat. deor.* III. xxvii. 68–9.

100.2. *Idæa*: image.

100.5–7. *Tereus mad wife*: Procne, who killed her son and served his flesh to Tereus after learning that he had raped her sister, imprisoned her, and torn out her tongue (Ovid, *Met.* vi. 587–600).

102–3. Spenser makes a similar distinction between true Love, the creative force, and lust, in *A Hymne of Honour of Love*, lines 176–82, and *Colin Clouts Come Home Againe*, lines 891–2. In both poems Love is said to implant the inclination towards beauty that Socrates defines as love in *Symposium* 204; Spenser describes it in *Hymne in Honour of Love*, 106–12:

> For having yet in his deducted spright,
> Some sparks remaining of that heavenly fyre,
> He is enlumind with that goodly light,
> Unto like goodly semblant to aspyre:
> Therefore in choice of love, he doth desyre
> That seemes on earth most heavenly, to embrace,
> That same is Beautie, borne of heavenly race.

108.2. *thys house*: Penelope's body, ruled by her soul. Its rule constitutes an invisible dance.

109.3. *Concord*: the state achieved when Love has reconciled conflicting elements. Renaissance emblems of Concord include a picture of two armed men shaking hands. It is associated with friendship (Spenser places Concord outside the Temple of Venus in *F.Q.* IV) and with musical harmony (its opposite is discord).

112.7. *transcend*: cross.

115.

When you see a statue or a painting, you recognize the exercise of art; when you observe from a distance the course of a ship, you do not hesitate to assume that its motion is guided by reason and by art; when you look at a sun-dial or a water-clock, you infer that it tells the time by art and not by chance (*De nat. deor.* II. xxxiv. 87).

121. Love looks forward 2,600 years beyond the time of Homer's Penelope to envision the British Isles in the time of Elizabeth. Britain was thought of as being triangular, the angles being at Land's End, the easternmost point in Kent, and the northernmost headland of Scotland; see William Camden, *Britannia* (1586), trans. Philemon Holland (1610), p. 1. Its geographical centre is roughly 54° latitude, or 'Thrise twelve degrees remov'd from the North star'.

The Greek islands of the blest were called the Fortunate Isles (Hesiod, *Works and Days*, 171). Vaguely located somewhere in the west, they were the Eden-like home of those upon whom the gods conferred immortality, such as Helen and Menelaos in *The Odyssey*. Although Greek geographers identified them with the Canary Islands, they continued as metaphors of paradise. Avalon, the misty isle where Arthur went from Britain, was later identified as the 'island of apples, called "fortunate" ' (*Vita Merlini*, 908); Giraldus Cambrensis (who is frequently quoted in Davies's prose works) then connected the Fortunate Isles with England by recording the discovery of Arthur's grave at Glastonbury (*De Principis Instructione*, I. xx). The accession of the Tudors, figuratively considered to be the return of Arthur, strengthened the connection. Camden tells how Pope Clement VI chose one '*Lewis of Spaine*' to be Prince of the Fortunate (i.e. Canary) Islands, whereupon the British, including their ambassadors at Rome, concluded

That he was chosen Prince of *Britaine* . . . as one . . . of the fortunate Ilands. . . . Neither will any man now judge otherwise, who thorowly knoweth the blessed estate and happie wealth of *Britaine* (*Britannia* (1610), p. 4).

Love's vision of England as the 'fortunate, triangled Ile' thus conveniently compliments Elizabeth in terms of legend appropriate to Homer's Penelope.

124.3. *Moone*: Elizabeth, often called 'Cynthia' by poets.

126.4. Lucian says, 'Like Calchas in Homer [*Iliad*, i. 70], the dancer must know "what is, and what shall be, and was of old" ' (*The Dance*, par. 36).

127.1–3. In concluding, Davies casts aside the light muse whom he had invoked for inspiration in stanza 6 and calls on the heavenly muse of prophecy and astronomy. In schemes that assigned a muse to each of the heavenly spheres, Urania was the muse of the firmament, the sphere of the fixed stars.

127.4. *tine*: perish.

128–31. Davies progresses from the great classical masters of epic, Homer and Virgil ('the man of *Mantua*'), to the father of English poetry, Chaucer ('old *Gefferie*'), to published contemporaries Spenser ('*Colin*') and Daniel ('*Delias* servant'), to poets evidently of his own circle, who are more difficult to recognize.

In *The Oxford Book of Sixteenth-Century Verse* (1932), E. K. Chambers tried
to identify the poets hidden here; scholarship has not advanced very far
beyond his conjectures. For the shadowy companion, three names have been
suggested. One may be dismissed, for, as P. J. Finkelpearl has pointed out in
a private letter, Edward Guilpin probably had not yet composed his *Skiale-
theia, or a Shadow of Truth* (1598), since it mentions the quarrel between Hall
and Marston, which developed after *Orchestra* was written. George Chapman
deserves consideration. His *Shadow of Night* was published in 1594, and in
1595 he published *Ovids Banquet of Sence* with two complimentary sonnets by
Davies. Another possible 'Companion' is Thomas Campion, who wrote a
Latin poem called *Umbra*, part of which, *Fragmentum Umbrae*, appeared in his
Poemata in 1595. This work contains an epigram to Davies:

Ad. Io. Davisium
Quod nostros, Davisi, laudas recitasque libellos
Vultu quo nemo candidiore solet:
Ad me mitte tuos; iam pridem postulo, res est
In qua persolvi gratia vera potest.

Salices is a reading preserved in *LF*, whereas *1596* has the misreading
Salues. Although *Salices* might suggest the genitive of 'willow', a traditional
symbol of sad lovers, the reference could be to Fulke Greville, who wrote a
collection of love poems to *Caelica*, published posthumously in 1633, but
probably in manuscript by the time of *Orchestra*. In Elizabethan Latin,
Caelica would have been pronounced with a soft initial *c*, like *s*.

Scholars have searched in vain for a poet who could be 'the Bay, the
Marigolds darling'. Grosart suggested Charles Best because of his poem on
a marigold in *Poetical Rhapsody* (1608), but it lacks a bay. Possibly Fitzjames in
LF and the compositor of *1596* both misread their copy, or perhaps Davies
used the sixteenth-century spelling 'bey' for 'bee' and was misunderstood.
'Bee' is evidently the correct reading, and is more appropriate to be covered
with Love's 'wing' than a bay tree. By this argument Davies here refers to
T. Cutwode's amusing and slightly salacious *Caltha Poetarum* [The Marigold
of the Poets]: *Or the Bumble Bee*. Its story concerns a bee which, nicked by
Cupid's arrow, falls in love with a marigold; deprived of his stinger, he is
provided with another from a hawthorn to assist his love-making. First
printed in 1599, *Caltha Poetarum* must have been extant in manuscript earlier
if this explanation is correct.

After Sidney ('*Astrophell*'), Davies concludes with 'the Swallow', clearly
Richard Martin, to whom the poem is dedicated, since a 'martin' is a bird of
the swallow family.

128.4. *Thunderer.* The reading of *1596*, 'thunder', is possible, but Jove's
traditional epithet is 'the Thunderer'. Since the final *er* is usually abbreviated
in Elizabethan handwriting, if the printer had seen *er* followed by the
abbreviation for *er*, he would probably have thought it an error, and printed
'thunder' instead.

Epigrammes

Textual Introduction

Elizabethan poems were often 'published', that is, made publicly known, before they came into print, and Davies's epigrams are one example of such publication. While only two copies of the first and one of the second printed editions now remain, there are, in addition to the sprinkling of epigrams appearing in scattered verse miscellanies, six principal collections of epigrams extant in manuscript. The present editor has described four of them, *Ro, R, H,* and *LF,* in an article in *R.E.S.* xii (1962), 118–24, and has included there the sequence in which the epigrams appear in those manuscripts. Some conclusions in the present discussion rest on evidence presented in more detail there.

Probably the earliest manuscript collection is *R,* a commonplace book containing forty-five epigrams by Davies under a title that imitates the phrasing of a popular Elizabethan almanac, to which Davies's epigrams are compared:

English Epigrammes much like Buckminsters Almanacke, servinge for all England, but especially for the Meridian of the honorable cittye of London calculated by John Davis of Grayes Inne gentleman Anᵒ 1594 in November.

R is significant in several ways: it has some readings that were altered later by the author; it provides texts generally free from corruption; and, most important, it preserves eleven epigrams that Davies did not print—for ten of these it is the only witness.

A second manuscript, *H,* is much later. On its last folio, 25ᵛ, is entered the date '1631' in a hand that appears to be that in which the manuscript was written, though smaller. Its contents include forty-two epigrams by Davies, some of which he did not print, fifty-six epigrams from Henry Hutton's *Follies Anatomy or Satyres* (1619), miscellaneous epigrams by John Harington, John Owen, John Heath, and others, and, in a fourth section, an anonymous poem and Davies's 36th epigram, 'Of Tobacco'. David C. Redding has pointed out in *N. & Q*. ccvii (1962), 31, 40, that the epigrams in the third section were copied from W. B.'s *A Helpe to Discourse*. A collation shows the text of *H* to have conjunctive errors with the printed editions of 1627–8.

Although *H* was evidently copied late, its epigrams by Davies are textually related to *R,* as is indicated in several ways. First, their titles are alike. The heading in *H* is

Epigramma in Musam Like Buckminsters Allmanackes servinge generallie for all England but especiallie for the meridian of this famous Cittie of London.

Second, the two manuscripts share conjunctive variants not found in other manuscript traditions; and third, the sequence in which their epigrams appear is similar. *H* is more corrupt than *R*, and has many blunders, but it includes at least one couplet, at 23.15–16, not found in other witnesses, which might reflect either Davies's first draft or perhaps only a scribe's ingenuity.

Related to *R* and *H* by both the sequence of its epigrams and their conjunctive readings is *F*. Its collection contains twenty-five epigrams by Davies, in texts generally not as corrupt as those in *H*, nor as reliable as those in *R*. Together, the three manuscripts may be referred to as Group I; they derive from a single archetype called γ, probably the earliest collection of Davies's epigrams. Each manuscript has separative errors indicating that it derives independently from the archetype. In those poems which the manuscripts share, the archetype may be reconstructed. By offering unrevised versions of the epigrams, γ preserves the readings of these poems in an early state.

A second group of two manuscripts probably descends from a collection later than γ. It may be called Group II, and its archetype δ. One of its manuscripts, *Ro*, provides texts for poems besides Davies's epigrams, and is discussed at more length in the Bibliography.

Ro has a collection of forty-four epigrams (two of them not printed by Davies) on fols. 2^v–9^r, and includes three other epigrams (one unprinted) later in the manuscript. Their order of appearance suggests that they are intermediate in time and organization between Group I and the printed texts. The readings of *Ro*, similarly, seem to represent an intermediate state of revision between Group I and the revised readings of the printed texts: sometimes *Ro* reads with Group I, sometimes with the printed texts, sometimes independently. It is possible, however, that *Ro* is earlier than Group I, and that δ is the earliest collection of Davies's epigrams, with γ a corruption of it. Although this seems unlikely, one cannot answer the question with certainty.

The other manuscript of Group II is *Ca*, with forty-three epigrams. *Ca* frequently reads with *Ro* against all other witnesses. Its handsome appearance, with epigrams neatly arranged in two columns and clearly entered in a careful hand, suggests that *Ca* was prepared by a professional scribe. Its text, unfortunately, is filled with blunders.

Another group of textual witnesses may be called Group III. It comprises *E1* and *E2*, the earliest printed editions, and one manuscript, *LF*. This group derives from a collection formed by Davies in preparation for the first printed edition.

LF was compiled by Davies's associate at the Middle Temple, Leweston Fitzjames, who evidently copied Davies's *Orchestra*, *Epithalamion*, and two satiric sonnets (NHA 15–16) from Davies's own papers. Two points suggest that Fitzjames's collection of epigrams derives from Davies's papers also. First, Fitzjames's date '95' for 1595 appears in only one other place in his manuscript—beneath Davies's *Epithalamion*: the unusual manner of entry suggests the texts derive from his source, probably Davies. Similarly, Fitzjames uses Latin titles for poems (here '*Epigrammata Io: Dauisij*') only for poems by Davies; evidently they derive from his copy. There are indications that his copy was a collection that Davies put together in preparation for printing. First, the order of the epigrams in *LF* (1–8, 10, 9, 11, 13–35, 37–44, 36) is almost identical to that of Davies's printed texts, whereas other manuscripts have quite different arrangements. Second, Fitzjames's collection contains all but five of the epigrams that Davies printed; four epigrams which it lacks, 45–8, were seemingly Davies's last compositions before printing. That they were composed last is indicated in several ways: Epigrams 45 and 46 are found in only one manuscript, *Ro*, where they are separated from the main collection; Epigram 47 refers to an event of 1595 and hence is demonstrably later than most of the epigrams, which according to *R* were written by November 1594; moreover, Epigram 47 does not appear in any of the manuscripts with full collections of epigrams; Epigram 48 appears only in print, and was clearly written to balance the first epigram as a farewell to the reader. Finally, the conclusion that *LF* derives from a collection made by Davies for printing is supported by the freedom of its text from obvious error, and its conjunctive readings with the printed editions.

The printing of the early editions presents a number of problems, including the nature of the copy used by the printers, and the order in which the various editions, all undated, were printed. These are discussed in detail in an article by the present editor and Roma Gill, 'The Early Editions of Marlowe's Elegies and Davies's Epigrams: Sequence and Authority', *The Library*, xxvi (1971), 242–9. The present discussion rests on evidence given at greater length there.

The title-page of the first edition, *E1*, gives the following information: *Epigrammes and Elegies. By I. D. and C. M. At Middleborugh.* It omits dates and names, though a second title identifies 'C. M.' and his elegies: *Certaine of Ovids Elegies. By C Marlow.* Davies's reputation as an epigrammatist was probably sufficient for his identity to be recognized; the Bishop of London and Archbishop of Canterbury recognized it in June 1599 when by their order 'Davyes Epigrams with Marlowes Elegyes' were among the books, many of them satiric, which were condemned to public burning; and it was specified 'that noe *Satyres* or *Epigrams* be printed hereafter' (*S. R.* iii. 677).

In spite of the orders, at least six editions (*S. T. C.* 6350 and 18931–3) appeared during the late sixteenth and early seventeenth centuries, all bearing the imprint 'at Middleborough'. Whether the early editions were actually printed in Middleburg is open to question. In 1940 William Jackson argued that the first two editions were printed by Waldegrave, the Edinburgh printer, because the signatures were in his peculiar manner and differed from those of the leading printer of English books in Middleburg, Richard Schilders (see *The Carl H. Pforzheimer Library: English Literature 1475–1700* (New York, 1940), ii. 664 n.). In 1961, however, Mr. Jackson responded to the present inquiry, 'As to Waldegrave's manner of signing, I am not now so firm as I was when I wrote that note.' Roma Gill in the article on the publication of the early editions believes them possibly to have been printed by James Roberts, since the type ornaments in *E1* are similar to those used by Roberts in printing Marston's *The Scourge of Villanie* (1598). The difficulty is that other printers used identical ornaments. Indeed, it is not impossible that the editions were printed in Middleburg. Davies himself visited there in 1592 and in a letter to Paul Merula in 1593 (Bodleian MS. D'Orville 52, fol. 50) Davies suggests that Merula might send letters by the Middleburg postman to Nicholas Martin, brother of Davies's friend Richard Martin, then lodging there.

Wherever the book was printed, *E1* was set up by a compositor who thought in English, for it has numerous errors of intrusion and unconscious alteration. For example, the compositor inserts '&' at 17.8, and at 27.3 prints 'But when doth he his' for 'But then doth he this', errors which are unlikely to have come from his copy. The printing itself is very shoddy, with haphazard spacing, inconsistent punctuation, and numerous misprints, some of which may result from foul case or an apprentice-compositor who had not yet learned his type-box: examples are 'dnth' for 'doth' at 15.4, 'hig' for 'his' at 45.4, 'stames' for 'states' at 47.10. In addition, there are many instances of misreading, such as *approue* for *reprooue* (1.7.), *out* for *cut* (26.8), *with* for *which* (30.11, 36.3).

E1 was followed by *E2*, a word-by-word, line-by-line reprint that makes frequent corrections. Davies was not personally responsible for the corrections, for too many errors remain to suppose he corrected *E1* for the printer of *E2*, nor is there evidence that the printer of *E2* received a new manuscript. The best explanation of the corrections is that they came from a more careful consultation of the manuscript that had been originally provided by Davies for *E1*.

Since *E1* alone of the printed texts derives directly from manuscript, and since the manuscript was provided by Davies, *E1* is most likely to preserve his accidentals. I have therefore chosen it as copy-text, but have corrected from *E2*. Further, although the punctuation and spelling of *E1* are generally preserved, I have emended more frequently than usual, either for clarity or to bring the pointing more in accord with Davies's usual practice.

The apparatus gives all departures from copy-text and includes all manuscript readings which may have been Davies's earlier efforts. Where at least two of the three manuscripts in Group I agree and are not obviously corrupt, their variants are given since they may reflect Davies's first draft. Similarly, readings of Group II manuscripts, where they agree, are given if they may claim to represent Davies's words.

Since the witnesses alter from one epigram to the next, they are listed in the apparatus for each epigram. The layout is that of the copy-text, which appears to imitate that of the printer's copy. In the few places that it has been normalized, this fact is indicated. The sequence of the epigrams is that of *E1* and all printed editions; the numbering has been silently corrected or supplied in a few instances where it was erroneous or had been omitted.

Date

Both external and internal evidence are available for the date of Davies's epigrams. The date in *R*, November 1594, indicates that all of Davies's first forty-eight epigrams except those which *R* omits, 5, 8, 9, 12, 14, 20, 24, 28, and 44–8, were written by that time. The date in *LF*, 1595, indicates that all but 45–8 were composed by then (although *LF* omits number 12, its enumeration accounts for it and suggests that 12 appeared in Fitzjames's copy). Some of Davies's epigrams themselves refer to datable events: the 'New water worke' in the sixth epigram, and the capture of Groningen in the fortieth, both refer to events of 1594. Epigram 47, one of the last to be written, refers to the war between France and Spain, declared on 17 January 1595.

If 'In Paulum' (41) refers to Raleigh's marriage in 1592 (see notes to the poem), and was composed soon afterwards, then Davies had begun writing by late 1592 or 1593; but the identification of Paulus as Raleigh is uncertain. A starting-point for the composition of epigrams that do not refer to datable events is necessarily equally speculative. Mr. J. M. Nosworthy in urging the date 1594 has correctly argued that 'Davies makes it quite clear that he is referring to recent events',[1] and although several poems were evidently written in 1595, the majority were probably composed in 1594. Certainly they are the kind of work that a man who boasted of writing *Orchestra* in fifteen days might easily have written within a single year, and there are no references to the epigrams before that time.

The publication date one proposes for the first edition depends partly on his interpretation of John Harington's reference to Davies's Epigrams 29 and 14 in *Metamorphosis of Ajax* (1596):

This Haywood for his Proverbs & Epigrams, is not yet put downe by any of our countrey, though one doth in deede come neare him, that graces him the more in saying he puts him downe. But both of them have made sport with as homely words as ours be; one of a Gentlewomans glove, save that without his consent it is no good manners to publish it (London (1962), pp. 102–3).

One may, like Harington's editor, Elizabeth Story Donno, interpret the statement to mean the poems have not been published. Or, like Mr. Nosworthy (*R.E.S.* xv (1964), 397–8), one may read Harington's words with the following emphasis: '*without his consent* it is no good manners [for *Harington*] to publish it', even if he knew it to have been printed elsewhere. In addition, one might maintain that Davies would be unlikely to wait at least a year after having formed most of his collection, evidently in preparation for

---

[1] 'The Publication of Marlowe's *Elegies* and Davies's *Epigrams*', R.E.S. iv (1953), 260–1.

printing in 1595, before actually publishing the work. The latter argument carries more weight; therefore a publication date of 1595 or 1596 seems likely.

The English Martial

The *O.E.D.* defines an epigram as 'a short poem leading up to and ending in a witty or ingenious turn of thought'. This usefully general definition bespeaks the influence of Martial, whose pointed epigram came to dominate the field, leaving behind the merely concise poem of, for example, Catullus, or the lapidary verse in which the epigram originated. The other uses of the epigram developed in other genres or acquired other names.

The term in English was used as loosely as 'sonnet' for a time; indeed, it has never been defined in terms of metre or form, only by length and subject. The usual concept of the epigram in the 1590s arises from the influence of John Heywood and from the study of Martial in schools like Winchester and Eton. Heywood's numerous and very popular epigrams helped to fix the genre as a short satiric poem. In Martial these schoolboys found a satirist who gave his epigrams a witty turn. Not all Martial's epigrams were satiric (as Jonson recognized when, in Epigram 18, he said that his own epigrams were written in 'the old way, and the true'): but it was Martial's satiric epigrams that were imitated in the 1590s.

In the revival of the epigram in the 1590s (a hiatus in the writing of epigrams followed the publication of Timothy Kendall's *Flowers of Epigrammes* in 1577), Davies is a major figure; Guilpin calls him 'our English Martiall' (*Skialetheia*, Epigram 20), and Harington says that he and Davies are accused of stealing from Martial. Davies's precedence over Harington, whose extant epigrams are far more numerous, must be attributed to his situation in the Inns of Court, when Harington's public life was more circumscribed, and also to Davies having published his work. Certainly Davies deserves credit for having adapted Martial to the English scene. His subject is the social group around him, his attitude is amusement; instead of merely translating Martial, as some others did, 'he has learned from Martial how to treat London as Martial treated Rome' (Thomas K. Whipple, *Martial and the English Epigram* (1925), p. 338).

Like Martial, he denies any interest in 'privat Taxing'; his denial contains an element of truth, but it is largely false. Probably the persons satirized were known to the immediate audience; the readers derived their enjoyment from the exercise of wit upon reality, and many of the least enjoyable poems greatly amused those who recognized the butts. On the other hand, many are still amusing as general comments on the ill-mannered individuals of a 'formall age'.

A word remains to be said of Davies's main contribution to literature, the gull as the would-be man of fashion rather than the mere dupe or simpleton.

The name took hold quickly, as the ensuing years show: there is a play *The Isle of Gulls* (1606), and a *Gulls Hornbook* (1609). But the character had to wait seventy years for its full development. Davies's gull who 'semes, and is not wise' is the would-be wit of the comedy of manners, described by a *persona* who belongs to the mannered world and approves its standards—thus Silla dares 'do what ever is unmeete'. Davies satirizes the failures of those who lack wit, or refinement, or the quality of judgement that would permit them to move with ease in the 'formall' society to which they aspire.

1.10–14. Cf. Martial, x. 33: 'This measure my books learn to keep, to spare the person, to denounce the vice.'

2. Martial contemptuously defines the *bellus homo*, the fop of his day, in the following terms:

> But, tell me, what is a pretty fellow? 'A pretty fellow is one who arranges neatly his curled locks, who continually smells of balsam . . .' A very trumpery thing, Cotilus, is your pretty fellow (iii. 63).

2.5–6. True velvet is an expensive cloth of silk, usually indicating wealth and position. *Brave* means 'finely dressed'. Samuel Rowlands, writing in 1609 about Davies's epigram, understood the velvet gown to be worn by the young woman of line 6 ('A Gull' in *The Knave of Clubbes*):

> His first Gull feares a silken wench,
> Her velvet gowne doth scare him.

2.11. *Indures the lyes*: tolerates being called a liar, an insult that a gentleman cannot accept without issuing a challenge.

2.14. *in presence*: in ceremonial attendance on a person of superior rank.

3.1–6. Elizabethan playhouses had several kinds of seating. The 'best and most conspicuous place' would probably be the Lord's room, the raised gallery at the rear of the inner stage. The 'grate' is a barred casement in a smaller, enclosed compartment in the Lord's room, through which Rufus looks. The 'privat roomes' are the boxes, generally occupied by the wealthy. The custom of sitting on stage became fashionable in the mid-1590s as the Lord's room declined in status; see *Elizabethan Stage*, ii. 531–7.

5.2. *Gella . . . Rodope*: famous courtesans of antiquity.

5.3. *Stanes*. Staines is a town near London that was popular for outings in Davies's time.

6.3. *lord Chauncellors tombe*. The large and elaborate tomb of Sir Christopher Hatton in St. Paul's Cathedral, completed in 1591, was one of the sights of London.

6.4. *New water worke*. John Stow mentions that a

> new Forcier was made neare to *Broken wharfe*, to convey Thames water into mens houses of West *Cheape*, about *Powles, Fleetestreet*, &c. . . . in the yeare 1594 (*Survey of London*, ed. C. L. Kingsford, i. 18).

6.4. *Elephant*. W. Milgate (ed.), *John Donne: The Satires, Epigrams and Verse*

Letters (1967), points out that the performing elephant is referred to in Jonson's *Every Man Out of his Humour*, IV. vi. 60–1, and Hall's *Virgidemiarum*, IV. ii. 95, as well as in Donne's first Satire, line 81.

6.6. *Counter*: a debtors' prison.

7.3. Two playhouses, 'The Theatre and the Curtain, both built in or about 1576, stood in "the fields" to the north of London proper' (*Elizabethan Stage*, iii. 357).

7.5. *Powles*. St Paul's Cathedral was a fashionable meeting place for lawyers and gallants.

7.5. *ordinarie*: a tavern at which a public meal was served at a fixed price.

8.2. *buffe jerkin*: a short military coat of 'a very stout kind of leather . . . having a fuzzy surface'—*O.E.D.* For a similar use of 'buff jerkin', see *1 Henry IV*, I. ii. 48.

10. *Medon*. Probably the poem refers to a contemporary, since John Harington, in *Metamorphosis of Ajax* (1596) refers to 'Captaine Medons grandfather' (ed. Elizabeth Story Donno (1962) p. 260).

10.4. *Henry Bulleigne*: Henry VIII captured Boulogne in 1544.

10.9–12. The saying attributed by Plutarch to Philip of Macedon, that any castle would open its gates to an ass laden with gold, was proverbial (see Tilley A356).

11. Martial (ii. 41) warns Maximina, who has only three teeth, all black, not to laugh or smile; Ovid gives the same advice in *The Art of Love*, iii. 279–80.

13. The hypocrisy of people who fasten on single Biblical texts to justify their vices is attacked by Sir Thomas More in two epigrams on priests (*The Latin Epigrams of Thomas More*, ed. Leicester Bradner and Charles Arthur Lynch (1953), epigrams 186, 244).

13.1. *Severus*: Latin for 'severe', and hence appropriate to a puritan.

13.2–4. Davies paraphrases Christ's injunction to the Pharisees in Matthew 15: 11, and alludes to the story of the self-righteous Pharisee in Luke 18: 10–14.

13.13. *Pharoes kine*: cf. Gen. 41: 2–4.

16.1. *hath a Lyon seene*: 'to have had experience of life'—*O.E.D.*, from the custom of taking visitors to the Tower to see the lions kept there.

16.3. *lost his hayre*: i.e. from venereal disease.

16.4. *Lyonesse*: a harlot.

17.5–8. E. K. Chambers quotes from 'An Order for supressinge of Jigges att the ende of Playes', prompted

by reason of certayne lewde Jigges songes and daunces used and accustomed at the play-house . . . divers cutt-purses and other lewde and ill disposed persons in greate multitudes doe resorte thither at th'end of everye playe, many tymes causinge tumultes and outrages (*Elizabethan Stage*, iv. 340–1).

19. *Cineas*. The name suggests 'cynic'. The Greek Cynical philosophers were so named because they originally met in a building (The *Cynosarges*) with a figure of a dog upon it, and because their behaviour was regarded as

bestial (*cyon, cynos*: dog). Martial bases an epigram (iv. 53) on this connection of Cynics with dogs: the poem describes a dirty, threadbare beggar who is thought to be a cynic, and concludes 'This fellow is no Cynic, Cosmus. What is he, then? A dog'.

19.2. *Mastie*: mastiff.

20.1. *Geron*: 'an old man'.

21.1. *Mins*. We have not traced the reference; evidently it was a dicing-house.

21.2. *come on seaven*: an expression used in throwing dice.

22. The overdressed young man attired in the latest fashion is a frequent object of satire; such a person is described by Martial in ii. 29.

22.1. *tierse*: spruce.

22.5. *hat*. Cf. Guilpin's Cornelius (*Skialetheia*, 53), a modish man who wears 'a hat scarce pipkin high'.

22.6. *treble ruffes . . . French*. The multiple ruff was a new fashion in the 1590s; the treble consisted of three layers, fastened to a band under the chin, and raised at the back so that the ruff rested on the doublet in front (in contrast to the earlier style, which was worn lower, but at right angles to the throat). The French doublet was distinguished by slashes in the sleeves to expose the shirt. The French cloak, also increasingly fashionable, was knee-length or longer (earlier cloaks fell only to the waist or hips).

22.7. *locke*. The love-lock, or Bourbon lock, was a tress of hair grown long, curled, often beribboned, and pulled forward from the nape of the neck to lie over the chest. Cf. NHA 19.7.

22.9–10. Ciprius's taste runs to old poetry; Gascoigne died in 1577, and may have been chosen for Davies's example because Gascoigne's satiric writing seems cumbersome if compared with Davies's epigrams.

23. Davies here imitates Martial's epigram (iii. 95), about Naevolus, who refuses to salute first, but excels Martial only in the grossness of his sexual practices.

24.1. *Friesland*: a province in the Netherlands where for many years a war of independence was waged against Spain with English help.

24.5–8. *counterscarfes . . . scaladose*: military terms.

24.11–12. *foorching . . . champartie*: legal terms.

25. Ben Jonson told Drummond that this epigram attacked Drayton, 'who in a sonnet concluded his Mistriss might been the ninth worthy' (*Works*, i. 137). Drayton does actually load ('lade') the mistress with this title in *Ideas Mirror* (1594), 'Amour' 8. The nine worthies are Joshua, David, Judas Maccabeus, Hector, Alexander, Julius Caesar, Arthur, Charlemagne, and Godfrey of Boulogne.

26.3. *morpheu*: a scurfy skin-eruption.

28.6. *spittle*: a hospital where a prostitute might be treated for venereal disease.

28.11–12. Raw beef and strong (red) wine were thought to increase bodily heat. Martial (xii. 17) writes of one Laetinus, whose fever persists because of the luxury of his diet.

28.14. *man*: accompany.

29. *Haywood*: John Heywood (?1497–1580), the leading writer of epigrams before Davies, who published six hundred of them in 1562. His satires are moral rather then social. This epigram is quoted in Jonson's *Cynthia's Revels* (v. iv. 252–3), where Asotus says

> *As buckets are put downe into a well;*
> *Or as a schoole-boy.—*

29.4. *hose*: breeches.

30. For a discussion of the identity of Dacus, see notes to Epigram 45. Davies refers to many popular sights of London, frequently mentioned by his contemporaries. Banks's horse Morocco is the most famous of the performing animals of the time; it could dance and count, among other tricks. It is referred to by Shakespeare (*Love's Labour's Lost*, I. ii. 57), Nashe (*The Unfortunate Traveller* in *Works*, ed. McKerrow (1958), ii. 230), Donne (*Satyres*, i. 80) and Hall (*Virgidemiarum*, IV. ii. 94). For references to the elephant, see note on Epigram 6. The ape is mentioned in Donne with the elephant (*Satyres*, i. 81) and by Jonson in the Induction to *Bartholomew Fair*. The keeper of the monuments at Westminster appears in Donne's *Satyres*, iv. 74–7.

30.8. *curtall*: a horse with its tail cut short.

32.5–8. Cf. Martial (ii. 16), on Zoilus who is ill in order to show off his bedding.

32.6. *wrought*: embroidered.

32.8. *Trollups*: apparently a pawnshop.

35. The more usual comparison is to a leek: cf. Martial xiii. 19, and Chaucer's *Reeve's Prologue* (*Canterbury Tales*, I (A) 3878–9), '. . . an hoor heed and a grene tayl, / As hath a leek'.

35.4. *burned*: infected with venereal disease.

36.1. *Moly . . . Nepenthe*. Moly is given to Odysseus by Hermes to protect him from Circe's charms (*Odyssey*, book x); Nepenthe, given to Telemachus by Helen (*Odyssey*, book iv), makes people forget their sorrows.

36.21. *Hectick . . . fever*. The Hectick fever is a wasting disease like consumption; the *quartain* an ague characterized by paroxysms recurring every fourth day.

36.26. *vile Medicine*. In Epigram 238, Sir Thomas More recommends eating onions to take away the smell of leeks, garlic for the smell of onions: 'But if your breath remains offensive even after the garlic, then either it is incurable or nothing but excrement will remove it.'

37.5. *Gaunt*: Ghent.

37.20. *an action . . . lie*: he will not be sued for libelling or slandering inanimate objects.

38.6. *auditorie*: audience.

38.15. *Serjeant*: bailiff.

39. Martial has two epigrams describing a day's activities division by division (iv. 8, x. 70), but unlike 'In Fuscum', they are not used for personal attacks. Guilpin's Epigram 25, 'Of Gnatho', also describes a day in the life of a gallant.

40. This epigram appears to be influenced by Martial's epigram on Philomusus (ix. 35), who, like Afer, gossips for his dinner.

40.1. *Burse*: the Royal Exchange. Like St. Paul's, it was a fashionable meeting place; as a commercial centre, it was a source of foreign news.

40.5–6. *Gronigen . . . Vere*. Sir Francis Vere (1560–1609) was the general of English troops in the Netherlands; Groningen, in north-eastern Holland, was captured by his forces in July 1594.

40.7–8. *Brest . . . Norris*. In November 1594, Sir John Norris (or Norreys) commanded a successful attack on a Spanish fort designed to cut off Brest from the sea.

41. Dr. Carolyn Bishop, in 'Raleigh Satirized by Harington and Davies' (*R.E.S.* xxiii (1972), 52–6) has suggested that Paulus is Sir Walter Raleigh (as he appears to be in Harington's epigrams on Paulus: see *T.L.S.* (1927), pp. 160, 355, 488), and that this epigram alludes to events of August–December 1592. She points out that Raleigh was envied, but powerful and at least apparently rich; his wealth came from his public offices (he was Lieutenant of Cornwall, Deputy Lieutenant of Devon, and Warden of the Stannaries) and from privateering. In 1592 he became tenant of Sherborne Castle, which belonged to the Bishop of Salisbury.

In consequence of his secret marriage to Elizabeth Throckmorton (probably in November 1591, discovered in May 1592), Raleigh was imprisoned in the Tower in August 1592. He was released in custody to supervise the distribution of spoils from the Spanish treasure-ship *Madre de Dios*, captured in September by his ships, carrying cargo valued at £200,000. He paid to the Queen not only her rightful share of £20,000, but £80,000 of his own share, which in a letter to Burghley he called his 'ransom'. Though the Queen did not act immediately, she ordered his release in December; his wife can therefore be called a gulf that swallowed Raleigh's wealth. If this identification is accurate, 'Of Paulus' is earlier than the epigrams which may be dated with certainty.

42.2. *gaine*. Travel was so dangerous that men used to accept odds on their chances of returning; safe arrival meant a man won the wager. The practice is often referred to, as in Fynes Morison's *Itinerary* (1617), and Jonson's *Every Man Out of his Humour*, II. iii. 243–51.

43.3. *Paris Garden*: the bear-garden across the Thames from the city of London.

43.6. *To head*: a spectator's cry meaning 'attack the head'.

43.10. *muted*: stained with hawk-droppings.

43.13. *Ployden . . . Brooke*. Edward Plowden, Sir James Dyer, and Sir Robert Broke were noted lawyers of the sixteenth century; their collections of case reports were used as textbooks.

43.14. *Harry . . . Sacarson*: famous bears at Paris Garden.

45. Scholars have often identified Dacus with Samuel Daniel, pointing out that *The Complaint of Rosamond* (1592) contains the expressions 'silent rhetorique' and 'dumb eloquence'. They accept the necessity of extending the identification to Epigram 30 (since usually an epigrammatist uses a name for only one person even if he is mentioned in several epigrams), adducing criticisms of Daniel (Jonson, *Works*, i. 132; Drayton, 'Epistle to Henry Reynolds', 123–6) as prosaic.

The evidence is unsatisfactory. First, the expressions in *The Complaint of Rosamond* differ from the words attributed to Dacus, and they do not designate the poet's mistress: they are part of Rosamond's attempt to define the power of beauty. Moreover, Daniel was not considered prosaic in 1594, by which time Epigram 30 was written. The criticisms of Jonson and Drayton postdate the publication of *The First Fowre Bookes of the civile wars* (1595), by virtue of which Daniel's lyrical work was overshadowed by his narrative poems; and one may question whether an expression like Drayton's 'historian in verse' approaches in severity the accusation that Dacus is a hack-writer of hucksters' speeches. In 1594, the year by which *Orchestra* and Epigram 30 were written, Daniel was still '*Delias* servant' whose rhymes Davies praised in *Orchestra* 128, a tribute that consorts ill with the charge that Dacus could 'never make an English rime'.

45.1. *collour*: show of reason.

45.3. *collours*: paint or make-up; also rhetorical figures, ornaments of style or diction.

46.6. *primero*: a card-game resembling poker; see NHA 4.

47.2. *hoode-winked*: concealed.

47.5. The 'war twixt France and Spaine' began in January 1595.

47.7 *Empire*: the German or Holy Roman Empire, under the Hapsburgs.

47.10 *states*: the Staaten generaal, legislative assembly of the Netherlands.

47.15. *blacke Feather*: an ostrich feather dyed black, perhaps gaining favour along with the pose of melancholy. Previously, the feathers men wore in their hats were brightly coloured ostrich feathers or peacock feathers; the poem implies that the black feather was a recent fashion. It is mentioned by Donne (*Satyres*, i. 55).

48.5–8. Martial also complains to someone who begrudges his fame that he is not better known than the racehorse Andraemon (x. 9).

48.6. *Cammels . . . hog*. Hall (*Virgidemiarum*, IV. ii. 96) mentions a 'rig'd Camell', among the performing animals. We have not been able to identify the western hog.

48.7. *Lepidus . . . dogge*. A picture of his dog, Bungey, appears on the title-page of Sir John Harington's translation of *Orlando Furioso*; Harington mentions its name in the notes to book xliii (to which Davies refers in NHA 10), and refers to Davies's Epigram 48 in 'Against Momus' (McClure, 219).

Epigrams from Manuscript

Canon, Text, and Date

Davies did not print any of these epigrams, which were first published by Percy Simpson in *R.E.S.* iii (1952), and by R. F. Kennedy in *T.L.S.* 7 August 1959. They appear in collections of Davies's epigrams in manuscripts of Groups I and II discussed in the previous Textual Introduction. All of them appear in MS. *R* or its archetype, and hence must have been composed by November 1594.

Epigram 49 appears midway in the sequences of the Group I manuscripts *R* and *H*, and reappears in the Group II manuscript *Ro*; it is therefore likely to have been available to Davies when he formed his collection for the press from which Group III witnesses derive. He may, however, have lacked Epigrams 50–9. Although some of them are coarser than or technically inferior to most of the printed epigrams, there is no reason to suppose Davies suppressed them all. He undoubtedly wrote more epigrams than have survived, and probably more than he kept copies of. Like Donne, he may have been forced to write to friends for copies of his own verse for printing (see *The Divine Poems*, ed. Helen Gardner (1952), p. lxiv). That Epigrams 50–9 appear together in sequence at the end of the collection in *R* suggests that the collection was copied from loose sheets; Davies may himself have lacked a copy of the sheet with these poems when preparing his collection for the printer.

The copy-text for each epigram in the present edition is the best available for that poem.

51. Cf. Harington's very similar refusal of a polyglot wife (McClure, 261).

52. Guilpin has a similar epigram 'Of Arion. 29'.

52.4. *cyterne*: a stringed instrument somewhat like a lute or guitar; the *Orpharion* of the next line is a form of it.

sackbutt: trombone.

52.6. *virginall*: a forerunner of the harpsichord.

52.8. *Regall*: a portable reed-organ.

Hoboy: 'hautboy' or oboe.

53.2. *beaten*: embroidered or embossed.

54.2. *jape*: joke; have intercourse.

56. *Bretton*: perhaps Nicholas Breton (?1545–?1626), a minor poet.

56.4. *murre*: a severe form of catarrh.

57. *Munday*: perhaps Antony Munday (1553–1633), a professional writer.

58.1. *vawting house*: brothel.

58.4. *Lotium*: vulgar form of 'lotion'; stale urine used by barbers to dress the hair.

59.1. *French disease*: syphilis.

60.20. *against the haire*: against the grain.

Gullinge Sonnets

Text and Date

The poems are found only in MS. *Che* (see Bibliography), a miscellany of prose and verse; the compiler, who was probably a member of an Inn of Court, attributes their authorship to 'Mr. Davies'.

Dating the poems is difficult. The eighth specifically mocks *Zepheria*, a ludicrous sonnet sequence using legal terminology that was printed in 1594. Probably the best audience for Davies's parody, as for *Zepheria* itself, was the Inns of Court, and the best time for parody is when the work being parodied is current. 1594 therefore seems the most probable time for Davies's composition, particularly since in that year Davies was popularizing the term 'gull'. If 1594 is correct, the copy of the poems sent to 'Sir Anthony Cooke', from which the transcript in *Che* derives, was not sent to Cooke until at least two years after their composition, for he was not knighted until 1596.

The text in *Che* probably derives directly from a scribal copy sent by Davies to Cooke; except for three minor slips, it is free from obvious error.

Introduction

The volumes of sonnets written after 1591 could easily have dulled the reader's ability to perceive the '*Energia*' which, Sidney assures us, will give amorous poetry the conviction of true passion; distinguishing the merits of even the best verse became difficult for a reader who had been rhymed in this fashion for 'years together, dinners and suppers and sleeping hours excepted'. The highly stylized treatment of love naturally made sonnets easy objects for satire, and the narrow line between Davies's parodies of sonnet conventions and the work even of some of the better sonneteers like Sidney, Spenser, Daniel, or Drayton (not to mention the laborious efforts of Griffin, Lynche, or the anonymous author of *Zepheria*), indicates how easily form could overtake matter. Davies is not mocking particular poems nor sonnets only, but those Elizabethan poems which either by over-use of technical conventions, or by over-literal extension of metaphor, became ridiculous. The following notes refer to some poems employing conventions that Davies plays upon; many of the references were kindly supplied by Professor P. Burwell Rogers, author of 'Sir John Davies' *Gulling Sonnets*', *Bucknell University Studies*, iv (1954), 193–204.

Dedication. Sir Anthony Cooke (1555–1604) was a cousin of Robert Cecil and Francis Bacon; he served under Essex at Cadiz, where he was knighted in 1596, and in Ireland. Drayton dedicated *Ideas Mirror* to him in 1594.

   3. *Antick*: clown

4. *lewde gulleries*: ignorant deceptions.

7. *whiskinge*: light, frivolous.

14. *begg him for*: call him.

Gullinge Sonnets

1. The Petrarchan conceit of the lover burdened by the weight of his love is found frequently, as in Sidney, *Astrophil and Stella*, 4, and at greater length in *Zepheria*, 36.

1.5. *fates*. The decrees of the Fates were irreversible; the gods could mitigate the circumstances.

2. Cf. Dorus's song, 'My sheep are thoughts' in *Old Arcadia*, book ii.

3. Davies combines the conventions of the eagle beholding the sun with that of the mistress's 'sunbrighte eye', as in Watson's *Hekatompathia*, 99, and Drayton's *Idea*, 56. The device of *gradatio*, frequently used in sonnets, as in *Astrophil and Stella*, 1 and 68, and *Hekatompathia*, 68, is expanded extravagantly and cleverly made ridiculous by Davies's carrying over almost half of each line of verse. He thus takes almost twice the necessary space to present a set of conventional contrarieties which succeed brilliantly in saying nothing.

4. For similar imagery, see Fletcher, *Licia*, 7, and Spenser, *Amoretti*, 18 and 30.

5. Correlative verse (*carmen correlativum*) was highly fashionable in the late sixteenth century. Some examples include Philoclea's song, 'Virtue, beauty, and speech', in *Old Arcadia*, book iii, Griffin's *Fidessa*, 47, and a poem sometimes attributed to Raleigh, 'Her face, her tongue, her wit'. William A. Ringler, Jr., in *The Poems of Sir Philip Sidney* (1961), p. 406, gives other examples. Hoyt Hopewell Hudson, in *The Epigram in the English Renaissance* (1947), points out (p. 161) that the device was intended to provide compression; Davies's parody succeeds partly by contravening this intent, and partly by increasing the number of correlatives to five, leaving no space to say anything.

6. The description of Cupid contains elements of two conventions. One is the blazon of Love, favourable, as in *F.Q.* III. xi. 47–8, and unfavourable, as in Dicus's description of him as horned and cloven-footed in 'Poore Painters oft' in *Old Arcadia*, book i, or Ronsard's 'Amour Oyseau'. The other is the allegory of courtly love, in which Cupid is associated with personifications of such qualities as pride, hope, and ire (these qualities of course appear abundantly in Petrarchan sonnets). Davies's parody consists in dressing Cupid in garments that have no connection with the qualities except alliteration; thus the sonnet is meaningless, and Cupid is wearing an unconscionable amount of footwear.

6.5. *bande*: collar.

6.8. *pointes . . . Iletholes*. Trousers ('hose') were attached to the doublet with points or ties which were drawn through eyelet holes either in the lining of the doublet at waist-level (invisible) or piercing the doublet along the waistline (visible); the latter, usual after 1595, is probably the custom to which Davies refers.

6.12. *pantofels*: overshoes worn to protect the pumps, soft shoes with thin soles, from dirt.

6.14. Socks were usually worn under boots (which Cupid is not wearing) to protect the stockings from being soiled or rubbed.

7–9. These sonnets mock the extensive elaboration of a single image in great literal detail, and the widespread use of legal conceits, as in Shakespeare, *Sonnets*, 87, 134; Barnes, *Parthenophil*, sonnets 8–10, madrigals 2, 16; Drayton, *Idea*, 2; Griffin, *Fidessa*, 5, 6; Percy, *Coelia*, 1, and especially *Zepheria*, 5, 6, 20, 37, and 38.

8.1. *Zepheria*: a reference to the anonymous sonnet sequence that appeared in 1594; it uses legal conceits.

8.6. *distrein'de*. A legal term; to distrein is to seize goods in order to force the owner to perform an obligation, such as paying a debt or appearing in court; or to punish him for not having done so.

8.9. *repleave*: to recover goods distreined, usually upon an undertaking to perform the duty required.

8.11. *Shreife*: a court officer whose duties include executing writs such as replevin.

8.12. *esloynde*: removed out of the jurisdiction of the court or sheriff.

8.14. *withername*: in an action of replevin, taking other goods in place of those eloigned.

9. The custom of wardship was a profitable one for the guardians and often a disadvantage to the wards. Technically, the Crown was the guardian of all minors who held land by knight-service (i.e. by a grant from the monarch in exchange for military service, which meant virtually all the knights and peers of the realm), all unmarried female orphans, and all idiots. In practice the Court of Wards granted guardianships to individuals, who could collect the income of the estates, and dowries, and whose consent was required for marriage and for selling the property. The number of appeals and complaints attests frequent conflicts of interest between guardians and wards.

Poems Not Hitherto Ascribed to Davies

Twenty-five poems are here ascribed to Davies, none of which has previously been ascribed in print to any author. Some are found in a number of manuscripts, but would have gone unnoticed had they not appeared in MSS. *Ro* and *Y*. Neither manuscript contains poems only by Davies, but both have far more poems by him than by any other author. The compiler of *Ro* very possibly knew Davies, for he seems to have been a member of an Inn of Court and to have received and copied Davies's poems in his manuscript at various times. Sometimes he attached the initials 'I. D.' to them, sometimes not. When he did not, as with his principal collection of forty-four epigrams, the reason could have been that his copy lacked them, or, perhaps, that he knew the author and saw no need to record his name.

In the same way, *Y* attaches Davies's name to *The Kinges Welcome*, yet omits it from his *Contention* and Epigram 47, and from most of the few poems it contains which are by other writers. *Y* is a scribal manuscript copied from the papers of Sir Christopher Yelverton; if the scribe found ascriptions in his copy, presumably he recorded them; if not, authorship known to Yelverton need not have been recorded. Moreover, Davies had good reason to leave his name off many of the poems copied in *Y* which are ascribed to him in this edition, for they satirize people in high places, and Davies might have shared a joke at their expense among friends and yet taken care not to give his name to the abuse in writing.

Some of the poems are attributed to Davies here because they have poetical characteristics unique to Davies's work: they are satiric sonnets used to attack contemporaries under Latin names. C. H. Herford and Percy Simpson noticed Davies's inclination toward the sonnet epigram:

The Sonnet had always been an epigram *in posse*, and Davies's epigrams are in effect sonnets, or easy variations upon the sonnet form, a series of one to four quatrains usually clinched by a stinging final couplet (Jonson, *Works*, ii. 346).

While only one-fifth of Davies's printed epigrams are in fourteen lines, all but four or five use alternating rhyme and fit the description of Herford and Simpson. Yet other epigrammatists did not adopt the sonnet. Only sixteen of Harington's 428 epigrams are in fourteen lines; half of them are written in couplets. Parrot, Rowlands, Hall, Bastard, Owen, and Jonson all avoided the sonnet form. Davies might almost, like Shakespeare in Sonnet 76, have complained that he had

> . . . [kept] invention in a noted weed,
> That every word doth almost tell [his] name,
> Showing their birth, and where they did proceed.

On the Marriage of Lady Elizabeth Hatton to Edward Coke

Canon

Several things identify these poems as Davies's work: their appearance in MSS. *Ro* and *Y*; a subject, which would be suitable to the lawyer Davies, the apparently unfortunate marriage of the Attorney-General; and, most important, their employment of the sonnet series for satiric purpose. Perhaps most telling is the use of the rhyme *abab baba cdcd ee*. A search of several thousand sonnets of the 1590s revealed only two examples of its use—in three of the first six sonnets appearing here, and in three of Davies's *Gullinge Sonnets*, which, like these, form a type of loose sonnet sequence.

The unique rhyme identifies only the first group of six sonnets. The second series, five sonnets found only in *Y*, is attributed to Davies because, although four of them are in his more usual Shakespearian rhyme, they attack the same marriage, and are clearly by the author of the first series. In *Y* they are separated from sonnets 1–6, and seem likely to have been received at a different time, an inference supported by the occasionally confused state of the text.

Text

Poems 1–6 appear in six witnesses, which show a variety of minor variants —usually prepositions or articles—but none of much interest, and most of them scribal, not authorial. The manuscripts show no interrelationship that would warrant the construction of a stemma, nor do all their variants warrant citation in the apparatus. I have selected three manuscripts for construction of the text: *A27*, *A28*, and *Y*. I thereby omit the individual variants of Bodleian MS. Rawlinson D. 1048, which by conjunctive errors shows relationship to *A27*. Also omitted are *Ro* and *Don*; their few variants would not assist in creating a better text nor would they reveal authorial revision. *Y* provides the copy-text because it is as correct as any of the other witnesses, though not necessarily superior to them.

The texts of 7–11 are from *Y*, the only witness. Its text is frequently confused, and I have hazarded one or two conjectures where the text was obviously wrong, though errors and gaps remain. Possibly not all the errors are scribal; Davies may not have completed the composition of these poems.

Subject

Edward Coke (1552–1634), having previously served as Solicitor-General, became Attorney-General in 1594. He was widowed in June 1598, and on 7 November of that year married Lady Elizabeth Hatton, the twenty-year-old widow of Sir William Hatton, owner of Corfe Castle (for which Davies sat as Member of Parliament in 1601). The wedding violated so many of the laws—

no banns were read nor licence obtained, the wedding was held in a private
house instead of a church, and at night instead of the lawful morning—that
the pair were threatened by Archbishop Whitgift with excommunication.

The unusual circumstances contributed to rumour, as indicated in a letter
of 22 November from John Chamberlain to Dudley Carleton:

The seventh of this moneth the Quenes atturney married the Lady Hatton to the
great admiration [i.e. wonder] of all men that after so many large and likely offers
[including Francis Bacon] she shold decline to a man of his qualitie, and the world
will not beleve that yt was without a misterie (*Letters*, i. 54).

How widespread was the rumour is indicated by an affidavit by Mary
Berham dated in the *Calendar of State Papers* 30 April 1599, in which she
testifies that William Denis, a servant to the Countess of Warwick, had
spread the story that at 'the beginning of Lent', as he arrived at Lady
Hatton's chamber to deliver a message, he was told she had given birth to
a son, though married only ten weeks.

Denis said . . . he had heard that she was forward with child before she was married;
and that it was no marvel Mr. Attorney wept sitting with the Judges, for he has
gone up and down ever since his marriage like a dead man discomforted. Also that
Mr. Attorney had been sick lately, and no marvel, and that the child was by one of
her servants, who was sent away with a piece of money; that Lady Hatton had never
lived in good name, and that it would kill Mr. Attorney to be so cozened as to assure
1,000 *l.* a year to a bastard (Domestic Series, 1598–1601, pp. 189–90).

The rumour was brought to rest. On 23 August 1599 John Chamberlain
wrote to Dudley Carleton:

The Lady Hatton is brought abed of a daughter, which stoppes the mouth of the
old slaunder, and about ten dayes since it was christened with great solemnitie
(*Letters*, i. 84–5).

Davies's poems were obviously written during the time between Chamber-
lain's two letters, when Coke was the butt of many jokes like these sonnet-
epigrams.

   1.1. *Caecus*: 'the blind man'.
   1.3. *Timpanye*: a swelling.
   1.7. *rowne*: whisper.
   1.10. *Brought . . . meate*: a reference to the proverb 'God never sends mouth
but he sends meat' (Tilley, G207).
   1.11–12. Coke was notoriously a buyer of land, a fact of which Davies
makes much.
   2.1–4. Asturias is a province in north-western Spain famous in Roman
times for its horses. According to Pliny (VIII. lxvii. 166), the mares of Spain
can be impregnated by inhaling the west wind, and in such cases produce
very swift, but short-lived colts.
   2.7. *Olympia*. According to a story that she herself told, Olympias conceived
Alexander the Great by Zeus, not Philip of Macedon.
   2.7. *spirte*: a short time.

3.1. *privement enciente*: pregnant but not known to be (Law French).

3.3. *grossement*: pregnant.

3.5. *dawe*: fool, simpleton.

3.10. *The . . . whelps*: proverbial; see Tilley, B425.

3.11. *crashe*: a short spell.

3.14. *Jeofayle*: the legal plea whereby one admits an error in pleading or procedure (AFr. *jeo fayle* 'I am at fault').

4. The game of primero is something like poker. Before the deal, a stake is agreed on and paid by all players: in addition a higher sum, the 'rest', is fixed. After the deal (four cards to each player), a player can drop out or pay his 'rest' into the pool. The remainder of the game is a matter of drawing and betting, the additional wagers being called 'the vie'. Much of the terminology has sexual implications as well.

4.3–4. *bommecard . . . sparrowes nest*: various ways of cheating at cards.

5.7. *Acteon* came upon Diana bathing; in punishment he was turned into a stag and killed by his own dogs.

5.8. *velvet*: the soft skin covering the budding horns before they break through.

5.10. *Solyman*: Suleiman 'the Magnificent' (1494–1566), Sultan of Turkey.

5.12. *mewing tyme*: the time when a stag sheds or casts its horns.

5.14. *pollard*: a horned animal that has cast its horns.

7.3. *pull*: like 'tug' in 10.14, a word for intercourse.

8.1. *Cooke*. Davies plays on Coke's name, pronounced 'cook'.

8.4. *snatche*: snack; sexual climax.

8.5. *pregnant*: resourceful. In the sixteenth century the primary meanings have to do with mental capacity; *O.E.D.* cites only one sixteenth-century example of 'pregnant' in the usual modern sense.

8.10. *kitchinne stuffe*: a contemptuous term for ends of food that would ordinarily be eaten by the servants; also, kitchen staff and low people in general.

8.12. *snuffe*: sniff at, be grudging about.

9.5. *triall*: 'experience'.

9.9. *Esculapius*: son of Apollo; patron of medicine and healing.

9.11–12. The meaning is obscure; the final couplet, missing in the manuscript, might have paraphrased something in Kings or the Psalms.

10.1. *bargemans*. In *Orlando Furioso* (xliii. 67–144) a bargeman tells the story of the eminent lawyer Anselmus, who marries the beautiful young Argia. She is seduced by Adonio, helped by the fairy, Manto. When Anselmus learns of her infidelity, he tries to have her killed, but she runs away. Looking for her, Anselmus comes to a magnificent castle, the property of a hideous blackamore (actually the fairy, Manto, in disguise), who offers to give him the castle in exchange for homosexual intercourse. Anselmus assents; Argia discovers him, and after she reproaches him for his fault, 'more vile' than her own, they forgive each other.

10.9. *Cocus*: cook. *Jocus*: uncertain; perhaps 'Jock', a common name, to indicate the universality of cuckoldry; or more likely a reference to Joconde (*Orlando Furioso*, xxviii), who, discovering himself to be cuckolded by a servant, learns to accept his wife's infidelity after travels which reveal to him that virtually all women are unchaste.

10.13–14. *case*: in addition to its usual legal meaning, 'vagina'.

tugger: 'tug her'.

11.1. *free*: of gentle birth; licentious.

11.9. *covetous*: not only acquisitive, but lustful.

11.11. Since rumour had Lady Hatton's lover to be a servant, he is here called *Ganimede*, cupbearer to Jove. 'Light' means either to lighten or to descend; the lady relieves him of his burden (semen, called 'Thrise decocted bloud' in NHA 19) which would hinder his vital spirit.

11.14. *paine*: perhaps sexual pain, or perhaps only an inexact word to avoid repeating 'burthen'; on the other hand, cf. 10.10 'pinne'.

12–16

On the Marriage of Lady Mary Baker to Richard Fletcher, Bishop of London

Canon and Text

This series of five popular poems is found in five manuscripts. The poems generally appear in the same order, though the two sonnet-epigrams, 15 and 16, were often copied in other manuscripts by themselves. The entire series appears in *Ro*, four of the five in *Y*, and 15 and 16 in *R* and *LF*—all manuscripts containing many poems by Davies. An internal reference most surely indicates their authorship: in poem 14 Davies writes 'Now tell me Martin...' an address making public his camaraderie with Richard Martin, the charismatic friend to whom at about this time he dedicated his *Orchestra*, and with whom he shared a group of friends at the Middle Temple who very likely formed the first audience for *Orchestra* and the poems on Bishop Fletcher.

The apparatus is selective, to avoid burdening the reader with trivial variants from many witnesses. The copy-text is *Ro*, with corrections from *Tan-I* and *A58*, and, for poems 15–16, from *LF* and *R*. Poems 12–16 also appear in hopelessly corrupt texts in Corpus Christi College MS. 327, while 15–16 appear in Harleian MS. 2127, *Tan-S*, *L740*, and *Y*.

Subject and Date

Richard Fletcher was ordained in 1550; he became Bishop of Bristol in 1589, of Worcester in 1592/3, and of London in 1594/5. Widowed in 1592, he remarried in 1594/5, shortly after his appointment to the See of London was confirmed. His second wife, born Mary Gifford, was the beautiful widow of Sir Richard Baker, and was a woman of high rank and low reputation. The Queen was so angered by Fletcher's remarriage that she suspended him on 23 February 1594/5; the poems, which refer to his notorious pride, but not to a loss of place, were evidently written shortly before then.

13.1–2. *Tarquine . . . Lucres*. Lucretia (Shakespeare's Lucrece), a virtuous Roman matron, was raped by Tarquinius Sextus; she killed herself rather than live with the dishonour of even accidental unchastity.

13.2. *Lais*: a famous prostitute of antiquity.

13.5. *confirmed*: the ceremony of confirmation includes the laying on of hands by the ministering bishop.

14.1. *John London*. John Aylmer, Fletcher's predecessor as Bishop of London, was accused of having depleted the income of his diocese by selling timber from the episcopal estates. He was censured by the Privy Council.

14.2. *Commons*: common or public land.

14.5–6. These lines resemble Martial's epigram on Artemidorus who, to satisfy his lust, exchanged his land for Calliodorus' slave boy: 'Say, which of those two made the better bargain, Auctus? Artemidorus has his pleasure, Calliodorus his plough' (ix. 21).

15.4. *occupier*: resident or possessor of premises; copulator.

16.2. Davies quotes St. Paul's statement in 1 Cor. 7: 9.

17–19

Canon, Date, and Text

Poems 17–19 were printed at the end of Davies's collection of epigrams in the first and second editions, *E1* and *E2*, and headed 'Ignoto'. Perhaps because these are among Davies's coarsest and potentially most offensive poems, they did not reappear in the editions of his epigrams printed after June 1599, when Davies's Epigrams and Marlowe's Elegies were among lewd and satiric works burned in public. This same coarseness must have prevented Davies from claiming them in *E1* and *E2*.

The poems were reproduced along with Davies's epigrams in the photo-facsimile copy of his poems prepared by Clare Howard (*The Poems of Sir John Davies*, New York, 1941), who took them to be Davies's work. So, perhaps, did Davies's contemporary John Marston in 1598. In editing *The Poems of John Marston* (1961), Arnold Davenport points out on pp. 228 and 357 that Marston ridicules Davies under the name *Curio* in several satires, most obviously in *Scourge of Villanie*, xi. 27–34:

> Prayse but *Orchestra*, and the skipping art,
> You shall commaund him, faith you have his hart . . .
> O wits quick travers, but *sance ceo's* slow,
> Good faith tis hard for nimble *Curio*.

Lines 15–20 from *Scourge of Villanie*, vi, which also attack Curio, warrant quotation:

> Think'st thou, that I, which was create to whip
> Incarnate fiends, will once vouchsafe to trip

> A Pavins traverse? or will lispe (*sweet love*)
> Or pule (*Aye me*) some female soule to move?
> Think'st thou, that I in melting poesie
> Will pamper itching sensualitie?

It seems possible that some of these phrases recall not only *Orchestra*, as does 'to trip/A Pavins traverse', but phrases in NHA 18:

> I cannot lispe . . .
> I cannot whine in puling Elegies . . .
> I am not fashioned for these amorous times,
> To court thy beutie with lascivious rimes.
> I cannot . . . sigh ay me,
> Ay me Forlorne: egregious Fopperie.

If so, they indicate that Marston took the poem to be Davies's work.

The appearance of NHA 17–19 in print with Davies's epigrams, and the fact that 17 is a sonnet-epigram and 18 and 19 similar to it, though written in fifteen and sixteen lines respectively, also point to Davies's authorship. The poems have Davies's characteristic features: the alternate rhyme, the colloquial diction and phrasing, the steady, deceptive parallels with their undercurrent of expectation, followed by a surprise couplet as a conclusion. The last was a characteristic of Davies criticized by Ben Jonson, whom Drummond quotes as saying:

A Great many epigrams were ill, because they expressed in the end, what s[h]ould have been understood, by what was said [—]   that of S. John Davies (Jonson, *Works*, i. 143).

Probably they were written about 1594 or 1595, in the same period as the epigrams and *Gullinge Sonnets*.

The poems are found in *E1*, *E2*, and several manuscripts, two of which are used in constructing the texts: *Dyce* and *Rosb* (Rosenbach Foundation MS. 243/4, a miscellany of the early seventeenth century; it contains poems 18 and 19 only). The manuscripts not used are all found in the Rosenbach Foundation, and are all verse miscellanies of the early seventeenth century: MSS. 1083/16 and 1083/17 contain poem 18; MSS. 1083/17 and 239/27 contain poem 19. None has variants worth considering that are not found in *Rosb*, however; hence these manuscripts are not cited in the apparatus. The copy-text is *E1*, corrected to read with *E2*, and occasionally emended from *Dyce* and *Rosb*.

18. It has been suggested by various scholars, most recently by G. A. Wilkes (*Shakespeare Quarterly*, xii (1961), 464–5) that the poem was influenced by the opening soliloquy of *Richard III*:

> He capers nimbly in a lady's chamber
> To the lascivious pleasing of a lute.
> But I, that am not shaped for sportive tricks,
> Nor made to court an amorous looking-glass;
> . . . and want love's majesty
> To strut before a wanton ambling nymph.
>
> (I. i. 12–17)

18.2. *base Viall*: also bass viol.

18.4. *Minikin*: treble string of a lute or viol.

18.10. *Oyling*: flattering.

19.4–5. *bezling . . . bowsing*. Both words mean drinking or guzzling.

19.7. *burbon locke*: the love-lock; see note to Epigram 22.

19.8 *pesant*: Davies may allude to the working-class gesture of tugging a lock of hair to express deference.

19.11. *shootires*: shoestrings.

19.14. *Thrise decocted bloud*: semen.

20

On Ben Jonson

Subject, Canon, and Text

Ben Jonson is clearly the subject of the attack, for he had been apprenticed to a bricklayer, and hence is similarly called a 'foule-fisted Morter-treader' by Marston in *Satiro-Mastix*. His *Sejanus*, first peformed in 1603, used Senecan commonplaces, and provoked violent outbursts from the audience, probably because of its political overtones, which caused Jonson to be summoned before the Privy Council to explain himself.

The epigram has been attributed to three different authors. It appears with the initials of John Hoskyns among his poems in MS. *Che*, but his most recent editor, Louise Brown Osborn, in *The Life, Letters, and Writings of John Hoskyns 1566–1638* (New Haven, 1937), rejects this and four others of the fifteen poems ascribed to him in *Che*. Hoskyns is unlikely to be the author since he and Jonson were close friends. John Aubrey reports that Jonson 'called him [Hoskyns] Father . . . [and said] " 'twas He that polished me" ' (quoted in Jonson's *Works*, i. 3*n*.). Further, while Hoskyns was known as a wit in his own time, the few poems known to be his are primarily Latin and English epitaphs, none so sharply satiric as this piece. This attribution cannot stand.

A second claimant is Henry Parrot, whose Epigram 163 in *Laquei Ridiculosi* (1613) is identical in lines 1–2 and 6 with the present poem. Parrot, however, was a notorious imitator, and admits in Epigram 132 (book ii):

> Some, that my lines have madded, make report
> What er I write is all by imitation.

His Epigram 216, comparing his epigrams to

> apparrell made in Birchin-Lane
> If any please to sute themselves and weare it,

imitates a lost epigram by Davies, referred to by Benjamin Rudyerd in an epigram attacking Davies in *Ro*, and by John Harington in *Metamorphosis of Ajax* (1596):

But as my good friend M. Davies said of his Epigrams, that they were made like dublets in Birchen lane, for every one whom they will serve . . . (ed. Elizabeth Story Donno (1962), p. 184).

Parrot's Epigram 163 is an imitation of the present poem.

Several points favour Davies's authorship. The poem was attributed to him in *Ro*, a manuscript nowhere demonstrably wrong in its attributions to him. Relations between Jonson and Davies seem not to have been cordial, if we may judge from Jonson's slighting references to *Orchestra* and Davies's epigrams. And the poem is like Davies's other epigrams—colloquial, personal, nasty; written in alternating rhyme with a final couplet.

The present text is from *Ro*, emended by *Che*.

21–2

The first little epigram about a country bumpkin obviously challenged a scribe's poetical ingenuity, for it is found (unattributed) in eight lines in a manuscript of Dr. James Osborn, New Haven, Connecticut, and in twenty-eight lines in Bodleian Rawlinson Poet. MS. 120, fol. 23. In *Ro* it appears beside Davies's Epigrams 45 and 46, all attributed to 'J. D.', in its obviously correct version of six lines. The compiler of *Ro* was an Inn of Court man who had frequent and close access to Davies's works, and his attribution of this epigram, as of the sonnet-epigram similarly subscribed 'J. D.' (NHA 22), may be accepted as accurate.

22.8. *Cypresse*: a light transparent fabric of silk or of silk and linen.

23–5

Canon and Text

The first poem appears in four manuscripts, the other two only in *Y*; all are unattributed. Their similarity in diction, style, and attitude to Davies's work, and their position in *Y*, immediately following *The Kinges Welcome*, point to Davies's authorship, especially since NHA 23 must, because of its subject, have been written within a few months of *The Kinges Welcome*, perhaps simultaneously with it. Their appearance together in *Y* makes it very probable that the poems were received at the same time from the same author.

The copy-text for the three poems is *Y*, the best witness for NHA 23, and the only one for NHA 24–5.

23.1. *Curio*: Henry Howard, first Earl of Northampton (1540–1614), as indicated in the titles of this poem in three manuscripts. Although a noted Roman Catholic, he won royal favour immediately after the accession of King James, who was the author of the theological work *Basilikon Doron* (hence 'Basilius' in line 7). On 4 May 1603, Northampton was made a Privy Councillor.

23.3. *jugling*: deceptive, tricky.

23.4. *shaveling*: contemptuous reference to a tonsured ecclesiastic.

23.11–14. Davies proceeds from continental, generally Lutheran theologians and reformers to Calvin and his Scottish followers Knox and Buchanan, tutor to King James, to the English theologians John Jewel, William Whitaker, and John Foxe, author of the 'Book of Martyrs'.

25. This poem is a translation of the *De Milone* ascribed to Martial (Loeb edition, ii. 523).

Love Poems

Ten Sonnets, to Philomel

Text and Date

These poems appear only in *A, B, C, D* (*Poetical Rhapsody*, 1602–21). The reasons for accepting them as Davies's work are given under the discussion of *Poetical Rhapsody* in the Bibliography. The text is from the Houghton copy of *A*, which exemplifies the third state of press-correction in forme inner K, which includes sonnets 3, 6, and 7. The Bodleian and Folger copies represent the second and first states respectively, with several variants in punctuation. In addition, the Folger copy reads *by* for *my* at 3.8; the Folger and Bodleian copies both read *behold* for *behold* at 7.4. The later editions provide a few corrections, but have no authority except that of the printer or possibly the editor, Francis Davison. Their variants are listed only if *A* seems doubtful.

Except for the date of *A*, 1602, we have no evidence for the time of composition. One may conjecture that Davies would not have written a conventional sonnet sequence after parodying such works in his *Gullinge Sonnets*, which probably date from the period 1594–5, yet he wrote the courtly but conventional *Hymnes of Astræa* in 1599. Nevertheless, these sonnets are less pointed, less accomplished metrically, and less original in imagery than most of his later work. A date when sonnet sequences were first in fashion, from 1591 to 1594, therefore seems likely.

1.1. Davies as Melophilus ('lover of song') distinguishes his mistress from those of other sonneteers by her remarkable voice; hence the name Philomel ('nightingale').

1.2. *assaile*. Hyder Rollins (ed.), *A Poetical Rhapsody 1602–1621*, ii (1932), 178 writes: 'Possibly *availe* means "to take advantage of", but I suppose *assaile*, the reading of *BCD*, is correct.'

3.4. *Favour*: attractiveness, beauty.

5. Theseus accompanied the Athenian youths and maidens who were destined to be sacrificed to the Minotaur. He promised his father that if he succeeded in killing the monster, his returning ship would replace the customary black sail with a white one; when he forgot, Aegeus, assuming that Theseus had died, jumped into the sea (or, from the Acropolis, according to another version) to his death.

6.1–2. Davies seems to be referring to the notion of the eyes projecting beams as Philomel glances at him.

7.5–6. According to Pliny (VII. xxxvii. 125) Alexander decreed that only Apelles might paint his portrait.

Elegies of Love.

The elegies appear here rearranged slightly from their order in *L*, the only textual witness for three of the four, and therefore the copy-text for the present edition. The elegy I have placed first is separated from the others in *L*, where it appears some folios later, without a number, though headed 'Elegies of Love'. The elegy I place second lacks a title or number in *L*; apparently the scribe's copy was torn, for the poem is a fragment without its beginning. It is followed in *L* by Elegies 3 and 4, numbered as here. The present arrangement therefore restores that originally intended.

There is no external evidence for a date of composition. The first two stanzas of the third elegy, however, are extraordinarily close to lines 37–40 and 45–8 of *The Kinges Welcome*, written on James's arrival in England. Possibly Davies was mining old material, borrowing from the elegies for his poem to the king, but even if he did, the elegies seem to date after *Nosce Teipsum* (1598–9), to which lines 17–18 of the first elegy appear to refer when Davies mentions

> . . . sadder studyes, and with grave conceite,
> Which late my'Immagination entertaynd.

4.20. I emend 'your' for 'the' in *L* because 'the' appears to have been carried over from the previous line, whereas 'your' is evidently the meaning intended.

Occasional Poems and Poems from Entertainments

All poems in this section were obviously written for a particular occasion or entertainment, but the actual occasions for the three poems printed last are unknown, as are their dates of composition.

To George Chapman on his Ovid and Another

Among five prefatory sonnets to George Chapman's *Ovids Banquet of Sence* (1595), the fourth and fifth are headed 'I. D. of the middle Temple' and 'Another', which in the context appears to mean 'Another by I. D.' These initials, sufficient to identify Davies's authorship of the *Epigrammes* published at about the same time, must therefore, when referring to a poet of the Middle Temple, mean John Davies.

Ovids Banquet of Sence is an erotic narrative of the type of *Venus and Adonis*. It teaches a neo-Platonic doctrine of love: sensual gratification is necessary to arouse the mind to spiritual love, but the mind cannot be satisfied with the merely physical. Chapman thus spiritualizes Ovid, singing 'deeper misteries' in Ovid's vein.

In *The Art of Love* Ovid calls himself 'praeceptor Amoris', the teacher of love; he says that he has been taught by experience, not by the muses, and invokes the help of Venus, not Phoebus. We have not traced the story of Venus kissing Apollo while hunting on Delos, referred to in 'Another', lines 5–8.

To Sir Thomas Egerton

The poem exists only in Davies's holograph, on the single sheet of paper which he sent to Egerton. His manuscript is reproduced exactly except that abbreviations have been expanded and Davies's lower case 'as' in line 2 has been capitalized. Sometimes his upper and lower case are indistinguishable.

The Ellesmere Calendar of Manuscripts, though not always accurate, correctly dates this poem 1599, when Egerton's second wife died and when Davies was directing his attention toward Egerton, who, as Lord Keeper, was particularly qualified to have Davies restored to the Middle Temple. The poem accompanied the gift of a book, as indicated by Davies's subscription to the poem, in which he refers to Montaigne's essay, 'Of Three Commerces or Societies' (III. iii):

A French writer (whom I love well) speakes of 3 kindes of Companions: Men, Women, & Bookes; the losse of the second makes you retire from the first, I have therefore praesum'd to send your Lordship one of the third kind, which (it may bee) is a stranger to your Lordship, yet, I persuade me, his conversation will not be disagreeable to your Lordship.

Epithalamion

The poem is found in only one witness, MS. *LF*, which was probably copied from Davies's own papers. Except for two obvious errors and three letters trimmed away in binding, the text requires no emendation.

The epithalamion celebrates the marriage of Elizabeth Vere, daughter of the Earl of Oxford and grand-daughter of Lord Burghley, to William Stanley, Earl of Derby. The wedding, attended by the Queen, was held at Greenwich on 26 January 1595, and was the occasion for lavish entertainment that may have included *A Midsummer Night's Dream*, sometimes thought to have been written for the marriage (see E. K. Chambers, *William Shakespeare* (1930), i. 359). Davies's epithalamion was probably used as part of a masque, with each of the muses presenting her separate sonnet. Masques were customary entertainment for important Elizabethan weddings, and we know that Arthur Throckmorton wrote to Robert Cecil asking to present a masque of the muses for this wedding:

If I may I mind to come in a masque, brought in by the nine muses, whose music, I hope, shall so modify the easy softened mind of her Majesty as both I and mine may find mercy. The song, the substance I have herewith sent you, myself, whilst the singing, to lie prostrate at her Majesty's feet till she says she will save me. Upon my resurrection the song shall be delivered by one of the muses, with a ring made for a wedding ring set round with diamonds, and with a ruby like a heart placed in a coronet, with this inscription *Elizabetha potest*. I durst not do this before I had acquainted you herewith, understanding her Majesty had appointed the masquers, which resolution hath made me the unreadier: yet, if this night I may know her Majesty's leave and your liking, I hope not to come too late, though the time be short for such a show and my preparations posted for such a presence. I desire to come in before the other masque, for I am sorrowful and solemn, and my stay shall not be long. I rest upon your resolution, which must be for this business to-night or not at all. (*Hatfield MSS.*, v. 99, quoted in *Elizabethan Stage*, i. 168.)

Possibly Throckmorton's masque, if it was held, was written by Davies, but Throckmorton's intent was to recover lost royal favour by presenting the Queen with a jewel, whereas Davies's poem is directed toward the wedding couple rather than toward softening the Queen's mind.

The identification of Davies's epithalamion with Throckmorton's masque is only conjectural; nevertheless, the epithalamion must have been written as an entertainment of some sort. This explains its concentration on a few epithalamic conventions to the exclusion of the others. The muses extol the nobility of the two families; they comment repeatedly on the excellence and felicity of the match; they wish the bride fruitfulness; they express their hope that the marriage will be a loving union, and end by wishing them long life and promising immortality.

While all these are important conventions well suited to the celebration of an illustrious public marriage, others are omitted: except for Terpsichore's reference to dancing, there is no mention of the events of the wedding-day such as the gathering of the procession and the bedding of the bride. Nor does the poet-speaker play his usual role of master of ceremonies.

Davies's poem is one of the earliest epithalamia in English, and one cannot define the form with only three or four possible exemplars. Only the refrain is common to all: Sidney's 'Let mother earth' (*Poems*, ed. W. Ringler (1962), p. 91), Spenser's *Epithalamion*, and Donne's 'Epithalamium made in Lincolns Inne', of uncertain date. Davies probably had not seen Spenser's poem (entered in November 1594 and printed sometime in 1595), but clear traces of Sidney are found, the most striking being the following lines, which resemble Davies's *Epithalamion*, 107–10.

> And like two rivers sweete,
> When they though divers do together meete:
> [Let] one streame both streames containe.

(After the above section had been written, and during the time that this volume was passing through the press, J. R. Brink published a note connecting Throckmorton's letter with Davies's *Epithalamion*. She observed, additionally, that the ruby to be given to Queen Elizabeth by Throckmorton, who was Raleigh's brother-in-law, may be referred to in *F.Q.* IV. viii. 6, lines 4–9; 7, lines 1–4. See 'The Masque of the Nine Muses: Sir John Davies's Unpublished "Epithalamion" and the "Belphoebe-Ruby" Episode in *The Faerie Queene*', *R.E.S.* xxiii (1972), 445–7).

1–8. Cf. *Orchestra*, stanzas 17, 102, and Sidney's epithalamion, which opens by saying that 'justest love doth vanquish *Cupid's* powers' (line 3).

15. *Clio*. The muses' songs are related to their special functions: Clio is the Muse of History; she is followed by the Muses of Comedy, Tragedy, Lyric Poetry, Dancing, Erotic Poetry, Sacred Poetry and Mime, Epic Poetry, and Astronomy and Prophecy.

15–18. The Stanleys held high offices under every king from Henry VI onwards, and married well. The bridegroom had succeeded his brother as Earl of Derby ('Raysd by the heavens') less than a year before the wedding.

20. *mother*: Anne Cecil, daughter of Lord Burghley.

47. *warlike Vere*: Sir Francis Vere, whom Davies praised in Epigram 40.6.

67. *palme trees*.

Pliny . . . attributes both Sexes and Wedlocke unto trees: and first he instanceth upon the Palme-tree; the love betweene whom is such, that if the female be far disjoined from the masculine, it becomes barren and without fruit (W[illiam] B[asse], *A Helpe to Discourse* (1638) p. 26; cf. Pliny, XIII. vii. 31–5 and Batman, p. 309).

Sidney's epithalamion mentions the elm and the vine (line 15), and turtle doves, which 'live one in two' (line 7).

79–82. Cf. *Orchestra*, 111–12.

An Entertainment at Harefield

The entertainment is in two parts, the first consisting of the Song and Lots, together referred to as *A Lotterie*, and the second consisting of *The Humble Petition*.

Canon and Text of A Lotterie

R. W. Bond, misled by a Collier forgery, erroneously attributed *A Lotterie* to John Lyly (*Works*, 1902). The reasons for recognizing it as Davies's work are given in the section on *Poetical Rhapsody* in the Bibliography, as are descriptions of the four textual witnesses: *A22*, *Mann*, *Con*, and *B*. The earliest version of *A Lotterie* is found in *A22*, a manuscript dating from about 1602–5 which has early versions of other poems by Davies. Although it omits the Song, it has thirty-eight lots, omitting one found in *Con* and *B*, and providing five not in the other witnesses. Although these five are among the last, they are not the final lots, and hence are unlikely to have been lost through physical damage to the last sheet of a manuscript. Three of the five omitted were lots for country wenches, and two were blanks. Probably Davies prepared a copy of *A Lotterie* to be read after the entertainment had been held, and elected to drop the lots of low members who were outside the court and outside his reading audience.

If *A22* is earliest, *B* and *Con*, which lack five lots found in *A22*, derive from a later common exemplar. One would expect them to read in agreement against *A22*, yet *A22* and *Con* often agree against *B* (the first printed edition). These differences in *B* may be explained not as errors, but rather as alterations for the press: some of the sharpness of the original is softened. For example, 'For you hate fooles and flatterers, her beste frendes' becomes 'For that you love not fooles that are her friends' in *B*. Were there reason to believe that Davies was himself responsible for the alterations in *B*, it would serve as copy-text. *B*, however, has a number of errors, some, such as *hit* for *fit* at 3.2, probably of misreading, but others more likely to derive from the printer's copy. I have therefore chosen *Con* as copy-text for the poems. It was probably written in 1602 or 1603, for its title refers to Queen Elizabeth as if she were alive. Like *A22*, it preserves the list of recipients of the lots, omitted from *B*. In the eight instances where recipients in *A22* and *Con* differ, I have kept the readings in *Con*.

I have also followed *Con* in its order of presenting the lots. *A22*, representing an earlier stage of the text, may in fact be more accurate here, but it is frequently so unreliable textually that I have not wished to follow it. The order in *B* is obviously arranged for the press, and does not reflect the disposition of the lots in the entertainment itself. *B*, however, has the only full description in prose of the manner of distribution of the gifts, and hence serves as copy-text for this material.

The remaining witness, *Mann*, has only sixteen lots, with attributions

identical to those in *Con*. Conjunctive and disjunctive readings indicate that
these two manuscripts are textually related but derive from an exemplar not
shared by *A22* and *B*. The following stemma shows their relationship.

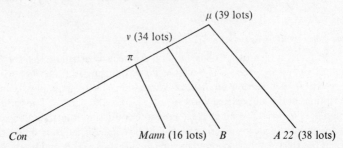

The readings of *Con* in the present text are abandoned whenever *A22*
agrees with one or more of the other witnesses; those of *A22* are listed when
they are not obviously wrong. All but the most minor variants of *B* are
listed, since, although they probably represent Francis Davison's alterations,
it is possible that *B* preserves some alterations made later than *Con* and *A22*,
though I think this unlikely.

The Song is printed with music in Robert Jones's *Ultimum Vale* (1608),
sig. E2ᵛ. Its text probably derives from *B*, and its few minor variants from the
composer's altering the verse to fit his music. A similar text, with music,
is found in British Museum MS. Add. 24665 (Giles Earle's book, 1615), fols.
19ᵛ–20ʳ.

Canon and Text of The Humble Petition

These verses are found in MS. *Con*, and in *Nichols*, where they are printed
from a manuscript containing *A Lotterie* and two prose dialogues, one
between a Bailiff and a Dairy-maid, another between Place and Time.
Grosart's reasons for attributing the prose dialogues and verses to Davies
are entirely convincing (*Poems*, i. cx–cxvi). Many of these lines to Elizabeth
echo Davies's prose and poetry elsewhere. For example, the first line may be
compared with 'Beauties fresh rose and virtues livinge booke', *Contention*,
line 220), and the remainder of the first stanza with the Dedication of *Nosce
Teipsum* to the Queen, lines 29–32, 1–2, and the fourth Hymn of Astræa,
lines 15–16.

There is little difference between the two extant texts; I have chosen to
follow *Con*.

Occasion

Davies wrote these verses for an entertainment given by Sir Thomas
Egerton, Lord Keeper of the Great Seal, during a visit by Queen Elizabeth
to Harefield, his house on the Colne, 31 July–2 August 1602.

It was customary to use masques and entertainments as opportunities for gift-giving. The Song that begins the entertainment allowed Egerton opportunity to present Elizabeth with a jewel. The prose introduction to the Song suggests that some type of stage device representing a ship was employed, for the Mariner appears from 'the Carrick'. Grosart identifies the carrick as a Portuguese ship captured by the English the previous June with a cargo valued at a million ducats (*Poems*, i. cxi–cxii).

The lots were not drawn by chance; the intended recipients were named. Most of the lots were designed to reflect some trait for which the recipient was noted. For example, Lady Anne Clifford received this lot:

[17] *A Lace.*
Give hir the lace thatt loves to be straite laced;
Soe fortunes little gifte is aptly placed.

She later wrote of herself: 'for I gave myself wholly to retiredness, as much as I could', and is described as

frugal in her personal expenses, dressing, after her second widowhood, in black serge, living abstemiously, and pleasantly boasting that 'she had never tasted wine and physic'. She was possessed of a very strong will, and was tenacious of her rights to the smallest point. (*D.N.B.*; for her own writings see *H.M.C.* 11th Report, part 7, *Hothfield MSS.*, p. 88.)

Most of the recipients were Elizabeth's Maids of Honour, though a few were probably friends of Egerton and his wife.

The *Petition* was read to Queen Elizabeth as she was presented with a robe on her departure from Harefield after the weekend, on Monday, 2 August 1602. It was very probably followed by the prose dialogue between Place and Time, written by Davies and printed by Grosart in *Poems*, i. 255–6.

Song, 6. There is no fishing comparable to sea-fishing nor service comparable to royal service. The line is proverbial; Tilley (F336) cites three earlier examples, to which Rollins (ii. 209) adds a fourth.

7. *Thetis*: a sea-nymph, daughter of Nereus and mother of Achilles.

The Lots. For explanations of unfamiliar clothes, see notes to Epigram 22 and Gullinge Sonnet 6.

Lot 5. *Snuffkin*: a muff.

Lot 23. *Coyfe*: 'a close-fitting cap covering the top, back and sides of the head'—*O.E.D.*

Crosscloth: 'a linen cloth worn across the forehead'—*O.E.D.*

Lot 25. *Falling Bande*: a white collar which is attached to a band under the chin and falls on to the doublet.

Lot 26. *stomacher . . . windowes*: a triangular ornamented cloth covering the V-shaped opening in the bodice; the windows are ornamental openings.

The Humble Petition

   Title: *Lady Walsingham*: wife of Sir Thomas Walsingham.

   7. *Saint Swithin*. According to legend, if it rains on St. Swithin's Day (15 July) it will rain for forty days.

   14. *Iris*: the personification of the rainbow; also a messenger of the gods.

   22. *the ladye*: Queen Emma, mother of Edward the Confessor. Accused of treason, she requested trial by fire: at Winchester Cathedral she walked barefoot over red-hot iron bars, led by two weeping bishops. St. Swithin, who had died two hundred years before, miraculously interceded to preserve her from pain and injury.

A Contention

Textual introduction

   There are three textual witnesses: MSS. *Υ* and *A22*, and the printed text *B* (*Poetical Rhapsody*, 1608). All are described in the Bibliography, and the reasons for accepting *A Contention* as Davies's work are also given there, under the discussion of *Poetical Rhapsody*.

   I base my text on *Υ*, the manuscript of Sir Christopher Yelverton, a judge who apparently received Davies's poems from Davies himself. Like *B*, it appears to be a revised version probably deriving from a scribal copy prepared at Davies's request soon after its presentation as an entertainment. Textually *B* and *Υ* are similar, but *Υ* has fewer errors in diction and the assignment of speeches.

   A22, a manuscript with an unrevised version of Davies's *Lotterie*, contains an early, unrevised version of *A Contention*, with variant readings and with the speeches arranged in eccentric sequence. The unusual speech-order might be explained by *A22* having been copied from loose prompt-sheets written for the performers, which reached the copyist of *A22* out of sequence, except that it is impossible to rearrange the groupings of speeches in *A22* into a coherent sequence. A more satisfactory explanation is that *A22* was copied from Davies's rough drafts, in which the arguments were composed often in four-line stanzas and then assembled and rearranged upon their completion. This explanation accounts for all units of speeches in *A22* (whether of one or several stanzas) being complete except for two stray lines, 129 and 224. It also accounts for the opening twelve stanzas having remained together: the first ten provided the narrative preparation necessary for the arguments and could not be rearranged. It means that three stanzas found in *A22* but omitted by *B* and *Υ* were discarded after composition, a satisfactory explanation since they cannot be inserted into the texts of *Υ* and *B* without disturbing the argument.

   The sequence in *A22* is as follows: 1–48, 137–40, 49–52, 161–4, 61–76, 93–6, 77–84, 97–100, 193–204, 145–8, 133–6, 165–76, 85–8, 53–6, 177–88, 101–4, 153–60, 109–20, 189–92, three stanzas omitted by *Υ* and *B*, 129,

213–22, 224, 149–52. It omits 57–60, 89–92, 105–8, 121–7, 130–2, 141–4, 205–12, 223, 225–40. The three stanzas omitted by *T* and *B* are given here:

Wife.

Is not the Sonne the worlds great hart & ey
a Bridegrome to the earth the earth his bride
Which makes hir flourish & to fructifie
Which causeth both hir plenty & hir pride.

Wid:

But when the Earth the Sonns great heate hath borne
she then at last putts on a widowes tyer
yet then she moste enjoyes hir fruite & corne
& though the Sonn be gone she wants no fier.

Mayd.

Yet would the Sonn be farr more bright & pure
But that suche vapors from the earth doth springe
Which Darkneth hir light & hir beames obscure
suche is the Dowre yea gentle wifes do bringe.

[*yea* is probably a misreading of yᵗ.]

The present text follows *T* except where it is obviously wrong or where *A22* and *B* agree against it and are not clearly incorrect.

Occasion and Source

The *Contention* was performed before the Queen on 6 December 1602.

On Munday last the Queene dyned at Sir Robert Secils newe house in the Stran. Shee was verry royally entertained, richely presented, and marvelous well contented, but at her departure shee strayned hir foote. His hall was well furnished with choise weapons, which hir Majestie tooke speciall notice of. Sundry devises; at hir entraunce three women, a maid, a widdowe, and a wife, eache commending their owne states, but the Virgin preferred (*Mann*, fol. 75ᵛ; *Diary of John Manningham*, ed. John Bruce (1868), pp. 99–100).

As Hyder Rollins noticed (ii. 215), Samuel Rowlands anticipated the *Contention* with his *Tis Merrie when Gossips meete*, entered in the Stationers' Register on 15 September 1602. His dialogue between a maid, wife, and widow is by comparison unrefined and distractingly colloquial.

66. *her . . . seene.* Daphne, daughter of the river-god Peneus, hated the idea of love and wanted to be a virgin forever. Apollo fell in love with her and pursued her; in her flight she called on her father for help, and was transformed into a bay tree. Apollo adopted the leaves as his emblem, bestowing on them the gift of perpetual greenness (Ovid, *Met.* i. 452–567).

109. *Dunmowe.* At Dunmow Priory in Essex, a married couple could claim a side of bacon if they swore that they had not quarrelled or regretted their marriage in the previous twelve months. The custom is referred to in *Piers Plowman*, C.xi.276 and the *Wife of Bath's Prologue*, 218; it lapsed at the dissolution of the priory, but has been revived frequently by the town.

110. *apes.* It was proverbial that old maids would lead apes in hell (Tilley, M37); Beatrice treats the idea amusingly in *Much Ado*, II. i. 37–45.

189–92. Davies revised these four lines but did not work out his speech headings. In *A22*, lines 189–92 follow lines 119–20 (using the line numbering of the present text); the six lines together read as follows in *A22*:

> M[aid] But happiest Maides who harts are calm & still
> whome hope nor feare nor love nor hate doth trouble
> For when they wed their merry daies are past
> Wife Nay then the Maide becomes sweete pleasure guest
> for maydenhead is a continuall fast
> and marriage is a continuall feast.

The above lines from *A22* probably reflect the original sequence. Davies then changed the line now numbered 189 from that of *A22*, 'For when they wed their' to 'If I were widowe my', and gave the speech to the Wife instead of the Maid. He then gave the speech which was originally the Wife's to the Widow; but in so doing he inadvertently made the Widow defend marriage as a 'continuall feast'. To avoid this anomaly I give lines 191–2 to the Wife, as did Grosart, but the emendation, which requires the Wife to complete a speech begun by the Widow, remains somewhat unsatisfactory.

197. *jewell.* We have not traced Davies's reference.

217. *Christall glasse.* Rollins (ii. 218) cites Sir Thomas Browne's *Pseudodoxia Epidemica*, vii. 17, for the legend 'that poyson will break a Venice glass'.

231. *chattring pyes.* The Pierides were changed into magpies for challenging the Muses to a singing-contest (Ovid, *Met.* v. 294).

Verses . . . upon . . . Trenchers

Text

The canonicity of these verses is discussed under *Poetical Rhapsody* in the Bibliography. They are found in six textual witnesses, three of them derivative and without textual importance. The first derivative witness is a set of wooden trenchers with verses inscribed upon them (not the original set of the title) in the Victoria and Albert Museum, case N. 30, 1912. Their text is corrupt, probably deriving from *C*, an edition of *Poetical Rhapsody* (1611), with which it has conjunctive errors. Its variants not found in *C* are only by chance supported by the manuscripts. The second is Bodleian Rawlinson Poet. MS. 84, fols. 44ᵛ–43, which has only four of the twelve sets of verses; their few variants are without authority. The third is John Maynard, *The XII Wonders of the World: for the Violl de Gambo, the Lute, and the Voyce* (1611), which derives from *B* (*Poetical Rhapsody*, 1608).

The three witnesses used to construct the present text are the printed edition *B* and MSS. *Dow* and *A22*. In *Dow*, a manuscript that was written consecutively, Davies's verses are found preceding an entry of 1605. Their title refers to the author as 'Mr. Davis', which he would not have been called by those who knew him after he was knighted in December 1603; the scribe, however, may have been following the title in his copy, so that he need not have entered the verses by 1603. The date of the transcript in *A22* is similar to that in *Dow*, between 1602 and 1605.

The witnesses reflect different states of revision in the poem. *A22* and *Dow* share conjunctive readings not found in *B*, and *B* and *A22* share conjunctive readings not found in *Dow*. Probably *Dow* preserves the earliest extant version, with *A22* and *B* descending from an archetype containing authorial corrections, which made the verses less offensive by removing certain criticisms—of wives going masked, and of priests serving the courts, for example. Since revisions in *B* blunt the satire even more, one might suppose that *B* represents Davies's final revision. Such a conclusion is difficult, however, because the other texts in *B* do not reflect Davies's alterations for the press. I think it more likely that the variants in *B* derive from the editor or printer, and therefore have based the present text on *A22*, the more revised of the two manuscripts.

The sequence of the speeches is similar in all witnesses, except at two points: *B* places the Lawyer before the Physician, and *A22* and *Dow* do not, though a seventeenth-century hand in *Dow* corrects to the sequence of *B*, entering by the Lawyer, 'This is misplasd, it should be before the Phisicion'; and, while all witnesses place the Merchant before the Country-Gentleman, the same hand writes by the Country-Gentleman in *Dow*, 'This is misplacd, in the originall it is before the Merchant'. There is no reason to suppose that by 'originall' he meant 'author's copy' rather than simply his copy; as *Dow* is unsupported by either *B* or *A22*, I have not followed its suggested sequence here.

Occasion

In the early seventeenth century trenchers were more widely used than plates at dinners. Sometimes they were embellished with epigrams, proverbs, or witty verses like those by Davies. The following description accompanies a set, dated about 1610, housed at the Victoria and Albert Museum:

Elizabethan dinner-parties, especially at the New Year, were often followed by a 'banquet' of marchpane and other sweetmeats, somewhat similar to dessert. The trenchers [flat serving plates, generally of wood] were decorated 'on their back sides' with designs and inscriptions intended to raise a laugh as each guest turned up his 'lot'. They were often made for amusement. . . . The trade of trencher-makers preferred old-fashioned themes . . . proverbs, and the like.

The title in *Dow* indicates that Davies's verses were written specifically for Thomas Sackville, Lord Buckhurst, the Lord Treasurer. Grosart (*Poems*, i. cxviii, quoting B.M. Lansdowne MS. 88, art. 2, fol. 4) noticed that a letter from Davies to Buckhurst's secretary, Sir Michael Hicks, apparently accompanied these verses:

Mr Hicks I have sent you heer inclosed that cobwebb of my invention which I

promised before Christmas; I pray you praesent it, & commend it, & grace it, as well
for your owne sake, as mine. bycause [~~you first~~]\by your / nominacion I was first putt
to this taske. for which I acknowledge my self beholding to you, in good earnest,
though the imployment be light & trifling; bycause I am glad of any occasion of
being made knowne to that noble gentl. whom I honour & admire exceedingly./if
ought be to be added or alter'd, lett me heare from you, I shall willingly attend to
doo it, the more speedily if it be before the terme./

> So in some hast I comend my
> best services to you
> Chancery Lane; 20 Janu 1600.
> Yours to do you
>
> > Service very willingly
> > Jo: Davys.

These present verses were written for a Lord Treasurer, are 'light & trifling',
and could have been a New Year's Day gift since New Year's Day might
be either 1 January or 26 March.

1.2. *sell . . . smoke*: to cheat with false promises. The use of 'smoke' in
this sense was proverbial; see Tilley S575–6. Thomas Nashe, in *Nashes
Lenten Stuffe* (1599; *Works*, ed. McKerrow (1958), iii. 225), says that 'the king
of fishers vouchsafed you [fishermen] for his subjects, that for your selling
smoake you may be courtiers'. Rollins (ii. 200) cites several other analogues.

2.2. *Chop-churche*: a person who makes a profit by exchanging benefices.

2.3. *mother*: a reference to the judgement of Solomon (1 Kings 3: 16–28).

5.4. *bill*: a medical recipe or prescription.

6.3. *for stall . . . engross*: ways of monopolizing goods so as to get higher
prices. To forestall is to prevent sales at the open market by selling the goods
in advance or by buying them before they reach the market; to engross is to
buy up an entire stock.

6.6. *Jewish use*: usury.

12.2. *leade an Ape*: see note to *Contention*, 110.

12.6. 'Rather a man without money than money without a man' (Tilley,
M361). Rollins cites several examples (ii. 202).

> *The Kinges Welcome*
> and
> *To the Queene at the Same Time*

Text

The first poem is found in an early version in *L*, and in a revised version
with three additional stanzas in *Y*, which serves as copy-text. The second
poem appears only in *L*.

Occasion

These companion poems were written to honour King James and his
consort, Anne of Denmark, on their arrival in England in 1603.

Kinges Welcome, 5–6. We have not found details about the eagle sent to the German Emperor from Nuremberg.

17–20. These lines refer to *Nosce Teipsum*, which James reportedly admired. According to Anthony Wood, Davies was among the first to reach the new monarch in Scotland in 1603, and being presented to him, was asked if he were '*Nosce Teipsum* Davies' (*Athenæ Oxonienses* (1815), i. 402).

37–40. Cf. *Hymnes of Astræa*, xiv.

46–48. Cf. *Elegies of Love*, 3. 5–8.

57–60. Cf. Hooker, *Laws* (VIII. ii. 12):

Where the king doth guide the state, and the law the king, that commonwealth is like an harp or melodious instrument, the strings whereof are tuned and handled all by one, following as laws the rules and canons of musical science.

Mira Loquor etc., Charles his Waine, Of the Name etc.,
Verses . . . with Figges.

These four poems all appear together in *L*, the only textual witness. The first three were certainly, and the fourth, by its position in *L* with the others, almost certainly written to King Charles soon after the death of King James on 27 March 1625. On 1 April 1625 Davies wrote:

As soon as I heard of the death of King James, I came up from Englefield to kiss King Charles' hands and renew my patent of King's Serjeant, both which I have done this day. . . . The young King doth already show many excellent tokens of a stout, a wise, and a frugal prince, and is like to restore the glory of our nation by his wisdom and valour (*H.M.C. Hastings* (1947), ii. 67).

Mira Loquor . . . Est: 'I speak wondrous things; the sun has set, but no night has followed'. This Latin verse, the epitaph of a medieval English king, was praised by Davies in his speech on epitaphs before the Society of Antiquaries in 1601.

Charles his Waine. In Ursa Major is Charles's Wain, a group of seven very bright stars forming a wain, or waggon; Arcturus is the driver.

Of the Name of Charolus. C(*h*)*arus* means 'dear' or 'precious'; the diminutive 'carulus' means 'darling'.

5. *Edgar*: king from 959 to 975, during which period the nation enjoyed a time of singular peace and national unity.

Verses . . . with Figges. Davies was a wealthy man with a number of estates. Possibly he is referring to a garden in his house in the parish of St. Martin-in-the-Fields, London, or more likely at Englefield, Berkshire, where his family lived in 1625–6.

To the Ladyes of Founthill

Founthill. The ladies of Founthill were the daughters of George Touchet, Lord Audley, who owned Fonthill Gifford in Wiltshire, near Davies's birthplace, Tisbury. Eleanor Touchet became Davies's wife.

A Sonnet

A Sonnet, 13–14. Batman, fol. 132ᵛ, records this idea of the sun: 'Though he be not hot of himselfe, yet he hath vertue of heating, of leeming [i.e. lighting up], & of burning'.

Other Poems

The poems in this section, all minor, are taken from the only textual witness for them, MS. *L*, except for the first and last of the group, which appeared only in printed texts. For several poems no evidence exists for specific dates of composition.

A Hymne in Prayse of Musicke

The reasons for including this work in the Davies canon are given in the Bibliography under *Poetical Rhapsody*, the four editions of which provide the only copies of the poem. The present text is from the first of these, *A*, which, being published in 1602, provides a *terminus ad quem* for the date of composition. The readings of the Bodleian and Houghton copies of *A* have been adopted in preference to the variants in the Folger copy at lines 21 and 24: *delighted*, not *delighte*; *doth*, not *with*.

Clare Howard's note in her edition, *The Poems of Sir John Davies* (1941), mentions that the ideas found here are all to be found in John Case's much longer prose work *The Praise of Musicke* (1586), and they are present in both works not because the poem is indebted to Case but because Davies uses entirely conventional arguments in defence of music. For the tradition of the musical *apologia*, see John Hollander, *The Untuning of the Sky: Ideas of Music in English Poetry 1500–1700* (1961), pp. 118–19.

Of Faith

Davies's description of faith is entirely orthodox; this conception of faith underlines *N.T.* 197–200, 257–64.

11. *virgins Lamp*: See Matt. 25: 1–13.
12. *Jacobs scales*. See Gen. 28: 12.

A Songe of Contention

The title recalls Davies's *A Contention between a Wife, a Widowe and a Maide*, written in 1602 to entertain Queen Elizabeth. To judge from its contents, this song was also written for an entertainment. If so, the years 1599–1602 are the likeliest period of composition.

A Maids Hymne in Praise of Virginity

Many of these lines seem particularly appropriate to Queen Elizabeth. The hymn appears likely, in view of the close similarity of many of its lines to *A Contention*, to have been written about 1602.

3. *Rosy Crowne*. The rose is often a symbol of virginity.

9. *baye*. See note to *Contention*, line 66.

11. *vine*. Cf. *Contention*, lines 53–6.

16. *unspotted garment*. Cf. *Contention*, line 223.

Part of an Elegie

9–23. The story of the androgynes is told by Aristophanes in Plato's *Symposium*, 189–92.

To the Queen

The poem is clearly written to Queen Elizabeth, probably between 1599 and 1603 when Davies was most assiduously courting royal favour.

Upon a Coffin by S.I.D.

This riddle appears in four witnesses. It is unattributed in two seventeenth-century verse miscellanies that have no other work by Davies: Bodleian MS. Rawlinson Poet. 172, fol. 9ᵛ (abbreviated *RP172*), and B.M. Sloane MS. 1446, fol. 37ʳ (abbreviated *S14*). It is attributed to 'S. I. D.' in two printed works. One is a prose pamphlet by William Parkes, 'sometime Student in Barnards Inne', an Inn of Chancery. Written in legal phraseology, his work, *The Curtaine-Drawer of the World* (1612), includes scattered verse, this riddle being among its four epigrams. The second is *Philosophers Banquet*, 1614 (abbreviated *PB*). The translator gives his initials as 'W. B.'; the author is identified in the *Short-Title Catalogue* as Sir Michael Scott. It is a small book of advice on morals and conduct with epigrams by Owen, Harington, Heath, and others. Some of its poems were taken from manuscript, as is evident from the compositor's misreadings, but the present poem may have come from Parkes. The initials 'S. I. D.' in 1612, when referring to an epigrammatist, would mean Sir John Davies.

The present text follows Parkes; it is identical with *PB* and similar to *RP172*.

3. *refuse*: relinquish, give up.

The Psalmes

Davies's metaphrase of the Psalms reflects his nature as a poet and as a thinker. Whereas Sidney sought metrical variety to make the psalter more lyrical, Davies reduced the psalms to closed couplets. Clearly his poetic talents lay somewhere besides lyricism.

The work reflects also Davies's essential conservatism. Unable, as far as we know, to read Hebrew, he was dependent on translations. The manuscript in which the Psalms are found indicates that they were composed in 1624. If so, Davies had a wide choice of translations, but he ignored the recent Authorized Version, the Geneva Bible of 1560, and the Bishops' Bible. Instead, he relied largely on Coverdale's 'Great Bible' (1540); there are echoes also of Sternhold and Hopkins's *The Whole Booke of Psalmes,* and some indication that he consulted the Latin translation by Immanuel Tremellius.

The clearest example of Davies's use of the Great Bible is the twenty-third Psalm, which Coverdale renders as follows:

> The Lord is my shepheard: therefore can I lacke nothing.
> He shall feede me in a greene pasture: & lead me foorth beside the waters of comfort.
> He shall convert my soule: and bring me forth in the paths of righteousnesse for his names sake.
> Yea though I walke thorow the valley of the shadowe of death, I wil feare no evill: for thou art with me, thy rod and thy staffe comfort me.
> Thou shall prepare a table before mee against them that trouble me: thou hast anoynted my head with oyle, and my cup shall be full.
> But thy loving kindnesse and mercie shal follow me all the dayes of my life: and I wil dwell in the house of the Lorde forever.

'Crooke' in Davies's line 10 was altered, perhaps in recollection of Sternhold's 'rod and shepheards crooke'.

Whereas Sidney's psalms were probably intended for publication, Davies's version represents perhaps the most private poetry in his canon. From that point of view his choice of the most familiar translations of his time is natural. The Psalter of the Great Bible was used in the liturgy and bound with the Prayer Book, and the metrical psalter of Sternhold and Hopkins provided the text and music for singing psalms in church. Davies versified the psalms as he knew them best.

18.59+The manuscript preserves here a line which Davies rewrote and intended to remove.

34.35 *Gods present helpe the [contrite heart] doth finde.* The necessary emendation is from the Great Bible; the scribe of *L* probably carried 'Lord' over from line 33.

Latin Poems

The text of Davies's epitaph on his son is from *Che*, and that of the anagram on his daughter from Wood, ii. 404. Wood mentions the occasions for both poems:

By this Elianor, sir Joh. Davies had issue a son, who was a natural idiot, and dying young, the father made an epitaph of four verses on him, beginning 'Hic in visceribus terræ, '&c. So that the said Lucy being sole heiress to her father, Ferdinando lord Hastings (afterwards earl of Huntingdon) became a suiter to her for marriage; whereupon the father made this epigram. [Text follows in Wood, loc. cit.]

The date of his son's birth and death is not known, but on 13 May 1617 Sir Robert Jacob wrote to Davies, who was in London:

I am of the opinion that if your son Jack were now put into the hands of some skilful man, he might be brought to speak. For he is wonderfully mended in his understanding of late, for he understands anything that is spoken to him without making any signs, so as it is certain he hath his hearing, and then the defect must be in his tongue. Your lady no doubt will use all means she may to recover him. (*H.M.C. Hastings*, iv. 17.)

Lucy and Ferdinando married in 1623, when he was fifteen years old and she not yet eleven. Davies's verses must have been written shortly beforehand.

Poems Possibly by Davies

The poems appearing here may be by Davies; the evidence available is insufficient to allow a firm conclusion. They are in two sections: the first containing poems ascribed to Davies in manuscript, the second poems which, though nowhere ascribed to him, occur in manuscripts of his work and seem for various reasons possibly to be by him. To simplify reference, I have numbered the poems.

I

Poems Ascribed to Davies in Manuscripts

I

This extraordinarily popular epitaph appears in thirteen manuscript copies in the Bodleian alone. Of more than twenty copies which I have seen, only one is attributed—to Davies, in Bodleian MS. Rawlinson Poet. 117, apparently compiled by someone at an Inn of Court. The specificity of the title, which identifies the child as that of Arthur Chichester, Davies's immediate superior as Lord Deputy of Ireland from 1604 to 1614, suggests that the attribution is probably correct, especially since other witnesses give no specific occasion. I have not, however, thought the one ascription, in a manuscript otherwise unconnected with Davies's work, sufficient reason to include the poem in the Davies canon.

2–4

These three poems are attributed to Davies in Bodleian MS. Rawlinson Poet. 148, the verse miscellany of John Lilliat, who used the subscription 'q^d D.' for Davies's Epigrams 14 and 29, which appear on fol. 4^r, and the three poems printed here, which appear on fol. 4^v. Miss Margaret Crum of the Bodleian has pointed out to me that Lilliat frequently attributes poems to himself which are by other writers, and that the manuscript is most unreliable. Poems 2 and 4 I have not found elsewhere. Number 3 appears anonymously in many manuscripts, though it is attributed to John Hoskyns in Bodleian MSS. Eng. Poet e. 40 and Rawlinson D. 1372 and in Camden's *Remaines*. (See Louise Brown Osborn's *The Life, Letters, and Writings of John Hoskyns 1566–1638* (1937), p. 281.) One of the most interesting references to the poem is in British Museum MS. Cotton Faustina E. v., fol. 171^v. There Davies, in his holograph copy of a speech delivered to the Society of Antiquaries in 1600, says 'The epitaph of the bellowes maker is in every mans mouth'. One cannot say whether his admiration is for the work of another or himself.

II

Poems Appearing Among Davies's Works

5–9

These poems have been found only in *Ro*; their location in this manuscript and their style suggest they may be by Davies. They are coarser than any poems to which Davies gave his name in print, but not coarser than some of his epigrams found in manuscript. Number 9 was imitated by Henry Parrot in *Laquei Ridiculosi* (1613), book i, epigram 164.

10

This poem is found in *Dyce*, immediately preceding NHA 17–19, and appears to have been entered at the same time as they.

11

This poem is probably by either Davies or the Earl of Clanrickard. It appears in three manuscripts.

MS. *Don*, in an entry dating between 1610 and 1620, entitles the poem, 'Of the last Queene by the Earle of Clanrickard'. One's difficulty in evaluating the ascription is that no other verse by Clanrickard is known, though he might, as a gentleman, have written verse occasionally.

MSS. *Y*, and *Burley* (described by Sir Herbert Grierson in *The Poems of John Donne* (1912), i. 437–8) have no attributions. In *Burley* the poem appears among Donne's work, though different from it. It may have been placed there by someone who saw a copy with initials 'J. D.' and understood 'John Donne', not 'John Davies'. In *Y* the poem was entered at the same time as a poem referred to in Edmund Lodge's *Illustrations of English History*, iii (1791), 146–7, which may be dated September 1602, a period when Davies wrote a number of verses to entertain Elizabeth.

The principal reason for suggesting Davies's authorship lies in the similarity between certain lines and images in this poem and those in Davies's known work. Its first stanza is almost indentical to Davies's Love Elegy 3, stanza 2, and is similar to *The Kinges Welcome*, lines 45–8; moreover, lines 15–16 resemble Davies's *A Sonnet sent with a Booke*, lines 13–14. If the poem is not by Davies, then probably Clanrickard wrote it, copying from Davies.

12

This poem appears unattributed in MS. *Y*. Lines 22–4, which somewhat resemble the concluding lines of Davies's Dedication to Elizabeth of *Nosce Teipsum*, indicate the poem was written to the Queen for Christmas, 1602. In the years in which he sought restoration to the Middle Temple, and after, much of Davies's writing was to entertain the Queen or pay tribute to her. The extravagant fancy of some of the metaphors and the easy movement in alternate rhyme are sufficiently like Davies's other work to justify making the poem available to his readers, though not to attribute it to him.

13

Too little evidence surrounds this 'Complaint' to allow a firm conclusion about its authorship. Grosart (*Poems*, ii. 256–8) followed Nichols in attributing it to Davies. Nichols took his text from an eighteenth-century copy by Ralph Churton of a seventeenth-century manuscript containing the complete Harefield Entertainment. Churton's transcript and the manuscript he copied are unknown today, but Nichols quotes Churton's description of his copy:

This 'Complaint' is on a separate leaf, and seems to be in a different hand, though little, if at all, more recent than the other. It does not appear when or how the 'Complaint' was introduced; and it may possibly be doubted whether it formed a part of the Entertainment, though it probably did. The title, 'Entertainment of Q. Eliz.;' &c. is written on the back of this paper: but the title as already said, is in a later hand (iii. 595).

The 'Complaint' is unlike the other known parts of the entertainment, Davies's *Lotterie* and 'Song' and his two prose dialogues. The dialogue between a Bailiff and a Dairy-maid was given on the Queen's arrival; that between Time and Place was a device to present the Queen with a jewelled anchor on her departure:

But now, since I perceave this harbour is too little for you, and you will hoyse sayle and be gone, I beseech you take this Anchor with you. And I pray to Him that made both *Time* and *Place*, that, in all places where ever you shall arrive, you may anchor as safly, as you doe and ever shall doe in the harts of my Owners. (Grosart, *Poems* ii. 256.)

The 'Complaint' could hardly have followed immediately after this farewell speech and gift, as Grosart and Nichols present it. It might have been used as part of an antimasque, but if so the masque is missing that might confirm such a conjecture.

The 'Complaint' is not found in *Con*, a manuscript in which the title given to the Harefield Entertainment does not suggest incompleteness:

The devyses [to] entertayne hir Majestie att Harfielde, the house of Sir Thomas Egerton Lord Keeper and his Wife the Countess of Darbye. In hir Majesties Progresse. 1602.

The only other appearance of the 'Complaint', in *H39*, a verse-miscellany, omits all mention of the entertainment and enters the poem without attribution, entitling it 'Satires'. Without more information about the 'Complaint', I should not want to say it was the work of Davies.

BIBLIOGRAPHY

BIBLIOGRAPHY

The Bibliography describes briefly most works used in determining the the canon and in constructing the texts of Davies's poems. It omits only those few works used once, for minor poems; they are discussed in the Commentary. Printed books are described in the Bibliography according to the sequence given below; descriptions of manuscripts follow, arranged alphabetically according to their sigla.

PRINTED BOOKS

Nosce Teipsum
   1599
   1622
Hymnes of Astræa
   HA1599
   (See *1622* under Nosce Teipsum.)
Orchestra
   1596
   (See *1622* under Nosce Teipsum.)
Epigrammes
   E1
   E2
Miscellaneous
   A, B, C, D (Poetical Rhapsody 1602–21)
   Chapman
   Nichols
   Wood

[*1599*] Nosce teipsum. This Oracle expounded in two Elegies. 1. Of Humane knowledge. 2. Of the Soule of Man, and the immortalitie thereof. London, Printed by Richard Field for Iohn Standish. 1599.

4°: A–L⁴ M²; [*8*] 1–64 '85–101' *82–4*.

Contents: A1 blank; A2 title, verso blank; A3ʳ⁻ᵛ dedication: To my most gracious dread soueraigne, *signed* 'John Dauies'. A4 blank. B1–4ᵛ text of first elegy with head title '*Of humane knowledge*'. C1–M1ʳ text of second elegy with head title: Of the soule of man, and the immortalitie thereof. M1ᵛ–2ᵛ blank.

Notes: the error of pagination begins with the new sheet K. Some copies lack full stop after 'Elegies'. The first setting of B has 'within' at B3ʳ, line 3, the second setting 'which in'. The first setting of C reads 'lights of' at C1^r, line 1; the second setting italicizes these words. For a full bibliographical description, see *The Carl H. Pforzheimer Library: English Literature 1475–1700* (1940) i. 259. The second edition, *1599(2)*, may be distinguished from the first by its comma rather than full stop after the date in the title, and by the following readings: 'emptie of' for 'of emptie' at B2^r, line 1; 'great' for 'gerat' at C1^v, line 7; omission of a comma after 'powre' at D1^r, line 4. Bodleian and Library of Congress copies of *1599(2)* have sheets B and C from *1599*.

Copies examined: *1599*, British Museum (2), Harvard, Huntington, Trinity College, Cambridge (3); *1599(2)*, Bodleian, Rylands.

Copy-text: British Museum C. 34. f. 22.

S.T.C. 6355; *S.R.* 14 April 1599.

[*1622*] Nosce Teipsum. This Oracle expounded in two Elegies. 1. Of Humane Knowledge. 2. Of the Soule of Man, and the immortalitie thereof. Hymnes of Astræa in Acrosticke Verse. Orchestra. Or, A Poeme of Dauncing. In a Dialogue betweene Penelope, and one of her Wooers. Not finished. London, Printed by Augustine Mathewes for Richard Hawkins, and are to be sold at his Shop in Chancery Lane, neere Serieants Inne. 1622.

8°: A–K^8 L^4; [6] 1–81, *82–161*.

Contents: A1 blank; A2 title, verso blank; A3^{r-v} dedication: To My Most Gracious Dread Soveraigne, *signed* Iohn Davies.

A4–7^v text of first elegy with head title: Of Humane Knowledge. A8–F4 text of second elegy with head title: Of the Soule of Man, and the Immortalitie thereof, verso blank. F5 second title: Hymnes of Astrea . . . 1622, verso blank. F6–H2^v text of hymns. H3 third title: Orchestra . . . 1622, verso blank. H4 dedication: To The Prince, verso blank. H5–L3^r text of *Orchestra* with head title: Orchestra. Or, A Poeme . . . of Dauncing. L3 verso, L4 blank.

Notes: Errata in some copies on L3^r; Folger copy (pressmark 6359.2) has variant title, with *Orchestra* in capitals, followed by a comma instead of a full stop.

Copies examined: Bodleian, British Museum, Trinity College, Cambridge.

S.T.C. 6359.

[*HA1599*] Hymnes of Astræa, In Acrosticke Verse. London, Printed for I.S. 1599.

4°: A–D^4 (–D3–4 ?blank); not paginated.

Contents: Ai title, verso blank; Aii–Dii^v text of poems.

Copies examined: Bodleian, Huntington.

Copy-text: Bodleian Malone 292.

S.T.C. 6351; *S.R.* 17 November 1599.

[*1596*] Orchestra Or a Poeme of Dauncing. Iudicially proouing the true obseruation of time and measure, in the Authenticall and laudable vse of Dauncing. Ouid. Art. Aman. lib. I. Si vox est, canta: si mollia brachia, salta: Et quacunque potes dote placere, place. At London, Printed by I. Robarts for N. Ling. 1596.

8°: A–C⁸; not paginated.

Contents: A1 title, verso blank; A2 dedication: To his very Friend, Ma. Rich: Martin, verso blank; A3–C8ᵛ text of poem with head title Orchestra. Or A Poeme of Dauncing.

Copies examined: Bodleian, Huntington.

Copy-text: Bodleian Malone 407.

S.T.C. 6360; *S.R.* 25 June 1594.

[*E1*] Epigrammes and Elegies. By I. D. and C. M. At Middleborugh.

8° in half-sheet imposition: A–G⁴ (–A1, G4 ?blank); not paginated.

Contents: A1 blank?; A2 title, verso blank; A3–D3ᵛ text of 48 epigrams, concluding: Finis. I, D. D4ʳ⁻ᵛ text of three poems (NHA 17–19 in the present edition) with head title, Ignoto, *concluding* Finis. E1 second title: Certaine Of Ovids Elegies. By C Marlow, At Middleborugh Verso blank. E2–G3ᵛ text of elegies, concluding: Finis.

Notes: British Museum copy wants A4. *S.T.C.* numbers *E1* and *E2* 6350.

Copies examined: British Museum, Pforzheimer.

Copy-text: no textual differences between the two extant copies.

[*E2*] Epigrammes and Elegies. By I. D. and C. M. At Middleborough.

8° in half-sheet imposition: A–G⁴ (–A1, G4 ?blank); not paginated.

Contents: A1 blank?; A2 title, verso blank; A3–D3ᵛ text of 48 epigrams, concluding: Finis. I. D. D4ʳ⁻ᵛ text of three poems (NHA 17–19 in the present edition) with head title, Ignoto, *concluding* Finis. E1 second title: Certaine Of Ovids Elegies. By C. Marlow. At Middleborough. Verso blank. E2–G3ᵛ text of elegies, concluding: Finis.

Copy examined: Huntington.

[*A, B, C, D*] Poetical Rhapsody, 1602, 1608, 1611, 1621.

Five works by Davies appear in the four editions of this Elizabethan miscellany originally compiled and edited by Francis Davison. These four editions, in their essential features, have been reduced and edited by Hyder Edward Rollins in *A Poetical Rhapsody, 1602–1621* (2 vols., Cambridge, Mass., 1931), and are referred to as *A*, *B*, *C*, *D*. He gives full bibliographical details of the works and examines the manner in which they were compiled, the authority of their texts, and their interrelationships. My references are to his edition. Rollins writes of the contributors:

The authorship of the various poems in *A Poetical Rhapsody* offers far more difficulties than is the case in any other Elizabethan miscellany. It is doubtful just what attributions are made, who made them, and how much faith is to be put in them. One will notice that Francis Davison, the collector and first editor of the book, expressly washes his hands of the attributions which, he insists, were made by the printer in defiance of his instructions. John Bailey [the publisher] is made to appear chiefly responsible for inserting the authors' names, though most of them must surely have been communicated to him by Davison. (ii. 36.)

Francis Davison's disclaimer of the attributions is given in his address 'To the Reader' in *A*:

Being induced, by some private reasons, and by the instant intreatie of speciall friendes, to suffer some of my worthlesse Poems to be published, I desired to make some written by my deere friend *Anomos*, and my deerer *Brother*, to beare them company: Both without their consent, the latter being in the low Country Warres, and the former utterly ignorant thereof. My friendes name I concealed, mine owne, and my brothers, I willed the Printer to suppresse, as well as I had concealed the other: which he having put in, without my privity, we must both now undergoe a sharper censure perhaps than our nameles works should have done, & I especially. . . . If any except against the mixing (both at the beginning and ende of this booke) of diverse thinges written by great and learned Personages, with our meane and worthles Scriblings, I utterly disclaime it, as being done by the Printer, either to grace the forefront with Sir *Ph. Sidneys*, and other names, or to make the booke grow to a competent volume. (i. 4–5.)

Davison does not say whether the printer has taken the additional poems from Davison's manuscript without his permission, or has supplied them from elsewhere. Possibly Davison allowed their printing, and wrote his address only to protect himself. It should be noted that he does not accuse the printer of wrong attributions. Whoever provided the attributions, in the first two editions he is never demonstrably wrong. Rollins concludes:

Careful study of the various editions convinces me that *D* is worthless in its attributions of authorship; that *B* and *C* are usually to be trusted for the new poems they include, while sometimes they corroborate (and once, in No. 170, correct) *A*; and that *A* shows signs of rather careful editorial supervision of authors' names or pseudonyms. (ii. 39.)

The appearance of Davies's poems may be set out in a table.

	A	*B*	*C*	*D*
A Hymne in prayse of Musicke.	I. D.	I. D.	I. D.	[Anon.]
Ten Sonnets, to Philomel.	Melophilus.	I. D.	I. D.	I. D.
Yet other 12. wonders of the world [*Verses upon Trenchers*].	[Omitted]	Iohn Davys	Sir Iohn Davys	Sir Iohn Davis

	A	B	C	D
A Lotterie.	[Omitted]	I. D.	I. D.	Sir I. D.
A Contention betwixt a Wife, a Widdowe and a Maide.	[Omitted]	Iohn Davys	Sir Iohn Davys	[Anon.]

A contemporary reference confirms Davies's authorship of *A Contention*. In a letter to Sir Dudley Carleton on 23 December 1602, John Chamberlain wrote:

You like the Lord Kepers devises so yll, [i.e. Davies's *Lotterie*] that I cared not to get Master Secretaries that were not much better, saving a pretty dialogue of John Davies twixt a maide, a widow and a wife, which I do not thincke but Master Saunders hath seen (*Letters*, i. 177–8).

Davies's authorship of *Twelve Wonders* is confirmed by the title in MS. *Dow*, 'Verses given to the L: Treasurer upon Newyeares day upon a dosen of Trenchers by Mr. Davis.' Although *A Lotterie* appears without authorial attribution in all extant manuscripts, *Poetical Rhapsody* provides clear evidence of Davies's authorship.

In *B*, *A Lotterie* is subscribed 'I. D.' and placed directly between *A Contention* and *Twelve Wonders*, which are there subscribed with his full name. An editor would not enter the initials 'I. D.' beneath a poem and place it between two others subscribed 'Iohn Davys' if he thought it to be by another author. That the initials 'I. D.' meant 'Iohn Davies' to Davison is indicated by his notes in British Museum MS. Harl. 280, which contains a 'Catalog of the Poems contayned in Englands Helicon' (fols. 99–101^v) in his hand. As Rollins points out, the catalogue was made 'not from personal knowledge, but from the pages of the printed book' (ii.70). In copying the list Davison expanded some abbreviations of the printed text. At John Dickenson's 'The silly Swaine . . .' he erroneously expanded 'I. D.' of the printed text to 'I. Davis', no doubt because he automatically associated Davies's name with these initials.

Two questions of attribution remain. *A Hymne in Prayse of Musicke* is attributed to 'I. D.' in *A*, *B*, *C*; *Ten Sonnets, to Philomel* is attributed to 'Melophilus' in *A*, to 'I. D.' in *B*, *C*, *D*. No modern editor of Donne considers them his work; the evidence pointing to Davies is succinctly outlined by Brinsley Nicholson in 'Donne, or Sir John Davies?', *The Athenaeum*, 29 January 1876, pp. 161–2:

Davison, with a full knowledge that he had already appropriated I. D. to the author of the 'Hymn in Praise of Music' [in *A*] affixed these initials to the 'Lottery,' [in *B*] and at the same time, and as if to distinguish the I. D. pieces from the others, and show their inter-connexion, altered the 'Melophilus' of the Sonnets to I. D.

John Donne himself seems to refer to Davies as the author of *Ten Sonnets, to Philomel* or as author of *A Lotterie*, or perhaps of both. In his mock-catalogue of books written about 1604–5, *The Courtier's Library, or Catalogus Librorum*

Aulicorum incomparabilium et non vendibilium (ed. Evelyn Mary Simpson, with a translation (1930), pp. 47–8), number 16 attacks Davies:

16. The Justice of England. Vacation exercises of John Davies on the Art of forming Anagrams approximately true, and Posies to engrave on Rings.

The anagrams are Davies's *Hymnes of Astræa*; the posies suggest both the ninth Sonnet to Philomel, entitled 'Upon sending her a Gold Ring, with this Posie [:] Pure, and Endlesse' and his third Lot:

> 3. *A Ring with this Poesye, As faithfull as I finde.*
> Your hande by fortune on this ringe doth lighte,
> And yett the word doth fitt your humor righte.

Donne may well have had both poems in mind.

If five poems in *Poetical Rhapsody* are by Davies, who provided the copies of the poems? It may have been Davison, or the printer, or someone else, but it appears not to have been Davies. Though the texts of *A Hymne* and *Ten Sonnets* appear to be free from corruption, no other texts are available to compare with those in *Poetical Rhapsody*. Its texts of *A Lotterie*, *Contention*, and *Twelve Wonders* are not as good as those of the best manuscripts. Although they might have come from Davies (whose manuscript, given to the printer of *Nosce Teipsum*, evidently had a number of errors), very likely they came from someone else.

Rollins credits Francis Davison with preparing many of the poems for the press and with correcting *A* to be used as printer's copy for *B*, an edition with some of Davison's own poems. Sometimes revisions of texts in *B* are acceptable, others are bad—in one case the rhyme is destroyed (ii.78). One cannot know whether the revisions restore original readings or simply alter the poems to conform with another taste. Davison seems to have had little to do with *C* and *D*; their corrections come from the printing house. *Poetical Rhapsody* provides good texts for miscellaneous poems, but its frequent and unexplained differences from the manuscripts, and our ignorance today of the reasons for its variants and alterations within different editions make it unreliable as a copy-text for Davies's poems in those cases where good manuscripts are available.

Copies examined: Bodleian, Folger, Houghton. *S.T.C.* 6373–6.

[*Chapman*] George Chapman, *Ouids Banquet of Sence*. 1595. *S.T.C.* 4985.

Five prefatory sonnets introduce the volume, including one headed 'I. D. of the middle Temple', beginning 'Onely that eye which for true love doth weepe', on sig. A3ᵛ, and one following it on A4ʳ headed 'Another', beginning 'Since *Ovid* (loves first gentle Maister) dyed'. Both are evidently by Davies.

[*Nichols*] John Nichols, *The Progresses and Public Processions of Queen Elizabeth*. 3 vols., 1823.

Volume three contains a copy of the Harefield entertainment, including the songs beginning 'Beauties rose and vertue's book' and 'Tell me, O Nymphes, why do you', on pages 586–93.

[*Wood*] Anthony Wood, *Athenæ Oxonienses*. ed. Philip Bliss, 4 vols., 1813–1820.

A life of Davies and the text of his Latin anagram on his daughter appear at ii. 400–5.

MANUSCRIPTS
(Arranged alphabetically according to their sigla)

[*A22*] British Museum. Additional MS. 22601.

4° 105 original leaves $5\frac{1}{2} \times 3\frac{5}{8}$ inches in a modern binding. Some leaves have a watermark with a pot and initials P. O. Most of the material copied in this miscellany of prose and verse relates to the years 1602–5: fols. 3–7^r contain letters dated 18 December 1604 and February 1605, fols. 10^v–11^r a petition dated 7 May 1603, fols. 17^v–18^r Raleigh's letter to King James after his arraignment in 1603, for example. Davies's *Verses upon Trenchers* appear without title on fols. 40–3^r, his *Lotterie*, dated 1602, on 49–51^r, and his *Contention* on 66–71^v.

It appears that the manuscript was written by or for someone at court, for it contains Davies's royal entertainments, letters and petitions to the King, tournament speeches by important peers, and, notably, on fols. 24–36^v, texts of many of King James's poems. These texts evidently are rare, since James Craigie's edition, *The Poems of James VI of Scotland* (Scottish Text Society, 2 vols., 1955–8) mentions only one manuscript containing them, British Museum Additional MS. 24195. The compiler seems to have had access to poems and court entertainments not often found in other manuscripts.

[*A27*] British Museum. Additional MS. 27407.

This manuscript consists of loose sheets of verse and prose, pasted into a modern binding, written in many hands from the sixteenth to eighteenth centuries. On fols. 51–2^r appears the series of six sonnets on Caecus, entitled 'In Caecum causidicum Epigr:' (NHA 1–6).

[*A28*] British Museum. Additional MS. 28253.

A large folio manuscript consisting of loose sheets of varying paper in varying hands. On fol. 7^{r-v} appear the six sonnets on Caecus, without title (NHA 1–6).

[*A58*] British Museum. Additional MS. 5832.

An eighteenth-century manuscript with transcripts of some sixteenth and seventeenth-century poems, entirely in the hand of the Revd. William Cole, who in 1783 left 92 volumes to the British Museum. On fol. 205^{r-v} Cole transcribed six poems on Bishop Fletcher from a manuscript he identified as 'MS. Crewe': NHA 12–16 and a sixth, beginning 'Marriage they say is honourable in all'.

[*AC*] Alnwick Castle, Northumberland. MS. 474. The Duke of Northumberland.

4° 52 leaves, $8\frac{3}{8} \times 6\frac{9}{16}$ inches, bound in original white vellum with the arms of Northumberland and the order of the garter stamped in gold on front and back. The paper bears Briquet water-mark 8423, which, though in use from 1582 to 1605, is most often found in manuscripts of the period 1597–1600. Special dedicatory verses to Prince Henry, Earl of Northumberland, are in Davies's holograph, but the text of *Nosce Teipsum* and the dedication to Queen Elizabeth are in a scribal Elizabethan secretary hand, written with five stanzas to each page. Throughout the manuscript Davies inserted some corrections, and most of the punctuation; his punctuation is distinguishable from that of the scribe because Davies's ink was black and the scribe's reddish. Where the scribe entered large words in bold italic, most often where new sections of the poem begin, Davies outlined the letters with his pen to enlarge them and thereby highlight their importance.

[*Ca*] Cambridge University Library. MS. Kk. 1. 3.

Folio, $11\frac{1}{4} \times 7\frac{5}{8}$ inches. A large volume in twenty-four parts composed of papers in several hands, mostly of the late sixteenth and early seventeenth centuries, treating a wide variety of topics. A collection of forty-three epigrams by Davies, written in two columns, appears on fols. 12–16^r of Part I.

[*Che*] Chetham's Library, Manchester. MS. 8012.

4° 122 leaves, $7\frac{3}{4} \times 5\frac{5}{8}$ inches, in a nineteenth-century binding. Watermark: pot with initials P. O. similar to that found in *A22*. This miscellany of prose and verse has been printed by Alexander B. Grosart, *The Dr. Farmer Chetham MS. being a Commonplace-Book in the Chetham Library, Manchester*, in the Chetham Society Publications (1873), vols. 89 and 90. *Che* is written in many hands, but the contents are so closely related to one another as to suggest it was compiled by one person who asked others to write entries in his manuscript. Its entries date from 1599 to the 1620s. The compiler probably had connections with an Inn of Court, for some of his entries are found also in manuscripts with Davies's poems compiled by lawyers, such as *Y*. *Che* has the largest extant collection of the poems of John Hoskyns, with whom Davies shared rooms at the Middle Temple. Hoskyns's verse is extremely rare, as he printed none himself and little has survived in manuscripts bearing his name.

The compiler of the manuscript may have known Davies personally or, more likely, knew of him in his years at the Middle Temple: he copied a series of epigrams by Benjamin Rudyerd mercilessly attacking Davies under the name of 'Matho'; these appear aiso in *Ro. Che* attributes two works to 'Mr.' Davies, neither of which has survived elsewhere: ten *Gullinge Sonnets,* and a Latin epitaph on Davies's son. A third poem (NHA 20) it attributes to Hoskyns.

[*Con*] Folger Shakespeare Library, Washington, D.C.

MS. V. a. 172. (Conway Papers)

Con, a small group of papers, was first described and printed by Peter Cunningham, in *The Shakespeare Society's Papers,* ii (1845), 65–75. *Con* then belonged to John Wilson Croker, but later passed to the Folger Shakespeare Library. A printed description from a bookseller's or auctioneer's catalogue now accompanies it:

On the envelope of the letter, Mr. Croker has written in respect to a portion of his collection. 'All those (letters) which once belonged to the Conway Papers, were given to me by Lord Hertford to make a volume for myself, like a very fine and curious one which I made for him. All the Conway Papers contained in the old chest are stamped with the words "*Conway Papers*" in printed characters.'

Part of these 'Conway Papers' are now British Museum Additional MS. 23229, a collection of loose papers of the Conway family dating from the seventeenth to the nineteenth centuries, now pasted into a modern binding. All the papers in Add. MS. 23229 that are from the early seventeenth century, including some miscellaneous verse, appear to descend from Sir Edward Conway, later Viscount Conway of Conway Castle, who held several important governmental posts in the early seventeenth century. Letters appear to him written from 1612 onwards from Lady Dorothy Conway, his first wife, and Lady Katherine Conway, his second. After his death they must have remained in the family until Lord Hertford gave them to Croker.

Con is undoubtedly from the same collection, of which Add. MS. 23229 is only a part, given by Lord Hertford to Croker, for each leaf bears the similar stamp 'Conway Papers'. Probably *Con,* like the seventeenth-century papers in Add. MS. 23229, also descends from Sir Edward Conway.

Con consists of six loose leaves. Fols. 1–4^r are blank. Fols. 4^v–6^r contain three parts of the Harefield entertainment: the poems 'Beauty's rose' and 'Cynthia queen of seas and lands', followed by thirty-four Lots which conclude with 'Finis'. The remainder of fol. 6^r is blank, but fol. 6^v has a poem on the five senses ascribed to William Haddon. The text is written in Elizabethan secretary hand; the names of the recipients of the Lots are entered in the margin in an italic hand. After revising the poem Davies probably ordered several scribal copies made, of which *Con* may be an example, or it may be a copy of Davies's scribal copy, which came into the possession of Sir Edward Conway.

[*Don*] Bodleian Library, Oxford. MS. Don. c. 54.

This handsome folio manuscript of 66 leaves, $14\frac{1}{8} \times 9$ inches, still in its original vellum binding, was compiled and owned by Richard Roberts, as Professor I. Ll. Foster has pointed out to me. Roughly the first half of the manuscript consists of poems in English, and the last half of poems in Welsh, though occasionally correspondence was entered as well. Many poems are from acquaintances in Wales, addressed to Roberts in London, asking him to send them things from the city, or seeking to introduce friends or relatives to him; in addition, some Welsh bards entered their verses in their own hand in the manuscript. Possibly more than one hand entered the poems in English as well, but I find no evidence that poets copied their own verses there. *Don* was apparently compiled at various times from about 1602 (fol. 45$^\mathrm{v}$) till at least as late as 1621 (fol. 2). Professor Foster informs me that the Welsh poems in *Don* identify Roberts as a justice and a wealthy man who spent much time in London. No doubt he knew of Davies, and he may have known Davies personally, for at fol. 2$^\mathrm{r}$, among poems on that folio dated 1619 and 1621, he recorded a couplet evidently directed at Davies and his wife, a notorious prophetess thought by many of her contemporaries to be mad:

> In my conceit Sir John you were to blame
> To make your quiet goodwife a madde dame.

On fol. 6$^\mathrm{v}$ he recorded six sonnets (NHA 1–6) attacking Edward Coke under the name *Caecus*, which are followed by several other poems attacking him as *Cocus*, a name used in NHA 7. They are written in a variety of forms; at the end of the *Cocus* series is subscribed 'FINIS. this last per Sir John Haidon as was thought'.

On fol. 7$^\mathrm{v}$ appears PP 11, followed by 'A servant of Diana as faithful as the best'; the only two known extant copies of the poem appear here and in *Y*, the manuscript of the judge Sir Christopher Yelverton. Since other material in *Don* appears also in *Che*, *Y*, and *Ro*, manuscripts connected with Inns of Court, and is seldom found elsewhere, it is evident that Roberts was in a circle of legal acquaintances that exchanged verses with one another. Roberts, however, entered some of his poems years after their composition. NHA 1–6 appear under the title:

A libell upon Mr. Edw: Cooke, then Atturney generall and sithence Cheefe Justice of the Comon pleas upon some disagreement betweene him & his wife being widow to Sr. Wm. Hatton Kt. and daughter to the now Earle of Exeter then Sr. Tho: Cecill.

The poems were not 'upon some disagreement' but upon her supposed pregnancy; they were written in 1598, but the title refers to Coke as Chief

Justice of the Common Pleas, a position he gained in 1606. Since Roberts evidently copied some of the poems into *Don* after having received them on loose sheets some years earlier, his attributions must be viewed with caution.

[*Dow*] Downing College, Cambridge. MS. 'Wickstede Thesaurus'.

Folio, $11\frac{3}{4}\times7\frac{3}{4}$ inches, in two parts of 174 and 150 leaves each. A preliminary modern note describes the manuscript as 'Partly in the hand of I. Wickstede formerly mayor of Cambridge &c.', apparently referring to Part 2 of *Dow*, which is concerned with Cambridge affairs. Davies's *Verses upon Trenchers* are the only poetry in a manuscript consisting otherwise of miscellaneous prose, entered consecutively over a period of many years. Fol. 6^r concludes a list of monarchs with a reference to Elizabeth, 'who hath reigned already 1597 39 yeares and long may she reigne', which was later altered to 'died the 24 of Marche 1602 when she had reyned 44 yeares 4 monthes & 7 daies'. Fols. 18^v–25^r contain entries from a journal dated 1598; fols. 25^v–7^r Davies's *Verses*; fol. 28^r a poor man's petition to the King, undated here but dated 7 May 1603 in the copy in *A22*; and fol. 29^r a copy of a letter dated 1605.

[*Dyce*] Victoria and Albert Museum. Dyce MS. 44.

4° $5\frac{11}{16}\times3\frac{9}{16}$ inches. 117 leaves, in a nineteenth-century binding. Inside the cover is a note 'Given to me by Mr. Bristow No. 19[,] 1800; Brought from Mr. Brockman's', which note is identified by a later hand as a 'memorandum by Todd'. Alexander Dyce wrote of the manuscript on an introductory leaf,

This valuable MS. belonged formerly to Todd; and from it were published in Park's ed. of *The Harleian Miscellany* thirty-eight Sonnets by Constable which do not appear in the printed copy. Todd received the MS. as a present from Alderman Bristow, who had been a bookseller at Canterbury, and who had bought it along with the library of a family in Kent.

Most recently the manuscript was used by Joan Grundy in her edition, *The Poems of Henry Constable* (Liverpool, 1960). She believed it to date 'probably from the early seventeenth century' (p. 84).

Constable's sonnets end on fol. 43^r, and the section of poems in that hand on fol. 56^v. On fols. 56^v–7^v a different hand has entered four poems printed in the present edition: PP 10, NHA 17–19; these texts derive from unknown manuscript copies. Miscellaneous poems follow, including on fol. 80^r three of Davies's printed epigrams; conjunctive errors show the texts of these three epigrams to derive from the third, fourth, or fifth printed editions.

[*F*] Folger Shakespeare Library, Washington, D.C. MS. V. a. 399.

A seventeenth-century commonplace-book containing twenty-five of Davies's epigrams grouped together in a collection on fols. 60–2^r.

[*H*] British Museum. Harley MS. 1836.

4° 25 leaves, 7⅝ × 5⅝ inches, pasted into a nineteenth-century binding, but the original sequence is preserved, as is indicated in the numbering of the leaves. The watermark throughout is a pot with flowers and the initials 'R. O.' The manuscript was probably written in about 1631. The compiler is unknown, but his hand is not the same as that which entered 'Ex spoilys Richardi Wharfe' on the outer leaf, nor is it the same as that of R. Wharfe, the Puritan divine who in 1644 compiled British Museum Add. MS. 42101. The manuscript was first used for Davies's epigrams by Alexander Dyce in *The Works of Christopher Marlowe* (1850), and later by Grosart in his editions of Davies's poems.

[*H573*] British Museum. Harley MS. 573.

4° 53 leaves, 6⅝ × 6¾ inches, on paper identical to that of *AC* and *HH*, ruled on all margins but the right. *H573* is a scribal manuscript that was rebound in 1875; except for its binding, its physical appearance so closely resembles *AC* and *HH* that, like them, it was probably a gift from the author, though without special verses. It contains the text of *Nosce Teipsum* with the accompanying Dedication to Queen Elizabeth.

[*HH*] Holkham Hall, Norfolk. MS. 758. The Earl of Leicester.

4° 54 leaves, 8½ × 6⅘ inches, bound in original white vellum. The watermark is identical to that of *AC* and *H573*. Like *AC*, the pages are ruled on all four sides. The manuscript was given by Davies to Edward Coke, Attorney-General, and contains the texts of *Nosce Teipsum*, the Dedication to Queen Elizabeth, and a dedicatory poem to Coke, the latter in Davies's holograph. Except for a few corrections in Davies's hand, the manuscript is in a scribe's Elizabethan secretary hand, written with five stanzas to each page, with stanzas two and four being indented.

[*L*] Edinburgh University Library. Laing MS. III. 44.

Folio, 56 leaves, 47 of them original, 12 × 7¾ inches. Rebound with original sides in brown calf. Watermark: fleur-de-lis with initials RLP beneath.

L is the most important single collection of Davies's poems; it was copied by several scribes, apparently from Davies's own papers, and clearly was first intended as a collection strictly of his verse. It belonged to Davies's daughter and sole heir, Lucy, who also inherited all his correspondence, and whose name is entered on fol. 28ᵛ, as is that of one of her servants, 'Thomas Bakewell' on fol. 31ʳ. Of the three entries other than Davies's poems and a funeral elegy on his death, one appears on fol. 35ᵛ headed 'The state of England before the Conquest. briefely By Henry lord Hastings mongst his notes found.' Henry Hastings was Lucy's brother-in-law. The second, on fols. 36–8^r, consists of notes on William the Conqueror. The other entry appears on the last written leaf, 43^v, where two answering poems by Henry Reynolds and Henry King appear in a hand later than those hands found elsewhere in the manuscript.

Fols. 1–25^v contain 'The Psalmes translated into verse ⟨?⟩ Anno dni. 1624.' Anthony Wood, who acknowledges having corresponded with Davies's daughter in writing his life of Davies, writes of Davies's psalms:

> Besides the before-mentioned things (as also epigrams, as 'tis said) which were published by, and under the name of, sir Joh. Davies, are several MSS. of his writing and composing, which go from hand to hand, as (1) *Metaphrase of several of K. David's Psalms* (ii. 403).

Probably Wood learned of Davies's metrical psalms from Lucy, who was praised by a contemporary for her knowledge of Hebrew, and who probably copied the Hebrew version of the first verse of the Psalms appearing in the margin beside Davies's first translation.

L was written during a period of at least several years. Its first folio records 'The Psalmes translated into verse ⟨?⟩ Anno dni. 1624'; a late folio includes a funeral elegy on Davies's death. In the first group of Psalms the hand, possibly that of Davies, makes a correction. Later entries obviously come from Davies's loose papers, and a few poems among them are incomplete—perhaps the copy was torn or lost. Had Davies himself overseen the transcription of the entire manuscript, he could have completed the gaps. It is likely the manuscript was begun during Davies's lifetime by one of his scribes; attempts to complete it with his poems were probably made by his daughter as she came upon his verse in loose papers. This account explains the occasional notes in prose, and the appearance of eight different hands. Their occurrence, and the order of poems in the manuscript, are given below (blank leaves and names entered in unidentifiable hands are omitted; reference is by short title): first hand, fols. 1–25^v, Psalms 1–46; second hand, 27$^{r–v}$, *Of faith* and *A songe of Contention*; third hand, 28^v–30^v, Davies's Psalms 67, 90, 100, 103, 91, 150; fourth hand, 31$^{r–v}$, *A maids hymne, Part of an Elegie . . . of marriage;* fifth hand, 32–4^v, Love Elegy 2, incomplete, Love Elegies 3–4, *To the Queen* ('What music shall we make to you'), *To the Ladies of Founthill, Upon a Paire of Garters, A Sonnet sent with a Booke, Epigram 36*; sixth hand, 35^r, *Elegies of love* [1]; seventh hand, 35^v, prose from Henry Hastings's notes; fifth hand, 36–8^r, prose notes on William the Conqueror; fourth hand, 39^v–41^v, *To the Kinge, To the Queene at the same time, Mira Loquor, Charles his Waine, Of the name of Charolus, Verses . . . with figges*, 'An Elegiecall Epistle on Sir John Davis Death'; eighth hand, 43^v, answering poems by Henry Reynolds and Henry King. A. B. Grosart, writing before a time when photostatic copies of works were readily available, thought the first hand in *L* identical to that of Davies's scribe in a letter found in British Museum Lansdowne MS. 78, but this is incorrect.

[*L740*] British Museum. Lansdowne MS. 740.

4° 8⅜×6⁹⁄₁₆ inches. An attractive miscellany dominated by a collection of Donne's poems appearing between fols. 58 and 127, with occasional poems by others occurring among them, including two sonnets attacking Bishop Fletcher, NHA 15 and 16, on fol. 94ʳ, and Davies's third love elegy on fol. 129. All are unattributed. The section with Davies's poems has a number of works dated about 1602 and 1603 (fols. 102–3), and would appear to have been compiled about the turn of the century. The section beginning on fol. 138ʳ, which contains poems by Dryden and his contemporaries, is in a later hand.

[*LF*] Bodleian Library, Oxford. MS. Add. B. 97 (Leweston Fitzjames MS.)

4° 64 leaves, 7⅛×5⅞ inches. Original vellum binding. I have described this manuscript in detail in 'Sir John Davies: *Orchestra, Epigrams*, Unpublished Poems', *R.E.S.* xiii (1962), 17–29, 113–24. It was compiled by Leweston Fitzjames of Leweston, Dorset, principally at two periods: in 1595 and between 1607 and 1609. Fitzjames enrolled at the Middle Temple on 6 November 1594, and Davies some six years earlier. He copied both prose and verse into his manuscript, including, on fol. 20ᵛ, two satiric sonnets (unattributed in the manuscript) which attacked Bishop Fletcher (NHA 15 and 16), and which were entitled 'In Londinense*m* Episcopu*m* iampride*m* Dominae & scortae nuptu*m*. 1595. Feb. 20'. Fols. 24ᵛ–38ʳ include the dedication and text of *Orchestra*; fols. 41–6ᵛ have a collection of forty-three of Davies's epigrams, numbered consecutively 1–44 but omitting number 12; fols. 49–51ʳ record Davies's *Epithalamion*, the only known copy of the poem, dated 1595, as were the Epigrams. Probably Fitzjames made his transcripts from Davies's own copies.

[*M23*] Bodleian Library, Oxford. Malone MS. 23.

8° 111 leaves, 6⅞×4 inches. A seventeenth-century miscellany in which many entries are dated in the 1620s, though fol. 6ᵛ bears the date 1615. A poem here entitled 'Upon Henry Howard Earle of Northampton. 1603' (NHA 23) appears on fol. 1ʳ, and is followed by the often-copied Censure of the Parliament Fart, sometimes thought to have been written by Richard Martin, Robert Cotton, and other one-time companions of Davies.

[*Mann*] British Museum. Harley MS. 5353 (Manningham's Diary)

An edited and expurgated version of *Mann* was prepared by John Bruce, *The Diary of John Manningham, of the Middle Temple, and of Bradbourne, Kent, Barrister-at-Law, 1602–1603*, Camden Society Publications (1868), no. 99. Sixteen of Davies's Lots appear unattributed on fol. 95ʳ⁻ᵛ, between entries dated 4 February 1602-3 (fol. 91ᵛ) and 6 February 1602-3 (fol. 96ʳ). Several notes in *Mann* refer to Davies.

[R] Bodleian Library, Oxford. Rawlinson Poet. MS. 212.

8° 155 numbered leaves 5⅜ × 3⅞ inches, with some, unnumbered, cut away. Original vellum binding. A miscellany of prose and verse with most entries dating from the first decade of the seventeenth century but with several referring to events of 1594–5. The manuscript was written from both ends, partly before binding and partly after. It includes several libels and speeches about Oxford (fols. 44ᵛ–42ᵛ, 118–124ʳ). A collection of forty-five epigrams by Davies appears on fols. 66ᵛ–57ʳ, and on fols. 100ᵛ–101ʳ, appear two un-attributed satiric sonnets (NHA 15–16), entitled 'In Episcopum London'.

[RD] Bodleian Library, Oxford. MS. Rawlinson D. 1048.

4° 90 leaves, 7⅝ × 5⅞ inches. Original vellum binding. A miscellany of mostly prose and some poetry, RD has a large amount of material relating to the Earl of Essex. RD and ϒ frequently contain the same prose material— correspondence between Egerton and Essex, names of people knighted at Cadiz on 21 and 27 June 1596, the speeches in the Star Chamber in 1599, and (on fols. 59ᵛ–60ʳ in RD) the series of six poems on Caecus (NHA 1–6). In addition, both manuscripts have letters signed 'J. S.'

The section of poetry begins on fol. 51 and continues to fol. 73ᵛ. A poem on fol. 55ʳ is dated 17 December 1613, while poems on fols. 71–2 are dated July 1623. Possibly RD was written from loose papers kept for some time, for fols. 55ᵛ–6ᵛ refer to events of 1599. The compiler remains anonymous, unless one of the acrostics on Margerie Williams and Robert Adyn on fol. 70ᵛ refers to the owner.

[Ro] The Philip and A. S. W. Rosenbach Foundation Museum, Philadelphia. MS. 186, pressmark 1083.15.

4° 93 leaves 7½ × 5¾ inches. Original vellum binding. This manuscript was item 186 in the sales catalogue issued by the Rosenbach Company in 1941, *English Poetry to 1700*, pages 46–7, and item 2495 in Sotheby's Catalogue of the library of William Horatio Crawford of County Cork, Ireland, *The Lake-lands Library* (1891), p. 206. The most complete description is given by James Lee Sanderson, 'An Edition of an Early Seventeenth-Century Manu-script Collection of Poems (Rosenbach MS. 186)', Ph.D. thesis, University of Pennsylvania, 1960. Dr. Sanderson has given helpful assistance with the manuscript in a number of points, and his thesis dates and identifies some of the libels in Ro.

Although Ro concludes with some poems of the 1620s, they are not in the careful Elizabethan secretary hand in which most of the manuscript is copied. Most entries date from the 1590s, and all of Davies's poems but one (NHA 23) appear before fol. 41, a section which can be dated before 1600. On fol. 12ᵛ appear epigrams published by Thomas Bastard in 1598; on fol. 18ᵛ a description of the devices at the wedding of Elizabeth Vere and the

Earl of Derby (the subject of Davies's *Epithalamion*) in February 1595; on fols. 24ᵛ–8ʳ, epigrams by Benjamin Rudyerd, some of which attack Davies, and one of which refers to *Orchestra*; and on fol. 31, a libel against Gray's Inn men on events of 1594. (The wedding devices and libel are discussed by James L. Sanderson in articles in *N. & Q.* ccviii (1963), 298–300, and *Modern Language Review*, lviii (1963), 217–19). On fol. 12ʳ *Ro* enters the poem 'When Phoebus first did Daphne love', subscribed 'Ch. R.' Seventeen other copies which I have seen give the poem as anonymous, but in *LF* the poem is subscribed 'Ch. Rives' in folios which can there be dated 1595.

The transcript of Rudyerd's epigrams in *Ro* is the only copy extant today; their rarity suggests the compiler may have received his copies directly from the author, who was a member of the Inner Temple. He must also have had close access to Davies's work, for, in addition to his principal collection of forty-four of Davies's epigrams in a sequence near that of Davies's own final collection, he later received copies of Epigrams 45 and 46, not found in other manuscripts, and written only shortly before printing.

Compilers are often irregular about indicating authorship: Fitzjames, for example, in *LF* indicated Davies's authorship of the epigrams and *Epithalamion*, but not of *Orchestra*, though he almost certainly copied *Orchestra* from Davies's own papers. Often when a compiler knew an author he did not bother to record his name. The compiler of *Ro* records authors for some entries, and is remarkably accurate wherever authorship can be proven, but does not indicate authorship for many other entries. He attributes several poems to Davies not found elsewhere, and I attribute several more to Davies that appear without attribution in *Ro*. The following poems appear in the present edition: fols. 2ᵛ–9ʳ, forty-four of Davies's epigrams, one unprinted; fol. 12ʳ⁻ᵛ, NHA 20 and 22, both subscribed 'J. D.', and PP 3; fols. 13ᵛ–14ʳ, PP 5–7; fols. 19ᵛ–20ʳ, Epigram 62, subscribed 'J. D.', PP 8–9; fol. 22ᵛ, NHA 21, Epigrams 45–6, each subscribed 'J. D.'; fols. 38ᵛ–9ʳ, NHA 12–16; fols. 40ʳ–1ʳ, NHA 1–6; fol. 77ʳ, NHA 23.

[*Tan*] Bodleian Library, Oxford. Tanner MS. 306.

A large volume consisting of loose sheets in many hands and from many sources. Two versions of the five poems on Bishop Fletcher (NHA 12–16) appear on fols. 188ᵛ–190ʳ in two different hands, one italic (*Tan–I*) and one Secretary (*Tan–S*). Both also have a poem on Fletcher beginning 'Marriage is honourable', which, with further evidence, may one day be attributed to Davies.

[*TE*] Henry E. Huntington Library, San Marino, California. MS. EL 76. (Thomas Egerton MS.)

A single leaf of paper 11×7¾ inches, in Davies's holograph, addressed to Sir Thomas Egerton on the death of his second wife.

[*Y*] All Souls Library, Oxford. MS. 155 (Yelverton MS.).

4° 413 numbered leaves 7⅝×5⅞ inches. Owned by Narcissus Luttrell, who entered the date 1679 on fol. 2ʳ, and left this and other books to All Souls. He called the manuscript 'A Collection of Speeches, Letters, Verses, & other remarkable things both publick & private'. It is a bigger volume than any single seventeenth-century miscellany in the Bodleian, and is written largely in one secretary hand, on papers of varied watermarks, one of which is a pot with flowers and the initials P. O. similar to the paper of *A22*, *Che*, and *Dow*, part 2.

This manuscript was used by Grosart to supply the text of *The Kinges Welcome*, by Percy Simpson in his edition of Ben Jonson (*Works*, vii. 153), and by Agnes M. C. Latham, for its unique copy of a letter from Raleigh to his wife in 1603, printed in *Essays and Studies*, xxv (1939), 39–58. *Y* was copied from the papers of Sir Christopher Yelverton, as is indicated in several entries. On fol. 111ʳ appears a copy of a letter from Thomas Cartwright beginning 'Good Mistress Yelverton'; fol. 68ᵛ describes a ring given to Queen Elizabeth, headed 'The Serjunntes ringe for the queene when I proceeded serjaunte'; on fol. 62ʳ is the heading:

When I was speaker of the parliament, A° 39, Eliz: and presented to the Archbishope of Canturburie to have his alowannce whoe stracke out the wordes that hereafter followe to be stricken out.

Yelverton became Speaker of the House in 1597, and the words which the Archbishop struck out were part of the prayer which Yelverton wrote for the opening of Commons, the prayer still in use today.

Y was undoubtedly written from Yelverton's papers, apparently largely at one time—it lacks the insertions, cramped areas, and blanks usual in a manuscript compiled over a period of years by one person. Moreover, most of the ink is of one consistency and colour. The dates, however, are varied; the manuscript does not proceed chronologically. The opening item is from 1600–1, the next is dated 7 May 1603, but on fol. 62ʳ is Yelverton's prayer of 1597. A few items appear in the manuscript twice, in different places, which indicates that it was compiled from papers collected for several years.

The manuscript consists largely of prose, part of which is found frequently in other manuscripts containing Davies's poems: the Advertisement of a Loyal Subject (fols. 15ᵛ–18ʳ) appears also in *A22*; the speeches in the Star Chamber, Michaelmas 1599 (fols. 20–5ʳ) appear in *RD*; speeches by the Earl of Pembroke and others at a tournament (fol. 248ᵛ) appear also in *A22*; and fols. 196–7ʳ contain a reply to propositions made by an atheist recorded in *A22*.

Some verses are scattered through the manuscript, including several known to be by Davies and others attributed to him in this edition. Several characteristics of these texts suggest that Yelverton received most of his copies of Davies's work directly from the author: their rarity—many are not found elsewhere; the high quality of the texts; the layout, or pattern of indentation of stanzas, a detail easily lost, but often similar here to the pattern found in Davies's holograph and in *LF*, which probably derived from Davies's papers; and the similar backgrounds of the two men—both were lawyers, Members of Parliament, and judges.

The following works appear in the present edition: fol. 12^r, PP 12; fols. 44^v–5^r, Epigrams 47 and 62; fols. 72–3^r, *The Kinges Welcome*, subscribed 'John Davis'; fol. 74a, PP 11; fols. 108^v–108a^r, NHA 13–16; fols. 118–22^v, *A Contention*; fol. 127^v, PP 11; fols. 262^v–3^v, NHA 7–11; fols. 272–3^v, NHA 1–6.

INDEX OF FIRST LINES

(The index is in modern spelling; poems of doubtful authorship are marked with an asterisk.)